THE INDUSTRIAL REVOLUTIO

CW01431512

Denny Smith
Decent 1 1114

The Industrial Revolution

A Macroeconomic Interpretation

Douglas Fisher
Professor of Economics
North Carolina State University

M

St. Martin's Press

First edition 1992
Reprinted 1993, 1994

Published in Great Britain by
THE MACMILLAN PRESS LTD
Houndmills, Basingstoke, Hampshire RG21 2XS
and London
Companies and representatives
throughout the world

A catalogue record for this book is available from the British Library.

ISBN 0–333–37935–7 hardcover
ISBN 0–333–61114–4 paperback

Printed in Hong Kong

First published in the United States of America 1992 by
Scholarly and Reference Division,
ST. MARTIN'S PRESS, INC.,
175 Fifth Avenue,
New York, N.Y. 10010

ISBN 0–312–07989–3 (cloth)
ISBN 0–312–10366–2 (paper)

Library of Congress Cataloging-in-Publication Data
Fisher, Douglas, 1934–
The Industrial Revolution : a macroeconomic interpretation /
Douglas Fisher.
p.   cm.
"First published in Great Britain 1992 by The Macmillan Press
Ltd"—Verso t.p.
Includes bibliographical references (p.   ) and index.
ISBN 0–312–07989–3 (cloth) — ISBN 0–312–10366–2 (paper)
1. Europe—Economic conditions—18th century.   2. Europe—Economic
conditions—19th century.   3. Europe—Industries—History.
I. Title.
HC240.F48   1992
338.094—dc20   92–1249
                                                            CIP

To Ann and Henry

Contents

Contents

Preface

This is a study of the European macroeconomy covering the period 1700 to 1910. There are two broad themes of this study, one involving the techniques of analysis and one involving the nature of the European economy itself. The methods of analysis feature techniques drawn from the time-series toolkit of the modern macroeconomist; this involves Granger-causality and unit root tests, although there are also other sorts of structural and specification tests and (even) several cases when a simultaneous-equations system is employed. With regard to the economics, quite simply put, the sustaining argument is the notion that much of Western Europe shares many of the economic processes at work over this period, speaking quite generally of course. In particular, we will be arguing that all of the countries in our sample are drawing at least some resources from a common pool and that certainly by 1700 or so positive per capita economic growth is the normal state of affairs in at least the most highly-developed parts of most of these countries. Here local conditions (soil, population dynamics, etc.) and events (weather, wars, revolutions, and the like), configure the actual rate of growth in particular countries. At the other end of the period (in 1910), on the other hand, all of these countries have clearly experienced an industrial transformation whose overall style is remarkably similar.

With regard to our emphasis on macroeconomics it should be pointed out that much of the material of economic history actually refers to economic aggregates – to inflation rates, the rate of growth of GNP, unemployment, the balance of payments, and the functional distribution of income – but in the historical literature less use is made of formal macroeconomic theory (or of its associated econometrics) than is possible, or so it seems to this writer. In the first instance this simply involves the use of standard macro-static and macro-dynamic reasoning, but at a deeper level it involves the struggle to demonstrate the identification and stability of economic relationships, and to establish the direction of causation among economic variables. These concerns are shared by all economists, whatever their interests, but it is notable that in the historical literature formal treatment of these topics rarely occurs, even though identification, stability and, especially, causation are often claimed for particular hypotheses. At any rate, in this study we shall try to be considerably more self-conscious about these matters, at least insofar as the data will bear the weight of our techniques.

In this study we will advance the proposition that growth and penetration is widely spread across Western Europe – although it clearly does not touch all parts of all countries equally – and that depending critically on local circumstances, the growth prior to and during the industrial revolution is a shared one. The industrial revolution did not arrive just in England alone in the 18th century, although there the conditions were certainly most appropriate and the developments most obvious, but all over the Continent as well, although local conditions give a significantly different twist to the story, as it unfolds. This hypothesis, then, downplays individual differences, particularly as they involve nationalities, and argues that a good approximation is that the industrial revolution was shared over much of Western Europe, arriving and conquering in a remarkably short time on a broad front.

To be a shade too specific, it is as if there were at the time a *de facto* 'common market' in Western Europe, involving England, Northern France, much of Holland, Belgium and parts of Western Germany and Northern Italy in the first instance, and much of the rest of Europe by 1910. Basic to our purpose, then, is to generate quantitative material describing how this common area developed and how it divided up its economic tasks, from data that are predominantly national in their scope.

The reader should probably think of the current study as a first pass at the problems just described. For one thing, the data are not sufficient to do much more than discuss the general case until just after the Napoleonic wars. We can get pretty far with the British data in the 18th century, and this is actually convenient (if a little misleading) in that much of the literature takes this line. Furthermore, it is certainly economical of the space in this study to use the British as the general case and the rest of Europe as examples of one thing or another. But we want to emphasize that whether or not the British experience is a good model for other countries is currently being debated and we are not taking a stand on that issue. Even when the data exist for other countries on an annual basis, usually after 1860 or so, they are generally of dubious quality for the sorts of sensitive tests that are employed here. Thus the reader is warned here, and repeatedly below, that he will be looking at the results of specific tests on specific data and that the stated results are conditional.

We also need to sound a warning about the techniques themselves. There is a certain amount of controversy surrounding the use of Granger-causality and unit-root tests and, for that matter, about the use of correlation and regression analysis. Part of the problem has to do with the weakness of the data (for example, certain test-procedures require longer runs of data than are available). Also important is the concern with tests such as the Granger-causality procedure that establish a kind of proximate causation (really a temporal ordering) but do not provide any information on how important the relationship is. To be sure, there are structural tests offered here, but in many cases, most especially in the tests for monetary neutrality, the Granger-causal influence is all that appears. This has to be taken as a piece of the puzzle: if some Granger-causal link has been established then that is an interesting observation; there are other steps to be taken (empirically), but these are not always on the agenda for this study. Finally, we should note that the regression methods employed here, whether the test is unit-root, Granger-causality or just linear multiple regression, are vulnerable to the claim that there are omitted variables of importance. This is readily admitted, of course, and the author welcomes correspondence on this (and on any other aspect of this study that troubles or interests the reader).

There is one final topic that ought to be addressed here and then neglected for the rest of the book. This is the question of whether we ought to be using the term 'industrial revolution' to describe the transformation of one or more of the countries studied. Over the 210-year period that we are considering, each of these countries went from a predominantly agricultural economy to one that was either predominantly industrial or soon to be. Two hundred years is a short time. Part of the heat in the long debate over this process is related to the notion that without a very rapid transformation – over a generation at most – the change is just not revolutionary. This position gets mixed up with the recent downgrading of the rate of change of industrial activity during Britain's industrial revolution; if Britain did not have an industrial revolution, then nobody did. What is proposed here is to ignore the debate in favour of merely describing the situation; when the term 'industrial revolution' appears in this study, it is used as evocative language, not as an apparent claim that a revolution has occurred.

I wish to thank Lee A. Craig and Walter N. Thurman who were my collaborators in several earlier projects that are summarized here. Lee Craig has also read substantial parts of the manuscript and I have profited enormously from his advice. Several of the component pieces have also been read to the members of the Triangle Economic History Workshop and I am grateful to the members of that group for their many comments.

DOUGLAS FISHER

1 The Background to the British Industrial Revolution

1.1 INTRODUCTION

To a considerable extent, the purpose of this study is to emphasize a particular way of evaluating both the causes and effects of the industrial revolution in much of Western Europe. This chapter takes a brief look into the nature of the economic system that produced the industrial revolution – on as macroeconomic a level of detail as possible – in order to isolate some of the principal influences on later development. The industrial revolution began in Britain in the 18th century and so the description of the British case occupies the largest space in this study. In fact, we will make simple chronological breaks in the 210 years of British economic history we consider, with Chapter 1 covering the period in which the event began (1700–1780), Chapter 2 covering the first revolution itself (1780–1850/60) and Chapter 3 covering the period of consolidation in the United Kingdom (1870–1910), when the rate of growth of the industrial sector also decelerated somewhat.

It is important for the reader to appreciate that Chapters 1 through 3 are parts of a unit on Britain (and the United Kingdom). In particular, certain topics introduced in Chapter 1 will be continued in Chapters 2 and 3, depending on their nature. Most notable in this respect are discussions of the agricultural sector, the nature of the national income data and the business cycle. It is hoped that the disadvantages of dividing topics will be outweighed by the advantages of dealing in chronological units (as one generally does in macroeconomics).

This chapter undertakes to work to the following general outline. The main task will be to lay out a macroeconomic framework for Britain for the period before the industrial revolution, with a rather patchy collection of macroeconomic topics necessitated by the similarly patchy data. Here are offered comparisons across all of Europe only on the growth of population, with the main point being simply that population growth seems to have been the normal condition (for all of the countries considered in this study) at least by the mid-17th century. In considering what this population growth might imply, it is suggested that two frameworks are appropriate. One of these is a simple macroeconomic growth model (neoclassical, in this case), which is clear on what happens if an economy grows at some stable rate, but less clear otherwise. That analysis is long run; in the short run, a method that suggests itself is to look at the components of aggregate demand and aggregate supply. This analysis produces ambiguous results for the influence of population growth on economic activity, but the overall conclusions of this section are, nevertheless, a good deal less pessimistic than at least some of the literature on this period.

With respect to the industrial record, we consider only British results. In spite of difficulties related to data availability, the chapter still attempts to maintain a focus on broad macroeconomic topics; as such it concentrates on certain very general issues – with details on national income, the price level and real wage behaviour at the head of the list. There are also available some useful data on the details of industrial production and on profit and interest rates to round out the picture somewhat. All in all, it is definitely possible to draw some broad macroeconomic conclusions about this period, but an equally important point of this first chapter is to establish certain broad themes of the book, especially those of a macroeconomic character.

1.2 POPULATION DYNAMICS BEFORE THE INDUSTRIAL REVOLUTION

Before looking at the population data, let us assert a very familiar proposition: along the equilibrium path of an economy that satisfies neoclassical stability conditions, economic growth will be at least as rapid as population growth and will tend to be more rapid in the event of technological change. The general neoclassical growth model is built on an aggregate production function; what makes a production function (and hence the resulting growth theory) neoclassical (and stable) are smooth, diminishing and positive marginal products for the factors of production. In addition, the general neoclassical framework assumes that markets are competitive with flexible prices. While strict satisfaction of these conditions is unlikely for any time period, it is within reason for an economic historian attempting to employ the framework on periods before the 20th century to argue that only partial adherence to these assumptions need not emasculate the general conclusion of the model; this is that economic growth and population growth are *not* natural antagonists (as so much of the literature since Malthus suggests).

Now what all of this has to do with the topic at hand is that a general result of the neoclassical model is that the economy (in its dynamic equilibrium) will tend to grow at the augmented rate of growth of the labour force. That is, if the labour supply grows at a rate of $\alpha + \beta$, where β represents the effect of 'augmentation' (technical change) on labour supply and α represents the growth rate of the labour force, then this rate is common to all variables that grow – including consumption, the capital stock and the rate of investment.[1] This feature is particularly useful in discussing events surrounding the industrial revolution; the reason for this is that the items just mentioned – especially labour supply, technical change and the rate of investment – are the most often mentioned topics in the historical literature.

Of course, the conditions required for the neoclassical model could easily fail to hold; consider the following. Suppose, for example, that consumption is actually growing at a slower rate than population (*ceteris paribus*),[2] perhaps because certain economic agents are simply unable to borrow in order to consume according to their expected lifetime income. We call this 'liquidity constrained consumption behaviour' in the literature on modern economies and it is very likely to be a factor in most economies of this historical era, when lending institutions were relatively immature (by modern standards). This situation would constrain overall growth to occur at a lower rate than would be available along the optimal path. Indeed, if some borrowers had access to credit facilities and some did not (does this sound familiar?), the overall result would be sub-optimal in terms of output growth, and so would the attendant functional distribution of the national product, for that matter.[3]

1.2.1 Notes on European Population Growth

By far the most obvious aspect of European development from at least 1500 until the industrial age was in place is the strong growth in population that seems to have affected every country in our survey. Population levels surely doubled and even tripled over much of Western Europe from 1500 to 1800 at rates of growth that sometimes

Table 1.1   The population of five European countries, 1700–1820
(thousands)

	1700	1760	1820	Annual growth rates	
				1700–1760	1760–1820
France	21 120	25 246	30 698	0.30	0.33
Germany	13 300	16 900	19 000	0.40	0.20
Italy	15 000	18 310	24 905	0.33	0.51
Sweden	1 260	1 916	2 574	0.70	0.49
UK	9 273	11 069	20 686	0.30	1.04

reached 0.5 per cent per year, although most of the time the rates of growth were lower. While world population has apparently always had a tendency to grow as far as one can say, and there are certainly other periods of significant growth in Western Europe (e.g., in the two centuries after 1100), in this particular period the growth is rapid enougn to have raised the question of whether there was a 'vital revolution' after 1500, that somehow contributed positively to economic growth.

The first thing one should appreciate about the population figures is that early numbers (before 1700) are little more than educated guesses. To complicate things, population growth seems to have been uneven in this period and, in particular, there was an 18th-century spurt throughout Western Europe, whose exact size is certainly a matter of conjecture (and thus highly likely to be revised with further research) and whose causes are a subject of considerable debate. Whatever the reason, population numbers are frequently revised and the changes are often of sufficient magnitude to have a major effect on any analysis that depends on their accuracy. But we still need to look at the numbers in order to establish some sort of economic base here, and so that is where we will start.

The population growth figures for Western Europe are remarkably similar across countries. In particular, while uneven population growth seems to have been general in the two centuries before 1700, most countries shared an upward trend at least. Indeed, in the earliest period where we have somewhat comparable numbers – the 18th century – an acceleration of population growth also seems to have been common property. For the 18th century, we can begin in Table 1.1 with some figures provided in Maddison (1982). The soundness of these numbers no doubt varies considerably, but the broad picture is certainly one of growth over the entire period, with the

Table 1.2   Population, England and Wales

Date	Population (m)
1450	2.4
1500	2.8
1550	3.6
1600	5.0
1650	5.8
1700	5.8
1750	6.2

most remarkable result being for the UK figures, where population growth was over 1 per cent per year for the 60 years that seem to contain the period of the acceleration of industrialization. This is clearly important.

Let us continue with some widely employed figures for the population of England and Wales for the 1450 to 1750 period (Table 1.2). Here we will begin with the 50-year average figures of Wrigley that formed the basis of Lee's (1973) econometric evaluation of the causes of population change. Except for the stagnation from 1650 to 1700, these figures are remarkable in showing a steady and strong increase in population that averaged a 0.32 per cent compound growth over the entire period and a 0.44 per cent growth rate up to 1650.

Lee and Schofield (1981) have published important revisions for the later part of the period just covered, up to 1800, based on recent detailed studies of Britain's population during the 18th century. These estimates are given in Table 1.3, where they are compared with the English numbers that are provided by Wrigley and Schofield (1981). The latter is an annual series that runs from 1541 to 1871. The rates of change here are very comparable, but show somewhat more rapid growth in England in the last thirty years of the period. More important, the English and Welsh figures show significantly more rapid growth in this period than do the previous (and now replaced) calculations of Brownlee (as reported in Deane and Cole (1967)). Those figures were for a population in 1701 of 5.83 million (and 9.16 million for 1801). This recalculation means that a half million people who (recently) were thought to have belonged to earlier centuries are now traced to a more rapid growth from 1701 to 1751. This, indeed, is where this research has been focused. It is disconcerting that the effect of research on the population is so great, but in any case, even

Table 1.3   Population in England and Wales

	Lee/Schofield: England/Wales		Wrigley/Schofield: England	
	Estimates	Growth	Estimates	Growth
1701	5.29		5.06	
1711	5.51	0.41	5.23	0.33
1721	5.66	0.27	5.35	0.27
1731	5.59	–0.12	5.26	–0.17
1741	5.94	0.61	5.58	0.59
1751	6.20	0.42	5.77	0.33
1761	6.62	0.66	6.15	0.64
1771	6.97	0.52	6.45	0.48
1781	7.57	0.83	7.04	0.88
1791	8.21	0.81	7.74	0.95
1801	9.16	1.09	8.66	1.12
Century growth rate		0.55		0.54

Source: Lee and Schofield (1981); Wrigley and Schofield (1981).

with the (now) steeper growth in the first half of the 18th century, growth is still faster from 1771 to 1801 than at any earlier time and this is the finding made most of in the literature. This later period is, of course, the period in which Britain's industrial revolution accelerated (as discussed below), so reference to our earlier propositions concerning the relation between economic growth and population growth seems appropriate.

1.2.2   Population Growth in the Macroeconomy

We simply do not have the space to dig into the causes of the increased population growth at this time, although they certainly are of macroeconomic concern, but we will not sidestep a discussion of the effects of population growth. Indeed, for the short run the natural thing for a macroeconomist to do is to look at the effects of population growth on aggregate demand and on aggregate supply. With regard to the demand side, the most obvious influence is that emphasized overly much in the literature – that there are more mouths to feed. In addition, there are broader markets as a result of population growth and this provides for economic opportunities, provided that the supply side responds and also generates sufficient incomes (as the neoclassical model – and Walras' Law – imply would tend to be the case). Furthermore, population growth provides economic opportunities that may even be associated with economies of scale, at least to the extent economic agents are able to respond. This is certainly one reason why we see the development of larger scale farming throughout the period (with more than a hint of acceleration at the end). Furthermore, in this first list of demand factors, population growth would tend to stimulate industrial activity directly and it certainly affects commerce in the same way.

There are also other kinds of effects of population growth that are largely on the demand side. For one thing, population growth increases the demand for governmental services, especially for aid in distribution, health, and the like.[4] In this respect the rapid growth of cities aided by the centralization of commerce and industry put some pressure on governments to deal with the increasingly obvious problems of poverty, disease, and the like. These problems were, of course, common in earlier times, but were more often treated by local or private means in the more rural society that predates the industrial revolution.[5] Finally, the demands of a growing population puts pressure on all sorts of other kinds of social and political institutions and surely accelerates the pace of social change, speaking fairly generally.

With regard to the supply side, the most obvious effect is on the supply of human capital (and on the supply of labour services). The labour force will grow at the rate of growth of the population – participation rates unchanged, of course – and it is certainly possible (and necessary along the golden path) for output and the capital stock to grow at the same rate. Population growth also affects the other factors of production. If the economy is growing along the optimal path, then the profit rate will not rise – as a result of competition among the owners of capital – but behind this event is the equivalent rise of the quantity of capital. There is also the likelihood of the more intensive and extensive use of land.[6]

Population growth, of course, can be excessive, especially in the short run, and it is likely that an economy that has long had a slow growth rate of population would have some difficulties with a rate of growth that is significantly accelerated. But even rapid population growth might have its positive 'supply-side' benefits by stimulating the introduction of labour-using (and land- and capital-saving) technology which could be superior to the technology already in use. Whether it did so on any scale at this time is likely to be debated for some time. Of course a growing population could also eat its capital, in effect, which would not stimulate much of anything. Where the balance of all of this turns out is not necessarily clear, but, in any case, one of the purposes of this study is to look at what the aggregate numbers tell us on some of these questions.

1.3   THE GROWTH OF AGRICULTURAL OUTPUT IN ENGLAND, 1700–1800

A sector that will not always get full coverage in this study is the agricultural. This is mostly because of lack of space for, after all, this is a study of the transformation of an agricultural society into an industrial one. In this early period, though, agriculture is certainly a considerable part of the story of GNP, and so it has a rightful place in the discussion. Even so, the details (most importantly, the story of technical change in the agricultural sector) really do not.

We will speculate here that the steady agricultural progress of the time had a broad interaction with overall growth, providing both stimulus and response to real and human capital development as well as serving as a supplier of products to industry and commerce. This is not really controversial. By the early 17th century, there were strong signs of vigorous agricultural growth and by the mid-18th century, the effect of rising demand was so great that dramatic changes – most notably the final erosion of the 'open field system' in England – were well under way. Not every observer sees the situation in this light, of course, and some awfully pessimistic conclusions are easy to find in this literature. The argument here, at any rate, does not require an especially rapid pace of technological progress in agriculture, but could be sustained if the pace of the application of existing knowledge proves to be adequate. Enclosures – clearly such an innovation – set the tone. In any case, the reader should be warned that the data are very provisional here, even compared with those considered to this point, as will be seen.

In a set of figures stretching back to 1500 (Table 1.4), Jones (1981) provides some recent estimates of the growth of agricultural output in Britain over the three centuries prior to 1800. These numbers are

Table 1.4   Overall agricultural output gains (%)

1500–1600	25–37
1600–1700	25–36
1700–1800	61

Table 1.5   Agricultural output in England and Wales, 1700–1800 (£m)

	Nominal agriculture	Real agriculture	% change	Population	% change	Per capita real
1700	20.0	20.0		5.29		3.78
1710	20.4	20.6	0.03	5.51	0.41	3.74
1720	18.2	24.1	1.70	5.66	0.27	4.26
1730	18.2	23.6	–0.21	5.59	–0.12	4.22
1740	18.4	26.1	1.06	5.94	0.61	4.39
1750	20.7	28.1	0.77	6.20	0.42	4.58
1760	25.1	28.9	0.28	6.62	0.66	4.36*
1770	33.5	29.0	0.03	6.97	0.52	4.16*
1780	34.1	31.5	0.86	7.57	0.82	4.16*
1790	40.6	33.4	0.60	8.21	0.81	4.07*
1800	74.3	36.2	0.84	9.16	1.09	3.95*

Source: Cole (1981) and Lee and Schofield (1981).

drawn by Jones directly from population figures (amended by trade figures from 1700), but not from the most recent population estimates (as described above). This clearly does not get us very far. Indeed, by tying agricultural growth to population growth, we prejudge the standard of living issue (it is assumed constant) as well as the issue of the effect of technical change and innovation on agricultural productivity (it did no more than permit agricultural output to keep up with population, by assumption). In some quarters, no doubt, arguing that the agricultural sector did this well would be labelled 'revisionist'. Labels aside, it is clear that the agricultural story needs to be revised, whatever else is done, in view of the newer and better population figures.

A more detailed set of agricultural figures is available for the 1700 to 1800 period, as proffered by Cole (1981). Table 1.5 shows a relatively steady rise in real agricultural output over the century, with per capita real output rising until the 1750s. Evidently, up to 1750 at least, agricultural output was adequate to cover population growth, even without the significant imports that appear after 1750. Indeed, there is quite possibly a rise in the 'standard' of the consumption of English agricultural products from 1700 to 1750 of at least 21 per cent, as judged by real agricultural output per capita.[7] After the 1750s, net imports of agricultural products occur – increasing significantly over the rest of the period – so that nothing firm can be inferred about the standard of living from these later data. Agricultural output, though, continues to rise (but not per capita).

Chapter 2 continues the discussion of agriculture as it bears directly on the period of more rapid industrialization in Britain (from 1780 to 1850). For the present discussion, we need to underscore our view that the transformation of the British agricultural sector in the first 80 years of the 18th century provided an effective and possibly necessary stimulus to the growth of the industrial sector. Partly it is a matter of releasing claims on the growing pool of resources in Britain, but partly emphasis also needs to be placed on the growth of the domestic capital stock and on the increasing internationalization of the European agricultural community. While there is doubt in some quarters that agriculture played that significant a role, especially in the first 40 years of the 18th century, that is not the position taken here.

1.4   ENGLISH INDUSTRIALIZATION PRIOR TO THE REVOLUTION

There is an abundant literature on the possibility of an industrial revolution prior to the acknowledged event in England sometime after the middle of the 18th century, but there is no reason to dig into that literature in this study, mainly because of the paucity of relevant macroeconomic detail. For the 18th century, there are somewhat better numbers available, and one can go at least part of the way. along the path of building up a picture of the aggregate situation, even without reference to the existing estimates of national income. The series that is most generally discussed in this context is the Hoffmann (1955) index of industrial production, which follows in Figure 1.1. Here one finds industrial growth throughout the century, with the well-known spurt that occurs sometime after 1780.

Unfortunately, these calculations are dated, incomplete, and possibly seriously flawed by errors.[8] Putting these issues aside, the most obvious event in the series is the spurt itself, of course, but it is surely important to recognize the doubling (roughly) of the index from 1700 to 1780. If, as the following discussion will suggest, the spurt should be muted by corrections, leaving the earlier numbers to stand, then the substantial earlier growth suggests that industrialization was proceeding relatively rapidly throughout the century; this requires a little rethinking for those who think there was no growth, no per capita

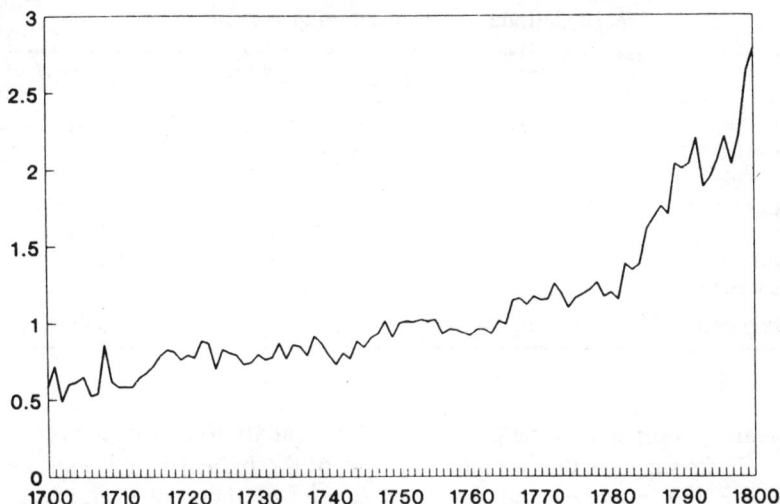

Figure 1.1   Hoffmann index of industrial production (1750 = 1)

Table 1.6   Growth rates (%)

	Hoffmann index	Population*
1700–1780	0.87	0.45
1700–1730	1.26	0.18
1700–1740	1.00	0.29
1700–1750	0.88	0.32
1700–1760	0.85	0.37
1700–1770	0.85	0.39
1700–1800	1.20	0.55
1780–1800	3.62	0.95

* One year later.

growth and/or no reason to expect growth in the period until the last decades of the 18th century.

One can look at the growth rates specifically, of course, and so the breakdown given in Table 1.6 of the general Hoffmann index is of interest. These establish a vigorous growth to 1780, running at a little less than twice the rate of population growth. After that, the spurt (now downgraded in the literature) is a very rapid 3.62 per cent per

Table 1.7   Industrial production growth rates (%)

	1700–60	1760–70	1770–80	1780–1801
Hoffmann	0.74	2.25	0.42	3.94
Crafts (1770 weights)	0.71	1.23	1.79	
Laspeyres				2.34
Paasche				2.14
Fisher Ideal				2.24
Divisia				2.11
Population	0.37	0.52	0.82	0.95

year, accompanied by a growth rate of population of 0.95 per cent.

Crafts suggests that a recomputation of the industrial indices is in order and compares the results of several methods of evaluation. Again we list some numbers drawn from his tabulation, along with the comparable Hoffmann numbers in Table 1.7. Here the preferred Divisia index shows the slowest rate of growth. Even so, the recomputation offered by Crafts (in comparison with Hoffmann) is also importantly a matter of adjusting the weights away from the rapidly growing cotton industry, although the identification of other products omitted in the earlier index has a role to play. It should be underscored, though, that growth of industry in excess of population growth is still the general result overall, and so this dispute has more to do with how to characterize the 1780–1801 period (actually a topic for discussion in Chapter 2) than it does with what happened up until 1780 (or, at least, 1760).

The Hoffman index up to 1780 does not contain all of the information currently available, and it contains sectors we might not want to include in an industrial index (such as patents, sugar, and ocean shipping) and so Table 1.8 presents a more recent and certainly more detailed tabulation for the 1700 to 1780 period, also as put together by Crafts (1983). Here we find that while for some products (beer, leather and soap) growth is at rates that are below population growth from 1700 to 1760 (which is at 0.37 per cent), the general result is for growth at rates well above that of population. In the 1760–70 decade there seems to have been depression in some of the consumer goods industries, but in the 1770s the boom was on in most sectors apparently, and population growth, which was running at 0.82 per cent per year, was generally exceeded by industrial growth.

Table 1.8   Real output growth rates in English industry, 1700–80

	1700–1760	*1760–1770*	*1770–1780*
Population	0.37	0.52	0.82
Cotton	1.37	4.59	6.20
Wool	0.97	1.30	. . .
Linen	1.25	2.68	3.42
Silk	0.67	3.40	–0.03
Building	0.74	0.34	4.24
Iron	0.60	1.65	4.47
Copper	2.62	5.61	2.40
Coal	0.64	2.19	2.48
Paper	1.51	2.09	0.00
Beer	0.21	–0.10	1.10
Leather	0.25	–0.10	0.82
Soap	0.28	0.62	1.32
Candles	0.49	0.71	1.15

Source: Crafts (1983).

1.4.1   Trade and Commerce in the 18th Century

There is another sector of the British economy that figures in such discussions and this is, broadly, trade and commerce. The overriding hypothesis about English trade in this period is, of course, the notion that it was a major contributor to economic growth that – by some – can hardly be underestimated in terms of its role in setting the stage for the industrial revolution. Deane (1979, pp. 69–70) says,

> it created a demand for the products of British industry; [it] gave access to raw materials; it helped to create an institutional structure and a business ethic which was to prove almost as effective in promoting the home-trade as it had been for the foreign trade; [it] was a prime cause of the growth of large towns and industrial centres.

She also points out that it was responsible for significant profits, some of which were turned to other uses, and that it helped promote the growth of the incomes of foreign countries. This is high praise.

The list just provided, then, emphasizes both exports and imports in the stimulation of the English economy although to what extent the

The Industrial Revolution

Table 1.9   English trade figures, 1700–1775 (annual averages, £m)

	Imports	Exports	Re-exports	(3) + (4)
1700– 9	4.7	4.5	1.7	6.1
1710–19	5.5	4.8	2.1	6.9
1720–29	6.8	4.9	2.8	7.7
1730–39	7.5	5.8	3.2	9.0
1740–49	2.3	6.5	3.6	10.1
1750–59	8.4	8.7	3.5	12.2
1760–69	10.8	10.0	4.4	14.4
1770–79	12.8	10.0	5.6	15.6

Source: Minchinton (1969).

whole process is export led (Kindleberger, 1962), led by the expansion of domestic British demand (Deane and Cole, 1962; Eversley, 1967) or simply the result of a general European-led expansion (as we have been implying) is yet to be determined. Moving slightly away from conjecture, there are some time-honoured figures for Britain, for the 18th century. Davis (1962) has published some of the best numbers currently in use and Minchinton's survey (1969) arranges them usefully; the numbers are, in any case, mainly those of E. Schumpeter (1960). They are carried in Table 1.9. These are real trade statistics.[9] Here we see that imports rose steadily, accumulating to a 172 per cent increase over the period, while the total of exports and re-exports shows a 156 per cent increase. Whichever way one looks at it, it is clear that growth was steady and was in excess of 2 per cent per year in these categories. This growth was probably greater than in the previous 50 years, but possibly not by much. Trade was growing somewhat faster than any other broad number in this period, and certainly faster than population and, as we shall see, real gross national product.

1.4.2   Commercial Banking During the 18th Century

An economic activity that also figures importantly in the macroeconomic stories we are about to tell is that of commercial banking. The financial sector is important in its own right, of course, because it creates a number of important financial products, permits a wider sharing of risks, improves the allocation of capital (markets) and provides credit information to both borrowers and lenders. With

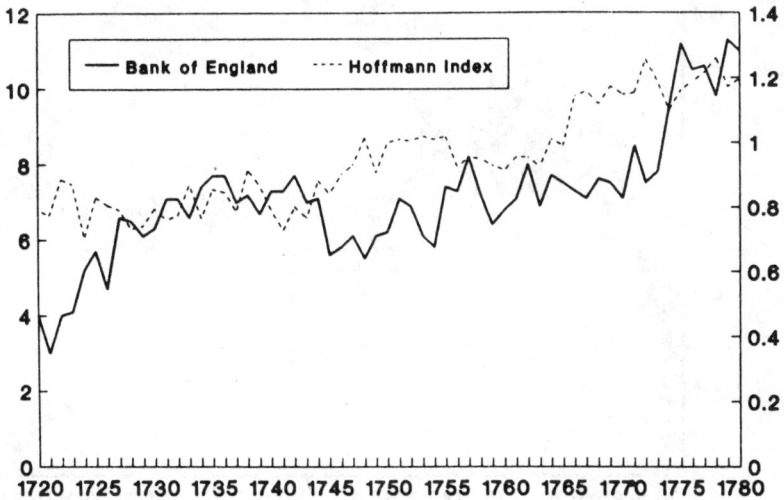

Figure 1.2   Bank of England circulating notes and drawing accounts, 1720–80

respect to macroeconomic issues, the money stock is a potential policy control variable and, in any period, what happens to the quantity of money is a useful indicator of financial pressures – and of crises.

The Bank of England from its inception operated somewhat as a central bank, even though it was privately owned and held private deposits. Its size, further, is a good indicator of general credit conditions in the British economy. Figure 1.2 contains the summation of circulating banknotes and drawing accounts for the period 1720–80; the source of the data is Ashton (1959). Here it is evident that Bank of England liabilities grow quite a lot more rapidly than the industrial sector (as measured by the Hoffmann index of production) and frequently moves in a different direction. The Bank of England liabilities also appear to stagnate from the mid-1740s to the mid-1770s. As we will note immediately, this is a period of considerable growth in the banking sector as a whole.

Of course there were many other banking institutions at this time, although a detailed accounting is not in order in this study. The base of the system was the coinage, and this was minted by the Treasury at set prices that never, it seems, quite conformed to world prices in

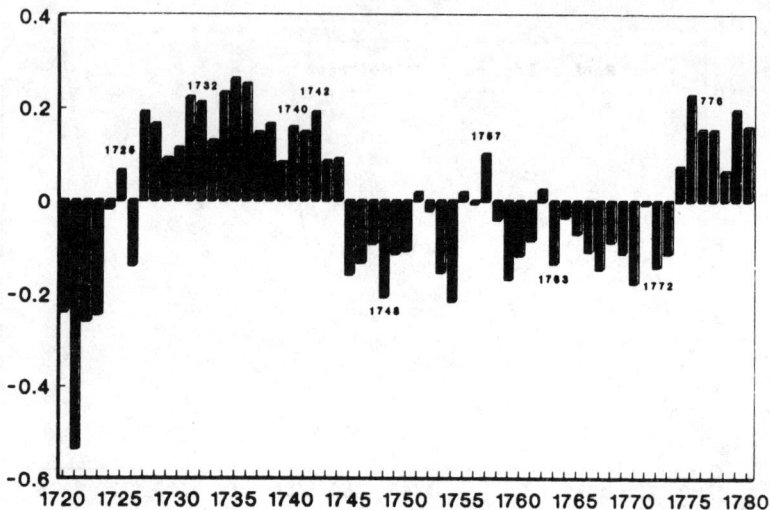

Millions, detrended

Figure 1.3   Bank of England detrended notes and drawing accounts

silver (sterling) markets. In any case, there is general agreement in
the literature that the coinage was inadequate for ordinary transactions through much of the 18th century. Commercial banks in a
modern form existed before the Bank of England (itself chartered in
1694), led by those of the goldsmiths. By the beginning of the 18th
century, private banks (e.g., Childs) were in existence as well and the
system consisted of London and country banks. By 1750–65 there
were 20 to 30 London banks and by 1770 there were 50 (Ashton,
1959). In the country, banking was tied more closely to trading
houses or retailers; banking-style operations were extensive, but by
1750 there were only about a dozen actual country banks in existence.
By 1797, in turn, 334 country banks were counted in England and
Wales; most seem to have sprung up during the prosperous years
during the acceleration of British industrialization, after 1750. While
some failed during the periods of credit stringency in the second half
of the 18th century, most did not. In any case, a kind of 'free' banking
is the rule and banking services, like many industries, generally
expanded during this period. We are not able, at present, to document this much more firmly, however.

In Figure 1.3 we illustrate a detrended series of notes in circulation
plus drawing account balances of the Bank of England.[10] This is not

the money supply, of course, but it would figure importantly in any measure of the money supply that is produced for this period. In the figure, the dates are set against those observations that are (later in this chapter) identified as years when the economy turned sharply down. Quite clearly, financial changes occurred at most such times, with about two thirds of the observations indicating peaks, and one third recession years. In some of those years (1745, 1763, 1769, 1773 and 1778) the Bank's bullion and coin reserves were also very low, indicating extreme pressure on the banking system. Part of this was simply due to the Bank taking on the responsibility of trying to help shore up the banking system.

1.5 BRITISH NATIONAL INCOME IN THE 18TH CENTURY

The best numbers belong to England and Wales; we employ the standard figures that appear in a summary by Cole (1981). The numbers in Table 1.10 show a real GNP growth rate for 1700 to 1780 of 0.76 of 1 per cent and, more surprisingly, substantial growth (0.68) in the 1700 to 1750 period (when population growth was only 0.32 per cent). As Figure 1.4 shows more dramatically, there is a spurt in the last decade, and a 'recession' in the war-plagued 1760s, but otherwise the pace of growth seems relentlessly upward throughout the century.

There is another aspect to the situation that might be remarked on,

Table 1.10   The national product of England and Wales, 1700–1800 (£m)

	Current prices				Constant prices			
	Agriculture	Industry/ Commerce	All other	Total	Agriculture	Industry/ Commerce	All other	Total
1700	20.0	16.5	13.5	50.0	20.0	16.5	13.5	50.0
1710	20.4	16.2	15.3	51.9	20.6	17.2	16.2	53.9
1720	18.2	17.1	12.2	47.4	24.1	19.6	13.9	57.5
1730	18.2	18.0	12.0	48.2	23.6	21.1	14.0	58.7
1740	18.4	18.1	13.8	50.3	26.1	21.6	16.4	64.1
1750	20.7	20.6	14.3	56.2	28.1	24.6	17.7	70.4
1760	25.1	27.1	21.4	73.6	28.9	29.6	23.4	81.9
1770	33.5	30.5	16.9	80.9	29.0	33.0	18.3	80.3
1780	34.1	33.1	29.1	96.4	31.5	32.2	28.3	92.0
1790	40.6	49.8	26.2	116.6	33.4	46.2	24.4	104.1
1800	74.3	84.6	53.6	212.7	36.2	61.0	38.6	135.8

Source: Cole (1981).

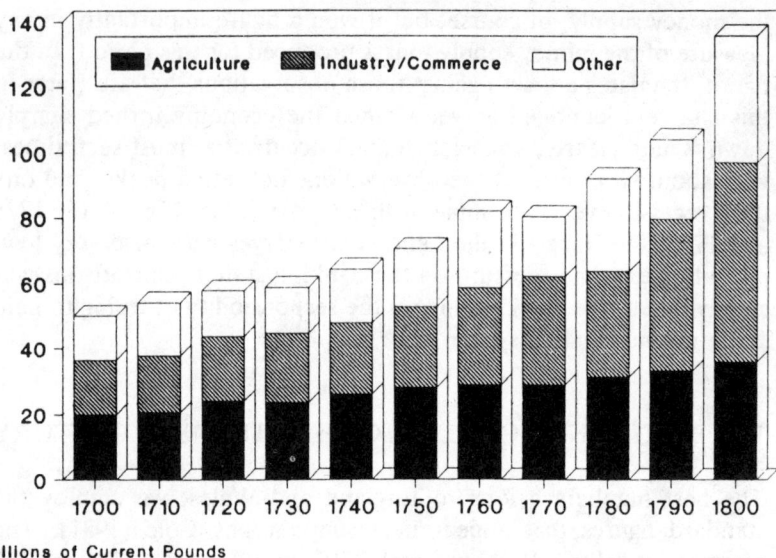

Figure 1.4   National product of England and Wales, 1700–1800

and that concerns the composition of English and Welsh output in the GNP figures. Here we can refer either to the right-hand columns of Table 1.10 or to Figure 1.4. It is readily apparent that all sectors were expanding steadily, but that industrialization (and 'other' activity) were growing slightly more rapidly than agriculture. Indeed, in 1700, agriculture had 40 per cent of GNP and industry 33 per cent; in 1780, they were about even at 34.2 and 35 per cent respectively. Then industry took off, reaching 44.9 (to agriculture's 26.7) per cent over the next 20 years. This was an exceedingly rapid transformation, albeit one that was already underway by 1700, and is quite unprecedented in history to that date. We will see, though, as we look at all of the other countries in this study, that such a rapid break from agricultural dominance is apparently characteristic of the period when the first important industrial acceleration occurs. This may seem obvious enough, but what is being underscored here is the rapidity of the event.

There is, though, a controversy over the British numbers and the sharpest criticism of these early figures has been raised by Crafts (1976). The index just described has an agricultural and an 'industry and commerce' sector and it is constructed as a weighted average. There are, of course, no direct figures on production in any sector and so a number of working assumptions are needed to produce general figures such as those reproduced in Table 1.10. For one thing, if one has population figures, then one can assume a constant per capita consumption of grain and thereby arrive (with a suitable starting figure) at an important part of the agricultural series; this is what Deane and Cole, whose calculations these are, did. This, of course, assumes that population figures are correct and that the standard of living (and hence grain consumption) was unchanged over the period. Deane and Cole also use export figures in order to arrive at estimates of industrial growth; these are erratic numbers at best and, in any case, are possibly quite unrepresentative of the general structure of commerce and industry in any period that one can think of.

On the basis of these and other problems, Crafts suggests that we return to the existing output statistics, such as they are, and try to arrive at a separate industrial output series. Crafts (1983) publishes the following estimates (based on 1770 weights) of the annual rates of growth per decade of industrial output.

1700–1760	0.71
1760–1770	1.23
1770–1780	1.79
1780–1790	1.60 (3.68)
1790–1801	1.33 (2.49)

Here the figures in parentheses refer to growth rates with the weights taken at 1801 shares. If these figures pass muster, then, the overwhelming impression generated is that growth just before 1800 was actually slower – and output already higher – than Deane and Cole surmised. Indeed, Crafts (1983, p. 199) makes the surprising claim that

> The economy did not experience a 'take-off' in the last two decades of the eighteenth century. The pace of growth quickened at that time, but not dramatically so. The investment ratio rose by about 1 per cent of national income and total factor productivity rose about .15 per cent per year compared with 1700–60. Consumption per head rose by only about 4 per cent in two decades.

This is certainly not the conventional view. We should note that this does not deny that the composition of commerce and industry changed dramatically, led by cotton and iron, but only that recalculated broad measures do not confirm earlier estimates of a late 18th-century revolution in British industrial output.

What conclusion can one draw from this material? While one is constantly reminded how empirical truths change over time, it seems a relatively safe position would be one that emphasizes that the entire period studied here was one of significant growth in Britain, sometimes even when judged by a per capita standard. At the same time, the redesigning of the index numbers has caused us to revise our views to the effect that we now think there was a less-than-revolutionary pace in the last 20 years of the 18th century. This is probably correct. To this writer, this does not take the excitement out of the study of the industrial revolution; rather, it more carefully quantifies an economic achievement that is surely one of the most remarkable in all recorded history.

1.5.1 Government Spending and Finances

This section introduces a topic – and a controversy – that will get some further coverage in later chapters; this controversy concerns the possible crowding-out of private expenditures by government spending. In fact, governments prior to the industrial revolution did very little spending compared with modern times, but when wars arrived they unleashed their fiscal machinery. Normally, governments would attempt to finance their expenditures through taxes, but partly because the tax base at the time was capable only of a moderate generation of extra revenues over the short run, the British government would either run its cash-creating machinery (as it did during the Napoleonic wars) or issue debt, as it did during all of its major wars. Of course these choices (taxes, money, debt) exhaust the broad possibilities for governments at any time, so what follows is a general discussion, even though couched in terms of specific events in British economic history.

In Barro's (1987) controversial analysis of the crowding-out effect of large temporary government expenditures in Britain, he notes that for the wars of the period up until 1780 there were significant deviations (from trend) of the ratio of military spending to national income in the following cases:[11]

War of the Spanish Succession (1707)	5%
War of the Austrian Succession (1748)	6%
Seven Years War (1761)	16%
American Revolution (1782)	10%

These provide significant cases of 'temporary government expenditure'. Furthermore, drawing on some numbers provided by Homer, government debt grew rapidly during the same war periods (1977, p. 188),

		Rise in national debt (m)
1688–1727	Various wars	£ 52.2
1739–1748	Austrian War	29.2
1756–1763	Seven Years War	52.2
1775–1783	American Revolution	104.7
		£238.3

At all other times during the period, the debt either declined or grew very slowly. Thus, in 1688 the national debt stood at £0.6 million and in 1783 at £231.8 million. As one can see, the total of the debt financing just described roughly equals the total debt by the end of the period, so that British wars are the proximate source of the permanent national debt until 1783.[12] Taxation, in turn, had little to do with the financing of wars, although it did generally rise in wartime.[13]

Now the first issue to consider is largely resolved in the literature; this concerns whether it matters how the debt is financed – by taxes or by debt, generically. Whether it holds in detail or not, it is very likely to be true that economic agents at any time realize that the appropriate way to think of government expenditures on war is as a form of social consumption in which the resources used in the effort are used up at the time of the war. Furthermore, argues David Ricardo and many others since 1817, it is probable that these same economic agents viewed taxes and debt as broadly equivalent methods of finance. For both methods of finance, of course, the government uses the claims on current resources and in both methods the private sector releases them. The tax measures hit directly; for bonds, the usual version of the theory stresses that the private sector merely puts aside funds (in the form of the current savings held in the form of government bonds) that are exactly equal to the present value of the future tax liability. This amount is exactly equal to the price of the bonds at the time of issue, *ex hypothesi*.

Now this is clearly an idealized situation and it is reasonable to hold to a less rigid interpretation of the theory. It is also important to recognize that both consumption and investment might well be reduced by such a crowding-out effect, and that the capital stock would tend to stand at a lower level than otherwise after the war is over.[14] In any event, there are two things one might want to look for as evidence of this effect in real world cases: direct evidence of the crowding-out of investment spending and higher real interest rates. As Barro puts it (1987, p. 221),

> Fluctuations in government purchases influence the economy in numerous ways. There are effects on real interest rates, and on the quantities of output, consumption, and investment. There are direct effects on the price level. . . . There are also effects on the current-account balance and on budget deficits, which may have additional influences on the economy.

Barro finds, for this period, that the real interest rate rose as follows,

War of Spanish Succession (1702–13)	2.7
War of Austrian Succession (etc.) (1740–48)	0.6
Seven Years War (1756–63)	1.2
American Independence (1775–83)	1.9

He uses annual Consol rates. This is, certainly, suggestive of the influence he is looking for, but one needs to remember that the real interest rate, like any price, has other things influencing it as well. Thus, this evidence is consistent with the existence of crowding out, but no more than that.

If one is to employ the correct real interest rate, then, of course, it is the *ex-ante* (expected) rate to which the theory refers. That is, in the Fisher Equation, the observed nominal rate of interest (i) is given by

$$i_t = r_t^e + \pi_t^e \tag{1.1}$$

where r^e is the expected real rate and π^e is the expected rate of inflation. For the most part, one cannot expect to get observations on the expected real rate, so the empirical game is either played out with inflationary expectations, or truly heroic assumptions are made to link nominal interest rates directly to real. In the modern literature the usual approach is to employ some sort of smoothed set of past inflation rates (or, even, past and future inflation rates) as a likely proxy for what economic agents might have had in mind about future inflation rates at the time. In some cases, though, especially if the rate of inflation is very low (as it was through most of the period 1700 to 1780), the nominal rate might actually be a reasonable proxy for the

Table 1.11   Quarterly interest rates in the 18th century. Nominal and (*ex-post*) real rates, 1718–1782

Date	War/Peace	Nominal rates		Inflation	Real rates	
		Short	Long		Short	Long
1718–39	Peace	3.986	4.287	−0.237	4.223	4.524
1740–48	War	3.227	3.931	1.009	2.218	2.922
1749–55	Peace	3.035	3.511	−0.510	3.545	4.021
1756–63	War	3.849	3.960	1.563	2.286	2.397
1764–74	Peace	3.177	3.709	2.507	0.670	1.202
1775–82	War	3.558	4.643	−1.328	4.886	5.971

real rate, at least under normal conditions (not, possibly, those of wartime!).

Barro does his experiments, which are suggestive at best, on annual data. We now have quarterly interest rates, to try to illustrate the effect; these are the work of Weiller and Mirowski (1990). Using the Bank of England dividend yield as the long-term rate and the East India bond rate as the short term, Table 1.11 captures the numbers for war and peace-time interest and inflation rates. The inflation series here is that of Phelps Brown and Hopkins (1956) and is a cost of living index; the protagonists in the debate tend to use a wholesale price index. In any case, it is an annual rate, unfortunately, so the calculation in the table is approximate.

It is hard to generalize, but one surely notices that the three war periods show nominal interest rates in excess of the following peace-time period (it would be the preceding period for the last set, of course). This is suggestive. Real rates are very high during the war for American Independence, speaking relatively, and the deflation of that period is certainly a contributor to that situation. On the other hand, real rates are lower during the first two war periods shown in Table 1.11, suggesting that we would not find significant crowding out then (although we might find savings rather low) if we only had the data.

Finally, let us comment on the tax situation. O'Brien (1988) has real tax receipts calculated as centred five-year averages for the 1700 to 1780 period.[15] The numbers in the last column of Table 1.12 drift upward over the century, and are relatively higher than (roughly) comparable late 19th-century calculations. They also show no clear pattern in relation to wars (marked with an asterisk), although the

Table 1.12

	Real tax receipts (£m)	Taxes as a percentage of income
1700	4.23	8.8
1705	5.61	
1710	4.71	9.2*
1715	5.46	
1720	5.93	10.8
1725	5.53	
1730	6.29	10.7
1735	5.79	
1740	5.50	8.7*
1745	6.66	
1750	7.12	10.5
1755	6.49	
1760	8.34	11.5*
1765	8.44	
1770	8.15	10.5
1775	7.94	
1780	9.79	11.7*

1760 and 1780 figures are marginally higher than the surrounding peace-time numbers. Some of this fuzziness is owing to the paucity of the data, but in any case it is evident that the range of 8.7 to 11.7 per cent of GNP for tax revenues would not provide much assistance in war-time financing, even if it were actually timed that way. This is what was claimed above.[16]

None of the empirical work of this section, it seems, comes out very strongly one way or the other with respect to the major theoretical issues. Possibly the safest generalization is that there certainly is some evidence of crowding out, at least in the form of a rise in the real rate of interest during the period of most intense deficit financing. This result held during war-time periods in the second half of the century. Beyond that we cannot go, and we cannot estimate any actual crowding-out effects (on investment spending for example), since we lack annual investment figures. But we are not through with this topic, and further evidence will be assessed in both Chapters 2 and 3, for the British case. Even there, however, the effect does not appear to be considerable, whether one looks at interest rates or actual expenditures.

1.6   WAGES, PROFITS AND INTEREST

What can one say about the functional distribution of income in the 18th century? Rather more than one might have suspected, particularly if one is willing to lean heavily on the wage, profit and interest rate data that are available. Part of this availability is the result of intense interest in the profession in the 'standard of living controversy' concerning the relative position of workers between 1750 and 1850; this is discussed at greater length in Chapter 2. The current section will have something to say on that topic in what follows, but since our survey stops around 1780, this part of the discussion should be regarded as preliminary.

1.6.1   Real Wages

The existing literature puts a lot of weight on a population-driven real wage rate story, with the influence coming either directly through relatively rapid population growth on the (excess) supply of labour, or indirectly through its effect on the price level. Clearly, both the demand for labour and the supply of labour would increase when population grows, so that a clear decision here is unavailable. Furthermore and moving to the next level of generality, as already discussed in this chapter it is impossible to establish an a priori case as to whether the net effect of population growth is to increase aggregate demand faster than aggregate supply, *ceteris paribus*. The fact is, it could. Indeed, since both inflation and population growth occur together frequently throughout history, there is enough fuel to keep this particular debate raging indefinitely.

There is another strand of the literature that enters here, although it is usually not phrased in terms of aggregate demand and supply; this is a population-velocity explanation of inflation that seems to tie up several loose ends in the simpler monetary explanation of inflation. This theory suggests that population growth would induce a change in the transactions velocity of money. What happens is that the spill-over on the farm would end up in the city (a clear fact!) which would produce more transactions (since the city has a much more developed market economy than the agricultural areas). Faced with the need for more transactions (but not with a sufficient rise in real income to stifle the inflation), and faced with a relatively inelastic money supply (the money supply is hard-money based and this is tied to the world production of precious metals), the velocity of money

Table 1.13   Real wages, population, and inflation in England, 1701–1801
(Index numbers, 1701 = 100)

	Real wage	Price level	Inflation	Population level	(Rate)
1701	100.0	100.0	. . .	100.0	. . .
1711	71.9	151.7	4.17	104.2	0.41
1721	107.0	103.1	−3.86	107.0	0.27
1731	107.0	102.2	−0.09	105.7	−0.12
1741	98.2	121.5	1.73	112.3	0.61
1751	122.8	98.0	−2.15	117.2	0.42
1761	114.0	104.8	0.67	125.1	0.66
1771	91.2	132.2	2.32	131.8	0.52
1781	112.3	129.7	−0.19	143.1	0.83
1791	96.5	148.5	1.35	155.2	0.81
1801	59.6	298.8	6.99	173.2	1.09

Sources: Cols 1, 2: Phelps Brown and Hopkins (1956); Col. 4: Lee and Schofield (1981).

would rise. This rise, it is argued, is actually larger than the increase (if any) in the real value of transactions and so, since MV=Py in the equation of exchange, prices must rise.

The major problem with this view is that this puts a lot of strain on velocity (a number often thought to be tied to payments habits), which must accelerate and decelerate with the rate of inflation (not the price *level*) for this to be an effective explanation. Indeed, in the history of prices of Europe before the industrial revolution, there are periods when inflation persisted for as long as 100 years, and there are always numerous examples of enormous price level spikes and dips in the data. Velocity would have to follow suit.

Now the reason this is relevant to the discussion of the standard of living is that the standard calculation of the real wage is the nominal wage divided by the price level. Thus, if there is inflation, *ceteris paribus*, real wages would fall. In modern times, nominal wages adjust with inflation, too, but in the 18th century it is at least arguable that nominal wages did not keep pace with inflation, at least in the short run, setting up a population–inflation–fall of real wages-decline of workers' living standards story that would seem to be complete.

There are some data bearing on these topics for 18th-century England, given in Table 1.13. It is noticeable here that the population story actually does not work all that well (for example, the second fastest population growth (1771–81) is associated with a rising real wage and a falling price level, instead of the opposite).[17] Actually, as the table makes clear, there is not much of a trend in real wages at all, with most of the decline coming in the last decade of the century.

More generally, because of a very small number of changes in the nominal wage, the real wage and inflation are negatively correlated over the period, whether (−0.83) or not (−0.74) the last decade is included. Population is similarly (positively) correlated with the price level (+0.76 and + 0.51) but, curiously, population and the real wage are essentially uncorrelated in the period excluding the last decade (but are negatively correlated (at −0.39) when that one observation is added in. This is not very strong support for the population pressure thesis when one additionally notes the extreme weakness in the money wage series and (see Chapter 2) the strong possibility that the end-of-century numbers are especially unreliable. We also note that the growth rates of prices and population (in Columns (3) and (5)) show only a modest positive correlation (+0.26) over the nine observations prior to the last decade.[18]

There are two aspects of the theory that can be explored empirically. For one thing, we can look for a direct link between population and prices. The other thing is to compare the annual data for real wages and prices, looking for evidence that prices might influence real wages. With respect to the relation between population and prices – in particular, the notion that population influences prices – we do have some reasonable data for England to enable a direct test. First of all, just to get things going, let us note that there is a strong correlation between the two series of annual data,[19] as shown in Table 1.14. While this is just a contemporaneous correlation and contains no causal information, it is surely interesting that the addition of the years from 1780 to 1800, when population and prices grew the fastest, produces a sizeable increase in what is already a significantly positive correlation.

In order to deal with the causal issues raised, a procedure exists – the Granger-causality test – that can be employed for the purpose of

Table 1.14   Consumer prices and population correlation coefficients

1700–1780	0.672
1780–1800	0.864

determining the extent of statistical 'causality'. We will compare the
results of the regression of

$$y_t = \alpha + \sum_{i=1}^{r} \beta_i y_{t-i} + \sum_{i=1}^{r} \delta_i x_{t-i} + e_t \qquad (1.2)$$

with the same regression restricted to the case of $\delta_i = 0$ $(i = 1, \ldots,$
$r)$. The test is an F-test and we will require a probability of 0.05 to
justify saying that the lags in the independent variable (x) predetermine y (holding the history of y constant in the first set of terms).

We will employ the Granger test elsewhere in this study, so, upon
its first appearance, we need to enter some important qualifications.
Most importantly, if the conditions of the regression equation are met
and the independent variables on the right-hand side of the equation
are themselves independent of the error term, then statistical causality (or exogeneity) has been established if the variables, as a group,
provide a statistically significant contribution to the explanation of
the dependent variable. Because the variables on the right-hand side
are predetermined variables (are drawn from time periods prior to
that of the dependent variable) the test is sometimes referred to as a
test of predeterminateness, although whether it is called that or the
Granger-causality test (as it is here) is immaterial as long as its
limitations are understood.

The causality (exogeneity) that is established by such a means is
just between the variables studied and does not imply causality in an
economic sense necessarily, although it may be consistent with one
(or, usually, more) economic theories in the literature. Other variables can, and often do, statistically cause the same dependent variable, and it is not unreasonable to expect rival theories to produce the
same reduced form test in the sense of the equation just illustrated.
Finally, we should note that the test does not provide any indication
of the degree of the influence, from trivial to all-encompassing,
although one does at least acquire the sign of the influence in this
particular experiment. This is a drawback, of course, but one should
take the test for what it does provide, evidence of a statistically
significant link between variates of interest to one or more theories,
where such a link need not have existed. That is the spirit in which we
continue with our discussion of the influence of population growth on
the price level.

Turning to the actual tests, Table (1.15) describes the results of a
battery of tests on log-level and differenced data for the population-
prices linkage. Note that the table provides the p-values (probabili-

Table 1.15 The influence of population on English prices, 1700–1800

| | Levels of significance (p-values) for lags of | | | | |
	1	2	3	4	5
Log level, 1700–1800					
Population → Prices	0.000*	0.000*	0.001*	0.022*	0.054
Prices → Population	0.003*	0.003*	0.065	0.116	0.060
First difference, 1700–1800					
Population → Prices	0.003*	0.011*	0.033*	0.076	0.027*
Prices → Population	0.002*	0.034*	0.075	0.077	0.129
Log level, 1700–1780					
Population → Prices	0.002*	0.002*	0.013*	0.082	0.142
Prices → Population	0.005*	0.014*	0.303	0.421	0.208
First difference, 1700–1780					
Population → Prices	0.011*	0.065	0.201	0.354	0.135
Prices → Population	0.005*	0.079	0.330	0.172	0.242

ties) and that we are generally looking for a value less than or equal to 0.05. When these are achieved, they are marked in the table with an asterisk. These results establish bidirectional causality between population and the cost-of-living index in England. The line of Granger causation between population and prices (with a positive sign that is not shown) is clearer on levels than first differences (the usual result) and stronger for the population-push line than for the prices-on-population (reverse link). Note that the first differences are presented here to deal with the possible criticism of the test in levels that the results of the F-test are possibly invalid if the data are non-stationary (as these are). A complete discussion of the issues involved in dealing with non-stationary data is presented in Chapter 3.

The strong evidence of reverse causation, running from prices to population, is a little disconcerting at first glance. The sign of this relation is negative and significant (and is measured by the sum of the lag coefficients on the independent variables) and suggests, directly, that price rises, *ceteris paribus*, are associated with something that reduces population in the 18th century. Bad harvests are one such known phenomenon. This is an interesting statistical result that ought to be further studied on other data and, even, at other times in the pre-industrial economy.

The other thing we might look at, with the same procedure, is the link between real wages and prices, looking to see if inflation, perhaps, reduces real wages in a Granger-causal sense. For England, the longest run of annual data we can dig out of the Phelps Brown

Table 1.16   Real wage growth and inflation[20]

	Real wage growth	Inflation
Germany (1701–1753)	−0.33	0.61
Austria (1701–1770)	−0.17	0.26
England (1736–1773)	−0.95	0.95

and Hopkins papers (1956, 1957) are for 1736 to 1773 and so the following summary must make do with that. Phelps Brown and Hopkins (1959) also report similar sets of calculations for Austria (Vienna, actually) covering 1701 to 1770 and Germany (Augsburg, really) for 1701 to 1753, and so these three sets of data are also considered in the following discussion.

Looking at the rates of change (to detrend the data), and calculating the growth rates via regressions, Table 1.16 presents overall growth rates for real wages and prices. Note that the time periods here are not arbitrary (except for the beginning date) but reflect the longest consecutive (annual) data periods available in the 18th century (from the above-mentioned sources). In any case, an apparent negative correlation appears to be common experience across the three countries, as things stand, with the English figures appearing rather extreme, really. This is not surprising.

Now correlation is not causation, and in view of the exceedingly sparse nominal wage data, little faith can be put in contemporaneous correlations like those just shown. In fact, the hypothesis we are considering suggests that inflation causes real wages to decline, i.e., that population pressure forces up prices and that the lag of wages behind prices produces a fall in real wages (as long as the gap is not eliminated). This being the case, a formal causality test might reasonably show inflation causing real wages. To search for this possibility, the Granger-causality test was applied to each of these data sets, for lags up to five years, but there was absolutely no sign of any causal relationship (or even a reverse-causal relationship) in these data. Of course the apparent strong effect at the end of the century is not included in any of this, but there was considerable population growth throughout, so this should not have destroyed such a relation, if it existed. On the other hand, these real wage data may, indeed, be essentially worthless, being a mirror image of the price level and little else, especially for England. On net, then, we have found an interesting and significant Granger-causal link between population and prices, but nothing between prices and real wages. While the latter effect may indeed exist for this period, the view is taken here that the nominal wage series is not of a sufficient quality to render the real wage series (of Phelps Brown and Hopkins) sufficiently useful for purposes of such tests. There could well be something to the population pressure theories on this evidence, although we must again caution the reader that the magnitude of the influence is not revealed here, and a powerful alternative, the quantity theory of money, has yet to weigh in for the contest.

1.6.2 Profits and Interest

Philip Mirowski (1985) has constructed an index of profit rates for almost a century (1728–1826) and a preliminary look at this index, which we will use below in our discussion of the 18th-century business cycle, seems appropriate here. Actually, there are two indices – adjusted profits and mean profits – in his collection. The *mean profit* index is the average profit rate for each year (the rather small sample size is different for each year, as firms come and go). The *adjusted profit* index divides each firm series by its mean and then averages across each year; the purpose of this adjustment is to eliminate fluctuations in the index due solely to the arrival and departure of firms.[21] The two series are graphed in Figure 1.5 for the period 1728 to 1800.

Curiously, although the procedure is not on the short list of obvious ways to detrend the data, the calculation of the adjusted profit index does just that, as Figure 1.5 suggests. In this comparison, the two series are converted to index numbers with a common base year (1754). Returning to the raw data, and calculating the trend formally (via Log $x = \alpha + \beta Date$), this impression can be confirmed, as in Table 1.17. The mean profit series has a strong trend, at 2.48 per cent per year, while the very choppy adjusted profit series evidently has no trend. One can conclude that adjusting the series for the arrival and departure of firms may well eliminate a trend that may have been induced by the way the data were put together rather than produced by rising profit rates.[22] In any case, we note that the possible cyclical information in the two series is not all that dissimilar – look back at Figure 1.4 – although Mirowski's motive was to produce a series that could be used to study the cycle. In fact, the two series are highly correlated (at 0.84); below we will suggest that the adjusted profit index does not serve that purpose particularly well because it is almost a random series.

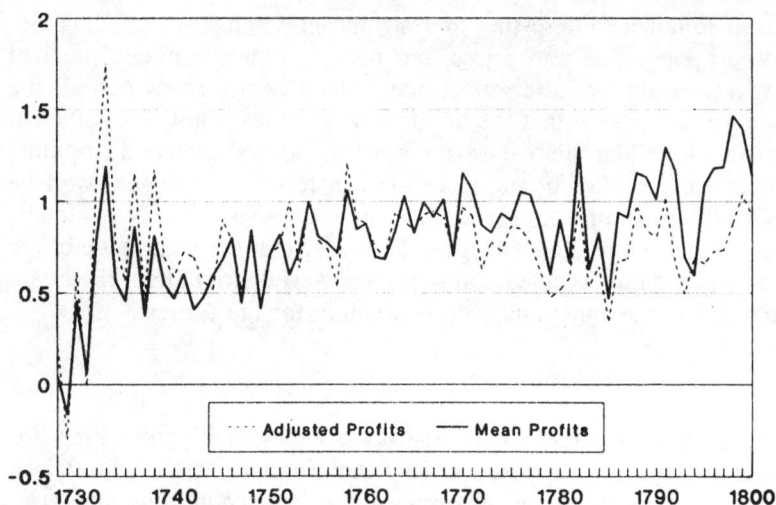

Figure 1.5   Mirowski's profit indices (1754 = 1)

Table 1.17

	α	β	R^2
Log mean profit	−41.28	0.0248	0.336
	(4.82)	(5.08)	
Log adjusted profit	−2.95	0.0016	0.006
	(0.58)	(0.57)	

t-values in parentheses.

Mirowski (1981) has also published an annual index of share prices – again for the discussion of business cycles – and we might as well append those figures here, since they, too can be inspected for trends. We note, though, that the index is simple-sum, over at most six share prices. In Figure 1.6, then, we have compared the yield on the 3 per cent Consol (it is the 3 per cent annuity before 1753) with the share index. The former series, drawn from Homer (1977), begins in 1729. Here we find no obvious trend in the share index, while the Consol rate appears to drift upward (at 0.5 per cent per year).[23] The two series actually seem like mirror images of each other, containing much of the same cyclical information; indeed, the simple correlation

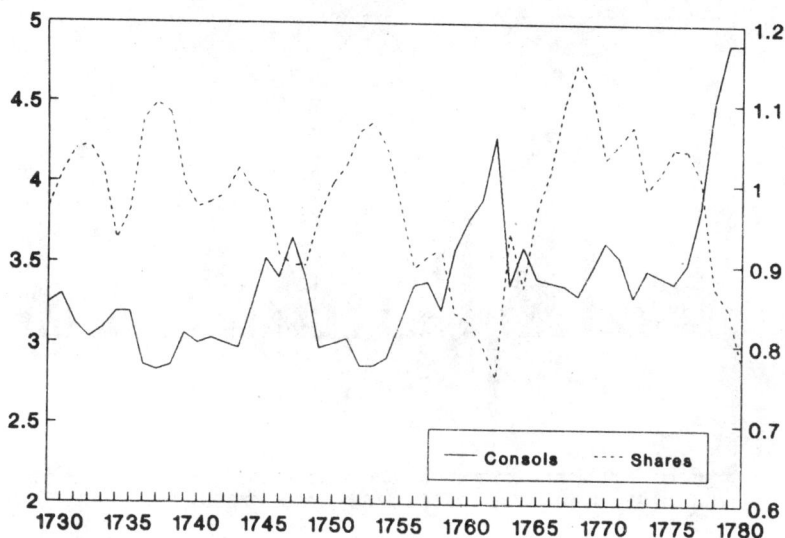

Figure 1.6   Consol rates and share prices, 1729–80

coefficient is −0.66. We will return to this in a moment, just noting that for now the important finding is that if there is an upward drift to the return on capital in this period – as measured by profits, share prices and interest rates – it is only nominal interest rates that indisputably show this.

Of course, nominal interest rates are not ideal for such purposes, in view of the possibility of the Fisher Effect. Thus, an *ex-ante* real rate of interest (r), calculated as the nominal rate less expected inflation is the correct rate for this calculation (see Equation (1.1) above). A well-known price series is available for this period (Phelps Brown and Hopkins, 1956), although it is a very choppy series, at least compared with modern annual price indices. One simple way to acquire an expected inflation rate – among the infinite number available – is to calculate a 10-year moving average of past inflation rates. When this is done,[24] the following graph (Figure 1.7) results. Here there is no obvious overall trend, but there is a slight upward drift in the real rate in the later years in the series. Note the labelling in the graph of upper turning points in the series (possibly denoting financial crises); these will be considered in the next section.

Weiller and Mirowski (1990) have also done something really unusual with the 18th-century interest rate data; they have tested the

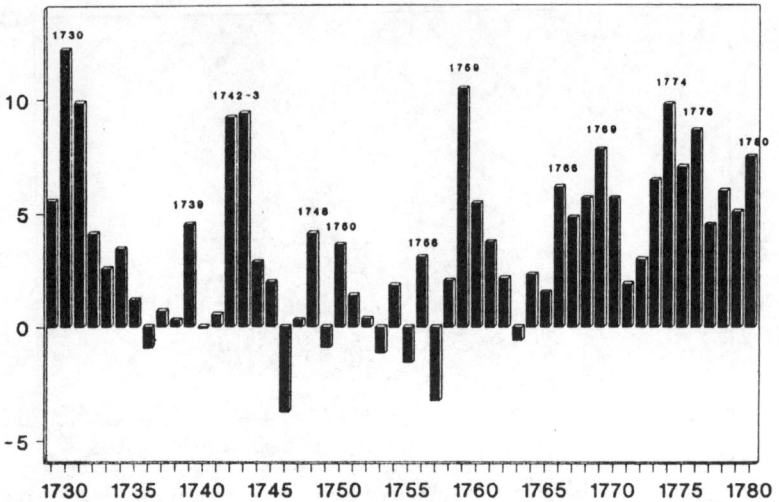

Figure 1.7   The real consol rate, 1729–80

rational expectations theory of the determination of the term structure of interest rates. This is done on newly constructed quarterly data running from 1718 to 1796. The rational expectations hypothesis argues that economic agents employ all of the information available to them – and as good a model as possible (usually implicitly) – to forecast variables that matter to them. They then use these forecasts (of, for example, the real rate of interest) to guide them in their investment strategies. Interest rates, in this context, are especially attractive to economists because they are *ex-ante* concepts by definition; for example, today's two-period nominal interest rate contains an implicit forecast of one-period interest rates a year hence. The question Weiller and Mirowski ask is whether this forecast has the properties of a rationally-determined variable and, further, whether it makes use of all available information.

On the whole, for the data set just mentioned, the rational expectations does not do all that well in their tests, which is certainly not surprising, although in at least one of their passes at the data there is some support (which is surprising). This is actually about the level of support the theory attains on tests of more modern data. We do not have the space to go into the details of their work here, but one result of theirs is directly related to Section 1.7 on business cycles, so a brief discussion here can serve as a bridge to that material. This is the

Table 1.18   Financial crises

	Bankruptcy crises	Term-structure inversions
1720	x	x
1726	x	x
1747		x
1761		x
1765		x
1772	x	
1778	x	

identification of financial crises in England by means of term-structure 'inversions'. These are periods during which the term structure is inverted, meaning that the short-term rate is greater than the long-term rate.

In the expectations theory of the term structure of interest rates, such an inversion is expected when current short term rates are relatively high, since an expected fall in interest rates would produce predictions (and *ex-ante* marginal rates) that are lower for the future period for which such a drop is expected. Even so, this may also be due to a liquidity crisis (that is, a sudden tightening of the supply of liquid funds). Comparing Hoppit's (1986) series on bankruptcies with Weiller and Mirowski's (1990, p. 9) list of inversions, we have two sets of financial crises in the period 1720 to 1780 (Table 1.18), the first by bankruptcies and the second by term-structure inversions.[25] The cases in which wars were involved are 1747, 1761, and 1778. In any case, these possible financial crises are not necessarily associated with real events, although in practice, most may well have been in this period (1761 and 1765 may not have shown real downturns, and the 1720 event was quite short, in real terms, as we shall see). This discussion is continued in the next section.

1.7   THE 18TH-CENTURY BUSINESS CYCLE (TO 1780)

There is work on the 18th-century business cycle, but only Mirowski's (1985) is conducted from a time-series perspective. Indeed, contemporary narrative evidence provides the sources of much of the professional discussion and, when there are no such descriptions, cyclical events sometimes appear to fall through the cracks. The established

Table 1.19　Cyclical turning points

	Mirowski	Deane	Ashton	Hoffmann	Real rate
1700–01	x			x	
1704	x				
1708	x			x	
1717				x	
1720	x	x	x		
1722				x	
1725–6	x		x	x	
1732–3	x		x	x	x
1735					x
1738				x	
1740					x
1743	x				
1745		x	x		x
1748				x	x
1752					x
1757–8	x				x
1761			x		
1762–3	x	x	x		x
1767				x	
1770					x
1772	x	x	x	x	
1776	x	x			
1778			x	x	x
Average	7.0	10.9	8.0	7.6	5.5

chronology shows considerable disagreement, as Table 1.19 makes clear. Here we have made use of Figure 1.7, where the real interest rate was graphed, and Figure 1.8, below. The latter series is that of the detrended logs of the Hoffmann index, with the upper turning points marked.

In Table 1.19, the Mirowski index has an average length of cycle of seven years, which the Hoffmann index, somewhat surprisingly, comes close to (at 7.6). The Deane and Ashton indices have rather long (and to this reader implausible) cycles, while the real interest rate index measure has cycles averaging only 5.5 years in length.[26]

If we accept that the share index could sometimes predict a cyclical turning point (the modern US index of leading indicators has a share price component), then there are common cyclical peaks in the three main sources, using Mirowski as the base, as follows:

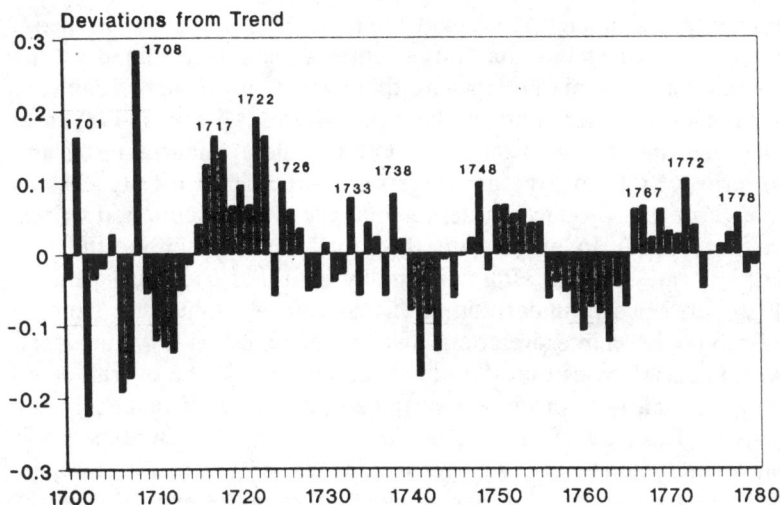

Figure 1.8   British business cycles, 1700–80 (based on Hoffmann production index)

1720
1725–6
1732–3
1743–5
1763
1772
1776–8

The three-year peaks in 1743–5 and 1776–8 are, quite possibly, 'double-dip' events, rather than continuous declines. Other information indicates that there was probably a peak in 1740, another in 1748 (as indicated by both the real rate and the Hoffmann index) and another in 1757. This is ten peaks in all, and these will form the basis of the following detailed chronology of what appears to have been behind these events.

We begin our story with the bursting of the South Sea Bubble in August 1720. This event was clearly a classic speculative binge that collapsed (the collapse was in shares in general, not just those of the South Sea Company). By January 1721, the South Sea Company stock was 15 per cent of its peak value and even the financially solid

East India Company stock had fallen to 38 per cent of its peak. Hoppit (1986) claims that this event was largely confined to the London financial markets, where there was a surprisingly small (but significant) increase in private financial failures. Mirowski (1985) also identifies this as a financial crisis, both in general financial terms and in terms of a term-structure inversion. Although history teaches us that this event produced a depression, the above mentioned writers do not appear to agree with this; furthermore, neither the real interest rate nor the Hoffmann index identifies a cyclical peak in 1720.[27] It is worth underscoring this, since it is a departure from an all-too-common interpretation, that economic history is well-stocked with financial crises that did not shock (surprise?) the overall economy sufficiently to produce a sustained depression of real economic activity. This may never be resolved for the South Sea Bubble, but, it must be remembered, we are sticking to largely macroeconomic interpretations here, and there is plenty of room for error, in view of the state of the data (if for no other reason).

Mirowski suggests that the decade of the 1720s might have been the 18th-century version of the Great Depression, even though even contemporary opinion does not seem to have noticed this. Certainly there were some partial crop failures late in the decade, but most noticeable in the real figures is the collapse of the export boom (this peaked in 1725) and the financial collapse (and subsequent monetary tightness) in 1726 that seems to have been associated with significantly increased bankruptcies in 1727 and 1728. Since the decade starts with the short but sharp 'bubble depression' and includes these other elements, there certainly seems to be something to Mirowski's view. Indeed, mulling over Ashton's (1955, 1959) figures on real output of various sorts, one finds a remarkable number of series that are no higher in 1730 than they were in 1720. Similarly, Hoffmann's industrial production indices are only marginally higher over the decade.

Moving on, Mirowski says (1985, p. 235)

The preceding boom and crash of 1733–4 must have been perceived as odious and dramatic as that of 1720. There is evidence of business failures and financial crises simultaneously in England, Scotland and Amsterdam.

Profit rates fell for two years (the peak was in 1733) with the financial crisis running from October to December 1733. The Hoffmann index of industrial production (without building) turned sharply down in

1734, to underscore the real dimension of this event. In 1739–40 (Ashton, 1959) in contrast, it seems that bad weather (in this case frost) produced two successive bad harvests, a fuel famine in London (in 1740) and high wheat prices in 1740 and 1741. Similarly, the building trades were depressed. Mirowski (1985) locates a profit dip in 1739, but there is no financial crisis at this time. Ashton (1959) does identify this downturn (1738), which is why we added 1740 to our earlier list.

Bonnie Prince Charlie's ill-fated expedition in September 1745 was associated with a run on the Bank of England (and many other banks) and the financial crisis that ensued went on into 1746. At the same time, wheat exports fell sharply upon the commencement of war with France in 1744, reaching their low point in 1746 (total exports do not seem to have been much affected). Even so, this does not appear to be a major event in real terms (stock prices did decline sharply in early 1746) as judged by bankruptcies (little changed) and the Hoffmann production index. The peak in 1848, in contrast, is clearly defined in real terms (bankruptcies increased for several years thereafter, and the Hoffmann index dropped sharply in 1849). The real adjustment here seems larger than in 1845–6, but the causes are certainly obscure (where is Bonnie Prince Charlie when we need him?).

In 1756 and 1757 there were harvest failures leading to high wheat prices, and Mirowski's profit indices plunged, especially the de-trended (adjusted) index. Ashton (1959) skips right over this event (there was no financial collapse, although there was a minor crisis in 1755) but bankruptcies are also up and the Hoffmann index is off slightly (it is depressed for much of this period). Ashton identifies a recession in 1762 and a financial crisis in 1763 (late in the year). This seems related to the end of the Seven Years War and also involves stock prices (Mirowski's quarterly indices show lower prices in early 1762 and late 1763). Bankruptcies, though, were up sharply in 1764 and the Hoffmann index declined in 1763. In general it seems that the trouble here was more financial than real, but that several shocks to the financial system did produce some real effects.

There was a run of bad weather in 1771–4 in England, but not enough to produce a famine (it did produce relatively high wheat prices from 1772–5). Ashton (1959) says that the export market collapsed in 1773 and the East India Company was particularly affected;[28] he identifies June 1772 to January 1773 as the period of financial crisis. Bankruptcies shot up in 1772 and 1773, reminding us of Mirowski's warning that bankruptcies also can rise during periods of boom, but more to the point, there was a significant amount of failure in the building trades in 1772 and construction was generally slow in 1773–5 (Ashton, 1959). The Hoffmann index (without building) also signalled a recession in 1773 and 1774. Finally, we have identified a real event in 1776–8. This Ashton identifies as a war-related financial crash-cum-recession. Here bankruptcies were up sharply, stock prices tumbled (in 1779) and the building trades entered a 'recession' that may have lasted into the mid-1780s. Mirowski's profit index is sharply lower in 1779 and the Hoffmann index is down somewhat in 1779. Shocks here are not easy to pinpoint, a circumstance that causes Ashton to say (1959, p. 162),

> but it is reasonable to believe that the boom, like the predecessor of 1771–2, had carried within it the seed of decay, and that economic forces were mainly responsible for the slump.

This view of the cycle as endogenous (of the system as inherently unstable) is associated with the Keynesian cycle theory of the mid-20th century. It is not as popular now as it once was, but lacking any better evidence of adequate shocks, we must let this argument stand for the time being.

1.8 CONCLUSION

Chapter 1, although an introduction to the study as well as a relatively loose collection of macroeconomic topics, does actually contain the elements of a theme. The period (1700–80) and the place (Great Britain) provides us with the proximate starting point for modern industrially-dominated economies. We lack the broad data to do detailed macroeconomic investigations, but we do have interest rates, prices and wages, as well as enough information on the behaviour of the real sectors of the economy to hazard some guesses as to what went on.

It appears, then, that the entire period was one of historically rapid growth and that industry and commerce rather speedily replaced agriculture as the larger component of GNP. While there is an ongoing dispute over the pace of growth at different times in this century, the key thing to notice is the growth itself and the historically rapid industrialization. This growth was accompanied by rapid financial development and, unfortunately, business cycles, and it was apparently slowed down (but only marginally) by expenditures on war. Thus, while the specific details of all this will be debated for years to come, it seems as if the British economy of the period has the tone and feel of a modern economy. It has, that is to say, many of its institutions (speaking quite generally) and certainly some of its more important macroeconomic characteristics and all, really, of its broad problems.

The only reason we did not use more of the modern techniques available to examine the 18th-century economy is the fact that the data would not bear their load. This situation is changing rapidly of course, so one must expect more tests in the future and, certainly, interesting changes in the conclusions about various of the issues provisionally summarized here.

2 The First Industrial Revolution in Britain, 1780–1860: National Income and Its Distribution

2.1 INTRODUCTION

The following pages continue the discussion of the British macroeconomy during the nation's period of industrialization, this time from 1780 to 1850/60. This is the period sometimes referred to as that of the First Industrial Revolution. We will spend some space on outlining the broad empirical record in this chapter, although our concern is more with topics already begun: on growth, cycles, crowding-out and the standard of living.

In what follows, we will work to the following outline. As usual, we will begin with a discussion of population and agriculture. The British population, quite simply, grew quite rapidly in this period. In turn, the agricultural sector obediently disgorged resources (relatively speaking), abetted considerably at the beginning (1780–1810) by the rapid spread of enclosures. This material is followed by a brief discussion of the industrial record, on an industry level. We should note that in this discussion the role of the railroad is considerably downgraded, since it arrived fifty-odd years into the industrial revolution, that is, if 1780 is the date of departure.

Turning to the macroeconomics, we encounter two of the most debated topics in all of economic history: how to characterize overall growth during Britain's industrialization (the subject of Section 2.4) and what happened to the distribution of income during the same period (the subject of Section 2.7). In between, we will look at material on the behaviour of (and influence of) investment and government spending, with the latter sub-section 2.5.3 featuring a reprise of the crowding-out debate considered in Chapter 1. In this case the data are much better, and the event – the Napoleonic wars –

much more decisive; the conclusions, however, are not particularly so. This chapter also enters the world of macro-dynamics in Sections 2.5 and 2.6. Section 2.5 seeks an interpretation of the overall growth record, and there is an attempt there to use a neoclassical growth model to outline the possibilities. In Section 2.6 the discussion turns to business cycles, again fortified by better data and a more consistent qualitative literature on the subject.

2.2 POPULATION AND AGRICULTURE: BRIEF NOTES

In view of what has happened to population dynamics since 1750 (really, since at least early medieval times) it would be excusable if someone thought that once you have a grip on the causes and consequences of population growth you have the subject matter of modern economic growth under control. There is much more to it than that, however, and we shall not be finished with population until the end of the chapter, but the simple numbers – and their sectoral composition – need to be laid out at the beginning.

Table 2.1 contains the basic figures for Britain over the entire period of the industrial revolution; we have separately included some numbers for England and Wales from Chapter 1 to take us back to 1761. Here one gets the distinct impression of a population spurt beginning sometime late in the 18th century and continuing as far as these numbers run, into the 20th century.

We are, in modern times, somewhat inured to numbers on rapid population growth, but, even so, British population growth in this period is markedly different from that of the other countries considered in this study, being consistently over 1 per cent per year. We have considered the effects of this in Chapter 1, and will say no more about that in this chapter. Note, though, that we will return to some of the effects of population growth (on real wages and the standard of living) in Section 2.7.

Turning to agriculture, let us consider the broad story of the role of agriculture in the transition. For the most part, the figures cover the 19th century in what follows, but in any case, certain broad patterns are certainly clear. Beginning with the employment figures, our first look is provided by Table 2.2. Here we find a steady decline of the relative position of agriculture in the employment of the British work-force, from 35.9 per cent of the total occupied population to 18.7 per cent sixty years later. This is a continuation of developments

Table 2.1   British population, 1801–1911 (m)

Date	British population	Annual growth rate	England/Wales population	Annual growth rate
1761			6.102	. . .
1771			6.448	0.55
1781			7.042	0.88
1791			7.740	0.94
1801	10.501	. . .	8.664	1.13
1811	11.970	1.31	9.886	1.32
1821	14.092	1.63	11.492	1.50
1831	16.261	1.43	13.284	1.45
1841	18.534	1.31	14.970	1.19
1851	20.817	1.16	16.736	1.12
1861	23.128	1.05	18.938	1.24
1871	26.072	1.20	21.501	1.27
1881	29.710	1.31		
1891	33.029	1.06		
1901	37.000	1.14		
1911	40.831	0.98		

Sources: Mitchell (1978) and Wrigley and Schofield (1981).

Table 2.2   Composition of the British work force, 1801-1861

	Per cent of total occupied population		Actual population (m)	
	in Agriculture	in Manufacturing	in Agriculture	in Manufacturing
1801	35.9	29.7	1.7	1.4
1811	33.0	30.2	1.8	1.7
1821	28.4	38.4	1.8	2.4
1831	24.6	40.8	1.8	3.0
1841	22.2	40.5	1.9	3.3
1851	21.7	42.9	2.1	4.1
1861	18.7	43.6	2.0	4.7

Note: Agriculture includes forestry and fishing and manufacturing includes mining and building.
Source: Deane and Cole (1967).

in the 18th century but, in fact, a continuation at a somewhat faster pace. While this is a widely recognized phenomenon, it is perhaps less widely known that the absolute numbers for agricultural employed actually increased until after 1851, by these estimates. Thus the labour resources released by agriculture over the course of the first industrial revolution were in the relative sense of Column (1) rather than in an absolute sense. We also note that agricultural capital increased more rapidly than the agricultural labour force in this period.[1] We will return to these comparisons below, when we have occasion to look at the incomes generated in the various sectors.

By far the most significant agricultural event of this time was the final end of the open-field system, which expired except for a small residual in a burst of government-encouraged enclosures in the late 18th and early 19th centuries.[2] What happened to the open field system ultimately is that it gave way to larger units, with the aggregation of small plots and the enclosure of common lands (and small plots) the generic agents of its demise.[3] As time wore on, more and more land was taken out of the open field system and aggregated into more efficient units. The pace of this development was stimulated by the pressure of demand and enabled by the decline of transportation costs and by the increased pace of technological change. It was constrained by the need to retain diversification to reduce risk, by whatever legal and other restraints there were and by the inability of economic agents to acquire lands at a reasonable cost due to the often confused nature of the property rights in land (see Dahlman, 1980).

Turning to the effects of enclosures, we move closer to the macro-economic concerns of this study. Indeed, enclosures have a special role to play, for a position often advanced (as, for example, by Deane, 1979) is that they are a significant (negative) influence on the standard of living of the working classes in the early years of the industrial revolution (at least up to 1815). Indeed, it is alleged that a cheap pool of semi-skilled workers was particularly useful in the early stages of the industrial revolution in that it permitted greater profits for the capital-hungry industrial sector. Enclosures, by redirecting population (relatively) toward the cities, even provided a ready market for certain types of products (e.g., low-cost housing, cheap cloths, etc.) that are typical of the early industrial revolution. All of this is, broadly, part of an overall hypothesis that rests on those familiar engines of oppression – the industrial revolution, the factory system and the enclosure movement.

Certainly the enclosure movement was surrounded by broad social changes that formed the basis for the new classes that were clearly visible by the mid-19th century. The rural middle class, especially those involved in handicrafts, was demoted in the process and an urban middle class that had long been around began to expand dramatically. Commerce and industry were their activities, on the whole. Unfortunately, there was also an increase in the number of workers crowded into increasingly uncomfortable urban areas (at least increasingly so up to the 1830s). More prosaically, the end of enclosures meant that a wider market could be served more efficiently and that Britain could grow with less dependence on imported grains. Finally, a newly prosperous and enclosed agriculture was better able to provide capital to the rapidly growing British capital market and, for that matter, to pay a sizeable share of the taxes to support the increasingly expensive British government (especially up to the end of the Napoleonic wars).

2.3   BRITISH INDUSTRIALIZATION

As already noted in Chapter 1, the main reason for bringing in a discussion at a level of disaggregation at the industry level is to create a necessary background for the study. In this connection cotton, iron and transportation (and coal) seem most important in the story, and in the aggregate actually provide a large slice of British GNP. Cotton, for example, is surely the representative British industrial revolution industry. Even so, it is a peculiar one to act as a leader because (in Britain) it is not an intermediate industry with a strong pull on factors (other than labour and capital) or a strong push (e.g., on costs of production for other industries). Iron is more to the point as an influential product, and Britain quickly moved into a dominant world position in the production of pig iron and finished iron products in this period. Iron (and the general application of steam power) pulled the coal industry along, as well. In any case, all of these industries – and quite a few more – had strong technological pushes at approximately the same time, making a general story easier at the same time leaving one in doubt as to which might be termed the most important industry, if that matters.

Raw cotton was imported into Britain, of course, so no important domestic industry was stimulated except for shipping. The rapid expansion of the cotton industry is remarkable and it certainly operated as a major creator of industrial capital (via its profits) and a stimulant to technological change.[4] To see just how quickly this industry emerged, consider the entries in Table 2.3. The table provides figures on cotton imports retained and used in English and Welsh factories. The growth rate over the 90 years is astronomical (at 6.02 per cent per year). Here we see an acceleration in the 1780–89 decade with a roughly tripled output over the previous decade. In the

Table 2.3   The cotton industry in England and Wales, 1760–1859 (£m)

	Raw cotton retained
1760–69	3.48
1770–79	4.78
1780–89	14.74
1790–99	27.92
1800–9	59.6
1810–19	96.3
1820–29	173.0
1830–39	302.0
1840–49	550.0
1850–59	795.0

Source: Shapiro (1967), p. 255.

19th century the growth of the cotton industry in Britain continued along its spectacular course as also shown in the table. Indeed, it continues to grow rapidly until 1880 (with the exception of the decade that contains the American Civil War).

The iron industry, providing an intermediate product on the whole, requires a demand further up the productive chain to get it going. One thing the iron series can do, then, is give us a good grip on real output, since it is so basic; it is also complete for the British case, in a series running from 1530 to 1914 (Riden, 1977). Table 2.4 lists the numbers available from 1790 to 1860. These are for estimated tonnage, at annual rates, but refer to the average for successive five-year periods.

In the story behind Table 2.4, technology looms large. For example, coke was widely employed after 1750, and as the century progressed, the charcoal blast disappeared in favour of coke; even later in the 18th century, the Boulton-Watt steam engine provided a hotter blast. In 1783–4, the Cort process was patented and it soon became standard. This process combined puddling, hammering and rolling, with the former eliminating impurities in the iron compared with the techniques currently in vogue. The Cort process also relied on coal rather than coke and so was cheaper to operate. From 1790, when the figures start in Table 2.4, the growth of the industry was often phenomenal; indeed, over the entire 1790 to 1860 period the compound growth rate of the output of the industry was 5.36 per cent, on these numbers. By 1800 the integrated iron foundry, including

Table 2.4   British pig iron production, 1790–1860 (000 tons)

Date	Output	Per cent change
1790	90	...
1795	120	6.67
1800	180	10.00
1805	250	7.78
1810	400	12.00
1815	340	−3.00
1820	320	−1.18
1825	580	16.25
1830	680	3.45
1835	930	7.35
1840	1400	10.11
1845	2200	11.43
1850	2250	0.45
1855	3220	8.62
1860	3830	3.79

Source: Riden (1977).

puddling and rolling, was the industry standard and the industry had finally moved into urban centres – near coal, ore, water and its labour supply. Of course the acceleration after 1830, itself significantly the result of the growth of the railroad, is also noticeable in these figures.

The railroad has always had a large part in the story of British industrialization and this fact has often been emphasized. The general idea is that the railroad is unusually important in that it lowers transportation costs for everyone while at the same time stimulating basic domestic industries (coal and iron). It is also involved in the complex of research and development that has so much to do with technical change in the industrial revolution. Even so, there is an obvious derived demand aspect of railroading that is especially clear in the British case. In a nutshell, population growth and industrial expansion create the demand for a better transportation network that is importantly filled by the railroad (after 1830). Before 1830 the same pressures stimulated the development of the available facilities – canals, harbours, and roads – in approximately the same way that they stimulated the railroad after 1830. This is less grand as a theme, but also less controversial.

In 1750, British roads were surely better than in 1650, but there was little application of advanced technology in road building and, of course, general maintenance was particularly uneven; in any case there were no really great differences from earlier standards. English road travel times were apparently cut in half between 1750 and 1780, partly as the result of the incentives associated with the collection of tolls and partly, surely, as a response to increases in demand. Surfaces improved steadily, and in the 1810 to 1815 period, the macadam process was widely adopted; this provided a smooth yet porous surface with a firm foothold. Undramatic, partly uncounted, and largely unremembered, roads steadily improved over the entire period from 1750–1910 and made a significant contribution to trade (much of which is local and similarly uncounted) and hence to GNP.

But in Britain much of the traffic in the major bulk products (grain, coal, pig iron) moved by water, which is cheaper as long as industry or market is able to locate by the waterside. The biggest part of this trade occurred along the British coasts, using the considerable penetration of the tides to carry the goods inland for distances that could reach a large percentage of Britain's population. British docks were constructed at a record pace from 1700 to 1800 (380 acres were built) and there was a virtual explosion from 1800 to 1838, when another 4230 acres were added to the total. But canals get the most attention and in this period they were effective because the British waterways needed relatively small amounts of canalling to produce sizeable declines in costs. Most importantly, some of these projects paid off handsomely to the private investors who formed joint-stock companies to finance them, many funded by local investors, thus ringing the starting-gong on modern capitalism. Factories sprang up in the new industrial centres so served, and a second wave of canal construction started in the 1780s and continued into the 1790s. By 1800, counting rivers and canals, fully 2000 miles of navigable waterways were in place in Britain, when no more than 800 were available in 1730. The canal system, like the docks, is countable, and we know that expansion continued at a rapid pace, with a further doubling of navigable waterways to 1858 (to 4250 miles).

2.4 ECONOMIC GROWTH DURING THE INDUSTRIAL REVOLUTION

There is a long-standing dispute over the pace of economic growth in Britain during this period that is interwoven with the argument over whether to call the whole business an 'industrial revolution'. We have sworn off the latter topic for the bulk of this study, but we should, at

Table 2.5 Composition and growth of British real national product, 1760–1861 (£m)

A. England and Wales (real product)

| | Agriculture | | Total real product | |
	Amount	Per cent (of total)	Amount	Index no.
1760	28.9	35	81.9	60
1770	29.0	36	80.3	59
1780	31.5	34	92.0	68
1790	33.4	32	104.1	77
1800	36.2	27	135.8	100

B. Great Britain

| | Nominal values | | | | | Real product | |
| | Agriculture | | Manufacturing | | Total | | |
	Amount	Per cent	Amount	Per cent		Amount	Index no.
1801	75.5	32.5	54.3	23.4	232.0	138	100
1811	107.5	35.7	62.5	70.8	301.1	168	122
1821	76.0	26.1	93.0	31.9	291.0	218	158
1831	79.5	23.4	117.1	34.4	340.0	312	226
1841	99.0	22.1	155.5	34.4	452.3	394	286
1851	106.5	20.3	179.5	34.3	523.3	494	358
1861	118.8	17.8	243.6	36.5	668.0	565	409

Sources: Cole (1981); Deane and Cole (1967).

least, lay out the extremes for the dispute over the data, since much of the discussion at later points in this chapter depends on having some sort of view as to the magnitude of the event. Let us begin by looking at a collection of Deane and Cole's figures for national income and its broad components over the entire century 1760 to 1861.

There are two sets of figures in Table 2.5, one referring to England and Wales and one to Britain. In the former, one sees the contribution of agriculture in real product decline from 35 per cent to 27 per cent in forty years, while in the latter part, the share declines even more rapidly, from 32.5 per cent to 17.8 per cent in sixty years, although these later comparisons are in nominal rather than real terms. The last columns in each part of the table present index numbers of real product; this is done to enable a comparison across the two sets of numbers (the base is 1800/1801). These figures show a real rate of growth of the economy of 1.28 per cent from 1760 to 1800 (but 2.61 per cent in the last decade) that almost doubles (to 2.35 per cent per year) from 1801 to 1861.

As discussed in Chapter 1, there is an important dispute over these numbers. It is now widely accepted that the Deane and Cole figures overstate the case for a revolution, and lower estimates by Harley (1982) and Crafts (1983) have replaced these earlier calculations. Part of the problem lies in the emphasis on certain sectors (notably cotton and exports) that are possibly over-weighted in the production index and part of the problem is related to the possible over-weighting of industrial production in the attempt to estimate an overall index of gross national income. Harley proposes using census data on the occupational structure of British industry and adjusting for relative price changes that mainly affected cotton (cotton cloth's price relative to manufacturing prices in general fell almost 50 per cent, from 1815 to 1841). The results of the recalculation by Harley for the annual growth rates are (using the Divisia technique):[5]

| 1770–1815 | 1.5–1.6 |
| 1815–1841 | 3.0–3.2 |

These are considerably lower than the comparable Deane and Cole estimates for the 1770 to 1815 period (the 1815–1841 estimates are in broad agreement). Their estimates, using linked figures from Table 2.5 are a growth rate of 1.93 per cent per year from 1770 to 1821 and 2.38 per cent thereafter. The latter is a lower rate, but comparisons are hard to make and the data are very provisional.[6]

Crafts (1983), as we have just noted, produces figures that agree with Harley on the early period (to 1801) but present a different picture for the later period. In an earlier paper Crafts (1980) suggests that the Deane and Cole figures for 1801–30 were incorrectly deflated and this factor is included in his re-weighting; furthermore, he argues that a 'value added' weighting scheme is better than an employment-based one (as used by Harley). In this case, the *industrial production index* that results shows (again taking the Divisia measure) the following annual growth rates:

| 1780–1801 | 2.11 per cent |
| 1801–1831 | 3.00 per cent |

Craft's chief contribution here lies in his re-estimation of the *national output* figures (this also involves agriculture, commerce, rent and services, and the government). These figures (see Crafts for the details, which are numerous) show growth rates as follows:

	Crafts	Cole (1981)	
1760–1780	0.70	0.65	
1780–1801	1.32	2.06	
1801–1831	1.97	3.06	(Deane and Cole)

The difference after 1780 is primarily the result of changing the weights in favour of commerce and industry, with the new index (already described) pulling down the estimates of GNP growth considerably. This seems to be about where we stand on these issues.

2.5   THE COMPONENTS OF NATIONAL PRODUCT

The most recent data that we have on the composition of GNP are from Feinstein (1978, 1981); we reproduce his numbers in Table 2.6. Here we see that real consumer spending grew during the period (although per capita growth is apparent only after 1800) and so did real investment. The government, on the other hand, grew in size up to 1811–20, when it declined relatively, to 4.1 per cent of GNP in the last decade in the period (even though a major war was fought in that period). In 1811–20 at its peak, the government was up to 12.6 per cent of GNP.

Table 2.6   Real GNP and its components, 1760–1860 (annual averages, 1851–60 prices, £m)

Date	GNP	Govern- ment	Invest- ment	Net foreign spending	Consump- tion	Consump- tion per capita
1761–70	93	7	7.5	0.5	78	9.6
1771–80	98	7	9.0	1.0	81	9.3
1781–90	111	8	13.0	1.5	88	9.5
1791–1800	134	15	17.5	1.5	100	9.8
1801–10	161	25	17.5	–2.0	120	10.5
1811–20	203	26	22.5	5.0	149	11.3
1821–30	278	14	32.5	7.5	224	14.6
1831–40	372	12	42.0	4.5	313	17.9
1841–50	460	16	54.5	6.5	383	19.4
1851–60	610	25	61.5	20.0	503	22.9

Source: Feinstein (1981). These figures are mostly from Deane and Cole, as adjusted by Feinstein.

Table 2.7 British growth rates, 1781–1860 (compound rates, per annum, for the decade)

Date	Population	GNP	Consump-tion	Invest-ment	Govern-ment	I+G
1781–90	0.67	1.24	0.83	3.68	1.34	2.72
1791–1800	0.92	1.88	1.28	2.97	6.29	4.37
1801–10	1.11	1.84	1.82	0.00	5.11	2.68
1811–20	1.47	2.32	2.16	2.51	0.39	1.32
1821–30	1.48	3.14	4.08	3.68	–6.19	–0.42
1831–40	1.34	2.91	3.34	2.56	–1.54	1.50
1841–50	1.18	2.12	2.02	2.60	2.88	2.67
1851–60	1.10	2.82	2.72	1.21	4.46	1.45

Source: Feinstein (1981).

We are now in a position to consider how some of the broad data that we have gathered for Britain conform to the expectations of the neoclassical model discussed in Chapter 1. Table 2.7 gathers all of the relevant growth rates from earlier tables; we are not expecting exact equality of growth rates across spending categories even though the theory predicts that, but we certainly could hope for some rough correspondence among the growing series.

These decades – covering roughly the period of the first industrial revolution in Britain, all exhibit growth rates of GNP in excess of population growth and are, somewhat surprisingly perhaps, consistent with each other, at least broadly. Note that because the government is somewhat of a wild card here, the appropriate way to treat that sector may well be to combine it with investment, as is done in the last column. In any case, it is readily acknowledged that the government does not play by the neoclassical rules. It is, indeed, noticeable that most big swings in the government figures are matched by opposite swings in investment growth in this period; consumption is similarly affected. This is a first sounding of the crowding-out theme that we will continue below.

2.5.1 Investment

A key number in any story of growth is, of course, the rate of domestic capital formation. If we keep to a broadly neoclassical framework, then a natural model to employ here is the Harrod–Domar growth model (Harrod, 1939; Domar, 1946); it is convenient partly because some of the protagonists in the debate over British growth seem to have it in mind, at least implicitly. The Harrod–Domar model is a simple demand-side macroeconomic model with a consumption function, $C = \beta Y$, an investment function, $I = \alpha(dY/dt)$, and an equilibrium condition, $Y = C + I + A$, where A refers to autonomous components of expenditure, including, usually the government and net foreign spending. In these equations β is the propensity to consume and α is the capital/output ratio (the accelerator coefficient). This system produces a simple first-order difference equation in Y (GNP) and, when solved for the equilibrium time path of income, yields the expression $(1-\beta)/\alpha$ $(= g)$ for the rate of growth along the equilibrium path. It is this latter expression, the ratio of the propensity to save $(1-\beta)$ to the accelerator coefficient, that defines the rate of growth in this simplest version of the model. If, for example, it takes £2 of new capital to produce £1 of new output, then $g = 2$; for $1-\beta = 0.05$, the indicated growth rate is 2.5 per cent. Heavier capital requirements and higher propensities to consume (lower savings propensities) tend to depress the indicated rate of growth.

To begin, there is a debate over the appropriate value of $1-\beta$ for the various subperiods of the period considered here. The first salvo in this debate was let off by Rostow (1962) who made this number the key to his 'take off' period. What Rostow said was (p. 20),

What you are talking about is a rise in the rate of investment and in the per capita stock of capital. Get the investment rate up to the point where the increase in output outstrips the rate of population increase – to, say, a rate of investment over 10% of national income – and the job is done. The difference between a traditional and a modern society is merely a question of whether its investment-rate is low relative to population increase – let us say under 5% of national income; or whether it has risen up to 10% or over. With a capital/output ratio of about 3, a 10% investment rate will outstrip any likely population growth; and there you are, with a regular increase in output per head.

Indeed, with a capital/output ratio of 3, a 10 per cent investment rate ($I=S$ in equilibrium) would produce a growth rate of 3.33 per cent in the Harrod–Domar model. This is well above any population growth rates in this period, and, it must be emphasized, also above all of the growth rates for real GNP that have been produced. But Rostow was an optimist.

Table 2.8   Investment in Great Britain, 1760–1860 (1851–60 prices)

	Fixed capital	Inventory invest-ment	Foreign invest-ment	Total invest-ment	Total as percentage of GNP	Crafts (1983) estimates
1761–70	6.5	1.0	0.5	8.0	8	5.7 (1760)
1771–80	7.0	2.0	1.0	10.0	10	7.0 (1780)
1781–90	11.0	2.0	1.5	14.5	13	
1791–00	14.5	3.0	1.5	19.0	14	
1801–10	16.5	1.0	–2.0	15.5	10	7.0 (1801)
1811–20	20.5	2.0	5.0	27.5	14	8.5 (1811)
1821–30	28.5	4.0	7.5	40.0	14	11.2 (1821)
1831–40	38.5	3.5	4.5	46.5	13	11.7 (1831)
1841–50	49.5	5.0	6.5	61.0	13	
1851–60	58.0	3.5	20.0	81.5	13	

Source: Mathias (1983) from Feinstein (1978).

The rate of capital accumulation during the industrial revolution has been the subject of several studies by Feinstein (1978, 1981) that are widely accepted (and debated); they are given above in Table 2.8. Here we see that the rate of capital formation is surprisingly high in 1760 and remains quite steadily at 10 to 14 per cent of GNP thereafter. Furthermore, fixed capital formation dominates the numbers in any period.

Turning to estimates of the capital–output ratio (and other things), we again look at some numbers constructed by Feinstein (1981) in Table 2.9. These figures contain a wealth of information on the utilization ratios of interest to us. In particular, we see that the capital stock grew faster than the labour supply (312 per cent to 208 per cent) and that average labour productivity grew faster than average capital productivity (as judged by the inverses of K/Y and L/Y).

More to the point, these figures show that in 1760, K/Y was 7.4 and $I (=S)$ was 8 per cent of GNP. Employing the Harrod–Domar model, this would be consistent with a growth rate of 1.08 per cent, which, when compared with the number of 0.70 above, is not far off the mark. For 1860, on the other hand, with $K/Y = 4.3$ and $I = 13$ per cent, the indicated growth rate is 3.02 per cent. That, too, is not far off the mark. This is very encouraging, although there certainly are problems with these numbers. Feinstein, in particular, uses the Deane and Cole figures for GNP and so, according to Crafts, underestimates GNP; accordingly, the ratio of investment to gross domestic product would be overstated. The numbers are shown in Table 2.8 in the last column; this recalculation considerably downgrades the

Table 2.9   Factor utilization ratios in the British economy (year end)

	1760	1800	1830	1860	Overall change (%)
Domestic reproducible capital	670	990	1510	2760	312
Real output (£m)	90	140	310	650	622
K/Y	7.4	7.1	4.9	4.3	−42
Labour supply (m)	3.5	4.8	7.2	10.8	208
K/L	191	206	210	256	34
L/Y	3.9	3.4	2.3	1.7	−56
Total factor productivity (index number)	49	53	79	100	104

Source: Feinstein (1981). Total factor productivity is the residual unexplained by the growth of capital or labour.

role of investment and capital formation, as already discussed, if one accepts Crafts's revisions. Crafts also questions the growth exercise that is noted in Table 2.9. In that set of calculations by Feinstein only two factors of production are employed, and their shares in the total are equal (at 0.5). If, says Crafts, we recalculate with a 0.15 weight to the missing residual share (with an assumed lower productivity), then the role of productivity growth as a stimulant to overall growth is considerably less than we have shown.

2.5.2   Consumption

The numbers on the overall rate of consumption demand have already been presented in Tables 2.6 and 2.7; they suggest that consumption grew along with the other components of aggregate demand but, surely, not in an unusual way. Below we will consider how this growth might condition the discussion of the distribution of national income, but for now we turn to a controversy over how much 'demand' itself stimulated the industrial revolution. Consumer and foreign demand are at the root of this debate and the broad proposition is that they are independent and important sources of pressure. This is from Gilboy (1932). What we would be looking for here, in view of our macroeconomic perspective, is factors that would shift the aggregate demand function; these could then be thought of as independent causes of industrial expansion (Mokyr, 1977).

The first problem we have to deal with is the role of income. In a partial equilibrium framework, such as this, income is a shift parameter for the demand curve.[7] As Mokyr says (p. 982) the rules we are operating by require that

> the shift in the demand curve must be caused by a rise in real income, and can therefore not serve at the same time as an explanation of it.

In short, either we need to correct the data for feedback from demand on to income or we need to find known *exogenous* factors that explain the shift. Mokyr, following Cole (1973) suggests that three factors could serve here, provided that they are largely independent of income. These are agricultural growth, the expansion of foreign demand and population growth. While it is probable that none of these are entirely free from feedback, it is at least arguable.[8]

For agriculture, Mokyr obtains a relative price series and argues (p. 983),

> The changes in relative prices thus account for at best 8 per cent of the industrial expansion, while it is quite possible that their net effect was on the whole negative.

He also dismisses a popular 'agricultural crisis' theory that a bad harvest stimulates overall demand since farmers spend more, proportionately, on manufactured goods because the argument requires that the overall demand for agricultural products be inferior. For the growth of exports we have an added difficulty because the technology of foreign trade changed considerably in this period. Even so, in a more casual way, the data examined by Mokyr do not paint a convincing picture of this effect, even if we could ignore the problem of causation. Finally, for population, using a simple single factor (labour) production function, Mokyr estimates that population growth could have contributed less than 10 per cent of actual industrial output growth (p. 989),

> Even if it is assumed that population growth was fully exogenous, its significance in generating the demand for increased industrial production was marginal.

Thus 'supply' dominates, residually, since the sum of these demand effects is not considerable.

Mokyr also provides a more conventional macroeconomic framework – of the IS–LM variety – to deal with another issue in the literature concerning the role of effective demand (and the multiplier). To begin, he argues that during the period of expansion there could have been a traditional 'multiplier effect' operating (p. 998) if the following condition were met.

> If there were large reservoirs of involuntarily unemployed labor, increases in demand would set into motion a multiplier mechanism, which, enforced by induced investment, could have led to the Industrial Revolution.

Mokyr quotes both Hicks and Keynes on the importance of insufficient demand in the industrial revolution in the terms just described. Hicks says (1946, p. 302)

> one cannot repress the thought that perhaps the whole Industrial Revolution of the last two hundred years has been nothing else but a vast secular boom, largely induced by the unparalleled rise in population. If this is so, it would help to explain why, as the wisest hold, it has been such a disappointing episode in human history.

and Keynes notes that (1936, pp. 347–8)

> there has been a chronic tendency throughout human history for the propensity to save to be stronger than the inducement to invest. The weakness of the inducement to invest has been at all times the key to the economic problem.

These notions Mokyr properly rejects. Instead he argues (p. 1001),

> as a *long-run* description of a normal state of affairs, involuntary unemployment in preindustrial Europe seems a dubious proposition. One reason is that in a barter economy Keynesian unemployment cannot occur.

He says this because the existence of unemployment in the Keynesian model requires a gap between savings and investment ($S > I$) that must be maintained by monetary accumulation – by a continuous upward shift in the *demand* for money – that produces higher interest rates and deflation.

There is, as yet, no direct evidence on this last proposition, although the evidence would be easy enough to assemble. In any case, it is one thing to argue that there was, in fact, an expansion of the money supply (from 1680) and that interest rates were actually *lower* – as Mokyr does – and quite another to rely on the irrelevance of the Keynesian model because the actual economic system uses barter rather than money (for S to be unequal to I we need financial assets of some sort). In particular, we should decisively reject the idea of a large-scale barter sector for this period as highly unlikely. In any case, Mokyr also argues that a good deal of the investment of this period was self-financed. This finesses the barter issue to some extent, and is undoubtedly correct, although it has been challenged in a different context by Black and Gilmore (1990), who correctly observe that this situation does not imply that one need abandon the neoclassical, factor-allocation model of savings and investment as long as firms correctly evaluate opportunity costs.

An alternative paradigm to the Keynesian theory would be to utilize the 'expectations augmented Phillips curve' as buttressed by a Lucas supply curve.[9] The Lucas supply curve is based on the notion that workers do not have all of the information they need to distinguish between the relative and absolute prices for their labour services and so they engage in a costly search procedure – that may involve joining the ranks of the unemployed – in order to acquire this information and thereby to maximize their expected utility. The upshot is that in the aggregate, supply will depend on the difference between expected prices and actual prices and on random factors that are, presumably, free of any systematic factors that economic agents could use in their forecasts of the price level. In this formulation errors in predicting the price level (whatever their source) produce aggregate supply responses (they produce labour supply responses in the first instance) that are positive if inflation is underpredicted and negative if inflation is overpredicted. The coefficient that describes the reaction to these errors reflects the relative dispersion in markets that produces the errors in the first place. It is but a short step, then, to a theory of unemployment in which the deviation of the actual rate of unemployment from its natural rate depends on errors in the prediction of inflation rates and on random factors, as above.

This model helps us in the debate by focusing on actual labour market dynamics. Here unemployment is based on the informational costs in the system. That is, a shock in one of the underlying functions – let us say in the production function – would generate a change in relative prices that would be hard for workers to pick up because they would have poor information about prices in areas and product lines other than those to which they have immediate access. Putting their best guesses on the line, they will make a labour supply decision that will, at times, be seriously in error. This would cause unemployment to deviate from its natural level (itself assumed to vary to some extent) as workers voluntarily become unemployed.

Now in the industrial revolution economy there were two factors at work that could easily have created the impression that aggregate demand was normally on the stagnant side, as Hicks and Keynes have argued. One of these lies in the shocks – of war and the industrial revolution. The other is in the obvious difficulty of access to effective information under the circumstances, a situation that was exacerbated as new products and activities came on line and was ameliorated as the information-providing economic agents developed; these latter are such as banks, newspapers, and the government. It is easy to imagine that for a time unemployment was often observed to be out of line with previous historical standards. It is, though, unnecessary to argue that it was a barter economy, in which case errors in the prediction of inflation would be irrelevant and the main explanation of unemployment would be in the natural rate of unemployment and in random factors.

Where do we stand on these issues, then? We can pretty much put aside population and agriculturally-inspired demand changes as recommended by Mokyr. That leaves the expansion of foreign demand. In a recent survey of this controversy, Williamson (1987b) notes that while the increase in the demand for exports is considerable over the course of the industrial revolution – and that there is some Granger-causality evidence in favour of such a line of causation (in Hatton, Lyons and Satchell, 1983) – we do not have any realistic notion of the actual magnitudes involved in the causal link. In effect, lacking magnitudes, we are still unable to say to what extent British industrialization was stimulated by a rise in exogenous foreign demand as compared with the line of influence that holds that the relatively rapid pace of British industrialization stimulated a more significant response in foreign economies that *fed back* on to the British economy through an increase in export demand. Better data and modern time series tests would be the best way to advance this discussion. Finally, the idea of a pool of unemployed workers as a prime agent also does not seem to be a compelling argument, at least on the available data.

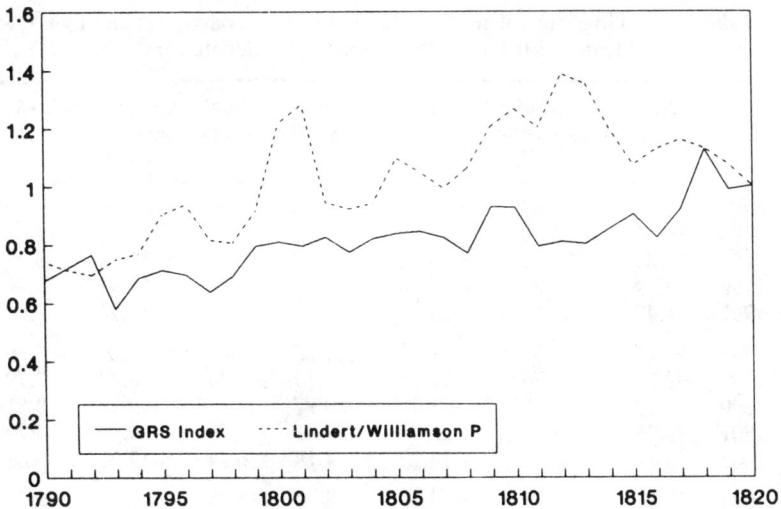

Figure 2.1   Inflation and growth in Britain, 1790–1820

2.5.3   Government Spending

In Tables 2.6 and 2.7, one can note significant increases in the level and rate of growth of government spending in the Napoleonic and Crimean wartime periods, speaking loosely, of course, since the data are ten-year aggregates. At this point, we should return to the discussion of Chapter 1 and further document the fiscal profile of this period. We will, though, limit our discussion to the period of the French wars, since it provides the most dramatic changes in both nominal and real data.

First of all, let us illustrate a phenomenon that has been widely remarked upon in the literature; this is the erratic behaviour of the price level. Figure 2.1, which also has the Gayer, Rostow and Schwartz (1953) index – GRS index – of business activity attached, illustrates the behaviour of prices for the period 1790 to 1820 (using the Lindert–Williamson cost-of-living index). From this it is clear that there were a number of sharp bursts in the price level, not always matched by the business activity index (although the simple correlation is 0.56). These bursts occur in 1795, 1799–1801, 1805, 1809–10 and 1812 and generally involve one or more years of double-digit inflation.

Table 2.10   Government receipts and expenditures and certain other statistics bearing on the crowding-out debate (£m)

	Net revenue	Net public expenditure	Deficit	Net borrowing	Bank notes	Government securities in BOE	GRS index
1793	18.52	21.82	− 3.30	3.68	11.38	9.97	0.58
1794	19.33	26.80	− 7.47	7.05	10.51	9.41	0.68
1795	19.05	38.31	−19.26	19.80	12.44*	13.21*	0.71
1796	19.39	38.25	−18.86	21.30	9.99	11.91	0.70
1797	21.48	46.93	−25.45	28.44	10.39	10.24	0.64
1798	27.24	49.51	−22.27	22.28	12.64	11.09	0.69
1799	32.51	49.76	−17.25	14.19	13.17	10.48	0.79
1800	33.10	54.22	−21.12	20.97	15.95*	13.78*	0.81
1801	32.75	58.48	−25.73	27.01	15.38	13.94	0.79
1802	35.17	48.46	−13.29	14.18	16.14	13.86	0.82
1803	37.81	47.24	− 9.43	8.43	15.65	11.38	0.77
1804	45.07	57.36	−12.29	13.73	17.12*	14.84*	0.82
1805	50.13	67.38	−17.25	17.78	17.13	14.15	0.84
1806	54.93	66.63	−11.70	11.40	19.38	14.49	0.84
1807	58.74	66.89	− 8.15	10.55	18.31	13.43	0.82
1808	51.31	71.11	−19.80	10.36	17.65	14.55	0.77
1809	62.72	74.53	−11.81	11.61	19.06	15.03	0.93
1810	68.39	78.21	− 9.82	9.01	22.91*	15.76	0.92
1811	66.55	82.29	−15.74	15.70	23.32	19.54*	0.79
1812	66.09	91.67	−25.58	24.45	23.22	21.65*	0.81
1813	72.57	106.15	−33.58	37.37	24.02	25.31*	0.80
1814	73.75	107.37	−33.62	32.47	26.58*	29.31*	0.85
1815	78.45	99.52	−21.07	21.50	27.25	25.85	0.90
1816	65.51	64.81	0.70	− 1.70	. . .	. . .	0.82

Sources: Bordo and White (1990) and Gayer, Rostow and Schwartz (1953).

One does not have to search very far for the causes of these events, since wartime finance was generally of the inflationary variety, but disentangling the wartime finance effects from possible business activity effects is certainly a challenge, especially in view of the nature of the data. From Table 2.10, compiled by Bordo and White (1990), we can take a first look at the government's budget, from 1793 to 1815. Here the connection between government finance and double-digit inflation (as just described) is especially obvious, with a big jump in the deficit beginning in 1795 and lasting through 1801, again (after a decline) in 1805, again in 1808 and again in 1811 (through 1815). This deficit is, of course, bond financed and, one notices, both Bank of England notes and government securities held by the Bank of England seem to accommodate this pattern. Taxation (not shown) has little to do with this story, in fact, being on an upward trend throughout the period (with an income tax introduced in 1799 providing steadily greater revenues).

Before turning to the literature on crowding out during this period, let us notice one other set of numbers in Table 2.10, the GRS index of business activity in the last column. The reason for including this series is to try to spot any possible adverse effect of government spending on aggregate spending. While both series are trend-dominated, which makes such calculations suspect, the correlation between government expenditures in Column (2) and business activity in the last column is a strongly positive 0.70. Since investment and consumption both expanded in this period a preliminary guess is that one might find little crowding out.[10]

As Barro (1987) notes, both the Napoleonic Wars and the Crimean War show significant increases in the ratio of real military spending to trend GNP; non-military spending has no such events. These are, of course, temporary blips, although the Napoleonic event is of sufficient duration for that interpretation to be questionable. As discussed in Chapter 1, the usual engine for crowding out is the effect on interest rates; in the Napoleonic period they rose, although so did the rate of inflation (sufficiently to call into question the usefulness of a nominal interest rate in this calculation). What is certainly true for this period, however, is that military spending led to money creation, as we can see in Table 2.10, but only because it first led to the suspension of the gold standard (1797 to 1821). This is a general result from the application of Barro's model.

Barro also considers whether tax-smoothing has occurred in this period. As discussed in Chapter 1, the hypothesis is that in the first instance, temporary government spending – such as is revealed in Table 2.10 – would be financed primarily by budgetary deficits. Tax rates (and presumably tax revenues) would not provide much assistance, although they would tend to rise steadily. We have already noted these patterns in the data in Table 2.10, so this effect is quite clear. Barro tests this formally, and finds strong confirmation of the effect of government expenditure on debt. A second test of tax smoothing for this specific period is carried out by Bordo and White (1990) to the same effect.

As far as the crowding out of private expenditures by government spending during the period is concerned, the literature is somewhat ambiguous, although recent work seems more on the side of the existence of the phenomenon. We have noted that investment expanded in the period, although not in 1801–10 (compared with the previous decade). Barro (1987) notes that nominal interest rates rose during the war period, and this is suggestive, but, as he also notes, he cannot rule out the effect of inflationary expectations on nominal rates (in the theory it is a rise in the real rate of interest that produces the crowding out). Heim and Mirowski (1987) attempt to isolate a real interest rate using several price indices to the opposite effect: there is not likely to be crowding out from this source. Williamson (1987a), in turn, suggests that a short-term rate (unfortunately unavailable on account of the usury ceiling) might be a more appropriate measure, while Black and Gilmore (1990) argue that the Heim and Mirowski model implies perfect foresight in forecasting inflation. They propose a test that rejects the assumption. In its place, they use adaptive expectations to produce a series of nominal yields (adjusted for inflation). The resulting rates prove to be dependent on lagged government borrowing and hence show possible crowding out. Finally, Williamson (1984), working on the question of why British growth was so slow between 1760 and 1820, employs a general equilibrium model to 'factor out', among other things, the effect of war debt on civilian expenditures. This, he feels contributed substantially to the slow growth of the economy, so he, too, opts for a significant amount of crowding out in this period.

There also have been other effects alleged in this literature. Thus Feinstein (1981) argues that the effect of the method of finance of the wars may well have been to shift the income distribution in favour of profits and rent earners; the higher interest rates would do this. Earlier, Hueckel (1973) argued that the effect was actually mostly in favour of landowners and that profits suffered. Our work with Mirowski's indices, below, does not corroborate this. Williamson (1984) also argues that workers' standard of living was adversely affected by the debt finance, much along the same lines. We will, in any case, return to these distributional issues below, although over a longer time period than that of the French wars.

2.6 BRITISH BUSINESS CYCLES

This section considers an analysis of the cyclical experience in England during the period from 1750 to around 1850. This material has

Table 2.11 British reference cycles, 1790–1850

Annual		Monthly	
Peak	Trough	Peak	Trough
1792	1793	Sept 1792	June 1794
1796	1797	May 1796	Sept 1797
1800	1801	Sept 1800	Oct 1801
1802	1803	Dec 1802	Mar 1802
1806	1808	Aug 1806	May 1808
1810	1811	Mar 1810	Sept 1811
1815	1816	Mar 1815	Sept 1816
1818	1819	Sept 1818	Sept 1819
1825	1826	May 1825	Nov 1826
1828	1829	June 1828	Dec 1829
1831	1832	Mar 1831	July 1832
1836	1837	Mar 1839	Nov 1842
1839	1842	Sept 1845	Sept 1846
1845	1848	Apr 1847	Sept 1848

Source: Gayer, Rostow and Schwartz (1953).

been carefully explored in an important work by Gayer *et al.* (1953), but in view of the developments in statistical technique since their work – and some additions and corrections to their data base – a fresh look is warranted. The result is a considerable difference in the timing of peaks and troughs especially during the middle of the period, from 1800 to 1820, roughly. As we will see, the re-orientation is the result of the use of a single profit series, rather than a weighted average of 'indicators' of the cycle.

Gayer *et al.* calculate broad price and output indices and construct a set of 'reference cycles' from these data.[11] The work involved is truly prodigious and, to this writer it seems unlikely that the broad patterns discerned are seriously wrong, partly because of the care with which the broad historical literature was consulted. To begin, the reference cycle data appears in Table 2.11.

Table 2.11, then, shows upturns that are significantly longer than downturns with major peaks (1792, 1802, 1810, 1818, 1825, 1836, 1845) coming (on average) every nine years and major depressions somewhat more frequently. In their view, the major cycles, trough to trough, are

1797–1803
1808–1811

Table 2.12   Decline in real GNP (factor cost)

	Per cent change	*Per annum*
1832	−0.07	−0.07
1837	−1.48	−1.48
1840–42	−6.92	−2.31
1850	−0.96	−0.96
1858	−1.98	−1.98

1816–1819
1819–1826
1832–1837
1842–1848

In this set 1816 and 1848 are particularly depressed years that actually followed one or more bad years. We can add some national product figures to these more impressionistic numbers with reference to the Deane (1968) data on real GNP from 1830 to 1860 (Table 2.12). These downturns are not particularly severe (see below) by this broad measure of economic activity. The numbers that overlap with the reference cycles also corroborate that earlier compilation perfectly.

In their comments on these events, Gayer *et al.* make it quite clear that they view these events as inventory cycles with monetary factors and events in international markets as the most frequent causes. In 1793, for example, they emphasize a collapse of the export boom to the United States (a collapse due partly to tightened monetary conditions in Britain itself). In 1797 there was a monetary crisis in Britain (and possibly an inventory collapse in the United States). The collapse in 1807 is credited to the imposition of the Continental System at the end of 1806, while the 1816 collapse in the United States followed an earlier post-war Continental collapse. In 1819 it is an inventory-overstocking in the United States (accentuated by monetary stringency in Britain), while in 1832 it is the export trade and the collapse of prices. World wide, 1837 was a major event and there was a major problem in the cotton industry in the United States (possibly stimulated by monetary stringency in Britain). The world-wide depression in 1848 is associated with revolutions around Europe and tight money generally.

The view that cycles have significant monetary causes is, of course, a contemporary one, but it strikes our modern 'real business cycle eyes' as a little arcane, nevertheless. We are not in a position to do

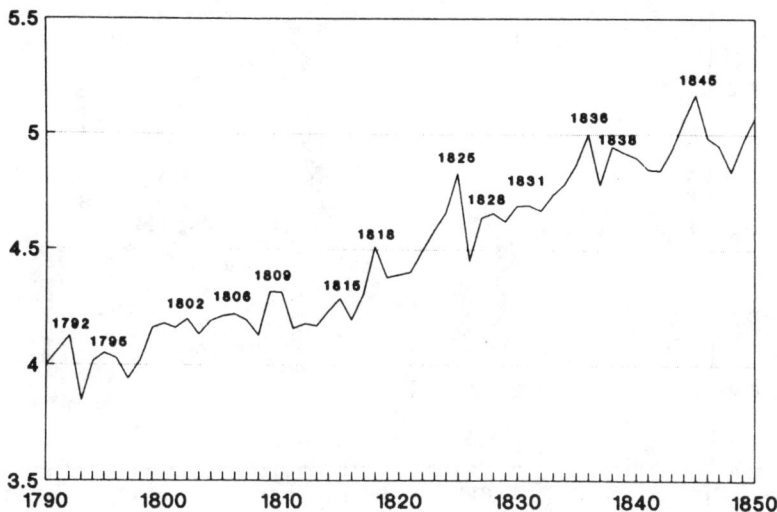

arithms of the Data

Figure 2.2   GRS business activity index, 1790–1850

Table 2.13   Per cent change in index

1792–1793	−24.2%
1816–1818	+37.0
1821–1825	+53.6
1825–1826	−32.0
1836–1837	−19.5
1842–1845	+38.9
1845–1848	−28.4

any effective causal testing here on account of the lack of monetary data, but certain aspects of their treatment warrant further comment. For one thing, it is apparent that Gayer *et al.* are relying on their 'index of business activity' to define the cycle.[12] This is a good start, and the graph of the series appears in Figure 2.2, with some of the more prominent peaks identified.

A major problem with the index is the violence of the swings; this is patently unrepresentative of business conditions in general. The largest swings are shown in Table 2.13. Indeed, one gets the impression from the literature on British cycles that many observers feel the

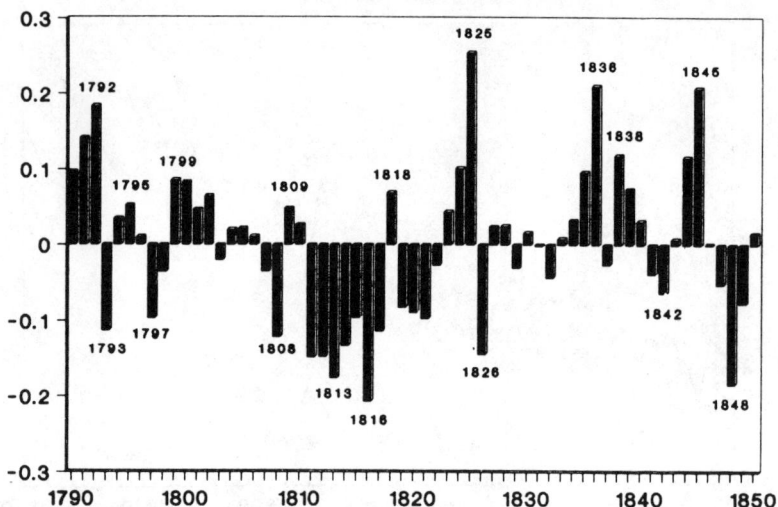

Figure 2.3   British business cycles-GRS residuals, 1790–1850

general cycle was also quite violent at this time, with accompanying unemployment on a comparable scale. This is also unlikely.

Let us take another look at the cycles, this time calculated as a set of deviations around trend. One way to do this is to detrend the data via the following regression:

$$\log I_t = \alpha + \beta_t \text{ Trend} + u_t \tag{2.1}$$

and then plot the residuals against time; here the value of β provides the growth rate while the plot of $\{u_t\}$ provides an impression of the 'cycles' in the data.[13] In this case the value of β is 1.93. From Figure 2.3 it is clear from the dates attached that the reference cycles and the chronology listed earlier are, in fact, reasonably well represented by the detrended business activity index. But the magnitudes should not be taken seriously as a general indicator of how bad or good things got during these events.

To attempt to get a stronger grip on the unemployment situation for at least part of the period, Lindert and Williamson (1983) use data on unemployment in engineering, metals, and shipbuilding for 1851–92 to estimate a structural relation and then use this to 'backcast' unemployment for 1837–50 (the 1840s were supposed to be generally depressed). The relation employed was *ad hoc* and had the following general form:

$$U_{\text{EMS}} = f\left(GNP^*, \frac{I}{GNP}, \frac{\dot{W}}{W}, \left(\frac{\dot{W}}{W}\right)^2, T, T^2\right) \tag{2.2}$$

Here GNP^* is the ratio of GNP to its average level over the previous five years, and I is gross domestic capital formation.[14] This is a Phillips relation, but here the trend variables turn out insignificant and R^2 was only 0.543. The figures for 'backcasted' unemployment are:

1837–9	2.70%	(0 to 7.70% range)
1840–50	4.41	(0 to 9.41% range)
1842, 1843	9.44	(4.44 to 14.44% range)

where the figures in parentheses represent two standard deviations around the point estimates. These figures are not large enough to produce the pessimistic conclusion of much of the literature and certainly represent swings that are considerably less violent than those for the business activity index.

The major work critical of the Gayer *et al.* interpretation is that of Mirowski (1985), continuing the discussion from Chapter 1. To begin, Mirowski offers a scathing denunciation of the Gayer *et al.* business activity index (p. 216).[15]

> It would be difficult to argue such a hodgepodge of timeseries could represent any one thing or idea. . . . It indiscriminately mixes financial and physical phenomena, domestic and foreign influences, quantities with prices, and objects with occurrences. And to think it is then vested with a spurious air of numerical authority through the assignment of weights!

In its place, Mirowski argues in favour of using an index of private-sector profit rates. The main advantage obtained by such an index is that it corresponds to something straight out of economic theory: firms maximize profits, and an index of their success (rate) is an index of the success (of the economy of firms). In modern times, indeed, profit rates are clearly related to the general cycle, so there is good reason to take this suggestion seriously (and to agree with Mirowski that the GRS index has no reasonable interpretation in theory). On the other hand, as Mirowski acknowledges, the profit index is subject to concern over whether accountants correctly measure economic

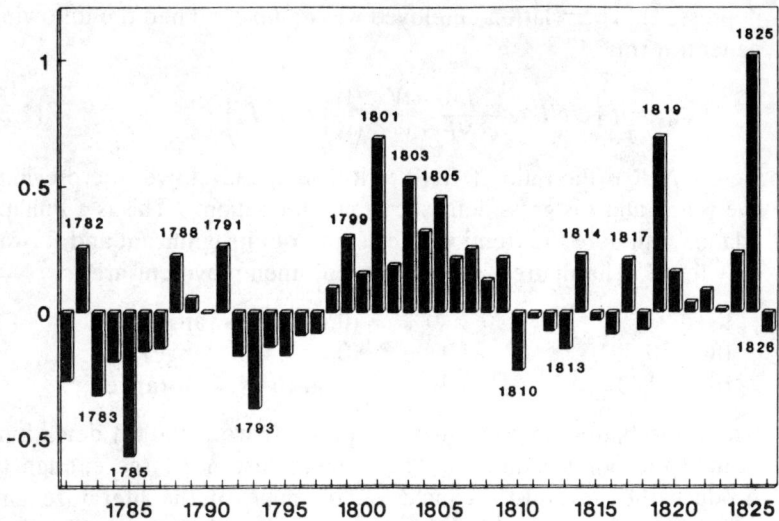

Average • 1.000

Figure 2.4   Mirowski's adjusted profit index, 1781–1826

profits and to aggregation problems (in common with all indices). It is also, in this case, a rather 'thin' index in the sense of the number of series included.

Considering all this, it is still interesting to look at Mirowski's own 'adjusted profit index' for 1781 to 1826 and consider the two series together for that period. Note that the manner of construction of the profit index is discussed more fully in Chapter 1. Figure 2.4 shows the adjusted profit index for the period 1781 to 1826; it is set up just like Figure 2.3, with similar labelling. Note that this is the adjusted index minus unity, to make the two series easy to compare.

Looking mainly at the issue of comparability, it is clear that while many of the major events are similar, there are also many exceptions, especially but not only among the lesser swings. The years 1793, 1813, and 1826 are identified as lower turning points in both series, and 1791 (or 1792), 1799, and 1825 as common upper turning points, but the profiles between 1800 and 1816 are significantly unalike. The difference is largely that of above average profits for the entire 1798 to 1809 period (missing one major downturn in 1808 in the Gayer index) and generally average profits from 1811 to 1818 (the Gayer index spends much of this period well below trend). These are major differences that are accompanied by appropriate text in each case.

Turning to the details in Mirowski, we note that 1783–7 is termed a depression although 1788, called by Ashton (1959) a very bad year, seems not so by the profit index. For the 1790s, there is a depression in share prices from 1793 to 1799, with the trough in 1793 not, as in the Gayer index, in 1797, largely on account of the financial crisis that produced a suspension of gold payments by the Bank of England. This did not appear to affect profits in any special way, although they were slightly below average that year. In the first ten years of the 19th century, say Gayer *et al.*, the war-related loss of trade (carrying the largest weight in their index) produces a lack-lustre decade with a major downturn in 1808; the profit index does not corroborate this story.

For the period 1810 to 1820, there are too many unusual events, mirrored in existing time series, for one to be confident about what is going on. The business activity index, reflecting exports and real series such as the production of bricks, is pretty pessimistic about this period, as shown in Figure 2.3. The profit index is not. Probably the jury is still out. While the timing of the peak in 1818 or 1819 is also a matter of dispute between the two approaches, it is at least comforting that 1825 is a peak and 1826 a trough in both cases. We will leave this topic in this unsettled state – for that is where it stands – reminding the reader that none of these series are ideal for these purposes and that the method of preparing the data (e.g., detrending by regression on trend in the case of the Gayer index) is quite arbitrary.

2.7 THE STANDARD-OF-LIVING DEBATE: MACRO ISSUES

Let us jump into the debate from a macroeconomic perspective with the broadest possible numbers, those for per capita national income and consumption, as given in Figure 2.5. The figures come from Feinstein (1981). Here we see per capita GNP rising steadily after 1775, while per capita consumption in 1795 is only marginally higher than it was in 1785. Indeed, there is not much gain in per capita consumption until the big jump from 1815 to 1825 (the 1815 figure is 17.7 per cent above the 1765 figure). This measure of the standard of living does not deal with distributional issues of course but it does fit quite a lot of the literature, although certainly not the most pessimistic case that has been

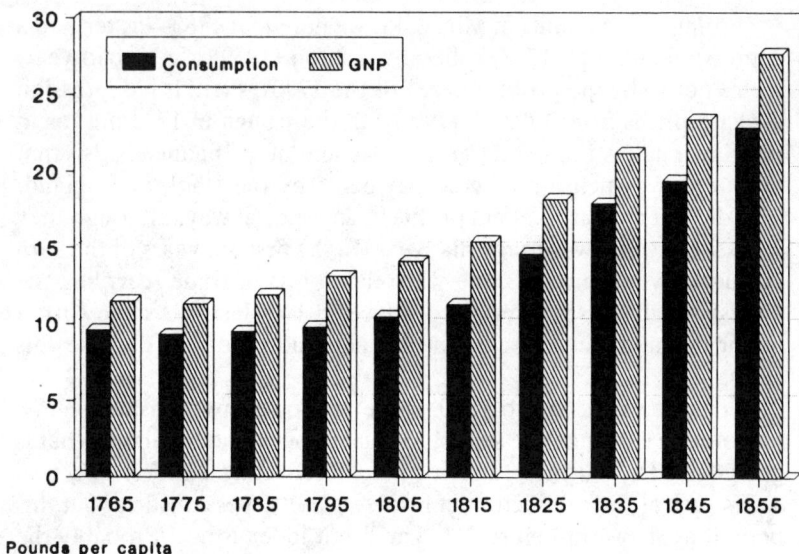

Figure 2.5   British GNP and consumption, 1765–1855

advanced. We submit it as a reasonable overall measure, and immediately move into the distributional issues.

One can provide a macroeconomic framework for distributional questions by defining the functional distribution of income. The functional distribution can be derived from the national income equilibrium condition for just two inputs ($Y = WL + RK$, where W is the nominal wage rate and R is the nominal rate of return on capital). Then,

$$1 = \frac{P_L wL}{Y} + \frac{P_k rK}{Y} + \ldots \tag{2.3}$$

where w and r are now equivalent real concepts. The above formula also admits of other factors of production (vaguely) since this has become an element in the debate. Looking only at the share for labour (the first term), we have

$$S_L \equiv \frac{P_L}{P} w \frac{L}{y} \tag{2.4}$$

Table 2.14   British real wages, 1750–1860

	Price level (1)	Real wage (2)
1751–60	633.5	63.6
1761–70	710.7	56.7
1771–80	806.9	57.0
1781–90	838.5	57.8
1791–1800	1067.3	52.2
1801–10	1484.3	45.6
1811–20	1569.3	51.7
1821–30	1200.7	67.1
1831–40	1159.8	69.3
1841–50	1104.3	73.6
1851–60	1188.2	74.9

Source: Phelps Brown and Hopkins (1956).

Here we use the fact that $Y = Py$, with P being the GNP deflator and y, real income. This formulation emphasizes that the share of national income going to labour depends on relative prices (the first term), the real wage, and the inverse of the (real) average product of labour.[16]

2.7.1   Real Wages during the First Industrial Revolution

We have used some annual data collected by Phelps Brown and Hopkins in Chapter 1 on real wages. This series shows a dramatic decline in real wages from 1751/60 to 1801/10 as shown in Table 2.14. There are, of course, good reasons for suspecting that real wages might actually have fallen from 1770 right up to 1815, the most obvious having to do with the population-induced rise of the supply of labour.[17] Tucker (1936) constructed an index of the real wages of London artisans which served as the empirical backdrop to Clark's famous comment that average real income fell 'from a fairly high level in the seventeenth century to an Asiatic standard at the beginning of the nineteenth'. Perhaps the strongest view in support of this position is that of Hobsbawm (1957) who attacked, among others, Ashton (1949) and Clapham (1926–38) as being excessively 'optimistic' about the standard of living of workers.[18]

To construct a real wage series one needs a series on nominal wages and a separate price level or cost-of-living index with which to deflate it. Perhaps the best recent summary of such figures in wide use comes from Flinn (1974). Flinn reports that the price level broadly rose from 1750 to around 1813 and then fell thereafter, until 1850, but that the variance in the 40 years around 1813 is troublesomely high; there is little dispute about this. Since there is general agreement as to the rise in real wages after 1840 or 1850, the century from 1750 to 1850 contains the controversy, at least with respect to this particular aspect of the debate.[19] It is a controversy over both price indices and nominal wage indices although, curiously, most of the discussion is over the former. It is curious because the nominal wage indices may be close to meaningless and, in any event are in much worse shape than the price indices, by almost any standard.

As Flinn points out, the real wage controversy (over the 1750 to 1840 period) could hardly have raged on if real wages had moved decisively. Furthermore, he also notes (p. 402),

Whatever criticisms might be made against this or that aspect of individual indexes, when juxtaposed it is their close similarity of behaviour both in the short and the long run that first impresses one.

All of these indices pick up the acceleration in the 1790s and all but one peak in 1813; 'short-run' peaks also agree broadly. For longer run trends, all produce a

rise	1788/92 to 1809/15 of	65–85%
fall	1809/15 to early 1820s of	25–35%
fall	early 1820s to late 1840s of	10–20%

Flinn expects any newly produced indices to fit into this pattern.

With respect to nominal wages, however, one is faced with changing regional patterns and with very poorly representative sources. Partly, this is on account of the fact that there are only two sets of underlying data, those of Gilboy (1932) or the even older numbers of Bowley and Wood (see the references in Flinn (1974)). Gilboy's are generally used, although those of Bowley and Wood are vastly more comprehensive – too vastly, in some ways, since upwards of a thousand series are available. Even so, and including a few more recent collections, Flinn feels that some broad generalizations are possible. Thus, all trends are upward from 1788/92 and downward thereafter. Thus, for nominal wages, the results show a

rise (9/12 cases)	1788/92 to 1810/14 of	50–100%
rise (6/12 cases)	1788/92 to 1810/14 of	65–86%
fall (10/13 cases)	1810/14 to early 1820s of	less than 20%

and no change after the 1820s. On net, then, little can be said about the period before 1788/92, while from then until 1813 perhaps the safest course is to say that (p. 410) '. . . wage rates in general broadly kept pace with rising prices' – that is, real wages are constant, so far as one can possibly say with certainty. Thereafter, though, they rose.

In the Flinn paper just discussed, it is pointed out that much of the gain in real wages in the entire century from 1750 to 1850 occurs just after the price level peaked in 1813. Von Tunzelmann (1979) accepts the uniformity of the price indices but, in order to deal with some of the statistical problems that Flinn faces, suggests applying the 'principal components' method to the wage data in order to generate another series that is itself (statistically) the best representative of the entire collection of series. In principal components analysis, each series is weighted during the computations in such a way as to minimize the variance of all of the series by the maximum amount possible. More than one series can be selected in this process (hence components). Von Tunzelmann emphasizes some of the peculiarities in the underlying data that Flinn looked at. Most peculiar in this connection is the Phelps Brown/Hopkins nominal wage data for 1810–50 which is essentially constant over the entire period, being based on 'contract-hire' rates and not on actual market nominal wages. Indeed, the only times these rates changed over the entire century (upward in this case) were in the 1775–1810 period. Tucker's (1936) series on London artisans changes downward once in 1762 and upward once in 1790/2 and is otherwise constant. Both series make real rather than nominal wages captives of the price level to an extreme degree. This, certainly, has no counterpart in the modern data and is implausible.

Von Tunzelmann produces upper and lower bounds for the real wage series that Flinn studies; his first principal component generally has an unexplained variance of 15 per cent and the addition of a second principal component lowers this to 5 per cent or less in all tests. One can read a combination of lower and upper bounds that produces the 'optimistic' finding of a gain of real wages of 150 per cent over the century or the 'pessimistic' finding of a fall until around 1810 and then a rise, to 1750 levels, by 1850. This undermines Flinn's confidence in the overall picture created by looking at all the series together.[20]

2.7.2 A Recent Effort on the Standard of Living Problem

Above we referred to the fact that recent discussions of the British standard of living have tended to undermine the pessimists. Mainly, this is a question of new data and the new evidence (Lindert and Williamson, 1983, pp. 1–2),

> suggests that material gains were even larger after 1820 than optimists had previously claimed, even if the concept of material well-being is expanded to include health and environmental factors. Although the pessimists can still find deplorable trends in the collective environment after 1820, particularly rising inequality and social disorder, this article suggests that their case must be shifted to the period 1750–1820 to retain its central relevance.

The new data in this paper are described there; suffice it to say that this represents quite the best recent collection of time series figures on British nominal wage rates. Perhaps the most interesting of these are estimates of 'service sector pay rates' some derived from the annual estimates of the House of Commons; these are dated 1755, 1781 and from 1797 onward. Gilboy and Bowley and Wood numbers are also used and there are adjustments for the regional disparities noted in these data (e.g., by Gourvish, 1972). This produces a sharper rise in nominal wages (in the building trades) than shown by Phelps Brown and Hopkins.

Taking the data points where the data are the best, Lindert and Williamson produce the set of numbers for nominal wages given in Table 2.15. These numbers are not for real wages but for the *earnings* of workers, so they reflect assumptions about hours of work, payment in kind, and the like. While this opens the door for all manner of adjustments in the data, the correct concept is 'earnings', as we have argued above. Thus, up to 1805, farm workers (and non-farm common labourers) gained compared with higher-paid workers, but thereafter they did not.

The price series used by Lindert and Williamson also reflects further work. There are new products and attention is paid to housing

Table 2.15   Nominal and real earnings in Britain, 1755–1851 (1851 = 100)

Date	Nominal				Real			
	Farm workers	All blue collar	White collar	All	Farm workers	All blue collar	White collar	All
1755	59.16	51.05	21.62	38.62	65.46	56.50	23.93	42.74
1781	72.62	59.64	26.42	46.62	61.12	50.19	22.24	39.24
1797	103.41	74.42	32.55	58.97	74.50	53.61	23.45	42.48
1805	139.12	96.58	38.88	75.87	74.51	51.73	20.82	40.64
1810	144.76	107.81	43.01	84.89	67.21	50.04	19.97	39.41
1815	137.88	106.18	46.55	85.30	75.51	58.15	25.49	46.71
1819	134.47	101.84	50.77	80.37	73.52	55.68	27.76	46.13
1827	106.89	97.59	55.09	83.11	75.86	69.25	39.10	58.99
1835	103.41	94.11	75.03	88.77	91.67	83.43	66.52	78.69
1851	100.00	100.00	100.00	100.00	100.00	100.00	100.00	100.00

Source: Lindert and Williamson (1983).

Table 2.16   Ranges of earnings for all workers

	1781–1851		
	Most pessimistic	Best guess	Most optimistic
Farm labourers	31.6%	63.6%	107.0%
All blue collar	61.8	99.2	154.4
White collar	294.5	349.6	520.3
All workers	103.7	154.8	220.3

costs; even so, the data are generally wholesale prices since retail prices simply are not available. Some attention is also paid to the need to have regional weights, but the final result is largely insensitive to varying these weights, so that in the final series southern/urban weights are used. The result is a new set of real wages which also appear in Table 2.15. This confirms the statement by Lindert and Williamson with which we started this section, to the effect that a clear break appears to start around 1820 while before that date constant (but definitely not declining!) real wages obtain. Using different weighting and price assumptions, they produce the ranges given in Table 2.16 for the first industrial revolution for all workers. As noted, the farm workers gained most in the early going and the other categories after 1815–20. These gains are sufficient, say Lindert and Williamson (p. 13) so that

> no conceivable level of unemployment could have . . . left the workers of the 1840s with less than their grandfathers had. Such a cancellation of gains would require that the national unemployment rate would have had to rise from zero to 50 per cent, or from 10 per cent to 55 per cent.

It is in this sense that the pessimists' case is seriously weakened by the new data.

2.8 CONCLUSION

One of the things that happens as one moves closer to modern times is that the data get considerably better. Up until 1780 we had little to work with except prices and population, but from 1780 not only do those two items exist, but there is also an index of business activity that permits a (controversial) estimate of the business cycle, as well as more realistic real wages and some fragmentary unemployment estimates. We are still short of adequate numbers for really interesting time-series tests, especially in the monetary area, but the range of macro topics is broadened somewhat in Chapter 2 compared with Chapter 1.

What we have found in this chapter is that while economic activity clearly expanded from 1780 to 1850, certain qualifications need to be considered. Most important, really, is the finding in the literature that the overall rate of growth of the British economy, at least up until 1815 or so, was not as rapid as the 'industrial revolution' school, now wellnigh defunct, once thought. Next in order of importance, but last considered in the chapter, is the finding, if that is the appropriate term, that the real wages of labourers – and possibly their standard of living – cannot be convincingly demonstrated to have changed much from 1760 to around 1815. After that, although the precise point of departure is not certain, there is a strong improvement in the overall position of labourers – and an acceleration in the overall growth rate.

There are other results in this chapter that also should be underscored in a summary. First, our continuation of the crowding-out and tax-smoothing propositions into the traumatic Napoleonic War period produces a rather strong conclusion in favour of the latter but not the former. Second, while a cyclical dating based on an index of economic activity is available, it seems that the period from 1800 to 1816 – again partly because of the shocks administered to the economy during the war period – is very much in dispute in terms of an agreed-upon cyclical profile. One can readily predict that further work will be done on these issues for this period, as the data become available.

3 The United Kingdom in the Second Half of the 19th Century: Maturity and Relative Decline

3.1 INTRODUCTION

The main task of this chapter is to explain and use a set of macroeconomic time-series tools to describe the performance of the UK macroeconomy in the 1850–1910 period. There are some new topics here, but the emphasis is on material (and controversies) already in the literature for the most part. We will have some cross-country comparisons, as well, but most of these will be with the United States, as is the fashion in the literature. Later chapters will make the obvious European comparisons where, indeed, Britain often provides the benchmark. This is particularly the case in Chapter 8.

The word 'relative' in the title of this chapter is meant to suggest that we will be making comparisons, both with earlier British growth rates and with other countries (usually over the 1870 to 1910 period). In the literature the meaning of the term 'relative decline' is a reference to the apparent slippage of the British economy in its rate of industrial growth, especially in comparison with certain successful rivals, but also with respect to her own past accomplishments. The usual way this is described is by means of detailed analysis of the performance of individual industries and the conclusions often emphasize the role of the entrepreneurs in these industries in transmitting what is sometimes called the 'British disease' to their own enterprises. We will look at some of this material to try to define the problem, but for the most part our data will be at a higher level of aggregation than these more microeconomic topics seem to require.

Most of the chapter deals with new tests of macroeconomic models designed to throw light on some of the existing controversies in the British literature. Before undertaking that, however, there will be some discussion of the individual industrial figures, in the remainder of this section. The macroeconomic story begins with a description of the figures on the growth of the British economy from 1830 to 1910 in Section 3.2; this shows a more modest performance for the entire 1830 to 1910 period than one might have expected for the leading nation in the industrial revolution. Our next exercise (in Section 3.3) is to introduce some time-series methods of analysis of the data, the purpose of which is to consider how the data might best be handled in econometric tests. This involves, among other things, Dickey–Fuller tests for unit roots. As a by-product, we obtain a characterization of the British business cycle that is surprisingly unlike the American, given what appears to be the tradition in this respect. This is discussed in Section 3.4.

The major concern in this chapter is with several hypotheses that have emerged in Friedman and Schwartz's *Monetary Trends* (1982). Friedman and Schwartz have argued in favour of a strong financial integration across the Atlantic – running both ways in a causal sense – while the real sectors of the British and American economies have moved more-or-less independently. This chapter will present a series of Granger-causality tests, designed to reveal the temporal ordering of variables; in this case the tests confirm much of the Friedman/ Schwartz story. Friedman and Schwartz also argue that the financial integration across the Atlantic involves the demand for money and its velocity. This actually may be true of the long run of data studied in *Monetary Trends*, but in the short period from 1870 to 1910, perhaps because the US financial sector can be described as unsophisticated relative to the UK, this integration hypothesis does not hold up very well. In a sense, this is what Friedman and Schwartz say, too, when they argue that these functions/variables need to be adjusted for changes in the degree of financial sophistication, but the details of this important difference tend to get swallowed up in the grand themes of their study. In any case, both money demand and velocity are studied in this chapter, with a variety of tests designed to contribute to a resolution of some of these controversies.

Turning to the microeconomic details on industrialization briefly, the most striking thing in the record is a general slowdown in the rate of growth of the individual sectors, as the First World War approaches. Table 3.1 collects figures for a broad set of representative (industrial-revolution) industries for the 1850 to 1909 period. Two things stand out in the table: the absolute figures are impressive (in many cases the gain in output in the last ten years equals or exceeds the total production in 1850–9 or even 1860–9) and there is a distinct slowdown in the rate of growth in the last 20 years pretty much across the board. This,

Table 3.1   British industrial growth, 1850–1909

	Railroad passengers (m)	Freight (m tons)	Steamship registrations (000 tons)	Iron ore produced + imported (000 tons)	Coal production (m tons)	Raw cotton retained (m lb)	Raw wool imports (m lb)
	(1)	(1)		(2)	(3)		
1850–9	111.4	. . .	319	9 128.0	58.50	795	85.8
1860–9	238.7	112.6	724	9 391.5	93.95	801	138.3
1870–9	490.1	196.2	1847	16 375.5	127.45	1244	192.9
1880–9	678.1	253.6	3783	19 014.0	160.80	1473	252.3
1890–9	903.5	329.5	5993	17 847.5	191.10	1557	354.7
1900–9	1170.0	455.4	8921	20 721.5	241.45	1733	374.0
Growth rates:							
50 years	4.70	3.49	6.66	1.72	2.84	1.56	2.94
Last 20 years	2.73	2.93	4.29	0.43	2.03	0.81	1.97

(1) Middle of period, (2) first figure is 1855–9, (3) first figure is 1850, 1855–9 evenly weighted.
Source: Mathias (1983).

clearly, is one of the meanings of the term 'relative decline'. Since some of these sectors grew more rapidly in *some* other countries, the other meaning of the term – the loss of relative industrial prestige across nations – is also implicit in these numbers. Indeed, as Table 3.1 clearly indicates, the two large industries that dominated the first industrial revolution – cotton and iron – show rates of growth that are sharply slower at the end and, in fact, lower than overall real GNP growth over the last 20 years. One should note, though, that the other industries, by exceeding the 2 per cent or so per year of real GNP growth, are pulling up the average. Indeed, declines from the very high rates of industrial growth of the early 19th century are surely to be expected since, for one thing, British demand is not likely to grow at a rate sufficient to absorb such an increase. Furthermore, it is the traditional industries that appear to do relatively poorly in this respect and this, too, is to be expected in a world that is developing these same industries partly with the assistance of the British. The rest of this debate, however fascinating, is peripheral to our interests, though, in view of its micro-economic context.[1]

3.2   THE GROWTH OF THE BRITISH MACROECONOMY, 1850–1910

The performance of the British economy over this period is really quite strong, however it might be measured, so the reader should be

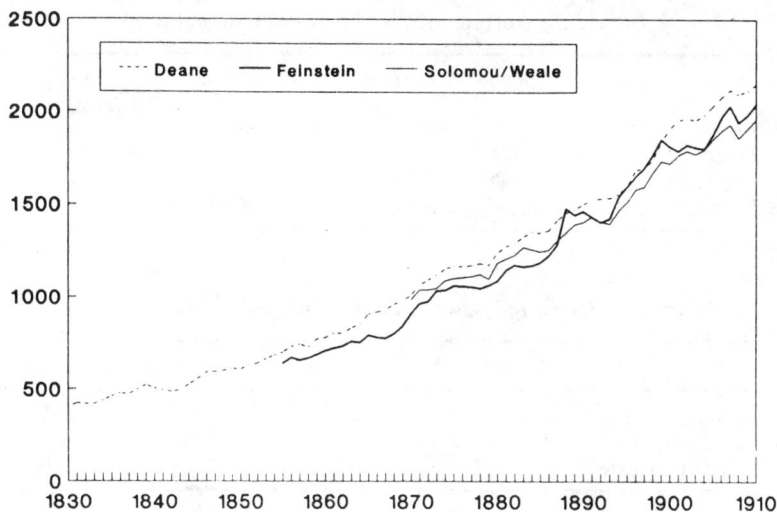

Figure 3.1   Three estimates of real product – UK, 1830–1910

alerted to the fact that to the extent there are problems in the performance of the British economy, they are basically in the nature of a slowdown – and a possible undermining of the traditional industrial sectors – rather than a dramatic collapse. Moving on to more general issues, let us look at some partly parallel figures on real product for the United Kingdom, those of Deane (1968), Feinstein (1972) and Solomou and Weale (1991). The first two series are estimates of GNP, while the third is a compromise estimate of Feinstein's real gross domestic product, where the method of constructing the compromise is consistent with statistical theory.[2] All three series appear in Figure 3.1, where efforts have been made to make the series comparable.[3] These series clearly grow at different rates, with the rate of growth of the newest numbers – the Solomou and Weale balanced estimates of real GDP – being the lowest and the real GNP figures of Deane the highest. This is apparent from a visual inspection of the graph. The series are, however, highly correlated as shown in Table 3.2. On the other hand, the standard deviation of the Solomou/ Weale figures is well below that of the other numbers. So there are sufficient differences to warrant checking across this set of estimates in particular tests, to see how sensitive the results are to the choice of series.

Table 3.2   Correlations: estimates of national product

	Deane	Feinstein	Solomou/Weale	Standard deviations
Deane	1.000			353.7
Feinstein	0.988	1.000		359.0
Solomou/Weale	0.997	0.992	1.000	306.3

Table 3.3   British real growth rates in the period of relative decline

	1830–1910	1850–1910	1870–1910	1890–1910
Deane	2.16	2.06	1.90	2.02
Feinstein	. . .	2.22	2.08	1.84
Solomou/Weale	. . .	. . .	1.75	1.81

Before going on, let us quantify the differences in growth rates in the series just described over the period; here, to return to our macroeconomic interests, we are looking for an aggregate estimate of the relative decline noticed in the industrial data in Section 3.1. Table 3.3 illustrates real growth rates for the three sets of numbers in order to establish a broad perspective on the performance of the British economy in this period.[4] These numbers, computed in each case by regressing the log of real GNP on trend, generally suggest a declining growth rate over the longer period.[5] On the other hand, the 1890–1910 period actually picks up a little in two of the three estimates, suggesting yet another way these calculations differ. In any event, an aggregate version of the relative decline of the UK economy is not especially obvious here (depending, as noted, on which series one looks at).

There are two sets of data available on the sectoral behaviour of UK national product, again from Deane and Feinstein. The numbers from Deane run from 1830 to 1910 and those of Feinstein from 1870 to 1910. What we are interested in are the broad trends in C/Y, I/Y and G/Y as well as any tendency for government expenditures to crowd out private expenditure in this period. Beginning with Deane's figures, we show in Figure 3.2 the behaviour of these ratios, here drawn on two different scales to make it easier to compare their movements.[6] Here we see a decline in the consumption ratio over the entire period, from 0.89 to 0.78, with the sharpest declines coming in

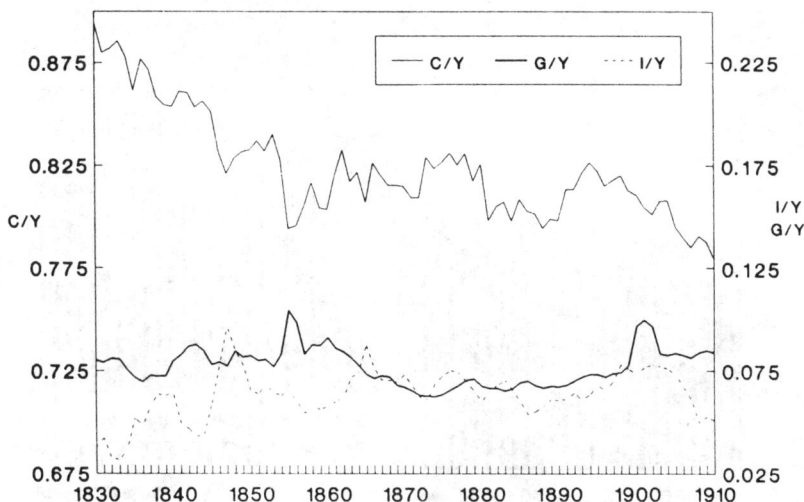

Deane's Data

Figure 3.2   C/Y, I/Y and G/Y in the United Kingdom, 1830–1910

the periods 1830 to 1855 and 1894 to 1910. The Feinstein figures show the same pattern for the latter period.[7]

Is there crowding out in the period? The Crimean and Boer wars represent major opportunities for this to show up and Figure 3.2 suggests that increases in the government spending ratio at these times were accompanied with declines in both the consumption and investment ratios, with the effect on consumption being more pronounced. As before, the investment and government spending data were differenced to remove trend, but for the entire period or for 1870 to 1910 (on Deane's data), the crowding-out phenomenon did not surface (the correlations were very small and positive). Consumption, on the other hand, is positively associated with increased government spending in both periods, and significantly so in the period 1870 to 1910 ($r = 0.34$). On this rather scant evidence it looks as if what crowding out there is, is restricted to the two major wars in the period.

These macroeconomic numbers also show the relative decline that we have identified in several ways already, but in a somewhat more dramatic fashion. As Figure 3.3 indicates, using per capita calculations for income and consumption for 1855 to 1910, there are several periods of stagnation in both sets of figures (especially in per capita consumption) in the 1870s and after 1900.[8]

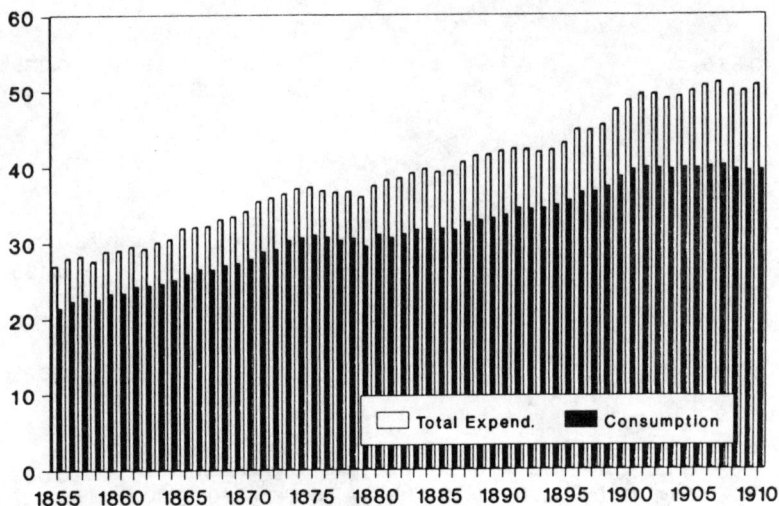

Figure 3.3   UK per capita consumption and income, 1855–1910

Table 3.4   Rates of growth (per capita)

	1855–75	1875–1910
Consumption	1.64	0.92
Expenditure	1.84	0.73

It is also noticeable in the graph that aside from a burst in the late 1890s, the whole period from 1870 to 1910 was at a rate of growth considerably below that for 1855 to 1874 for both series. The actual growth rates, using the endpoints for the calculations, are given in Table 3.4. This is the macroeconomic equivalent to the industry-level relative-decline story. Note that 'relative' here refers to recent UK history, but it could also refer to comparisons with some other countries (in this study), at least for the 1895 to 1910 period. These comparisons are discussed in Chapters 4 to 7 and summarized in Chapter 8.

3.3   SOME TIME-SERIES PROPERTIES OF THE INCOME DATA

The income and monetary data used in later sections of this chapter – and comparable data used in the study of other countries in other chapters – is going to be used fairly intensively in both structural and astructural tests of macroeconomic models. This being the case, there are certain prior questions that need to be dealt with in this section – involving mainly how the data are to be transformed to put them into a form amenable to such time-series testing without either corrupting the data or despoiling it of its interesting economic properties.

The main issue concerns whether or not the data are stationary. The concern is actually whether the 'process' that drives the data is stationary (because if not it will tend to produce non-stationary patterns in the data) but the tests are, of course, on the data themselves. A *stationary* series of the variable x_t has

$$\text{COV}\ (x_t, x_{t-k}) = \mu_k$$

for all k; this would be violated (be *non-stationary*) if

$$\text{COV}\ (x_t, x_{t-k}) = \mu_{k,t}$$

In particular, dependence on 'time' of the autocorrelations in the series in question provides for non-stationarity. Usually, trend in the basic series (or in its variance) is the likely and usual proximate cause of non-stationarity in economic time series (although seasonal factors are also relevant in this context). Since many macroeconomic time series exhibit trends, we could clearly seriously prejudice a test involving several of these series if, at the same time, the trend were not an integral part of the hypothesis. Indeed, usually it is population growth that is the suspected *proximate* case of the dependence of macro variables on time. In this section we propose to judge stationarity in terms of a formal test procedure (the Dickey–Fuller test) and to illustrate it by less rigorous, but nevertheless revealing, time-series plots. We begin with the time-series plots, mainly for the intuition they provide.

Figure 3.4, is a plot of the Feinstein data for net national product in real per-capita form.[9] It is here regressed on a constant term and the residuals are plotted, with the ':' lines indicating a 5 per cent confidence interval. Lack of stationarity, here, is clearly trend related and

Figure 3.4 Feinstein data for real NNP (data less a constant)

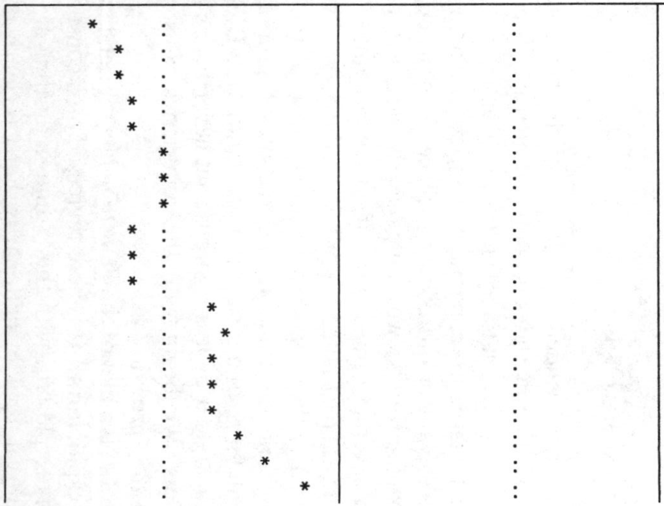

obs	RESIDUAL	ACTUAL	FITTED
1870	−7.81902	28.2025	36.0216
1871	−6.59939	29.4222	36.0216
1872	−6.77172	29.2498	36.0216
1873	−6.00069	30.0209	36.0216
1874	−6.07919	29.9424	36.0216
1875	−5.58054	30.4410	36.0216
1876	−5.64553	30.3760	36.0216
1877	−5.39384	30.6277	36.0216
1878	−6.10560	29.9160	36.0216
1879	−5.72202	30.2995	36.0216
1880	−5.96930	30.0522	36.0216
1881	−4.42063	31.6009	36.0216
1882	−3.97403	32.0475	36.0216
1883	−4.24130	31.7803	36.0216
1884	−4.43869	31.5829	36.0216
1885	−4.29541	31.7261	36.0216
1886	−3.32450	32.6970	36.0216
1887	−2.35745	33.6641	36.0216
1888	−0.34079	35.6808	36.0216

Data With Constant Removed

Year			
1889	1.55669	37.5782	36.0216
1890	1.45509	37.4766	36.0216
1891	0.74656	36.7681	36.0216
1892	-0.58679	35.4348	36.0216
1893	-0.54166	35.4799	36.0216
1894	2.21811	38.2397	36.0216
1895	3.32885	39.3504	36.0216
1896	4.11017	40.1317	36.0216
1897	4.70089	40.7224	36.0216
1898	6.28563	42.3072	36.0216
1899	7.58466	43.6062	36.0216
1900	5.61067	41.6322	36.0216
1901	4.86800	40.8895	36.0216
1902	5.68100	41.7025	36.0216
1903	4.77069	40.7922	36.0216
1904	4.00675	40.0283	36.0216
1905	5.30604	41.3276	36.0216
1906	7.04432	43.0659	36.0216
1907	8.13807	44.1596	36.0216
1908	5.54902	41.5706	36.0216
1909	6.00996	42.0315	36.0216
1910	7.23700	43.2585	36.0216

the pattern of the data, as it crawls off the page at the bottom, is typical of a non-stationary series.

What happens when data are non-stationary is that the variance of the data is potentially infinite. Since statistical tests generally require a finite variance – and, in particular, since the F-test does – it is necessary to protect against non-stationarity by removing the trend. One way to do this is to include a trend term in the basic regression (of, for example, the demand for money); this is often done. A variation is to remove the trend directly by using as our measure of income the residuals from the following regression.

$$\text{Log } y = \alpha + \beta T$$

where T is a date variable. After processing the Feinstein NNP data in this way, the pattern of residuals given in Figure 3.5 results. This detrended series certainly looks much better, although the series does appear to wander off from time to time and, more seriously, to exhibit a greater variance in the later observations (say from the mid-1890s). The Dickey–Fuller test, described below, actually confirms that this particular transformation is non-stationary.

There is a feeling among macroeconomists that detrending data in the way just described tends to produce the impression of more cyclical activity in the data than is actually there. In particular, slowdowns in NNP might appear as declines if the data are detrended in the way just described, and so the detrended series should not be used to establish firm cyclical dating, at least of the milder recessions. Since we will do so, but only in comparisons with data that have been similarly abused, we have been forewarned. As an alternative, as described, for example, by Nelson and Plosser (1982), one might use the first differences of the data – either the raw data or the logs of the data (producing growth rates) – to try to induce stationarity. In Figure 3.6, the differenced Feinstein data do appear to be stationary at least in the sense that the series tends to return to zero over time. It is, though, still hard to judge whether these numbers are stationary or not, since the variance, again, appears to be somewhat larger at the end of the period. This procedure, does, however, pass the Dickey–Fuller test, as we will see, implying that the data are stationary.

A precise statistical test also exists for judging whether a series needs to be transformed to induce stationarity; this is the Dickey–Fuller test, as described in Fuller (1976). Basically, what we are looking for is the presence of a *unit root*, in which case the data can be presumed to be non-stationary. What one does is to run a regression of the data on a lag of the data and trend, as in

$$Y_t = \mu + \alpha T + \delta Y_{t-1} + e_t \qquad (3.1)$$

and then test to see if δ is significantly different from unity. We also test for whether the data contain trend – hence the appearance of T in the regression equation. (That is, the test is of the joint hypothesis that $\alpha = 0$ and $\delta = 1$.)[10]
    Table 3.3 collects the results of Dickey–Fuller tests for the real *per capita* NNP and real *per capita* money variables used in this chapter. Indeed, we also perform Dickey–Fuller tests for the logarithms and first-differences of the data to provide comparisons. The equation estimated is (3.1), as just given, and the Dickey–Fuller statistic (appearing as 'DF Stat' in Table 3.5) is calculated as

$$DF = (\delta - 1)/S_\delta$$

where S_δ is the standard error of the coefficient δ. This is not distributed as t, as one might suspect, but has its own 'Dickey–Fuller' distribution. For an n of 50, for example, if the DF statistic is greater than -2.93, then we are not able to say (at the 5 per cent level) that the data do not have a unit root. These cases are marked with an asterisk in Table 3.5
    These results establish, quite clearly, that all forms of the 'raw' NNP data may well have unit roots and are, thereby, potentially non-stationary; even the regression-detrended logarithms of the data do not successfully eliminate the possibility of a unit root, as we have already mentioned. For NNP and log NNP there is also a significant trend term. Note that when the first differences of the data are employed – for both money and NNP – there is no sign of a unit root (as shown by the relatively high values of the DF statistic in the last two rows). This is the typical result for macroeconomic time-series variables.

3.4 BUSINESS CYCLES IN THE VICTORIAN AND EDWARDIAN ECONOMY

British business cycles in the period we are studying are well-documented in the literature, of course, but we will again rely on

Figure 3.5 Regression detrended logarithms Feinstein real per capita NNP

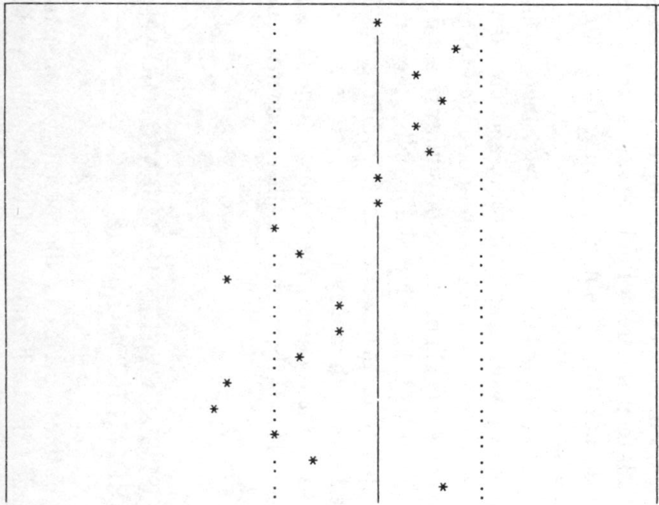

Date	RESIDUAL	ACTUAL	FITTED
1870	-0.00148	3.33941	3.34090
1871	0.02920	3.38175	3.35255
1872	0.01168	3.37587	3.36420
1873	0.02605	3.40189	3.37585
1874	0.01178	3.39927	3.38750
1875	0.01665	3.41579	3.39915
1876	0.00286	3.41365	3.41080
1877	-0.00054	3.42191	3.42245
1878	-0.03570	3.39839	3.43410
1879	-0.03461	3.41113	3.44575
1880	-0.05446	3.40294	3.45740
1881	-0.01586	3.45319	3.46905
1882	-0.01348	3.46722	3.48070
1883	-0.03350	3.45884	3.49235
1884	-0.05138	3.45262	3.50400
1885	-0.05850	3.45714	3.51565
1886	-0.04001	3.48728	3.52730
1887	-0.02251	3.51643	3.53895
1888	0.02402	3.57461	3.55060

Detrended Data

1889	0.06418	3.62643	3.56225
1890	0.04982	3.62372	3.57390
1891	0.01909	3.60463	3.58555
1892	−0.02950	3.56769	3.59720
1893	−0.03988	3.56897	3.60885
1894	0.02338	3.64387	3.62050
1895	0.04036	3.67251	3.63215
1896	0.04837	3.69217	3.64380
1897	0.05133	3.70678	3.65545
1898	0.07786	3.74496	3.66710
1899	0.09645	3.77520	3.67875
1900	0.03848	3.72887	3.69040
1901	0.00883	3.71088	3.70205
1902	0.01687	3.73056	3.71370
1903	−0.01685	3.70849	3.72535
1904	−0.04741	3.68959	3.73700
1905	−0.02712	3.72153	3.74865
1906	0.00244	3.76273	3.76030
1907	0.01586	3.78781	3.77195
1908	−0.05620	3.72739	3.78360
1909	−0.05683	3.73842	3.79525
1910	−0.03970	3.76719	3.80690

Figure 3.6 Differenced data Feinstein real per capita NNP

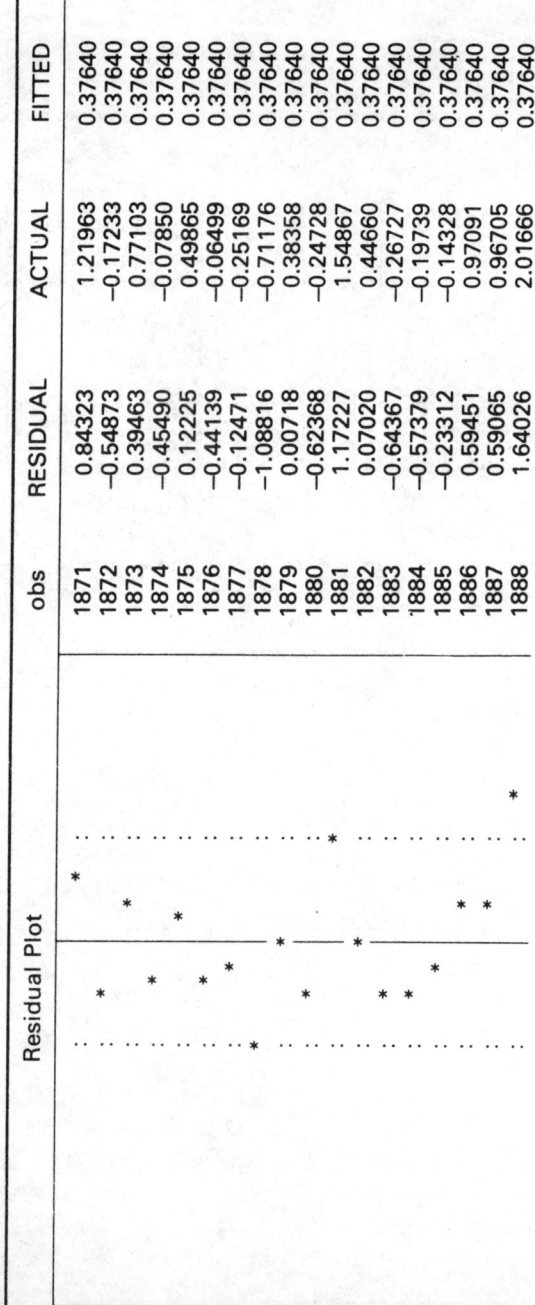

Residual Plot	obs	RESIDUAL	ACTUAL	FITTED
	1871	0.84323	1.21963	0.37640
	1872	-0.54873	-0.17233	0.37640
	1873	0.39463	0.77103	0.37640
	1874	-0.45490	-0.07850	0.37640
	1875	0.12225	0.49865	0.37640
	1876	-0.44139	-0.06499	0.37640
	1877	-0.12471	-0.25169	0.37640
	1878	-1.08816	-0.71176	0.37640
	1879	0.00718	0.38358	0.37640
	1880	-0.62368	-0.24728	0.37640
	1881	1.17227	1.54867	0.37640
	1882	0.07020	0.44660	0.37640
	1883	-0.64367	-0.26727	0.37640
	1884	-0.57379	-0.19739	0.37640
	1885	-0.23312	-0.14328	0.37640
	1886	0.59451	0.97091	0.37640
	1887	0.59065	0.96705	0.37640
	1888	1.64026	2.01666	0.37640

1889	1.52108	1.89748	0.37640
1890	-0.47800	-0.10160	0.37640
1891	-1.08493	-0.70853	0.37640
1892	-1.70975	-1.33335	0.37640
1893	-0.33127	-0.04513	0.37640
1894	2.38337	2.75977	0.37640
1895	0.73434	1.11074	0.37640
1896	0.40492	0.78132	0.37640
1897	0.21432	0.59072	0.37640
1898	1.20834	1.58474	0.37640
1899	0.92263	1.29903	0.37640
1900	-2.35039	-1.97399	0.37640
1901	-1.11907	-0.74267	0.37640
1902	0.43660	0.81300	0.37640
1903	-1.28671	-0.91031	0.37640
1904	-1.14034	-0.76394	0.37640
1905	0.92289	1.29929	0.37640
1906	1.36188	1.73828	0.37640
1907	0.71735	1.09375	0.37640
1908	-2.96545	-2.58905	0.37640
1909	0.08454	0.46094	0.37640
1910	0.85064	1.22704	0.37640

Table 3.5   Dickey–Fuller tests of British data (real *per capita* form),
1870–1910

Dependent variable	Intercept (μ)	Trend (α)	Lagged Dep. (δ)	DF Stat	DW	Obs.
Money	2.838	0.024	0.864	−1.56*	1.51	39
	(1.64)	(1.31)	(9.90)			
NNP	10.210	0.112	0.727	−2.39*	1.47	40
	(2.48)	(2.24)	(6.36)			
Log money	0.437	0.001	0.856	−1.58*	1.56	39
	(1.67)	(1.30)	(9.40)			
Log NNP	0.904	0.003	0.750	−2.23*	1.97	40
	(2.25)	(2.02)	(6.69)			
DT log money	−0.001	−0.000	0.856	−1.58*	1.56	39
	(0.31)	(0.37)	(9.40)			
DT log NNP	−0.001	−0.000	−0.750	−2.23*	1.47	40
	(.17)	(.31)	(6.69)			
Differenced money	0.132	−0.002	0.191	−4.87	1.85	38
	(1.51)	(0.21)	(1.51)			
Differenced NNP	0.298	−0.002	0.161	−5.09	1.84	39
	(1.58)	(0.12)	(0.98)			

Notes: DW is the Durbin–Watson statistic; the values in parentheses are t-values.
Source: Friedman and Schwartz (1982).

Friedman and Schwartz to get things started. They are interested in a comparison with the United States, and the *impression* one gets from their discussion is that aside from the two world wars, and aside from different trends, both the cyclical phases and the log level figures for real income are similar across the two countries (the latter has a 0.96 correlation for their entire period). Indeed (p. 307),

> of thirty-nine United Kingdom turning points in the 109 years from 1867 to 1975, twenty come in the same year as a United States turning point of the same kind (i.e., a trough in the same years as a trough; a peak in the same year as a peak); eleven come one year later; four come one year earlier; and only four have no corresponding turning points within one year. Of these four, three are in the post-World War II period, one in 1926.

This argument is supported by a detailed set of 'phase reference' datings from which Table 3.6 has been abstracted (and redesigned, with my brackets). Certainly on this reading, the broad experiences are similar, although the United States shows a series of events

Table 3.6   British and American cycles. Friedman and Schwartz's calculations

Type	United States	United Kingdom	Type
E	1867–1869		
*C	1869–1870	1868–1874	E
E	1870–1873		
C	1873–1878	1874–1879	C
E	1878–1882	1879–1883	E
C	1882–1885	1883–1886	C
E	1885–1887		
*C	1887–1888	1886–1890	E
E	1888–1890		
C	1890–1891		
*E	1891–1892	1890–1893	C
C	1892–1894		
E	1894–1895		
*C	1895–1896		
E	1896–1899	1893–1900	E
*C	1899–1900		
**E	1900–1903	1900–1904	C
C	1903–1904		
E	1904–1907	1904–1907	E
C	1907–1908	1907–1908	C
E	1908–1910	1908–1913	E

(mostly short contractions) – marked here with a single asterisk – that depart from the unanimity. Only one cyclical event, in 1900–1903, offers a clear contrast (it is marked with a double asterisk). Indeed, the two economies appear to head out of the period in 1913 in almost perfect lockstep.

Be all this as it may, the foregoing is possibly a little misleading, especially in being unquantified (although Friedman and Schwartz do produce some phase-related numbers). A different way to provide quantification, on a narrower statistical base, to be sure, is to use the data we have generated – i.e., either the detrended logs of NNP, which possibly exaggerate the cycles, or the first differences, which may well minimize them. Looking first at the detrended logs (in Figure 3.7), we see that until around 1900 or so, the real cycles in NNP are dramatically different in the two countries. That this remarkable difference is not, somehow, a statistical aberration is

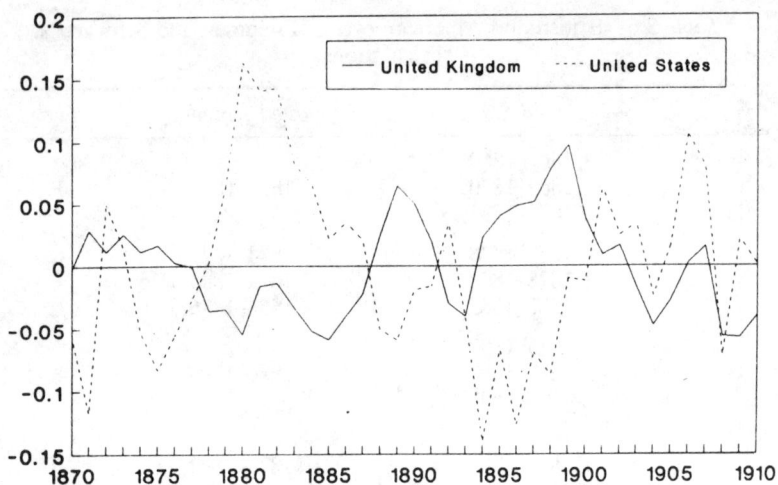

Detrended Logarithms of the Data

Figure 3.7   British and American business cycles, 1870–1910

apparent in Figure 3.8 since when the differenced real, per capita numbers are compared across the two countries, somewhat the same pattern shows up.

It is probable that real shocks shaped the course of these events and that these differed in the two countries, as the popular literature really implies. We emphasize real shocks – or, loosely, 'real business cycles' – in anticipation of both our results and Friedman and Schwartz's that the monetary sectors were so intertwined that monetary shocks, if they affected real income (which is not obvious) would do so in both countries at, or nearly at, the same time. If this is not convincing at this point, where only a portion of the evidence is assembled, read on (also into Chapter 8).

Another way one might look at the cycle is by listing the actual years in which national product declined. In this case we abandon our interest in US/UK comparisons and move into a discussion of the UK figures by themselves. Above we noted that there are several major compilations of the national product data and so we return to that topic, briefly, before discussing the details of the UK experience. Thus Table 3.7 lists the recession years from the Deane, Feinstein and Solomou and Weale calculations of real national product. Not surprisingly, the Solomou and Weale and Feinstein versions are quite similar. On the basis of the three sets of numbers one could possibly

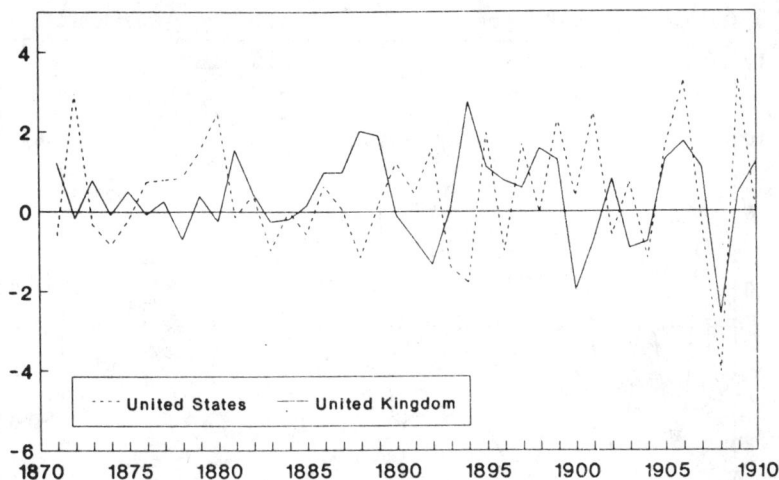

Differenced Data

Figure 3.8   British and American business cycles, 1870–1910

Table 3.7   Recessions in the United Kingdom: three measures compared

Deane (1)	%	*Solomou/Weale* (2)	%	*Feinstein* (3)	%
1850	0.95				
1858	2.25				
				1872–3	1.26
1876	0.43				
1879	0.86	1879	2.21	1879	1.82
				1881	0.16
1885	0.34	1984	0.86	1884–5	0.88
		1892–3	2.76	1892–3	2.11
		1900	0.63	1900	1.79
1903	0.57	1903	0.94		
1908	1.02	1908	3.75	1908	2.81

(1) GNP at factor cost; (2) GDP balanced estimate; (3) GNP at factor cost (Table 5, Column 12).

argue that major downturns occurred in 1858, in 1879, in 1884–5, in 1892–3, in 1900, and, certainly, in 1908. This is six major downturns in 60 years.

There are also some unemployment figures for the 1855–1910 period in the United Kingdom, as produced by Feinstein (1972).

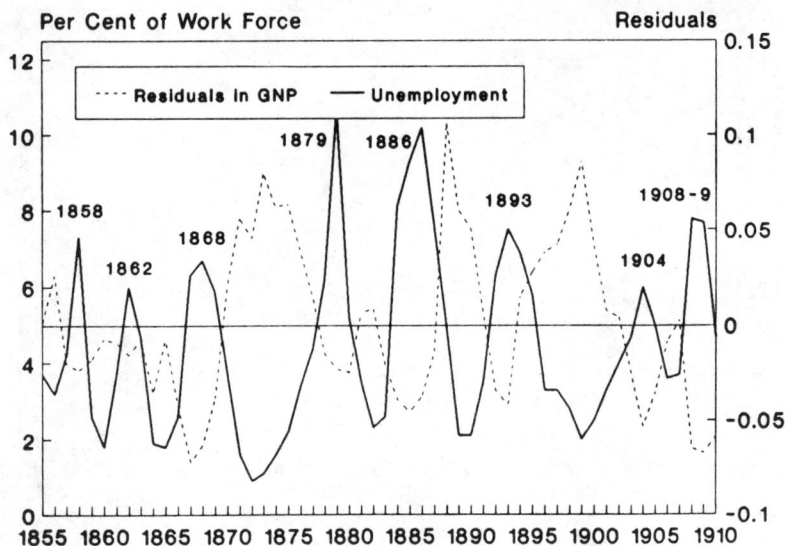

Figure 3.9   Unemployment and business cycles, 1855–1910

Possibly the best way to look at these is in comparison with the residuals (from the Feinstein estimate of GNP at factor cost), and this is done in Figure 3.9.[11]

In the figure the unemployment series is the percentage of the labour force unemployed, while the residuals of GNP are from the regression detrended logs of the original series. One would expect these series to be negatively correlated – and they are at −0.60. The troughs are labelled in the figure, and they are very distinct, indeed. These put lower turning points at 1858, 1862, 1868, 1879, 1886, 1893, 1904 and 1908–9. These generally correspond to turning points in Table 3.7, although the unemployment troughs occasionally lag by a year. This lag is common in modern cycles, as well, and has to do with the layoff patterns of business firms, in all likelihood. In any case, this discussion provides further evidence on the exact timing of cyclical events in this period.

A standard (modern) view of the business cycle is that it is the result of a shock-persistence mechanism. A system that is shocked – for example by a financial crisis – will react to the shock by spreading out the real effect over time. The latter – termed 'persistence' – might go on for some time, but typically does not. It also does not seem to be the case that the reaction to the shock is unstable (in the sense of an economy spiraling helplessly downward). All of our work in this study is consistent with stable reactions to quite a few shocks (of both a real and a monetary origin).

Beginning with the financial shocks in the period, we also begin with the earliest major recession of the period, in 1857 and 1858.[12] This particular downturn began with a financial crisis in October 1857 that was initiated in the United States and spread to British firms that had substantial interests in American companies. In this case the drain on the Bank of England almost exhausted its reserves (it had increased its lending substantially) and disaster was possibly avoided by the suspension of the Bank Charter Act of 1844 with respect to its limitation on the note issue. The reason that a limitation on the note issue was a problem is that a liquidity crisis was underway, but without suitable collateral, the Bank of England was unable to meet the abnormal demand for bank-notes. This forced financial institutions to sell assets in a declining market, to accommodate the needs of their customers. This event, and the troubles in the 1890s, represent the best examples of the textbook 'financial shock, real reaction', mechanism that is a popular explanation of 19th-century downturns.

Continuing with the theme of financial failures, now into the 1860s, we note that there was a financial panic in May 1866 upon the failure of the prominent brokerage firm of Overend-Gurney (on May 10th); a Black Friday ensued (on May 11th) in which there was an enormous general sell-off. In this case, the Government acted immediately to suspend the note restrictions of the Bank Charter Act (on the same day, actually) so that while there were some business failures, the overall disruption was relatively slight; indeed, Deane records no downturn in the 1860s, and Feinstein's two year event in 1866–7 is quite minor, in terms of the percentage real GNP fluctuation. Finally, in November 1890, the Baring Brothers financial firm came under suspicion; in this case the Government directly rescued the firm, which counted unsuccessful Argentinian ventures among its problem loans. There was no general panic or depression.

In terms of real shocks, the major events are in the mid-1870s (after the American railroad failures of 1873), the mid-1890s, and 1908. These are all international in scope, with an American orientation. There were downturns in other years (1884–5, 1900), with the first having no really clear-cut cause in the literature and the latter probably associated with the Boer War. The upshot of all this is that the shocks appear to come from three sources: international, where the contact is both through the financial markets and the export markets, domestic financial disruptions and special cases (e.g., wars). The major events seem fairly evenly balanced among these cases, suggesting that a single-theory methodology (e.g., a Granger-causality test of exports) would not work particularly well.

3.5 THE UK FINANCIAL SECTOR

In this section we investigate three interrelated issues in connection with the UK financial sector, involving topics suggested or actually dealt with in Friedman and Schwartz's *Monetary Trends*. The broad hypothesis they propose is that of the possible international integration of the financial community (across the Atlantic in this single instance). They demonstrated this in a variety of ways, the most provocative of which is possibly a pooled money-demand function for the two countries.

What we will argue in this section is that whatever else might be true of the long run of data studied by Friedman and Schwartz (to 1975), in the shorter period from 1870 to 1910, this hypothesis is essentially premature: the financial sectors of the two countries are too dissimilar for this to be a totally useful perception, although, admittedly, there is a clear trend toward integration over the period. Since money demand is at the centre of this debate, we will feature this in Sub-section 3.5.2 with a detailed look at the demand for money in the United Kingdom. The tests will be both ordinary least squares and two-stage least squares, and the effort will be to pin down the appropriate variables and their elasticities.

A second somewhat less structural comparison is the subject of Sub-section 3.5.3. Here we are concerned with the behaviour of velocity in the two countries and, after a brief illustration, we turn the topic over to the relatively well-developed literature on the subject, offering a survey in the place of original empirical work, on the whole. Finally, in Section 3.6, recognizing that the Friedman–Schwartz financial interaction hypothesis has causal tones – with the United Kingdom as a primary source of funds for US industry – we embark on a series of Granger-causality tests that are designed to reveal just such influences. Through all of this, incidentally, the Friedman–Schwartz hypothesis stands up reasonably well in the final analysis, at least if rephrased as a strong trend toward greater financial integration in this period. Let us begin, however, with a discussion of the institutional background.

3.5.1 Financial Institutions, 1850–1910

The following material is a summary and not meant to be a substitute for the many fine works in the literature on this subject. What is needed here is some background for the macroeconomic discussion, with special emphasis on the overall size and volatility of the banking system, on the practices of the Bank of England during the period and on the nature of the UK involvement with the late 19th-century gold standard. This discussion keeps to a macropolicy line for the most part, with the empirical studies later in this section (on money demand and velocity) broadening the discussion somewhat.

An important consideration, to begin with, is that the United Kingdom was on the gold standard, and as the reserve-creating country simultaneously enjoyed the advantages of the system while being unencumbered by its manifest inflexibility. The UK money supply, accordingly, was determined jointly by endogenous factors – that is by the decisions of commercial bankers (when they determined the quantity of reserves they held against their notes and deposits), by the actions of individuals (when they determined the quantity of gold and currency they held relative to their bank deposits) and by the portfolio decisions of the Bank of England (which were a combination of profit-maximizing and policy-oriented decisions).

The English banking sector from 1850 consisted of a wide variety of institutions in addition to the proto-typical joint-stock banks (London and provincial). The list includes building societies, merchant banks, savings banks, discount houses and foreign banks, and they all participated in banking activities, variously, including in some cases the issuance of bank-notes. One accounting of the main actors, the joint-stock banks, is given in Table 3.8 for the period up to 1880 (Collins, 1983, p. 391).

In the case of both sorts of banks, it is clear that expansion was vastly greater in branches than in newly formed banks and that the trend was upward, at least at the five-year intervals detailed in the table.[13] The contrast with the US banking system at the time could not be greater, with growth in the number of US banks running at a very high rate, and failures quite numerous during and after the major cyclical peaks there. In a very real sense, relative financial

Table 3.8   Banks and bank offices in England and Wales, 1850–1880

	Banks	London offices	Liabilities	Banks	Provincial offices	Liabilities
1850	4	77	£12.4m	22	153	£30.1m
1855	6	193	32.4	25	168	38.9
1860	6	224	38.5	29	196	46.6
1865	12	369	77.7	36	320	72.8
1870	12	369	80.6	41	388	79.4
1875	13	435	117.6	44	542	131.1
1880	14	539	128.3	44	653	120.4

maturity is indicated for the United Kingdom. We note though (as does Collins) that the growth of the liabilities of these banks increased as a ratio of money national income (using Deane's figures) right through to 1880.

Turning to the central bank, the question is what role the Bank of England played both in the stability of the financial system and in its steady growth.[14] First, we need to recall that the Bank of England was a private bank with public responsibilities. Long before 1850, the other London banks had given up the note issue and throughout the banking system the liabilities of the Bank of England were the principal reserve of these (and all other) banks. This brought considerable control to the Bank of England and, ultimately, the need to operate as the lender of last resort in order to protect its own interests, if nothing else. But the currency supply was relatively inflexible, partly on account of the restrictions of the Bank Charter Act of 1844, and there were liquidity crises – and bank failures – in 1847, 1857 and 1866. Even so, for most of the period, the Bank of England operated effectively as a modern central bank, using both lender of last resort functions and discount rate policy, with one eye on the bottom line. The discount rate policy was primarily used to produce a quick increase in the gold reserves of the Bank of England (drawing from domestic and foreign sources), but this policy did have a tendency to undermine Bank profits and so was not employed in a routine fashion.[15] The Bank became increasingly powerful over this period and it is likely that treating Bank of England notes and liabilities (to other banks) as high-powered money is an analogy with modern times that could be maintained.

There has been considerable discussion of whether the Bank of England played by the 'rules of the game' of the international gold standard during the period when most major countries were on this system (say 1880 to 1910). One set of rules was originally defined by Bloomfield (1959) in terms of whether central bank liabilities were adjusted so as to permit the domestic price level to stay in line with world prices. In this scheme, central bank policies (open market operations and discount rate changes) would be judged in terms of whether they reinforced the effects of gold flows on domestic money supplies or counteracted them (Dutton, 1984). Following an independent policy aimed toward domestic objectives would be construed as a violation, insofar as it comes into conflict with the requirements of international equilibrium. In this literature, it is open market operations rather than discount policy that receives the emphasis because the former suggests a long-run strategy while the latter provides a temporary fix to an exchange rate imbalance (usually).[16] It is the latter, though, that receives most of the attention in the non-quantitative literature.

Bloomfield did not give high marks to the Bank of England for its adherence to the gold standard rules, but studies of interest rate policy by Dutton and separately by Goodhart (1972) suggest quite strongly that their responses were stabilizing. Indeed, it would be surprising if they were not, since such a policy dominated central bank thinking for a very long time. With regard to their portfolio adjustments, however, Goodhart, Dutton, and Pippinger (1984) all argue that the adjustments were procyclical. Goodhart (1984, p. 223) takes the position that the Bank 'accommodated the demand for cash by buying more securities at times when the reserves were low and interest rates were high'. Dutton (1984, p. 192) argues that 'Instead of amplifying the effects of reserve changes on the money supply, the Bank seems to have sterilized them'. Pippinger (1984, p. 209), finally, suggests that 'The Bank systematically reduced liquidity in order to earn income'. This last view reflects a continuing suspicion that the Bank's private ownership influenced its decisions – which is certainly likely – at the cost of significant macropolicy inefficiency. This latter point may well be untrue. In any case, as we shall see in each of the remaining chapters of this study, central bank adherence to the rules of the gold standard is not always obvious in this period.

3.5.2 The Demand for Money

Let us begin with a set of estimates of a conventional money-demand function for the United Kingdom.

$$m_t = \beta_o + \beta_1 y_t + \beta_2 i_t + e_t \qquad (3.2)$$

The equation tested has the logs of real, per capita, money holding (and income) and the level of interest rates. Several interest rate experiments are recorded in each case. The results in Table 3.9 show the demand for money for the United Kingdom to be reasonably well determined, with (usually) a significant interest rate.[17] The need for an autoregressive adjustment was anticipated, if only because of the non-stationarity of the data when handled in log-level form, as it is here. It is worth underscoring in these tests that the two results in lines (5) and (6), where US rates perform very well in a test of the British money demand, provide evidence of the international character of the demand for money, as suggested by Friedman and Schwartz. Also note, for later reference, that the income elasticities, while greater than unity, are not as high as those for some of the other countries in this study.

Aside from the general fit of the model, our chief interest here is in the income elasticity of the demand for money. Friedman and Schwartz note that the income elasticity of money demand is considerably higher in the United States than in the United Kingdom (where it is around unity) and associate this with a lack of relative 'financial sophistication' of the United States. By this we mean that the general lack of financial services makes those that do exist (in banks) relatively valuable to Americans. Our results agree with this interpretation, at least in that the UK measures are relatively low (and lower than Friedman and Schwartz found for the United States).[18] What Friedman and Schwartz say about the United States in the 1870s (compared with the United Kingdom) is (p. 146),

> The United States, by contrast, though wealthier and more populous, was still financially backward, conducting its international trade largely in sterling. Nearly three-quarters of the population was classified as residing in rural areas, and half of the working force (male and female) was still in agriculture. . . . These differences meant a much higher demand for money relative to income by United Kingdom than by United States residents.

Indeed, say Friedman and Schwartz, much of the change to a sophisticated economy occurred between 1870 and 1906. The word 'sophisticated' may be misunderstood, as it was just used, but it should be noted that we are merely comparing a characteristic of

Table 3.9   Money demand in the United Kingdom, 1871–1910

Equation (interest rate)	Income (β_1)	Interest (β_2)	$\bar{R}^2$	DW	AR	Income elasticity
1. Call money	0.830 (16.25)	–0.016 (2.51)	0.964	1.61	(1,2)	1.565
2. Deposit rate	0.826 (16.61)	–0.017 (2.61)	0.965	1.64	(1,2)	1.527
3. Treasury bill	0.829 (16.25)	–0.015 (2.60)	0.965	1.62	(1,2)	1.580
4. Consol	0.750 (12.86)	–0.093 (2.36)	0.964	1.79	(1,2)	1.275
5. US-Com bond	0.493 (4.16)	–0.063 (2.69)	0.965	1.70	(1,2)	1.836
6. US-Ind bond	0.485 (4.02)	–0.057 (2.73)	0.964	1.69	(1,2)	1.761

Notes: DW is the Durbin–Watson statistic; numbers in parentheses are t-values. AR designates autoregressive terms.

money holding in the two cases. In the United States the marginal dollar appears to be worth more in income to the user, reflecting, it can be argued, a relative scarcity of such forms of payment (and certainly of the accompanying banking services).

A way to visualize the relative financial sophistication of the two countries – and how this concept changes in this transitional period – is to use a 'financial sophistication index' as suggested by a procedure in Friedman and Schwartz. This is calculated by multiplying the inverse of velocity (i.e., M/Y) by 52 (the number of weeks in the year). The result is the number of weeks of national income financed by (or covered by) money balances. The comparison of the two countries is given in Figure 3.10.

In the United States, money holding grew from 11.2 weeks of NNP in 1871 to 23.9 weeks in 1910, while in England it actually declined slightly from 28.9 to 27.3. This method of comparison avoids the different currency units – and the attendant exchange rate adjustments – and, most importantly, highlights the relative sophistication of the British monetary system. This financial sophistication index appears at later points in this study, and comparisons of the United

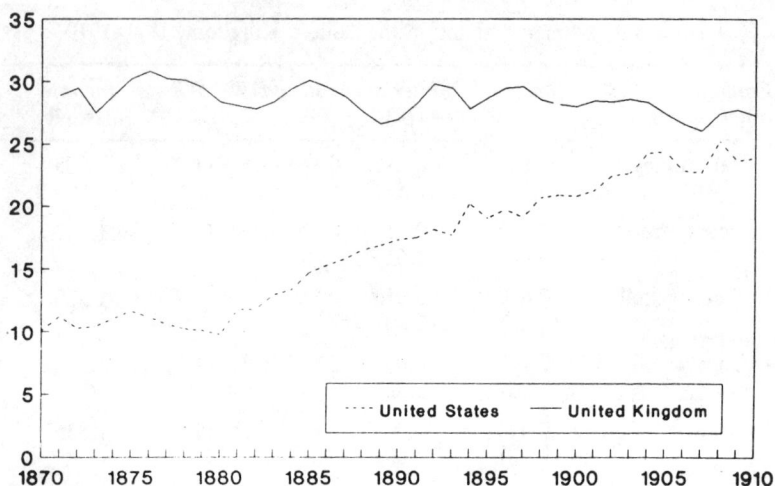

Figure 3.10   Financial sophistication indices, 1870–1910

Kingdom with Sweden are discussed in Chapter 6, where causality tests are conducted on this statistic, as well; some cross-country comparisons over the entire sample of countries are presented in Chapter 8. There it is abundantly clear that the UK is different from all other countries during this period. It is, if this is an acceptable usage, the most financially sophisticated country in the world.

3.5.3.   Velocity and Atlantic Financial Integration

The concept of velocity has already intruded into our discussion and it is now time to consider the literature on that topic for the United Kingdom. Indeed, the behaviour of velocity, (say Friedman and Schwartz) is a major part of their financial integration hypothesis. They argue that the levels of velocity are highly correlated across the two countries and (p. 6),

> The common movements of velocity reflect a unified financial system in which monetary variables such as prices, interest rates, nominal income, and stocks of money are constrained to keep largely in step. . . . The highest correlation for the two countries is for prices; the lowest, for real per capita income.

This is strong stuff, and it involves causality across the Atlantic as well as the specific statement about velocity.

To be blunt about it, the velocity argument is incorrect for the period 1870 to 1910. Friedman and Schwartz are, of course, speaking of an entire 100 year period and they note some differences in the first 40 years (put off to differences in financial sophistication), but this is not a sufficient caution. For one thing the trends in velocity are quite different in the two cases (as we have seen with the financial sophistication indices), being 0.17 per cent per year ($t = 3.73$) in the United Kingdom and -2.58 per cent ($t = 23.11$) in the United States. Furthermore, the correlation coefficient between the two velocity series is actually negative, at -0.464 in this period. Now Friedman and Schwartz presumably know all this. The explanation, as in Bordo and Jonung (1987), is to attribute the difference to institutional factors (is the income elasticity of money demand 'institutional'?) related to the stage of development of the economy (i.e., to financial sophistication). We do not disagree, exactly, but one must be careful to note that the financial institutions are endogenous in the long run if not the short, so that the long-run demand for money (for example) does not stand by itself in this respect.

Before looking at the evidence on the velocity numbers, we need to consider some additional time-series procedures. If an economic time series can be represented by a moving average of order one (MA(1)), then it can be written as the following, where e_t is white noise.

$$Y_t = e_t + \beta e_{t-1} \tag{3.3}$$

For a non-zero value of β, this successful estimation of a moving average parameter will smooth the original series. Indeed (Wold's Theorem), any stationary time series can be described by a deterministic part and by a moving average component (series) of possibly infinite order. Without the deterministic part, a moving average of order q is given by

$$Y_t = \beta_0 e_t + \beta_1 e_{t-1} + \beta_2 e_{t-2} + \ldots = \sum_{i=0}^{q} \beta_i e_{t-i} \tag{3.4}$$

This is a useful fact if the q required is quite small (since moving average processes are difficult to estimate) because it provides a possible decomposition of the data into a deterministic (permanent) and a stochastic (transitory) part.

If an economic time series depends on its own past values, as is frequently claimed to be the case for data generated under rational expectations, then it might be represented as an autoregressive process of order one (AR(1)) as in

Table 3.10   Autocorrelation and partial autocorrelation

	MA (q)	AR (p)	ARMA (p, q)	White noise
Autocorrelation function	$D(q)$	T	T	0
Partial autocorrelation	T	$D(p)$	T	0

$$Y_t = \delta_1 y_{t-1} + e_t \tag{3.5}$$

Again, e_t is white noise. Many economic time series are at least AR(1) and, as we have seen, the estimates of the demand for money presented in this chapter were actually AR(2).[19] The generalization of Equation (3.5) is

$$Y_t = \delta_1 Y_{t-1} + \delta_2 Y_{t-2} + \ldots + e_t = \sum_{i=1}^{p} \delta_i Y_{t-i} + e_t$$

where the AR process is of order p. Indeed, and even more generally, both processes can occur together, as in the ARMA (p, q) model of

$$Y_t = \sum_{i=1}^{p} \delta_i Y_{t-i} + \sum_{j=0}^{q} \beta_j e_{t-j} \tag{3.6}$$

where, as before, e_t is white noise.[20]

In order to identify a model for a time series, one thing that can be done is to look at the autocorrelation and the partial autocorrelation functions. What we are looking for is summarized in Table 3.10. Here, for example, $D(q)$ means that the function drops off after lag q, T in the first column means that it tails off exponentially after a lag of q, and 0 in the last column means that the function is zero at all non-zero lags. The autocorrelation records the correlation between the error at t and $t-i$, while the partial autocorrelation is the correlation between successive error terms.

What we are looking for is the 'proximate' process that drives the data using these methods, and we are interested in whether these processes are the same or sufficiently dissimilar across the two countries to invalidate the notion of a common velocity. We can do this most easily by looking at a graph, as we do in the two parts of Figure 3.11. The two parts refer to the United States (a) and the United Kingdom (b). In the top half of the figure, the partial autocorrelation for the United States drops off after one lag; here $p=1$ would be a good guess. For the United States, the autocorrelation tails off exponentially after the first lag. A short AR process is indicated. For the United Kingdom, there is a second significant partial autocorrelation (an observation lying to the left of the 5 per cent line), while the autocorrelation function just collapses. There are clearly quite different processes driving these two sets of data.

This impression is confirmed by estimating the various possible AR processes out to AR(3) for the two cases, as in Table 3.11. The numbers here should be read from top to bottom and they show the United Kingdom with a second lag in the AR process (in Columns (2) and (3)). Only one lag figures in the US case. It is clearly untenable to take the position that a common process drives these series in this period, and that is the upshot of this discussion.[21]

3.6   INTERACTION ACROSS THE ATLANTIC

In a previous citation from Friedman and Schwartz we recorded their feeling that prices, money, nominal interest rates, and nominal income were largely in step with each other across the Atlantic, while real variables were not, on the whole. Since the project of this section is the financial linkages, we should note that in the previous results important financial variables – interest rates – while correlated are not highly so. A set of pictures, in the two parts of Figure 3.12, illustrate these distinctions. Thus, while short-term rates (Part (a)) are at about the same level throughout the period, the US call money rate is considerably more volatile than the UK Treasury bill rate (admittedly a rate that would be expected to be smoother). More significantly, and mirroring our comments on relative financial sophistication, it looks as if the US long-term interest rate is approaching the UK rate from above, reaching some sort of steady relation by 1900 at the latest. On the surface it would appear that the relatively sophisticated (and abundantly stocked) UK capital market was responsible for a narrowing of the long-term gap, probably by means of the infamous capital outflow of this period.

We will now employ the Granger causality test to implement the causal statements, both in the original literature and in the revision attempted here; Friedman and Schwartz provide us with most of our hypotheses. We will compare the results of the regression of

$$y_t = \alpha + \sum_{i=1}^{r} \beta_i y_{t-i} + \sum_{i=1}^{r} \delta_i x_{t-i} + e_t \qquad (3.7)$$

Figure 3.11 US and UK autocorrelations

A. Velocity in the United States

	Autocorrelations	Partial Autocorrelations	ac	pac
1			0.944	0.944
2			0.876	-0.134
3			0.796	-0.145
4			0.733	-0.144
5			0.669	-0.068
6			0.599	-0.146
7			0.513	-0.134
8			0.421	-0.084
9			0.323	-0.122
10			0.227	-0.080
11			0.154	0.160
12			0.077	-0.147
13			0.015	0.059
14			-0.044	0.053
15			-0.093	-0.012
16			-0.139	-0.034
17			-0.183	-0.088
18			-0.219	0.036
19			-0.255	-0.134
20			-0.289	-0.096

B. Velocity in the United Kingdom

	ac	pac
1	0.673	0.673
2	0.242	-0.385
3	-0.004	0.063
4	-0.068	0.001
5	-0.039	0.019
6	0.038	0.079
7	0.131	0.092
8	0.146	-0.041
9	0.087	-0.002
10	-0.018	-0.082
11	-0.092	-0.008
12	-0.145	-0.102
13	-0.201	-0.125
14	-0.213	-0.040
15	-0.070	0.193
16	0.155	0.151
17	0.227	-0.069
18	0.184	0.095
19	0.105	0.022
20	0.072	0.107

Autocorrelations

Partial Autocorrelations

Table 3.11   UK and US AR processes

	United Kingdom			United States		
	AR (1)	AR (2)	AR (3)	AR (1)	AR (2)	AR (3)
t–1	0.694	0.961	1.059	0.976	0.881	0.858
	(5.71)	(6.21)	(6.53)	(28.92)	(5.68)	(5.05)
t–2		–0.402	–0.531		0.081	0.275
		(2.58)	(2.49)		(0.52)	(1.27)
t–3			0.113			0.086
			(0.70)			(1.14)
Const.	1.832	1.830	1.823	1.085	1.222	0.086
	(65.47)	(99.68)	(84.40)	(0.84)	(0.66)	(0.71)

t–values in parentheses.

with the same regression restricted to the case of $\delta_i = 0$ ($i = 1, \ldots,$ *r*). The test is an F-test and we will require a probability of 0.05 to justify saying that the lags in the independent variable (*x*) predetermine *y* (holding the history of *y* constant in the first set of terms). Note that since level figures rather than first differences of the data are employed here, we should restrict any claims of Granger-causality to higher-order causal links (at lags of two or greater). This, too, is not foolproof. We do make some comparisons of the methods in Chapter 8, although not along these lines.

Friedman and Schwartz, to begin with, argue that there was no direct effect, in either country, of money on real economic activity. This is, indeed, an example of the empirical *neutrality of money*. To see confirmation of these results from the point of view of a Granger-causality test, consider the top half of Table 3.12. That is, in the first two rows we have no sign of money affecting real income (but the reverse holds, in lines 3 and 4). This is what Friedman and Schwartz say (they do note a transitory effect of money on real income for the United States, but none is shown for this particular subperiod). The bottom half of Table 3.12 demonstrates that monetary neutrality holds across the Atlantic, but there is also an international aspect to this relation for US real income does appear to Granger-cause UK money. The mechanism, possibly, is by means of the stimulation to the UK capital markets to fuel the more rapid expansion in the United States and to close the long-term interest rate gap. This, of course, is what we would expect (the sign of the effect (when summed)

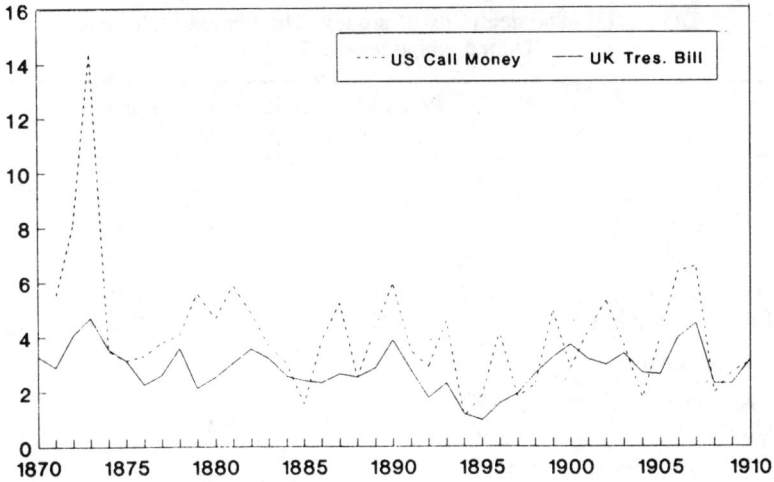

(a) UK and US short-term interest rates, 1870–1910

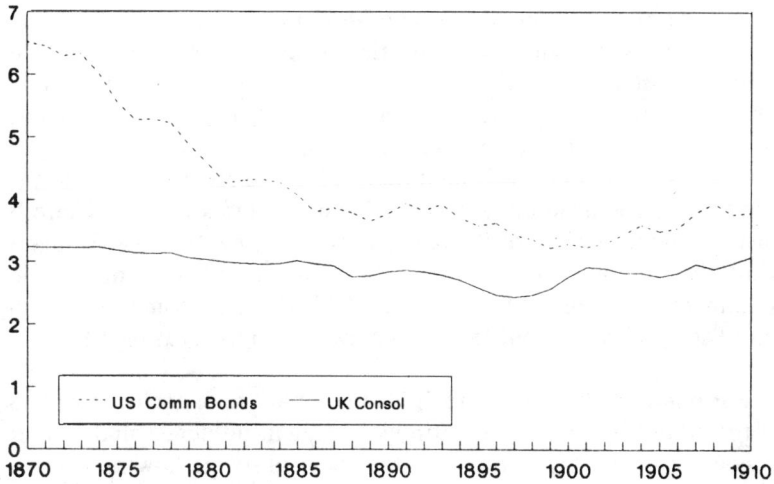

(b) UK and US long-term interest rates, 1870–1910

Figure 3.12

Table 3.12   The neutrality of money. The United States and
United Kingdom, 1871–1910

| National: | *Probability that the restriction is not significant (for lags of:)* | | | | | |
	1	2	3	4	5	Sign
UK money → UK y	0.280	0.800	0.560	0.777	0.805	
US money → US y	0.078	0.978	0.390	0.474	0.401	
UK y → UK money	0.007*	0.000*	0.025*	0.005*	0.002*	+
US y → US money	0.044*	0.115	0.070	0.126	0.260	+
International:						
UK money → US y	0.187	0.182	0.123	0.117	0.208	
US money → UK y	0.491	0.520	0.680	0.494	0.659	
UK y → US money	0.190	0.153	0.309	0.536	0.708	
US y → UK money	0.944	0.014*	0.266	0.084	0.204	+

is, indeed, positive (as are the intra-country effects in the top half of
the table)). So there are no surprises here.

With respect to nominal income and money, however, there are
differences within the two countries – and internationally – that
require explanation. Friedman and Schwartz suggest, simply, that
nominal money is a strong Granger-causal agent on nominal income
within each economy. This effect, as the top half of Table 3.13
illustrates, occurs in the United States, but the *reverse* is true in the
United Kingdom: nominal income Granger-causes money. There is
also (in the lower half of the table) very strong evidence of Granger-
causation running across the Atlantic – that is, of UK money on US
nominal income and of US money on UK nominal income. Friedman
and Schwartz say, about their comparable results, that (p. 6):

For nominal income before 1914, the influence of each country on
the other was manifested entirely through its influence on the other
country's quantity of money – the classical specie-flow process.

For prices between the two countries, Friedman and Schwartz say
the following (p. 6):

the influence of each country on the other operates not only

Table 3.13   Money and nominal income. The United States and the
United Kingdom, 1871–1910

National:	Probability that the restriction is not significant (for lags of:)					
	1	*2*	*3*	*4*	*5*	*Sign*
UK money → UK *Y*	0.949	0.234	0.406	0.960	0.980	
US money → US *Y*	0.144	0.987	0.032*	0.080	0.033*	ns
UK *Y* → UK money	0.002*	0.003*	0.026*	0.175	0.270	+
US *Y* → US money	0.854	0.583	0.683	0.407	0.603	
International:						
UK money → US *Y*	0.098	0.059	0.046*	0.064	0.145	+
US money → UK *Y*	0.092	0.035*	0.055	0.088	0.074	+
US *Y* → UK money	0.779	0.521	0.777	0.642	0.471	
UK *Y* → US money	0.934	0.885	0.993	0.999	0.999	

ns indicates no significant sign

through effects on the other country's quantity of money but also more directly. . . . This is an expression of the 'law of one price.'

To see the law of one price in operation, at least on this aggregate level, we should recall, firstly, that the correlation between UK and US price levels is 0.892 for the entire period. Since the statement by Friedman and Schwartz also refers to causation, we can turn, once again, to our Granger tests. In Table 3.14 we see illustrated the remaining interactions among the nominal variables of the two economies. The most obvious thing to look at, of course, is whether money drives prices. In the United States it does (and not the converse), but in the United Kingdom prices actually drive money (and, again, not the converse).

Internationally, there is only one relation that stands up in both countries, and that is that foreign money drives the domestic price level. This is evidence of the specie flow mechanism, to be sure, but there is one serious problem. There is (not shown in the table) no evidence

(a) that money stocks cause each other (or conversely)
(b) that price levels cause each other (or conversely)
(c) that high-powered money stocks cause each other (or conversely)

Table 3.14   Nominal interactions between the United Kingdom and the
United States, 1871–1910

National:	Probability that the restriction is not significant (*for lags of:*)					Sign
	1	*2*	*3*	*4*	*5*	*Sign*
UK money → UK P	0.461	0.148	0.279	0.138	0.138	
US money → US P	0.026*	0.074	0.021*	0.032*	0.002*	+
UK P → UK money	0.246	0.137	0.009*	0.014*	0.030*	–
US P → US money	0.188	0.065	0.204	0.425	0.662	
International:						
US money → UK P	0.495	0.094	0.074	0.072	0.004*	+
UK money → US P	0.032*	0.255	0.404	0.166	0.067	+

There is, though, some evidence (also not shown) that US high-powered money Granger-causes UK money. All-in-all, the international evidence is very much in favour of the interaction hypothesis, but the specie-flow mechanism is not well-supported, at least by this sort of test. In view of doubts, generally, that countries adhered to the 'rules-of-the-game' of the international gold standard – thus endogenizing their money stocks to some extent – this is not all that surprising.

3.7   CONCLUSION

This chapter pretty much abandons any serious interest in the industrial revolution – largely because during this period it is on the wane in the United Kingdom, relatively speaking – in favour of a battery of time-series tests of various sorts. This choice reflects both the controversies in the literature as well as the (better) state of the macroeconomic data for the United Kingdom. The time-series discussion begins with material on the properties of the data themselves; it is readily apparent that they are non-stationary in levels (or log-levels) and that first-differencing is probably the best way to handle them, at least in tests that do not in some way internalize the lack of stationarity.[22]

Turning to substantive issues, our first major finding is that there is a possibility of significant crowding out of private investment by government spending in this period, but only during the Crimean and Boer War periods. The tests here are not rigorous, though, and this is why it is referred to as a possibility. Business cycles in the United Kingdom in this period are not particularly violent, but our main interest here is in the Friedman and Schwartz view that the United Kingdom and the United States develop increasingly similar cyclical patterns as the 19th century wanes. This is corroborated, as is (broadly) the Friedman and Schwartz finding of the increasing financial integration of the two countries. As we move through France, Germany, Sweden and Italy in later chapters, the financial (and real) integration of the late 19th-century European economy will continue to receive coverage. Chapter 8, then, is devoted entirely to that subject.

4 Industrialization without Revolution: the French Case

4.1 INTRODUCTION

This chapter begins a series of individual country studies of the macro-economic aspects of the industrial revolution. The broad proposition is that each of the major European economies actually faced roughly similar economic pressures during the period 1700 to 1910, but that economic endowments, population growth and the political style of the individual countries sometimes produced distinctively different responses to the economic pressures unleashed by the industrial revolution. Even so, the parallels are obvious, since not only did Western Europe lead the way toward industrialization, but the nations of the group considered here did so in ways that are actually strikingly similar on the whole. This, in itself, is sufficient to suggest that broad models – macroeconomic models in this case – might produce broadly similar results across countries. After all, the countries considered are almost the complete set of advanced countries at the time of the first industrial revolution and hence were not subject to domination economically, except among themselves.

A common view concerning French development is that it was neither rapid enough to be called a revolution nor early enough to qualify France as an active partner in the first industrial revolution (to 1850). To be more specific, there are those who think France never had an industrial revolution (Clapham, 1921); those who see no revolution because they cannot locate a decisive starting point (Kindleberger, 1964; Milward and Saul, 1973; Fohlen, 1970); those who suggest that France was simply a laggard (the above and Cameron (1958), Clough (1972), Kemp (1962)); and those who find a distinct drive toward industrialization, but date it toward the middle of the 19th century.[1] Taking the latter position, Price says (1981, p. xi),

> The period is conceived as one of growth in production within pre-industrial economic structures, succeeded from 1840–50 by

120

rapid structural transformation and the creation of an industrial economy.

This pre-industrial structure is the economic part of the *ancien régime* and it

> was characterised by the predominance of a low yield agriculture devoted to meeting local needs and by the preponderance in the industrial sector of the production of consumer goods, primarily by means of artisanal techniques. (p. 1)

In this view, the French economy is certainly not stagnant, nor does it necessarily compare unfavourably with the British. Even so, according to Price, it took a fundamental disruption of the transportation infrastructure – in the form of the railroad – to launch the modern French economy. This movement begins in the 1840s and 1850s.

In contrast, a vocal minority of opinion feels that France was competitive with England in many of the traditional industrial sectors in the 18th century (Crafts, 1977 and Roehl, 1976); that French commodity output grew at the same pace (per capita) as the British in the 19th century (O'Brien and Keyder, 1978) and that French agriculture was not only competitive (given the nature of its demand, crops, and soil), but that the agricultural spurt came long before the middle of the 19th century (Newell, 1973; O'Brien and Keyder, 1978). This establishes a multifaceted controversy to which a macroeconomic perspective could contribute, although it must be pointed out that most of the available evidence in this literature is on a level of detail that is unsuitable for the present study. We will, though, present some of these micro-details, in order to establish the specific nature of the debate.

The following sections set up an expositional structure for the discussion of French development that will be followed as later chapters move on to German, Swedish, and Italian material. The population story will come first; in the case of Fance this is really quite different from that in the other countries (it grew very slowly and was less urban than the average, throughout the period). It comes first primarily since population growth may well set the floor to growth (normally) and, for that matter, has a lot to do with how the economy structures itself. The natural follow-up, in Section 4.2, concerns questions surrounding the agricultural development of France. This story runs clear back to 1700, on an admittedly flimsy empirical base, although the margin of the current debate is in the early 19th century. At this point a discussion of the aggregate data is appended, since a breakdown is available for the agricultural and industrial components of French GNP from 1815.

A snapshot of France's industrialization appears in Section 4.3; this is at a microeconomic level of detail whose purpose is to establish the industrial background. Section 4.4 looks at the recent macroeconomic data that has been produced by Toutain (1987); the interest here is in trends and cycles in the 19th-century French economy. The most interesting findings concern the dominant influence of agricultural shocks on French cycles and the ubiquity of stagflation in this period. Finally, Section 4.5 contains an extended discussion of the role of money in the French economy. Here are discussions of the institutional setting as well as empirical tests of monetary neutrality and the demand for money in 19th-century France. The results are unusual (for this study), as well, with rather less support for typical monetarist models than is the case elsewhere. This is not a particularly firm conclusion, however, since the data are more than normally suspect.

4.2   THE BACKGROUND TO FRENCH INDUSTRIALIZATION

Chapter 1 has stressed how important population growth is to the general pace of economic growth, since in this period it generally appears to establish a floor to the overall growth rate. For the French case, though, the details of population growth are actually a little distracting, because the rate of growth is so low in this period that very little impetus to growth and change could have been generated in this fashion. What it does make perfectly clear is that in many cases per capita calculations are necessary when one is comparing countries – and especially so when the French are included. In fact, after the recalibration, the French per capita performance is generally respectable, and this is not always conceded in the literature.

We also need to consider French agriculture – and its place in the French macroeconomy – partly because an agricultural acceleration is apparently a constant companion to the quickening industrial pace in 18th and 19th-century Europe, and partly because the agricultural sector is the largest sector of the French economy for most of the

Table 4.1   French and British populations

	France	Growth rate	Britain	Growth rate
1750	21.0		7.40	
1800	27.3	0.52	10.69	0.74
1850	35.8	0.54	20.88	1.34
1910	39.6	0.17	40.89	1.12

Source: Mitchell (1978).

period. As already noted, there is a lively debate concerning the actual contribution of this sector in the 19th century.

4.2.1 Population Dynamics in France

In 1750, France's population was actually three times the British; indeed, in the 80 years prior to the French Revolution, French population growth was at the same rate as the British. The numbers given in Table 4.1 refer to the 1750 to 1910 period; here it is clear that a huge lead was gone by 1910. What is most remarkable, clearly, is the 0.17 of 1 per cent annual growth rate of French population over the last 60 years. To see more clearly what happened, consider Figure 4.1.

What is immediately apparent is that the two countries were actually running on almost parallel tracks until around 1860 and then France slowed down, relatively. The sudden drop in the early 1870s is due, of course, to the terms of the Franco-Prussian war, but, even so, an extension of the line for the French would have the two crossing just after 1900 rather than in 1890, so the unsuccessful war is not, as it appears, as decisive as it might seem in the comparison effected here. What is certainly clear is that there is a very slow rate of population growth in France in this period. For want of space, we will forbear to discuss the reasons for this situation, although there are some macroeconomic issues involved.[2]

Now population growth is not the only topic one might consider under the heading of population dynamics, for *where* the population is located has some influence on the general performance of the economy. It is also an indicator of progress, obviously, since commerce and industry are urban activities in this century. Crafts (1984)

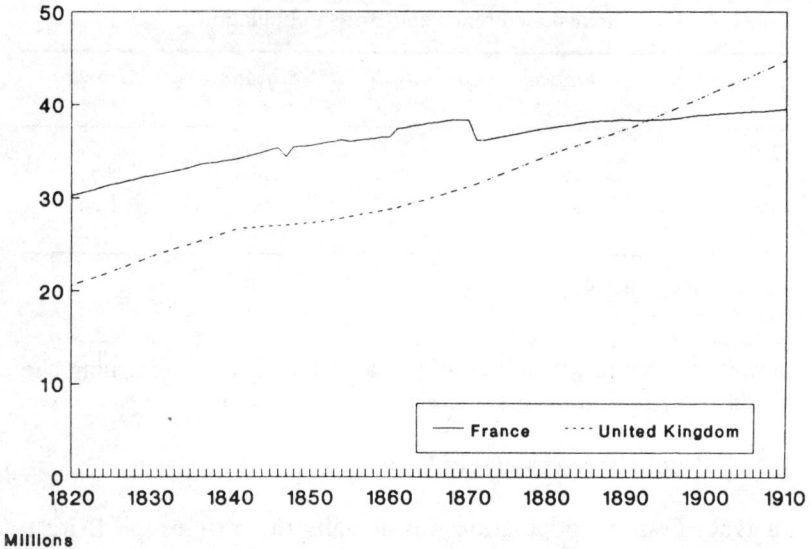

Figure 4.1   French and UK population, 1820–1910

points out that France was considerably less developed than Britain
at any time in the 200 years we are looking at, basing this judgment
partly on the rural/urban character of the two populations. The
figures provided by Crafts suggest that by 1750 England had 49.6 per
cent of its population engaged in agriculture and extractive industries
while a century later France had 51.8 per cent similarly employed,
indicating by this measure of development that the French might
have lagged the British by as much as a century. This is not Crafts'
overall position, certainly, but it is proof of a dramatic structural
difference between the two economies, as they moved along their
respective paths of industrialization.

France has a relatively large agricultural population during this
period and this means that its urban population is proportionately
lower, but several qualifications must be filed. For one thing, in the
relatively industrial parts of France, urbanization is actually more
along the lines of the British. Some data given in Table 4.2 on
individual cities emphasize this factor, over the 1800 to 1910 period.[3]
These were all of the French cities that had at least 500 000 inhabitants in 1910 (or 75 000 in 1800). Note that the figures on growth rates
for 1850 to 1910 are lower than for comparable German cities, but
higher than for the British. Since there was a very low rate of overall

Table 4.2 Population of certain French cities (in thousands)

	1800	1850	1880	1910	Annual % 1800–50	change 1850–1910
Lyons	110	177	376	472	0.95	1.63
Marseilles	111	195	360	551	1.13	1.73
Paris	547	1 053	2 269	2 888	1.31	1.68
Total	768	1 425	3 005	3 911	1.24	1.68
4 German	392	758	1 787	4 114	1.32	2.82
5 British	1 422	3 942	6 652	10 026	2.04	0.93

population growth from 1851 to 1911 (at 0.17 per cent per annum) the relative rapidity of urbanization in France at this time is surely impressive. This implies, to attempt a brief summing up, that we might look for a significant transformation in the structure of the French economy after 1850, based on the finding of a relatively rapid urbanization. Otherwise, population apparently is less of an influence on growth in France than it is elsewhere in Europe.

4.2.2 French Agricultural Development during the Transition

A basic – and controversial – question about French agricultural development concerns the extent and flexibility of French agriculture before a well-documented late 19th-century increase in agricultural productivity. At the other end, an almost overwhelming volume of literature has described the period before the French Revolution (or, at least before 1750) as a stagnant one for French agriculture, with a rigidly structured social system and virtually no technological change. The style for this view has been set by prominent and persuasive French writers (Le Roy Ladurie, Lefebvre, Soboul, Jacquart and Braudel), who often appear in English, as well as by a legion of British and American writers who have accepted at least part of this tradition.[4] Indeed, much of the literature extends the malaise up until 1850, although to do so requires an intellectual juggling act since French agricultural production is known to have increased fairly rapidly from 1815.

The rival camps are not close on these issues, and there is an extensive period of time to consider in order to encompass the entire argument (1710 to 1850). To begin, it is certainly not possible to present a totally clear picture of French agriculture prior to 1800 – on account of the data – but certain facts nevertheless stand out. For one thing, the notion that the period from 1700 to 1790 was a totally stagnant one is surely preposterous. Of course, if we are looking for dramatic changes we will surely be disappointed; even so, cumulatively powerful changes took place in the French marketplace that involved the agricultural sector in an active role (Roehl, 1976). Agriculture was generally commercial (local, commercial, of course), but there was a strong export sector, in addition. This was possible because of 'substantial reserves of potential productive capacity' (Goldsmith, 1984, p. 185) that were apparently easy to tap with simple adjustments in agricultural practices. This process is especially obvious from the mid-18th century, even though it was once thought not to be the case. There is evidence for inefficiency, of course, especially in the contemporary literature, and there is also some uncomplimentary data on yields (per acre or per unit of seed). The comparison is usually with England, where the yields are invariably higher, but this is often a superficial point that should be carefully qualified in terms of differences in production functions, the cost of inputs and, of course, in the cost of transportation. To force the point, a level of technology sufficient to permit a Frenchman to raise his grain yield per acre to British levels may well bankrupt the Frenchman. One supposes, then, that the Frenchman generally was well advised to ignore any but market signals in his choice of technique; this definitely admits that information of economically relevant new techniques is useful and was employed in the French agricultural sector, but that it was guided by optimizing decisions that were constrained by a much less flexible and extensive market system.

On net, then, it is perhaps agreeable to say that French agriculture in pre-industrial times was relatively less productive than its counterpart in England, but had, at the same time, considerable unexploited capacity. Agriculture apparently was also adequate to deal with population growth – which was relatively modest – and was capable of participating in overall economic growth as necessary; it also had significant technological change.[5] It was probably not a bottleneck sector. The commercial part of agriculture expanded as opportunities presented themselves and it is obvious that overall growth was slow enough, and the international grain market vigorous enough, to produce relatively little pressure on the agricultural sector.[6] In a way, this accounts for the impression that the agricultural sector held up progress. These observations could well make the 'productivity gap' that undoubtedly existed consistent with the obvious ability of the French agricultural sector to cope with the general rise in population and living standards that it faced throughout this period.[7]

In the 19th century, one needs to examine the situation making due allowance for the slow growth of French population. Price (1981) argues that while no area lay completely outside commercial circuits (p. 43)

> until the mid-nineteenth century the market structure remained characterised by fragmentation. It was composed of a series of semi-closed local and regional markets with only limited irregular relations between them.

This was especially the case in the south of France.[8] Indeed, he argues (p. 55),

> French agriculture at the mid point of the nineteenth century was still characterised by its fragility. A political revolution had occurred but not an agricultural one.

The problem, he alleges, is distribution (Price mentions disparities in cereal prices across the country as evidence of this) and, he feels, the arrival of the railroad in the south in the 1850s knit the markets together and brought an end to the dual sectors in the French agricultural sector.

Price's work is very detailed and is certainly persuasive at many points, but is nevertheless not the only view available. It is Newell (1973) who is most responsible for the alternative view here and his (and others') results continue to generate controversy. Newell feels that the data (Toutain's, again) show that the actual acceleration in total and per capita agricultural output begins in the 1815–24 period, in spite of two very bad years in 1815 and 1816, and lasts until 1865–74. Newell feels that it was mostly a result of increased productivity that occurs across all crops and areas (especially in the central and southern regions). He believes that the data show (p. 730)

> that the introduction and subsequent diffusion of mixed farming – characterized by decline in fallow, growth of planted meadows, and use of manure fertilizers – is responsible for the regional difference in both the yields at the beginning of the period and the increase in yields.

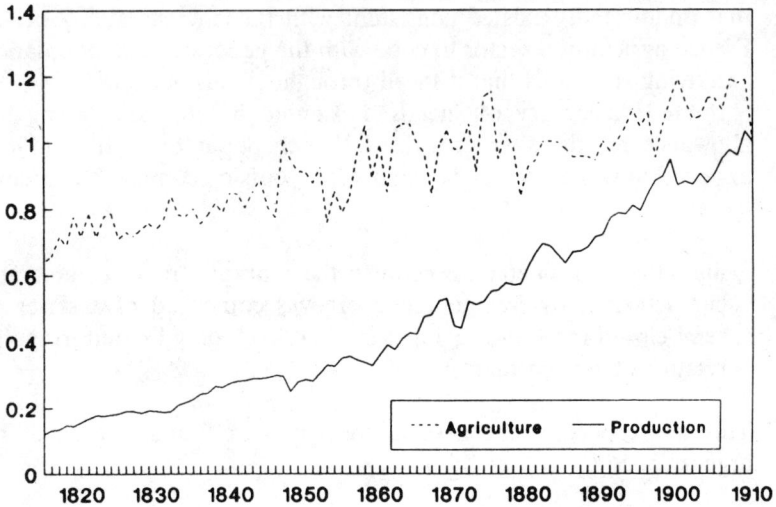

Figure 4.2   Agricultural and production indices, 1815–1910

The pattern of labour usage, then, is dictated by the fact that the mixed farming of the time is actually relatively labour intensive. This view, broadly, also appears in a controversial study by O'Brien and Keyder (1978).[9]

Let us turn to the macroeconomic data. The numbers are those produced in the process of calculating France's Gross National Product from 1815 (Toutain, 1987) and appear as indices of agricultural and industrial production; Figure 4.2 shows these for the period 1815 to 1910, calculated on a per capita basis. In this period, then, from 1815 to 1910, the per capita agricultural index grew (to 100 per cent) from 64 per cent of its 1910 level, not an astonishing amount of growth to be sure, but, being per capita, one suggesting an adequate response to the general growth of the economy.[10] Actually, as indeed suggested by Newell, much of the per capita growth occurred in the 1815 to 1847 period, with the remaining years showing a lot of year-to-year variation, but no clear trend until after 1890. This would support Newell's position rather than Price's as to when the major agricultural response occurred (in the 19th century). Even so, we must be clear to emphasize that the word 'revolution' ought not to be used to describe any of this.

Table 4.3 Compound annual growth rates

	Agriculture	Industry
1815–1870	0.68	2.24
1880–1910	0.67	1.59

Actually, it could be argued that Figure 4.2 shows another pattern and that is a rather steady trend in the agricultural index up until the 1870s, and then a series of sharp reversals in production, followed by a return to the trend. These two trends can be estimated, if one is willing to be arbitrary about the end points; Table 4.3 provides one possible comparison of the growth rates. This result (for agriculture) does not depend materially on the choice of year (e.g., 1869–71) and suggests that a long-term view (dropping the 1870s) is that per capita agricultural output (and possibly productivity) grew steadily and unspectacularly throughout the 95-year period.

We have included industry in this comparison partly because of the somewhat surprising result that industrial production actually grew more rapidly – at a substantial rate per capita – up to 1870 than from 1880 to 1910. Actually, the comparable rate from 1815 to 1850 is 2.4 per cent per annum (even faster!); this almost disposes of arguments that the French industrial revolution had to await a late agricultural revolution (or, possibly, any French agricultural revolution at all).[11] These numbers are remarkable considering the literature on the industrial revolution, where claims to the contrary are quite common.

One final point about the agricultural sector concerns the relative eclipse of this sector by the industrial sector. It turns out that the ratio of agricultural to industrial production is a useful index of structural change (in the study of money demand, below), so it is interesting to generate such a number for France for this period. Actually, as Figure 4.3 makes clear, the story for France is a little unusual. Panel (a) here, drawing on Toutain's (1987) numbers again, shows the behaviour of the *nominal* components of GNP attributed to the agricultural sector and the industrial sector. Quite remarkably, they are roughly parallel until the early 1880s, with industry finally pulling ahead of agriculture for good a little earlier (in 1878).

The impression just given, of no really decisive move toward industrialization in France, is not really quite right; the problem is that the nominal figures conceal a dramatic change of the terms of

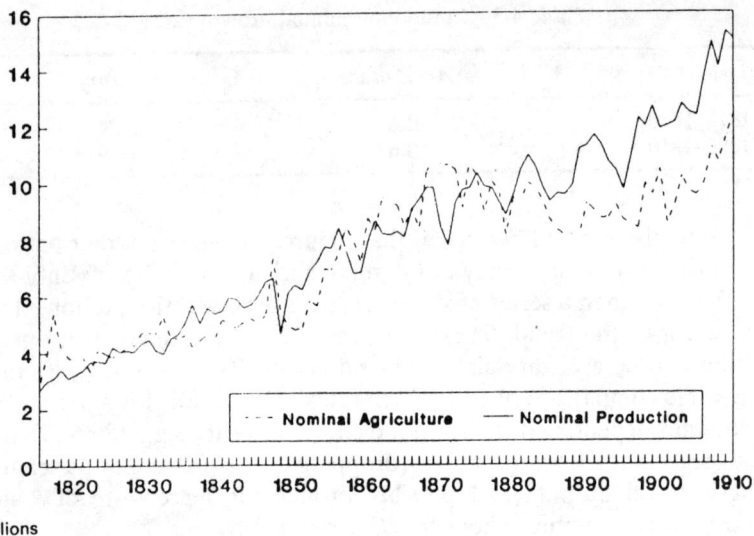

(a) Nominal agriculture and production, 1815–1910

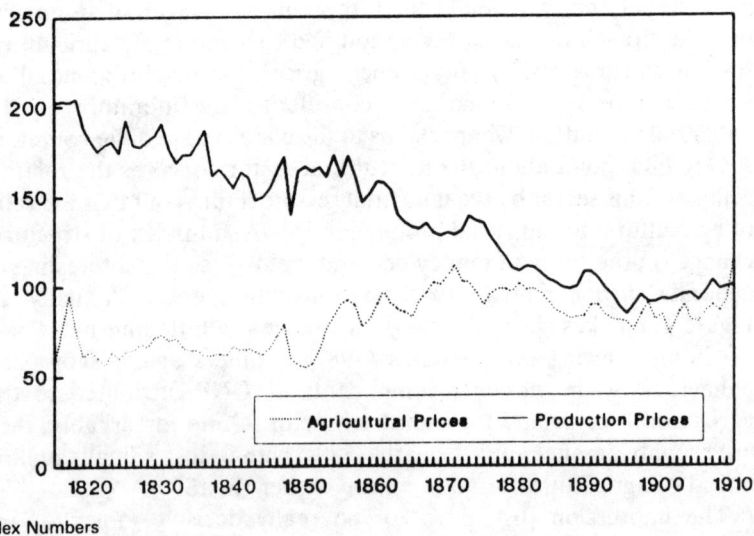

(b) Agricultural and production prices, 1815–1910

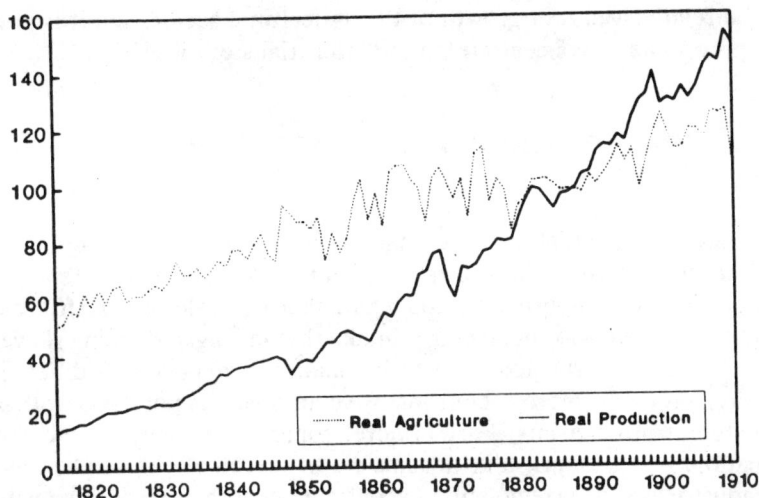

Millions of 1905–13 Francs

(c) Real agriculture and production, 1815–1910

Figure 4.3

trade between agriculture and industry in this period, in favour of agriculture. To see this, consider Panel (b) in Figure 4.3, which exhibits the behaviour of the price indices for these two sectors. Accordingly, the real contributions of these sectors to real GNP are required, and these are provided in Panel (c). Here we see that the relative ascent of the industrial sector is much more decisive from the 1850s (with an interruption in the next decade); in 1888, then, the agricultural component of GNP was finally dominated by the industrial. That is, the ratio of these two series, which stood at 3.77 in 1815, was 0.99 in 1888, and never afterwards exceeded unity; in 1910 it was 0.71 (a figure that is abnormally low because that was a very bad year for the agricultural sector).

Evidently, France can be referred to as an industrial nation from 1888 with the clear implication that an important amount of industrialization occurred earlier. For all we can say on the basis of the aggregate numbers examined so far – and illustrated in Figure 4.3 most tellingly – France spent the entire century (1815 to 1910) on the path to industrial maturity. But these comparisons are coloured by the relatively slower growth of the agricultural sector, and it is now appropriate to concentrate on the industrial story itself.

4.3 THE INDUSTRIALIZATION OF THE FRENCH ECONOMY

There is a parallel story to that of French agricultural told with respect to French industrialization. Without going into the details, we note that it is important to appreciate that the style of industrialization in France was, on average, unlike that in England, being slower in heavy industry, tied up with population dynamics in a different way, probably more labour-intensive in some sectors and with a different product mix. Furthermore, comparisons between the two nations – of dubious value in some ways – become confused because industrialization is regionally concentrated in both countries, but with France's considerably larger area burdened with its massive non-industrial heartland.

There is not a lot of information available for the 18th century, but several writers have hazarded guesses as to what went on in France. One well known comparison is that of Crafts (1977), who argues that French industrial output actually grew more rapidly than English, at least up to 1780.[12] The French did employ current technology of a style similar to the English, but they did not generate the volume. According to Fohlen (1970) English cloth-making processes appeared in France from 1752, with a mule-jenny put in use in 1782. France had its first coke blast furnace in 1785 but charcoal was the standard fuel well into the 19th century. Even so, general figures are hard to come by [13]

For the 19th century, there is some comparative data on per capita commodity output in the two countries, as constructed by O'Brien and Keyder (1978) and shown in Table 4.4. While commodity output would include things not actually made in 'industries', this comparison is still relevant, since much is; it is also very controversial. In Table 4.4, it looks as if the French misfortunes on the battlefield might be the only real reason their per capita (commodity) output did not actually stay ahead of the British throughout the industrial revolution. Of course, doing the numbers up in per capita form turns the trick, but this is appropriate. To look at the industrial situation yet another way, and to broaden the comparison, consider how France's basic industries fare as leading sectors in the 19th century.

Table 4.4   British and French commodity output (per capita)

Date	Great Britain	France
1781–90	6.94	9.53
1803–12	13.38	17.20
1815–24	12.27	11.31
1825–34	11.86	12.24
1835–44	13.32	13.28
1845–54	13.80	14.27
1855–60	15.31	17.30
1865–74	17.64	19.33
1875–84	17.28	17.65
1885–94	18.09	16.22
1895–1904	19.82	16.69
1905–13	21.53	22.43

Source: O'Brien and Keyder (1978).

Price (1981) points out that the French coal producers were actually way above average (for the French economy) as industrial producers for most of the period from 1786 to 1870.[14] Among the other major industries, cotton was above the average from 1786–1840, silk from 1807 to 1850, metals from 1830 to 1870, and chemicals from 1860 to 1870.[15] It is really quite interesting to see cotton leading the way in the French industrial revolution right from the beginning and to see that mining is dominant over the entire stretch of the 19th century. In any case, there seems little doubt that the event took place, although in a less dramatic fashion possibly than in some other European countries.

For the 19th century, we can return to a more macroeconomic perspective to provide a slightly different perspective to these propositions about relative development. Crafts (1984), as already noted, argues that Britain is a different case from all of Europe, France (especially) included. The numbers appear in Table 4.5 for the five countries we are considering. This table uses the arbitrary standard of $550 US (per capita) as a benchmark. It is cast in real terms (1970 dollars). Thus, in 1840, when Great Britain reached this standard, she had 25 per cent of her labour force in agriculture and extraction. Here it is clear that France was an average European developer in a broad sense, reaching a per capita real income of $550 (1970 US dollars) in 1870, at which point her agricultural (including extractive)

Table 4.5   The development of five European countries ($550 per capita US, 1970 dollars)

	Date	Agriculture and extraction % Labour in	% Income in	% of gross expenditure in Invest- ment	Consump- tion	Govern- ment
Great Britain	1840	25.0	24.9	10.5	80.4	7.9
France	1870	49.3	33.5	12.5	78.4	7.0
Germany	1870	50.0	39.9	15.2	81.0	4.3
Italy	1910	55.4	38.2	16.4	74.3	9.5
Sweden	1900	53.5	27.2	12.0	82.0	5.9

Source: Crafts (1984).

sector still had 50 per cent of total French resources (producing 33.5 per cent of total income). This method of analysis provides an arbitrary – but surely reasonable – measure of development that illustrates just how different Great Britain was from the others at that comparable stage of development. It certainly establishes France as structurally different at a comparable stage, as well.

On the other hand, the basic macroeconomic numbers on spending flows provided by Crafts in the same paper do not show equivalent differences among these countries, as we also can see from Table 4.5 in the last three columns. That is, the range of numbers showing the spending ratios for the three countries are more similar than one might have expected based on the development statistics just described. Indeed, France is very close to an average performer and actually invested only slightly more (I/Y = 12.5 per cent) and consumed slightly less than the British at this comparable stage of development. Furthermore, the investment ratio of 12.5 per cent in France is certainly enough for an industrial revolution rate of growth; it is also evidence of a developed capital market (and economy) by 1870. We now turn to the point of this exercise, which is to discuss the situation in France.

4.4   FRANCE'S MACROECONOMY IN THE 19TH CENTURY

There are some GNP numbers for France before the post-Napoleonic period, but they are little more than educated guesses. Be that as it may, let us look briefly at the data reproduced in Price (1981) and given in Table 4.6. The compound annual rate of growth over the first

Table 4.6   France: GNP and population

	GNP (million 1905–13 Fr.)	Population (millions)	GNP (per capita)
1701–10	2818	20.0	141
1781–90	4760	26.8	178
1803–12	5693	29.0	196

eighty years here is 0.66 per cent for the real income in the first column, and 0.29 for real GNP per capita. These numbers are not very solid, of course, but in comparison with the equivalent British calculations available in various sources, they do show a comparable growth in the two countries over the first eighty years of the 18th century of this broad measure of economic activity.

The really good French data are available from 1815 onward, as recently published by Toutain (1987). Actually, two different collections of French data have been published in recent years, both on the same base (Toutain's work). The Lévy-Leboyer/Bourguignon (1990; henceforth LLB) versions are possibly slightly older estimates than those of Toutain himself, but most importantly, they do not contain an overall calculation of gross product in real terms.[16] Indeed, there is no general measure of prices in the economy in this set of numbers, although one could presumably come pretty close to generating one from the agricultural and industrial price indices that are provided. This is not necessary, fortunately, because of the presence of a real GDP estimate (and a deflator) in the Toutain series. We will, accordingly, concentrate on these numbers, although the LLB numbers come into play when we have occasion to refer to the levels of consumption, investment, and government spending in the French economy, simply because they are the standard source for that particular breakdown.

Figure 4.4 shows the Toutain data for real gross domestic product for the entire period, 1815 to 1910; this is produced on a logarithmic scale, with the growth rates estimated by regression on trend for various periods also provided (at the bottom of the figure). It is apparent that overall French growth was very steady in this century – as the industrial sector replaced the agricultural in importance – with the remarkable result that the seventy years from 1840 to 1910 showed an approximately constant rate of growth in real terms. Also remarkable, considering the literature we have discussed to this

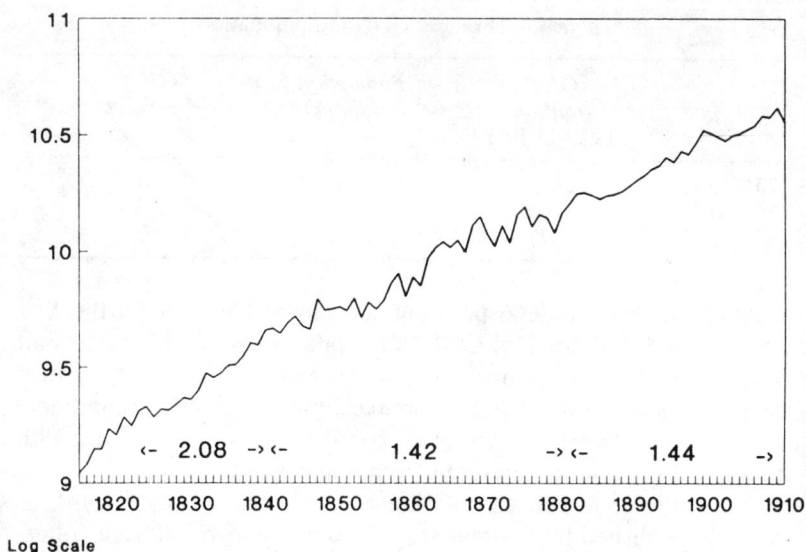

Figure 4.4   French real domestic product, 1815–1910

point, is the fact that the growth rate of GDP was actually higher up to 1840 than it was thereafter. Indeed, no signs of the significant influence of railroads or of the breakdown of traditional agricultural techniques in the South is evident here, either, on these general numbers. It must be noted, though, that these are new numbers, so no criticism of earlier work is intended.

4.4.1 French Business Cycles in the 19th Century

In Figure 4.4 there are numerous downturns in the French data visible; the years of sharpest decline in real GDP are listed in Table 4.7. Looking not at the logarithms, but at the actual real GDP data behind them, Table 4.7 represents a complete record of the years of decline in the French economy from 1815 to 1910. These results clearly indicate that the middle period – the forty years from 1840 to 1880 – definitely contains most of the unpleasant cyclical experience for the French economy, with the average decline of GNP (peak to trough) being 5.71 per cent, and with declines in 44 per cent of the years. The 25 years before and the 30 years after this period show declines in slightly less than a third of the years (more in keeping with 20th-century figures); further, the later period shows an average amplitude of the cycles of less than 3 per cent per cycle.

Table 4.7 Downturns in the French economy

	1815–1840			1840–1880			1880–1910	
Date	%Decline	Years	Date	%Decline	Years	Date	%Decline	Years
1820	2.8	1	1842	2.3	1	1884–5	2.9	2
1822	3.8	1	1845–6	5.4	2	1895	2.1	1
1825	4.3	1	1848	4.8	1	1897	1.3	1
1827	0.4	1	1851	1.6	1	1900–2	4.3	3
1830	0.7	1	1853	7.9	1	1907	0.5	1
1833	1.9	1	1855	2.8	1	1910	6.1	1
1839	0.8	1	1859	9.6	1			
			1861	3.5	1			
			1865	2.5	1			
			1867	5.1	1			
			1870–1	11.8	2			
			1873	7.1	1			
			1876	8.1	1			
			1878–9	7.4	2			
Average decline per cycle:								
	2.10			5.71%			2.86%	
Average number of years of decline:								
	0.28%			0.42%			0.30%	

The downturns that seem to require an explanation, being either long or deep are shown in Table 4.8. Table 4.8 also includes the peak-to-trough changes in the agricultural and production indices that were employed in Figure 4.1. Thus, for 1822, the overall index (repeated from Table 4.7) declined 3.8 per cent, while the agricultural index fell 8.1 per cent; the industrial index for the same year *rose* 6.4 per cent. The asterisks, then, indicate the cases in which the marked sub-index contributed to the decline in the overall index, in the sense of declining further than the average. Mostly, it is agriculture which earns the asterisks, with all but the 1845–6 and 1870–1 cyclical experiences made worse by the decline in agricultural production. Generally, in turn, the industrial sector tended to smooth the cycle, at least until the more recent period (1880–1910). Otherwise, only during the revolution in 1848 and in the war-determined decline in 1870–1 did the industrial sector add to the average instability of the economy; in those two cases, the finger points elsewhere, of course.

There are, then, two things that stand out here. First, the story of the French business cycle in the bulk of the 19th century is a story of what went on in the agricultural sector. This is a contemporary causation story, quite probably involving the weather in the general

Table 4.8 The role of agriculture and industrial production in the major declines in French real GDP

Date	Overall	Agricultural production	Industrial production
1822	– 3.8	– 8.1*	+ 6.4
1825	– 4.3	– 9.2*	+ 0.4
1845–6	– 5.4	– 3.2	– 0.8
1848	– 4.8	– 2.7	– 13.4*
1853	– 7.9	–17.6*	+ 7.8
1859	– 9.6	–14.4*	– 2.7
1861	– 3.5	–12.1*	+10.6
1867	– 5.1	–12.4*	+ 1.6
1870–1	–11.8	–10.4	– 21.5*
1873	– 7.1	–13.1*	– 1.1
1876	– 8.1	–17.1*	+ 0.8
1878–9	– 7.4	–17.6*	0.0
1884–5	– 2.9	– 3.8*	– 7.0*
1900–2	– 4.3	–10.0*	– 7.5*
1910	– 6.1	–15.5*	– 2.8

case. The second thing is that as the century wanes – and the industrial sector gains relative position – it is the industrial sector that destabilizes the economy relatively. This is especially true of the major downturns in the last 30 years. It is important to notice, though, that the cycle itself is much less severe (see Table 4.7) during the last period, a reflection, it seems, of the growing influence of the relatively stable industrial sector. The notion that the industrial growth of the French economy is associated with increasing stability may not go down well in certain quarters but, is none the less, quite hard to dispute on this evidence.

There is another aspect of French cycles, aside from the agricultural dominance in the 19th century, that Marczewski (1988) emphasizes. This is that situations of stagflation (rising prices and declining real GDP) are actually the norm in the 19th century. Table 4.9 lists these stagflations along with the episodes of depression (defined as falling prices and falling real GDP). Marczewski dismisses the other declines listed in Table 4.8 as minor events (although 1867 should also be included). Stagflation, it is clear, is nothing new in the West, although the modern business cycle literature (since the 1960s) tends to create the impression that it is a post-World War II phenomenon. Even more interesting, in some ways, is the finding that all of the long periods of expansion in 19th-century France are associated with

Table 4.9   Stagflation and depression

Stagflation	Depression
1825	1848–51
1845–6	1876–9
1853	1884–5
1859	
1870–71	
1900–2	
1910	

falling prices (on average). The periods he identifies as having this characteristic are

1815–24
1826–44
1860–69
1886–99

In total, 56 per cent of the expansionary years in the 1815–99 period show deflation. There are certain quarters in which this, too, might not go down well.

The role of the money stock in these events, according to Marczewski, is as follows. A rise in agricultural production will produce lower farm prices and induce industrial expansion; the overall price level will fall as a result of the rise in aggregate output insofar as the quantity of money does not keep pace with growth in income; this is what the equation of exchange $(MV=Py)$ implies. Of course, this assumes that velocity does not change enough to offset this influence. A bad harvest, on the other hand, reduces agricultural output and overall growth and causes agricultural prices to rise (and industrial output to decline). The equation of exchange in the second case merely predicts the opposite: prices will rise insofar as the accompanying monetary contraction is not as great as the decline of overall output. Again, this assumes that any change in velocity does not counteract these pressures. Why the monetary sector would, in effect, respond less than the real sector, pulling against the tide in both circumstances, could be related to the particular institutional structure of the French financial system. In particular, if the supply of money is (interest) inelastic, one might anticipate an inadequate response here. This general description casts money in a passive role in this period with respect to prices. It also implies that causation might run from output to prices (and money). Below we will look at some Granger-causality tests that might be showing just that. But the present section is about business cycles, and so we now turn to a more detailed explanation of those events in France.

The standard literature on French cycles makes much of the financial crises that sometimes accompanied these events, and these, as it turns out, have a more international flavour. To begin, then, 1817 provides an immediate counter-example because it is a 'classic subsistence crisis' (Caron, 1979), unaccompanied by a major downturn in real GDP. In 1825 the agricultural decline was sufficient to produce a recession, while a financial crisis in 1829–30, involving the failure of all of the newly formed English-style iron-making companies, failed to dent the aggregate figures.[17] In the late 1830s, a financial crisis again involved the industrial sector, but, as shown in Table 4.7, this made almost no dent in the agriculturally-dominated annual real GDP figures.[18] Harvests were poor in 1845–6, apparently, but the numbers in Table 4.8 do not show this as a major event for the economy. There were disastrous harvests in 1847–8 (say Lévy-Leboyer and Bourguignon, 1990), but a period of progressively worsening agricultural production actually runs from 1848 to 1851. In any case, this event features an international financial crisis (in 1848) and a domestic financial crisis (which wiped out the newly formed 'caisse' style of banks); a succession of European governments also were toppled in this period. Industry was involved in the 1848 collapse significantly – look back to Table 4.8 – but rebounded sharply in 1849.[19] The industrial decline was echoed in other European countries (for which we have firm data), and so depression, agricultural decline and, as it turns out, revolution, was spread quite widely around Europe at this time. This event might not qualify as the first major post-industrial revolution crisis (1837–41 having a claim as well), but it certainly has all of the flavour of one of those complicated (international) events. Continuing with the French story, though, we note that the contractions of the 1850s and 1860s all show very sharp agricultural declines and two of these years (1853 and 1861) actually exhibit perversely strong gains in the industrial sector. The decline in 1867 was coincident with the collapse of the Crédit Mobilier, but there was no general financial collapse at this time.

International events loom a little larger – and poor harvests smaller – as we consider the last forty years up until 1910. Unsuccessful wars, especially the disaster in 1870, produced considerable financial pressures (including a sizeable indemnity in that case). Thus the industrial collapse of 1870–71 hardly needs further explanation, with political factors standing as the chief culprit. The international financial crisis of 1873 does not seem as important in France as the agricultural decline of that year (of 13.1 per cent); similarly, the sharp downturns in 1876 and 1878–9 seem agricultural, primarily, although LLB note that the investment market toppled in 1876, as well. From 1878, there was a financial and speculative boom – as well as a rather steady industrial expansion. Behind the financial collapse beginning with bank failures in 1882 and culminating in a recession in 1884–5, there seem to be several factors working at once. The expansion itself may have got out of hand (in the traditional over-investment sense); evidence for this exists in the rise of investment as a per cent of nominal GDP to 9.1 per cent in 1882, and then an abrupt decline to 6.3 per cent, thereafter.[20] In fact, these events occurred alongside an international money crisis that 'lastingly weakened the Banque de France and brought about the collapse of the main banks in the Lyons market in January 1882' (LLB, p. 83). As if this were not enough, Caron (1979) and Marczewski (1988) argue that sharpened international competition in the agricultural markets (especially floods of American and Russian wheat) undermined the French agricultural sector. Certainly, agricultural production was only marginally higher in 1892 than it was in 1884 (a peak) – and significantly lower than in 1875), but there is not a lot of cyclical flavour to these facts, and, in truth, there is no downturn here that we feel compelled to explain (the 1884–5 slowdown being only 2.9 per cent, peak-to-trough). Even so, the peak in real GDP in 1883 was not exceeded again until 1888, so the complex of events did work some considerable harm on the French economy, collectively.

The stirring international financial crises of the 1890s seem to have by-passed France and, in particular, there are only recessions in 1895 (2.1 per cent) and 1897 (1.3 per cent) to mar this period. An industrial collapse in the 1900–02 period did contribute to a general decline (the agricultural contribution here was also considerable) but worldwide cycles followed a different pattern (1903–4 and 1907–8) than French (1900–2, 1910). The last cited was a full-blown agricultural event, however, the last of its kind in modern French history. The conclusion, clearly, is that little detailed evidence exists to tie French cyclical experience to world events, at least in real terms, since domestic agriculture is so large a part of the story. The industrial sector is usually a stabilizer in these events, and international influences seem sparse here too. On the financial side, though, the

French seem to have shared in the international crises of 1848, 1873, and 1882–4, with revolution and war a factor in the first of these two events. One might expect, on this evidence, that the French might well be causally linked to European financial shocks, but that real events in France would only be related to other European real events in a contemporaneous sense, since the weather seems to be the main culprit.

4.4.2 A Brief Discussion of the French Macro-Sectors

In Table 4.5 we noted that by one accounting the broad sectors (C, I, G) of the French economy in 1870 were very like those of the other countries considered in this study when they reached an equivalent and arbitrary level of development. This suggests, of course, that the European economies are broadly similar in this respect. In this section, then, we want to look at the time-series behaviour of these entities for France – of consumption, investment, and government spending – for clues as to how they interacted with growth (and the French business cycle) in the 19th century. This will not be a full scale investigation, although one is long overdue, mainly because the basic numbers are only available in nominal form. The potential for error here, accordingly, is enormous, and we will try to be suitably cautious in any interpretations proffered.

One way to handle nominal figures like these is in ratio form; this would even be formally correct in the unlikely event that the ratios of prices for these sectors were constant. In Panels (a) and (b) of Figure 4.5, we illustrate four variables – exports, imports, investment and consumption – as ratios of *nominal* gross domestic product; these are drawn from the LLB (1990) figures. It is, of course, unfortunate that these are not in real terms.

The first thing to note in Panel (a) is the steady C/Y ratio. This actually drifted slightly downward in this period, although most observations lie between 85 per cent and 78 per cent; it ended up, in 1910, at 82.03 per cent, having been 83.83 per cent in 1824. Evidently the growth that did occur in this period was not at the expense of consumption. On the other hand, investment as a per cent of nominal GDP actually rose over the period, from its low of 8.97 per cent in 1820 to 14.76 per cent in 1910. While this last was not changed much from the 1880s, it does show an important influence on growth.

The two remaining comparisons are considerably more dramatic. In Panel (b) of Figure 4.5 we show exports and imports as percentages of nominal GDP. Here it is clear that there was a long mid-century boom – from the mid-1840s to the mid-1870s – that died out in rather dramatic fashion for both series. Increased worldwide agricultural competition is a large part of this story, but so is the rising industrial power of the rest of the world. The upsurge part of the graph, from the 1850s to the 1880s is, in any case, remarkably strong. It is worth recalling that the overall level of both exports and imports does grow from the mid-1870s until 1910, so that this pattern should not be interpreted as a decline, but rather the achievement of a rate of growth roughly equivalent to that of the economy. If there is any failure in this it is only related to the drop off from the 1870s to the 1890s. Before and after the foreign sector grew vigorously.

The last panel of Figure 4.5 touches on an issue that we discussed in the British case: the possibility of the 'crowding-out' of private investment by government expenditures. In this case, we can look at Figure 4.5c, where a slight change of focus occurs because the relationship we are looking for appears sharper with the figures for net investment and net national income (in the denominator). In this case there does appear to be something to the crowding-out hypothesis for the French, especially at revolution or war-time, although this judgment is partly the result of the sharp spike in 1870–71 that tends to draw the eye. The following set of correlation coefficients is helpful.

Overall	−0.33
1820–1869	−0.39
1872–1910	0.05

Here we find the phenomenon prior to 1870, but not afterwards, in this very simple test. Of course, with investment growing over the entire period and government spending fairly constant, we would not expect to see much of this effect in any case.

There appear, in summary, to be enough problems with the French national income data to warrant some caution in any tests that would employ them. Even so, the broad upward trend in real product at a comfortable rate (1 to 2 per cent) and the apparent instability (in terms of frequent and sometimes deep recessions) seem to stand out. The trend in real growth is the result of the industrial revolution, of course, while developments in the agricultural sector provide the cause of many of the downturns in the 90 years for which we have data. Finally, we note that much of the evidence assembled in this and previous sections implies that growth was relatively stable over the entire period (1820 to 1910); certainly the spending ratios were

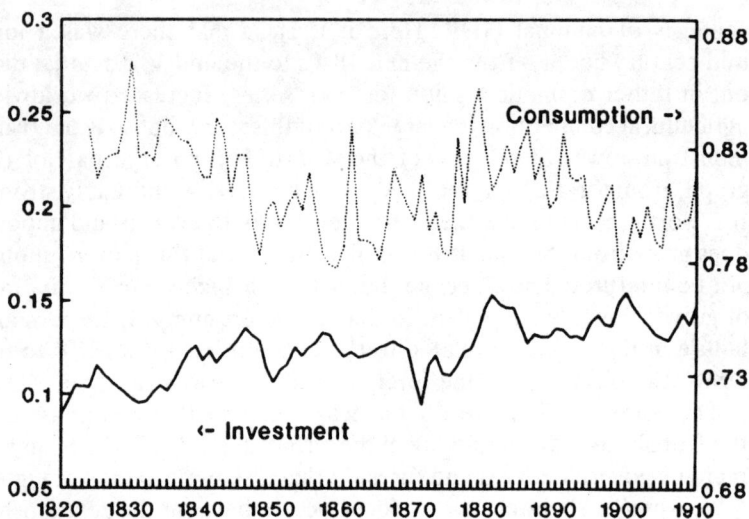

Ratio of Gross Domestic Product

(a) Investment and consumption ratios, 1820–1910

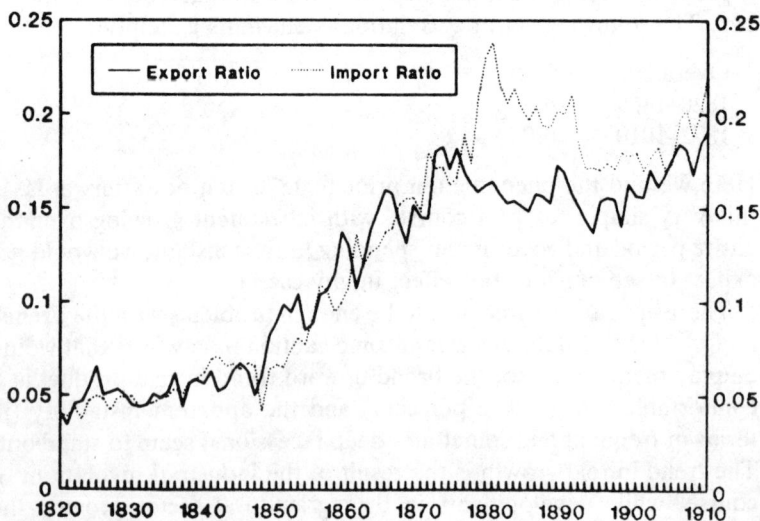

Ratio of Gross Domestic Product

(b) Export and import ratios, 1820–1910

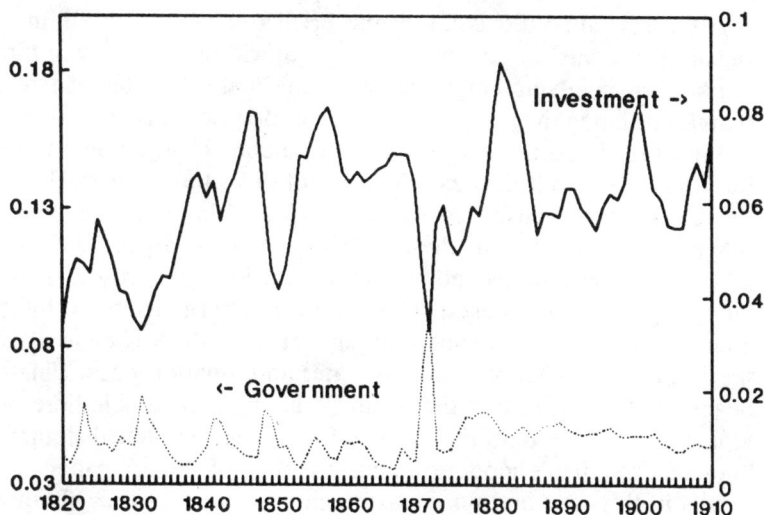

(c) Government and investment ratios, 1820–1910

Figure 4.5

also reasonably constant in the same span. On the whole these results corroborate the contention of earlier sections that growth was self-sustaining over much of this century and that the industrial revolution (or some sort of self-sustaining transformation, at least) may well have been in place by 1820. This is, of course, a contested view.

4.5   THE QUANTITY THEORY OF MONEY IN 19TH-CENTURY FRANCE

The largely verbal story of French business cycles in Section 4.4 clearly suggests that money may well have been neutral in the 19th century, at least in the sense that aside from the contraction of 1848–51, monetary shocks had no noticeable effect on real income. Actually, neutral is not a well-chosen word here, since monetary neutrality is an implication of the quantity theory of money and, as we shall see, the quantity theory of money does not do at all well on the French data for this period, at least in terms of some of the test results that will be reported below.

After a detailed discussion of the French monetary system in the remainder of this introductory section, we will tell the story in three parts, each involving empirical tests. The first set of tests involves searching among the real income, money and price variables for signs of Granger causality. We certainly find monetary neutrality in this, but it also turns out that money does not drive the price level while the converse actually holds. This is odd, at least if one takes a monetarist viewpoint. In the second set of tests, a procedure suggested by Lucas is employed to discern if the long-run growth rates of money, prices, and interest rates follow a pattern suggested by the quantity theory. They do not, although, at least, there is some sign of the Fisher Effect between interest rates and inflation rates. Finally, beginning to suspect that the quantity theory is in trouble here, we look at the behaviour of the demand for money – modelled along the lines of Friedman's modern quantity theory of money paper. The results in this case are more encouraging for monetarism, although certain periods (1815–30 and 1870–80) remain stubbornly outside the monetarist pale. Instability in the financial sector, at the least, might be conceded on this evidence.

Modern banking in France begins with the Bank of France, which began operations in February, 1800.[21] It was an invention of the government and primarily operated to discount bills of exchange for, and make advances to, the government. For a time it had a national monopoly of bank-note issue (from 1803 to 1814), which was subsequently restricted to the Paris area until 1848, when it once again obtained the national monopoly of issue. From 1817 to 1838, a small number of private banks were chartered in France, mostly in other economically important cities (e.g., Bordeaux, Lyons), and in 1836, the Bank itself began to spread out, with 13 branches in operation by 1848. In the financial crisis of 1848, when all other banks suspended, it absorbed all of the private commercial banks.

The Bank of France followed a very restrictive discount policy and so there were quite a few private discount operations in place around the country, although very little of this was formally money, in the legal sense.[22] A group of banks – 'la haute banque Parisienne' – beginning for the most part after 1815, operated as investment banks (especially concentrating in international trade), although they also dealt in insurance and (even) operated savings banks.[23] From 1837, a new type of institution, a kind of credit bank, was founded.[24] These were significant in the early days of the industrial revolution, but did not survive the financial crisis of 1848. The deliberate policy of the Bank of France also had something to do with their fragility.

Following the financial crisis of 1848, the government permitted the establishment of 'comptoires d'escompte', this time with a formal link to the Bank of France. In 1852, a nationwide mortgage bank (Crédit Foncier de France) and the famous Crédit Mobilier were founded; both had government support. The latter was involved in lending to industry (especially railroads) but was forced to liquidate in 1867 on account of unsuccessful real estate loans. Until the early 1860s, many new sorts of banks were founded, but cheque writing was slow to develop (it was legalized in 1865). The government was still hostile to English-style banking after 1851 and discount banks, as earlier, filled the gaps. Three banks of special importance are the Crédit Industriel et Commercial (1859), the Crédit Lyonnais (1963), and the Société Général (1964); they were national in scope and offered demand-deposit accounts. Their lending functions were concentrated in short-term securities, however.

The Bank of France continued to expand throughout this period, reaching 60 branches by 1870 and 411 by 1900. According to Cameron (1967), by 1870 one might refer to the French financial system as mature (p. 109),

> by 1870 the basic pattern of the modern French banking structure had been fixed. It included the Bank of France in the center, the sole source of paper currency and supreme regulator of the system; a relatively small number of joint-stock deposit banks – four or five – operating on a national scale; a much larger number of small local and regional banks in the provinces; a few *banques d'affaires* and a number of specialized institutions, . . ., some of which . . . had semi-official status.

As we shall see, our velocity (and crude financial sophistication index) calculation confirms that sometime shortly after 1870, the French monetary system could be referred to as mature in that restricted sense.

4.5.1 Monetary Neutrality: Granger Tests

We may investigate monetary neutrality by employing the Granger-causality tests already used earlier in this study. The Granger test – to

Table 4.10 Monetary neutrality in the French economy first differences of
the per-capita data

Causal test	p-values for lags of					Sign
	1	2	3	4	5	
1830–1870						
M → Y	0.022*	0.150	0.493	0.644	0.882	+
Y → M	0.151	0.012*	0.012*	0.024*	0.095	+
M → P	0.014*	0.054	0.163	0.304	0.534	+
P → M	0.152	0.154	0.054	0.104	0.176	
1880–1910						
M → Y	0.973	0.828	0.867	0.846	0.918	
Y → M	0.088	0.190	0.324	0.176	0.301	
M → P	0.022*	0.061	0.070	0.261	0.380	+
P → M	0.558	0.904	0.799	0.665	0.596	

Note: The relations between money and real income are calculated in per
capita terms; all variables are calculated as first differences of the logarithms
(see the discussion in Chapter 8).

repeat – searches for a significant influence from the lags of a proposed causal agent (e.g., money) on a particular variable (e.g., real
income). The tests are often run on level, log-level or detrended data,
with the detrended data most often employed to avert any suspicion
that non-stationarity of the data might have influenced the results.
The findings are usually stated in terms of the probabilities (p-values)
from an F-test employed to find out if the lags of the causal variable
as a group contribute significantly to an autoregression involving the
dependent variable and its own lags. The p-values are often judged to
be significant (and are so marked in Table 4.10 with an asterisk), if
they are 0.05 or less (indicating a 5 per cent or less chance of asserting
causality when it is not true). Table 4.10, thus, contains the basic
results for this section. The results listed are for two periods, 1830 to
1870, and 1880 to 1910.

Attached to the table is a column indicating the sign of the relationship as judged by a *t*-test on the sum of the lag coefficients (on the
Granger-causal variable). These are as anticipated, with 'ns' in the
table indicating that while a significant effect existed, the sum of the
effects for individual lags was zero, statistically. The reader should
also notice that the periods chosen are not overlapping, but exclude
the 1870s (and the period from 1815 to 1829). The reason for the

exclusion of the early data is that the monetary data appear to be in error; see the discussion below. The reason for the exclusion of the post-war period of the 1870s is that there appears to have been financial (and even economic) chaos following the war, until late in the decade. In the study of the demand for money, below, the same strategy is employed. In that case the differences in the estimation are not important, but here they are.

Turning to the specific results, we note, first, that the first period in Table 4.10 shows monetary non-neutrality (in the first row); this is a relatively unusual result (and holds for a shortened period running from 1840 to 1870). The influence of real income on money in the second row is not unusual, however, and neither is the quantity theory result in the third and seventh rows, involving the influence of money on the price level. Why income affects money in the 1830–70 period and not in the 1880–1910 period is not clear, however. Perhaps the ten fewer degrees of freedom in the later test is a factor. This is not, though, a contradiction for the theory.

Part of the reason for isolating the 1880 to 1910 period is to see if in that gold standard world the quantity theory of money is upheld. In fact, money is neutral (row (5)) and there is a Granger-causal link from money to prices (both measured as log first-differences). Thus for that period a conventional result holds, as predicted by the theory. Nevertheless, for the whole stretch of 95 years, patching back the bits cut out and considering the violation of monetary neutrality for the first period, the overall results are not particularly good news for the quantity theory. We note, though, severe concern with the quality of the monetary data before 1850 and, for that matter, of the income data before 1830.

4.5.2   A Formal Test of the Quantity Theory in the Style of Lucas

In the recent literature on the possible real effects of changes in money on real variables, a certain amount of attention has been directed toward exactly how to test for monetary neutrality. What we have done so far in this chapter basically contributes to the discussion of monetary neutrality, insofar as we have searched for a causal link between money and prices (generally unsuccessfully), while establishing that one between money and real income can be denied. In fact, we find a period when money was driven by prices, if anything, although neutrality itself did appear to hold for at least part of the time. In this work, the variables are studied as growth rates, principally because of suspicions that unit roots might exist in the level figures (rendering the F-test employed in the comparisons suspect). The growth rates of the variables are also the subject of tests in Lucas's (1980) paper on the quantity theory, where the following implications of that theory are proposed:

that a given change in the rate of change in the quantity of money induces (i) an equal change in the rate of price inflation; and (ii) an equal change in nominal rates of interest.

The former is a typical observation in this literature, while the latter is an implication of the operation of the Fisher effect between inflation and nominal interest rates.

There are, then, three possible lines to explore here. For one thing, we could examine the long-run relation between the growth rate of prices and the growth rate of money, searching for a (positive) proportionality; this is, as Lucas says, an implication of the quantity theory of money. For a second, again as in Lucas, we could examine the growth rate of money and the nominal interest rate; we would anticipate a proportionality again. Finally, we could look to the Fisher effect itself, examining the relation between the inflation rate and the nominal interest rate. Lucas does not do this, but, then, he did not need to, in view of his success in establishing proportionality between the monetary growth rate and the nominal interest rate in his tests (on US post-World War II data).

How Lucas implements the test – between the growth rate of money (m) and the growth rate of the price level (π) – is to smooth the data in order to isolate the long-run effect. What he uses, and what is employed here, is the following two-sided exponential 'filter':

$$X_i\,(B) = \left(\frac{1-B}{1+B}\right) \sum_{k=-j}^{j} B^{|k|}X_{i,\,t+k} \qquad (4.1)$$

Here B is the parameter that controls the extent of the smoothing, with the characteristic that a value of B near unity smoothes the series considerably compared with a number close to zero. The backward-looking part of the double-sided 'lag' is justified in terms of the use of prior information on, for example, inflation rates in forming an expectation of future inflation rates; the forward side can be argued to contain economic agents' best guesses as to what the future will bring. We might want to assume that economic agents form such forecasts – even in 19th-century France – because *if* money is neutral, their best long-run strategy is to assume that it is, in any negotiations where an incorrect estimate would hurt them (as in any contract stated in nominal terms). They will try to predict the future, then, although whether they do so well or not depends on a lot of things, including their skill and, we might as well admit, the nature of the economic process that is driving the data they need to monitor. In view of the fairly consistent patterns of inflation rates already noted in 19th-century France, agents would not have found it difficult to profit by forming accurate expectations of these rates, insofar as their nominal contracts could be revised in response to new forecasts (as any could, of course).

How this test is implemented is to calculate the smoothed series of m and π, for different lag lengths (presumably very long) and different values of B. For B fairly small, then, the scatter plot of the two series would be expected to look very dispersed – almost shapeless – forming a picture of the short run for which the quantity theory propositions are not expected to hold. For B near unity, the theory predicts that the data would lie along a smooth 45° line, although in view of the dubious quality of the data we are working with, anything resembling a smooth (proportional) pattern presumably would be of interest.

The first illustration, in the first panel of Figure 4.6 is of the Lucas test when $B = 0.5$ and refers to the relation between inflation and money growth; this is, as expected, quite random-looking, although it does cluster around the point (0,0). This test was performed with a relatively long lag, of 50 years.[25] In the other three panels of Figure 4.6 – where $B = 0.95$ is assumed – a different story unfolds. In Panel (b), we find that the relation between inflation and money growth is quite amorphous. Indeed, as Table 4.11 shows, the relation is negative, and significantly so ($t = 2.08$). This is definitely not what the quantity theory would predict. In Panel (c), to continue the dissolution of the theory, the relation between money growth and the nominal interest rate is also highly irregular, and, in Table 4.11, shows no definite pattern.

The Fisher equation between inflation and the nominal interest rate is a venerable concept now, as it nears its 100th birthday. Basically it argues that an implication of the rational behaviour of economic agents in capital markets is to add a premium on to the

B = .50

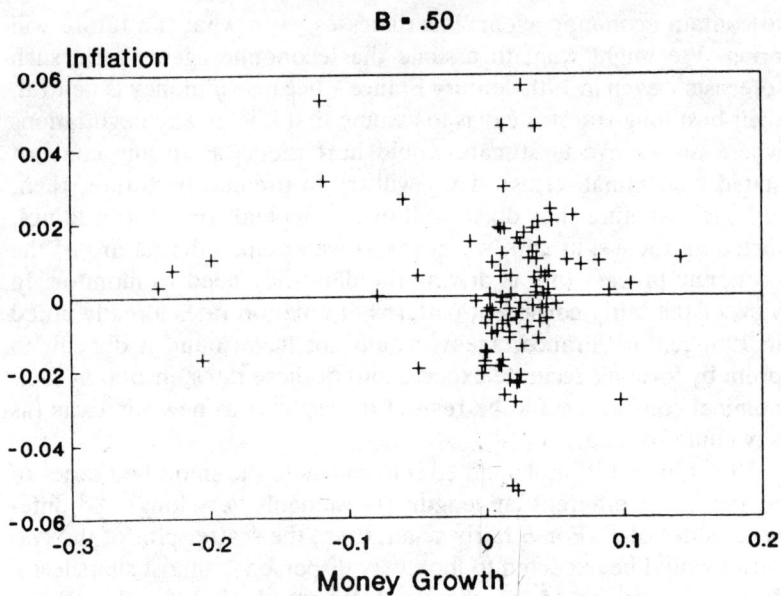

(a) Inflation and money growth

B = .95

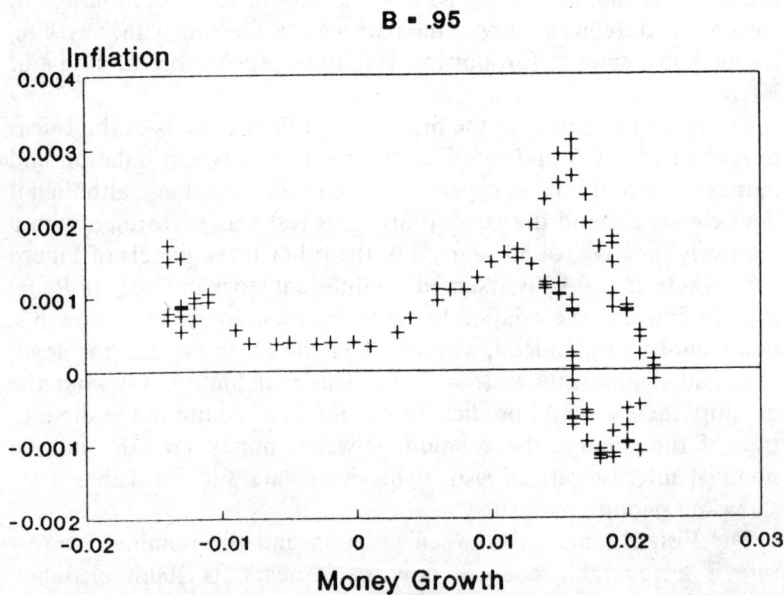

(b) Inflation and money growth

B ▪ .95

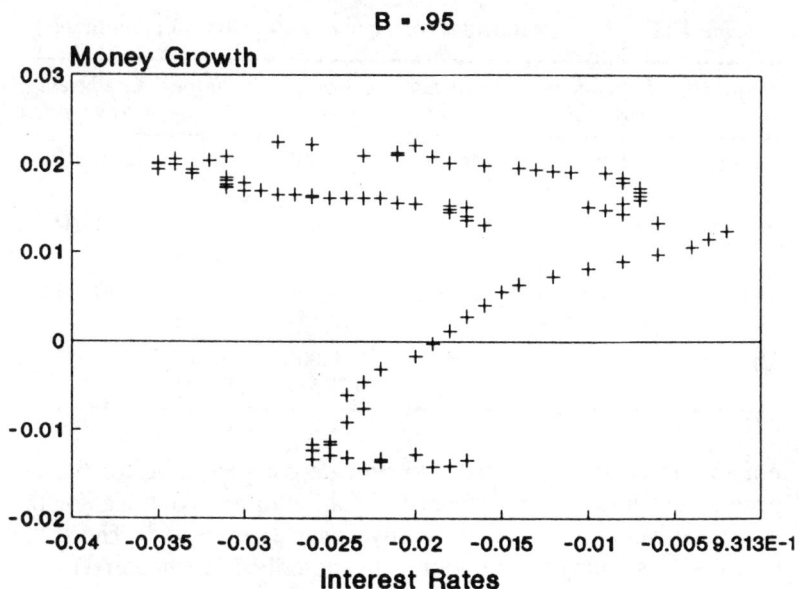

(c) Money growth and interest rates

B ▪ .95

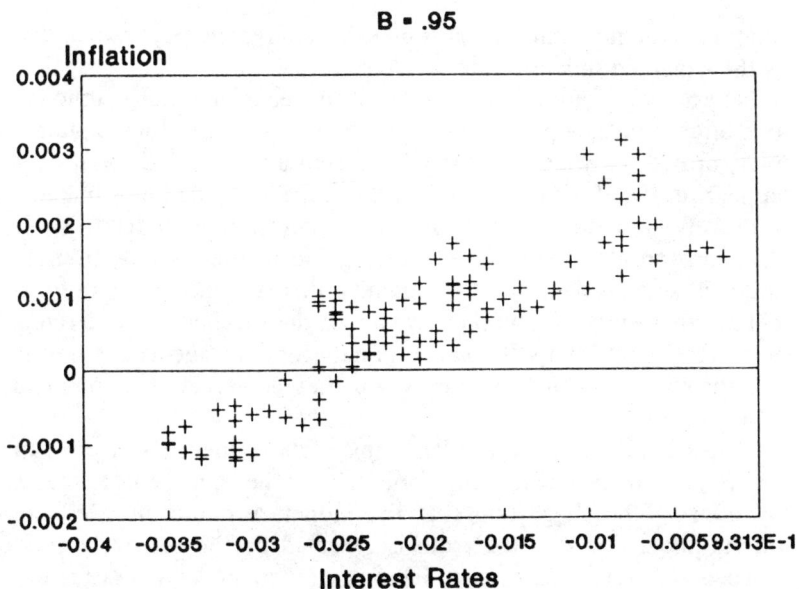

Figure 4.6

(d) Inflation and interest rates

Table 4.11   Linear regressions for Figure 4.6 (*t*-values in parentheses)

Figure (b)	Dependent variable	Independent variable	Constant	Slope	Coefficient of determination
(a) 0.5	Inflation	Money	0.001 (1.67)	0.01 (0.20)	–0.010
(b) 0.95	Inflation	Money	0.001 (6.05)	–0.018 (2.08)	0.034
(c) 0.95	Money	Interest	0.010 (3.15)	0.011 (0.08)	–0.011
(d) 0.95	Inflation	Interest	0.003 (21.32)	0.106 (17.85)	0.772

nominal interest rate in order to provide compensation for the expected deterioration on account of inflation of any contracts for the future delivery of a nominal entity (such as money).[26] The usual equation describing this relation is (as described in Chapter 1),

$$i_t = r_t^e + \pi_t^e \qquad (4.2)$$

where i is the nominal rate, r^e is an expected real interest rate and π^e is the expected inflation rate.

Now actual inflation is not necessarily expected inflation – although it is often used as a proxy – but it certainly is arguable that Equation (4.1) provides a valid measure of expected inflation. Indeed, it does appear, in Panel (d) of Figure 4.6, that expected inflation is linked – positively – to the nominal long-term interest rate. Indeed, Table 4.11 corroborates that this is a highly significant effect. Thus, after all, there is some solace for the quantity theory, since such rational behaviour in financial markets is part of the mechanism underlying the quantity theory itself (since rational economic agents apparently see through the veil of money when they construct their nominal financial contracts).

Considering all of the results of this section, then, the avenue of escape, for the beleaguered quantity theorist here, it seems to me, is by offering the suggestion that the monetary data employed are questionable and that the truth is revealed by the relatively good price and interest rate data. This is not an entirely satisfactory answer, of course, and one might like to test the shorter period (1880–1910) for which the data might well be considered adequate, but the Lucas technique employed here really requires longer runs of data in view of the very long lags hypothesized. But let us suspend any final judgment until the results for the demand for money are considered, in the next section.

4.5.3 The Demand for Money in 19th-century France

For the literature on modern economies, there is a standard form for the demand for money, as a log-linear function of real income and one or more nominal interest rates, but in recent years, this representation has come under fire for various reasons. Most important, for our purposes, is the frequently-voiced view that the function is unstable over time, at least on modern data.[27] The oft-stated converse, that the function was a stable function of a few key variables, is widely thought to hold for annual data prior to World War II (and possibly for a few years thereafter), at least for 20th-century tests. For the 19th century, there are further doubters concerning its stability (e.g., Komlos (1987), for Austria-Hungary), but a very influential view (Friedman and Schwartz, 1982; Bordo and Jonung, 1987) is that once one adjusts for the effect of an altered financial structure on the velocity of money, the traditional relation holds up well, at least for the countries they studied (which did not include France).

For France, we have a very long run of monetary data that we have already used in data-intensive time-series work. This might seem an advantage, but, as Figure 4.7 illustrates, the behaviour of the income velocity of money is decidedly irregular at times, particularly up until 1830. On this evidence it would be hard to have any faith in the data before the 1830s, at the least.

Figure 4.7 also shows a long decline in velocity from 1830 into the 1870s and, thereafter, no strong trend. This pattern is fairly typical in countries that are developing their financial markets; indeed, in this study, we invert this relation and call the resulting index a measure of the 'financial sophistication' of the economy. In this light, France gradually achieved financial maturity by the late 1870s, earlier than Germany, Italy, Sweden and the United States, but certainly not earlier than the United Kingdom. This specific comparison is spelled out in Chapter 8.

Returning to the standard demand for money, the following function is fit by ordinary least squares.

$$\text{Log } m_t = \alpha + \beta_1 \text{Log } y_t + \beta_2 i_t + \beta_3 x_t + e_t \qquad (4.3)$$

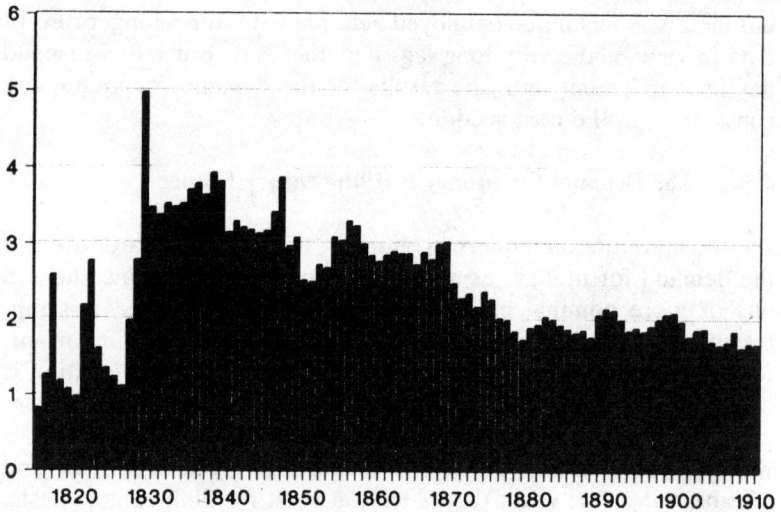

Figure 4.7   Velocity in France, 1815–1910

Here real money balances and real GDP (y) are measured in per capita terms. There is an additional variable in the equation (x_t), which is the ratio of agricultural production to industrial production. The purpose of this variable is to control for the effect of structural change on money demand. In particular, as the economy industrializes, it also urbanizes. In urban settings, more money is used per capita, and so a reasonable expectation for the sign of β_3 is that it is negative: a decline of agriculture/production (that is, a rise of urbanization) produces a rise in money holding per capita.[28] Table 4.12 contains the results of a set of runs for this function, over the period 1830–1910, as well as for several obvious subperiods. Note that an autoregressive correction – for first order autoregression (AR (1)) – was necessary in each test.

The fits described in Table 4.12 are pretty good, for the most part, and they show comparable results for income elasticities both before and after the gap in the series for 1870–80. As noted in the table, this gap defied estimation and could well indicate instability in demand, supply or both, for all one can say.[29] Be that as it may, the greatest interest here is in the income elasticities; these estimates are all over unity (although the 1880–1910 result is not statistically so). This finding, of real per capita money holding being a mildly superior good when financial markets are first taking their modern form is a

Table 4.12 The demand for money in 19th-century France (*t*-values in parentheses)

Dates	Constant	β_1	β_2	β_3	AR(1)	$\bar{R}^2$	DW
1830–1910	−2.517 (3.23)	1.306 (11.41)	−0.011 (0.75)	−0.154 (3.15)	0.681 (7.24)	0.975	1.680
1830–1870	−7.539 (3.63)	1.315 (5.86)	−0.000 (0.00)	−0.000 (1.20)	0.354 (2.38)	0.893	1.401
1880–1910	−1.287 (0.73)	1.121 (4.44)	−0.047 (2.01)	0.027 (0.15)	0.679 (4.56)	0.895	1.896

Note: Attempts to include the period 1870–80 in either the second or third equation produced strange results (i.e., β_1 = 0.281 in an 1830–80 test and −0.151 in an 1870–1910 test).

common one (as we shall illustrate in later chapters). Even so, we must note that the estimate is only marginally above unity; it is also lower than the comparable numbers produced for the other countries in this study. In any case, to sum up, whatever else we might have suggested here, the results in Table 4.12 do not indicate any obvious shift in the demand for money in this period. There is, though, a troublesome and unidentified structural change (in the coefficient β_3), as well as several periods – 1815 to 1830 and 1870 to 1880 – that are possibly financially unsettled, at the very least.

4.6 CONCLUSION

France is a major factor in the story of the industrial revolution in Europe, but to this writer, at least, it is an unusually ambiguous story. Part of the problem lies with the quality of the data, for both the income and money data, while available over an unusually long time, appear to be suspect at certain points. The most prominent of these periods are 1815 to 1830 and the post-war decade of 1871 to 1880. In the former case, it is clearly the numbers that are at fault, while for the later period, the data might be describing correctly a very unsettled economy. As we will see, this state of affairs is not unique to France in this period.

What can one say that is reasonably likely to survive further inspection? Nothing, probably, to satisfy everyone, but certain things do appear to stand out. For one thing, the agricultural sector seems to have been on a reasonably steady upward path from 1815; so too was the industrial sector. Indeed, so was real national product, which should settle the point except, of course, for the legion of writers who have thought otherwise. Thus, unless one can undermine the data discussed here in some significant way, this result seems sustainable on the 'evidence'.

France's cyclical record is not like the other countries we will be looking at, being more violent and more dependent on agricultural events and, for that matter, possessing more frequent downturns. This seems especially true of the period before 1870 at least; after that date the settling influence of the industrial revolution is apparent, as it is in the other countries. Even so, while the French economy was far from mature in the mid-18th century – and certainly had fluctuations far in excess of the British – it is nevertheless reasonable to think of the two countries as marching side by side in this period of rapid transformation. They are not similar, really – although some interesting commodity output figures, and the financial sophistication comparisons are surprisingly alike at time – but both countries are clearly responding to the challenges of industrialization throughout the period. As we will see, this comment can certainly be extended to Germany and Sweden – and possibly Italy – although the last two join the race a little later.

5 The Development of the German Macroeconomy

5.1 INTRODUCTION

This chapter deals mainly with the remarkable upsurge of the German economy in the 19th century. The most often-mentioned characteristic of modern Germany in discussions of its economic development is the political fragmentation of the country; this appears extreme until well into the 19th century, at least compared with all but Italy in our sample of countries. At one time it was argued that the really strong economic acceleration in Germany came sometime after the formation of the *Zollverein* in 1834, but more recent data suggest that one can just as easily go back to the immediate post-Napoleonic period – or quite possibly earlier – to locate the source of modern growth. The difference, transparently, is crucial in the interpretation of what went on in Germany, since the earlier start might easily suggest that the oft-praised and certainly more visible mid-19th century bureaucratic control in Germany might have had less to do with the rapid economic progress that country experienced than is commonly supposed. This view is certainly a controversial one. It needs to be underscored, though, that the macro-details are not often directly relevant to this dispute and, in any case, there is obviously a lot to set down about the general macro-profile of modernizing Germany – and that is the main task of this study.

The remainder of this chapter will follow the outline already established for France, but with deviations to consider topics unique to the German literature. The story begins with background material – on industry in 18th-century Germany and on population growth from 1700 to 1910 – before considering (still as background to the macroeconomics), the record of 19th-century German industrialization. Here we establish the dating of the German acceleration, which is certainly before 1850, and we also present some comparisons with France that are a little surprising, at least if one considers what the historical literature has to say about the period (for both countries). There is no agricultural discussion in this chapter, partly for want of space, although the agricultural component of the national product is singled out at an appropriate point.

The formal macroeconomic material begins with description, first of the behaviour of consumption, investment and government spending, as components of national income and then of the business cycle. In Germany, in contrast to France, there is no sign of the crowding out of investment by government spending, even in the pre-war period of the first decade of the 20th century. This is a little surprising, really, but, of course, the tests offered here are not very powerful. The German business cycle, on the other hand, has much the same character as those in the other countries in this study, in being more severe and more frequent in the earlier period (1850 to 1880) than later (up to 1910). This may well be a stabilizing effect associated with industrialization (or of the more stable markets that grew up in the wake of the industrial revolution).

With regard to the financial side of the German experience, the chapter concludes with an extended discussion of a considerable controversy over just what role commercial banks played in German expansion; it also presents some original tests. The controversy centres on the *Kreditbanken* – lenders to and sometimes controllers of industry – and whether they helped or hurt the very rapid German drive to economic maturity in this period. We find, much as we find for most of the countries considered in this study, that money is neutral, utilizing the usual Granger-causality procedure. Actually, money does not drive real income (or even the converse!) but it does, rather curiously, drive real investment in the period after 1880. In a way, this is a fence-straddle, since it is consistent both with the notion that large-scale investment was encouraged – perhaps excessively – by the particular arrangements between the banks and the large-scale firms and with the notion that banks, as usual, do not stand out as a special influence on the overall economy. Finally, there is a series of tests designed to probe the financial sophistication of Germany over this period, with several attempts to locate a satisfactory demand for money function. It seems, pretty convincingly, that this function is unstable, with Chow and CUSUM tests helping us to pinpoint a break around 1878. It should be recalled that this is the period when the French financial sector also seems unstable.

5.2 THE BACKGROUND TO GERMAN INDUSTRIAL GROWTH

Without casting any aspersions on earlier achievements, it is probably fair to say that at all times since the 12th century, Germany has had a significant role to play in the development of the European economy. In the 12th and 13th centuries, German farmers operated an efficient agricultural system that put them into the international grain trade; this was based on relatively large units and the heavy plough. By the time of the Magna Charta, Feudalism was *passé* in Germany, but Germany did retain a strong nobility and a landed aristocracy that survived into the 19th century in some instances – probably not as a feudal remnant, as is sometimes claimed, but as a free-standing economic-and-political system that participated in the broad agricultural market. This can be said in spite of the survival of serfdom in Germany into the 18th century simply because serfdom is not, *per se*, a feudal arrangement, however much it is associated with that period in Western history. Germany once had relatively abundant silver and copper deposits and from the 14th century it possessed a number of great trading and banking families, with the latter reaching their peak of influence just before the time of the influx into Europe of American silver (and gold) in the 16th and 17th centuries. Throughout this period, Germany also exported the gothic style of architecture and, in the 16th century, the Reformation.

During the wars of the Reformation, German political units were involved on both sides, with the North favouring the Protestant position and the South the Catholic, to over-simplify. A number of campaigns were fought on German soil and as a result of the Peace of Westphalia (after the Thirty Years War), the French acquired the prize territory of Alsace and Lorraine. In the period that followed, prior to the efforts of Frederick the Great of Prussia, Germany was certainly not a unified country in a political sense, but consisted of some 300 significant political units meeting in a *Reichstag* to deal with certain common problems. Centrists see in this period the roots of an apparent retardation in German growth, but it is not entirely clear, at least to this writer, that Germany (however one might want to define that term geographically) was not moving with the times in this period, with a characteristic emphasis on trading, shipping and, of course, agriculture. In any event, a degree of centralization came with Frederick's attempts to build a northern union to counterbalance the Austrian Habsburgs; at this time, 'Germany' included a sizeable piece of Poland, as well.

Napoleon, curiously, is given some credit for setting Germany on the path of its final (19th century) political cohesion, partly by design, since he literally helped to redraw the German political map in favour of more unity. Napoleon's decline left Prussia in charge of a virtual empire of the North, stretching to Westphalia and the Rhine; since this area was the source of the first industrial revolution in Germany, the stage was adequately set for further decisive political and economic developments. These came in the form of the elimination of internal tariffs in the *Zollverein* in 1834; in the development of a first-rate railroad system (beginning in the mid-1830s); in the final unification following the successful war with Austria in 1866; and in the re-acquisition, for a time, of Alsace and Lorraine (with their important coal and iron deposits) after the Franco-Prussian War in 1870. How important these political events were to the final outcome is not entirely clear, however. They do confuse the data, though, especially in the 1870s.

5.2.1 Population During German Industrialization

For our purposes, what is most relevant, considering other comparisons we have already made in this study, are the 18th and 19th-century population figures for Germany. In fact, the German story in the 18th century is parallel to that of the other prosperous parts of Western Europe, with an agricultural revolution, increased urbanization, an apparent sharp fall in the death rate but a fairly modest population growth, overall. In Chapter 1 we noted that German population growth was somewhere around 0.3 of 1 per cent from 1700 to 1820, with the last sixty years running at 0.2 per cent per year. While these rates of increase, if they are correct, are somewhat lower than the other countries studied here, it is still important to note that Germany was sharing in the general population growth of the period. Perhaps that is all that needs to be established at this point.

For the 19th century, from 1817, a much clearer set of numbers is available, as drawn from Mitchell (1978). Table 5.1 presents the basic figures, along with a set of annual compound growth rates.

Over the entire period, then, population grew at a 1.02 per cent per year rate, although somewhat unevenly, with the most rapid growth (ignoring the little spurt after the Napoleonic wars) coming during the period of most rapid industrial expansion in the last two decades

Table 5.1   German population and its growth, 1817–1910

Date	Population (ms)	Annual growth rate
1817	25.009	. . .
1820	26.101	1.42
1830	29.392	1.19
1840	32.621	1.04
1850	35.312	0.79
1860	37.611	0.63
1870	40.805	0.81
1880	45.095	1.00
1890	49.241	0.88
1900	56.056	1.30
1910	64.568	1.41

Note: These figures are for the Empire of 1913.

Table 5.2   The population of four German cities 1800–1910 (thousands)

	1800	1850	1880	1910	Annual % Change 1800–1850	Annual % Change 1850–1910
Berlin	172	419	1 122	2 071	1.78	2.66
Cologne	50	97	145	516	1.32	2.78
Hamburg	130	132	290	932	0.03	3.26
Munich	40	110	230	595	2.02	2.81
Total	392	758	1 787	4 114	1.32	2.82
5 UK cities	1 422	3 942	6 652	10 026	2.04	0.93
3 French cities	768	1 425	3 005	3 911	1.24	1.68

of the period. A relative slowdown in mid-century is also noticeable, but in any case, this is a rapid population growth, towards the upper end of rates in Western Europe at the time.

Table 5.2 presents some figures for four major German cities from 1800 to 1910 and this can provide a reasonable snapshot of the degree of urbanization in the 19th century (and a look at some data back to 1800); these data appear in Mitchell (1978). Note that Table 5.2 includes all cities having populations of 500 000 or more in 1910 in each case. Here we find German urban growth after mid-century extremely rapid compared with the other two countries, although

such comparisons mainly emphasize the speed of German urbanization during the strongest part of her industrial revolution. Indeed, the
comparison must deal with the facts that England was comparably
urban a century earlier than Germany and that France had a very
slowly growing population (and a relatively labour-intensive agricultural sector compared with the other industrial powers).

5.2.2 The Industrialization of Germany: a Sketch

Germany's industrialization begins in the 18th century, presumably
on a limited scale, at least if one disregards the view that anything
before 1850 is 'preliminary' (as in Borchardt, 1976). This early activity involved a spinning mill (1784), a coke blast furnace (1792) and
several steam engines. Around 1800, Germany was in a good position
to industrialize, but by most accounts she did not, at least at anything
like the pace of the British or the Belgians. Part of the reason this is
alleged is that important technical 'backward linkages' (to use Rostow's terminology) ran to the English mainly because that country
had a sufficient technological lead to make it appropriate to buy
machinery and even finished iron products from them. From an
international viewpoint, this is merely a detail, since the German
market was growing quite rapidly and German firms were well-
represented in certain kinds of manufacturing, as well as in commerce
and finance. But for Germany, one has to deal with the legion of
writers who see a problem in all this and, worse, who look for causes
of what is alleged to be a serious 'relative backwardness' of the
Germans.

Still considering Borchardt, the following are often given as specific
reasons for the relatively weak position of Germany. As mentioned,
a prominent factor is the pressure of British efficiency on any
attempts to initiate new enterprises. Inevitably mentioned, in addition, is the political fragmentation of Germany that led to insufficient
(official) attempts to develop economic interdependence. There
were, to be sure, over 300 independent German territories in 1789,
but perhaps this number is misleading considering that many of these
were politically (and more importantly, economically) dependent on
their larger neighbours. In any case, charges of 'feudalism' and
heavily encumbered trade routes fill the air, sufficiently, it seems, to
rank this as a serious potential cause of slower German development.[1] Vestiges of serfdom, of large landed estates, an alienation

between the ruling classes and the merchants and the partly related failure of the market economy to flower in Germany, are also mentioned in the spirit of rationalization that such a search engenders. Even so, and this is the main counter-argument, by 1780 certain significant parts of Germany – notably Saxony, the Ruhr and Westphalia – were already well on their way to industrialization. A comparison with France, where industrialization was also regionally concentrated, comes to mind at this point.

There appears to be little agreement as to whether the 1814 to 1850 period is one in which the stage was set for industrialization or whether a relatively slow industrialization was underway then. The ultimate problem, of course, lies in the absence of really good numbers – especially those for broad aggregates – and, we might as well own, a tradition in the literature that later bureaucratic reforms led the way to more rapid growth. No doubt the issue will never be resolved to everyone's satisfaction, but this is certainly the place to lay out some of the industrial numbers, partly to provide substance and partly because a careful look is just a little disquieting to the traditional perception. Although it is somewhat misleading, as we have already argued in the French case, we will base this discussion on coal, iron, and cotton, although, to be sure, no one would want to leave these out in any story of German economic development.

Table 5.3 contains a collection of figures for coal and pig iron production, comparing the German numbers with the French in this case.

Putting aside the guesses for the early part of the period, these show parallel growth in the two industries, across countries, for coal through the 1840–44 period and for pig iron through the 1855–9 period. Calculated in logarithms to facilitate the comparison of growth rates, these same numbers appear in Figure 5.1. The relationships just described stand out, but so does the upward drift of both series throughout the century. Put in more exact terms (drawing on Table 5.3 again), we find output growing as shown in Table 5.4, at compounded annual rates. If coal is the stuff of which industrial revolutions are made, then the French seem well-supplied (recalling, in this connection, that the French imported an increasingly large volume of coal as the century progressed). It is, in any case, evident that both economies were growing rapidly after 1820 and continued to do so for the rest of the century. While the German performance ultimately eclipsed that of the French, it must be remembered that coal and iron were something of a German specialty and, of course,

Table 5.3　German and French coal and iron production 1815–1910
(metric tons)

Date	Coal (ms)		Pig iron (000)	
	Germany	France	Germany	France
1815–19	1.2	0.9	70**	150
1820–24	1.2*	1.1*	75†	150
1825–29	1.6†	1.5*	90	212
1830–34	1.9	2.0	111	244
1835–39	3.0	2.9	146	327
1840–44	4.4	3.5	160	395
1845–49	6.1	4.4	184	488
1850–54	9.2	5.3	245	561
1855–59	14.7	7.6	422	900
1860–64	20.8	10.0	613	1 065
1865–69	31.0	12.7	1 012	1 262
1870–74	41.4	15.4	1 579	1 211†
1875–79	49.9	17.0	1 770	1 462
1880–84	65.7	20.2	2 893	1 918
1885–89	78.1	21.5	3 541	1 626
1890–94	94.0	26.3	4 335	1 998
1895–99	120.1	30.6	5 974	2 386
1900–4	157.3	33.0	7 925	2 665
1905–9	201.2	36.4	10 666	3 391

* First of five years, only.
† 1823/24 average.
‡ Excludes Alsace-Lorraine.
** A guess!
Source: Mitchell (1978).

that per capita calculations would bring the later numbers of the two countries somewhat closer together in view of the dramatically slower growth of the French population by the end of the century.

The figures on the third staple of the industrial revolution, the cotton industry, end up somewhat more in favour of the French in similar comparisons. Thus, in Table 5.5 we see comparisons of figures for three countries – Germany, France and the United Kingdom – expressed in thousands of metric tons (and in per cent changes). Here we see the particularly strong performance of the German economy from the 1830s, although German production is little more than half of the British total by 1913. Note that the French performance in the late 19th century is particularly strong, especially when a per capita

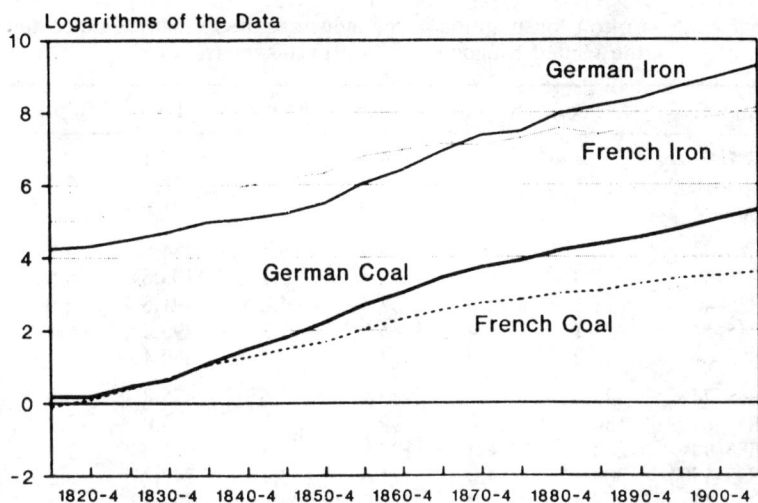

Figure 5.1   German and French iron/coal production, 1815–1910

Table 5.4

	France	Germany
Coal		
1815–19 to 1830–34	5.32%	3.06%
1815–19 to 1840–44	5.43	5.20
1840–44 to 1905–9	3.60	5.88
Iron		
1815–19 to 1830–34	3.24	3.07
1815–19 to 1840–44	4.48	4.49
1840–44 to 1905–9	2.65	6.46

adjustment is made (French production would be roughly equal to German from 1885 to 1913). These are, in any case, remarkable numbers for the German cotton industry.

Finally, and most important for the two continental economic powers we are comparing, we come to the railroad. The first German steam engine appeared in Bavaria in 1835, although the Ruhr had a horse-drawn railroad in 1828. The early German lines were government run and there was a famous plan drawn up in 1833 by the

Table 5.5 Cotton consumption in the industries of Germany, France and the United Kingdom, 1781–1913 (000 metric tons)

Date	Germany	% p.a.	France	% p.a.	UK	% p.a.
1781–91	. . .		4.0		8.1	
1791–1800	. . .		. . .		13.9	5.4
1801–14	. . .		8.0*		31.8	5.9
1815–24	. . .		18.9	8.6	54.8	4.9
1825–34	3.9*		33.5	5.7	105.6	6.6
1835–44	11.1*	14.9	54.3	4.8	191.6	6.0
1845–54	21.1	6.4	65.0	1.8	290.0	4.1
1855–64	42.0	6.9	74.1	1.3	369.4	2.4
1865–74	85.6	7.9	85.9	1.5	475.8	2.5
1875–84	134.3	4.5	99.5	1.5	605.0	2.4
1885–94	208.2	4.4	127.0	2.4	691.8	1.3
1895–1904	309.3	4.0	174.0	3.1	747.7	.8
1905–13	435.4	3.4	231.1	2.8	868.6	1.5

* The date to which this number refers differs slightly from that listed in the date column.
Source: Mitchell (1978).

economist Frederich List; the plan was not followed in detail in favour of a somewhat more easterly concentration than List had suggested. In any case, although the government initiated many projects, private enterprise provided the biggest push to the railroad industry and, coming after the *Zollverein* as it did, the railroad ran right across state lines.

Obviously, cross-country figures on railroad construction are potentially misleading, since topography, size, and the nature of the payload will vary considerably, but the unmistakable impression one gets is that the major European economic powers took to the railroad quite rapidly, once it was introduced. The figures for three countries are compared in Table 5.6, and illustrated in Figure 5.2.

In Table 5.7 we show that during the take-off for the railroad in the three countries there is virtually no difference in the rate of growth. Great Britain appears to have a five-year lead on the other two countries, but if we use the 1835 figure for Great Britain and the 1840 figures for the other two countries, their records are remarkably similar. This point has not really received much emphasis in the literature. We should emphasize here, though, that this discussion has been conducted entirely in terms of the track laid; without a

Table 5.6   Railroad track open at year end in Germany, France, and
Great Britain 1835–1910 (km)

Date	Germany	France	Great Britain
1835	6	141	544
1840	469	410	2 390*
1845	2 143	875	3 931
1850	5 856	2 915	9 797
1855	7 826	5 037	11 744
1860	11 089	9 167	14 603
1865	13 900	13 227	18 439
1870	18 876	15 544	21 558†
1875	27 970	19 357	23 365
1880	33 838	23 089	25 060
1885	37 571	29 839	26 720
1890	42 869	33 280	27 827
1895	46 500	36 240	28 986
1900	51 678	38 109	30 079
1905	56 739	39 607	31 456
1910	61 209	40 484	32 184

* Includes Ireland.
† 1871.
The figures for 1870 reflect the shift of Alsace-Lorraine.
Source: Mitchell (1978).

doubt, if one were to use tonnage and/or passenger mile statistics, the more concentrated British system would pull away from the German and French systems (in that order), at least until late in the century. Thus it appears as if railroad construction, at any rate, proceeded at a comparable pace (Table 5.7), once the systems started up, even though the engineering of European railroads initially had a lot to do with the British.[2] The annual rates of growth here are astronomical, really, and it is clear that the forward and backward linkages that the railroads must have provided were considerable. It is, in any case, as close to a parallel growth as one could reasonably expect, qualified, of course, by the geographical and demographic differences among the three countries.

km of Track Laid (Thousands)

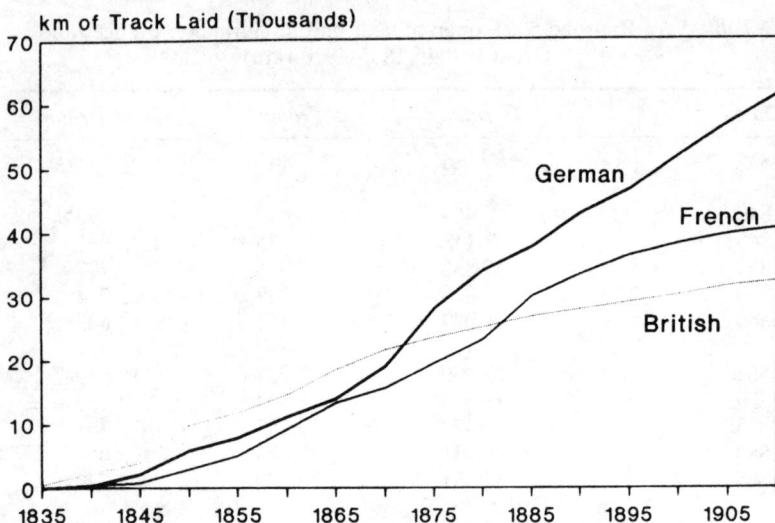

Figure 5.2   German, French and British railroads, 1835–1910

Table 5.7   The growth of the railroad systems of Germany, France, and
               Great Britain during their respective take-offs

	Average track laid per year	*Annual % change*
Germany (1840–60)	531.0	15.8
France (1840–60)	437.8	15.5
Great Britain (1835–60)	560.0	15.4

Source: Mitchell (1978)

5.3   THE DEVELOPMENT OF THE AGGREGATE ECONOMY IN GERMANY AFTER 1850

Germany in 1850 was already growing industrially, as we have seen,
but the period we are describing contains what is undoubtedly one
of the strongest spurts in the endogenous economic growth of any
country at any time in history. This provides ample reason for looking
at the (aggregate) details. We have already remarked that rapid
population growth was important to the German performance; while
this is inevitably hard to demonstrate, Table 5.8 shows that the more

Table 5.8   German growth

	Real production	Compound growth rates in Money	Prices	Population
1850–1910	2.674	3.853	0.402	0.995
1850–1870	2.531	4.200	0.758	0.764
1871–1910	2.674	3.721	0.095	1.156
1881–1910	3.016	5.677	0.475	1.126

rapidly growing periods also had more rapidly growing population. The relation with the growth of the money supply is not particularly distinct, in contrast. In any case, German growth is quite rapid throughout this period, and not much more rapid at the end than at the beginning. It is also noticeable that while German inflation rates were in line with those in the rest of the world, as befits a country playing by the gold standard rules, German money stock growth surely was not. Evidently, the rapid rate of growth of the German economy and the manner in which the German central bank managed the gold standard enabled the Germans to bypass this pressure on prices. We will return to this topic below, and offer a review of the literature, some causality results and some estimates of the demand for money that bear on the question of how the relatively rapid monetary growth was absorbed.

Next, consider the growth of real national product in Germany. Figure 5.3 plots real net national product (on the left axis) and real capital formation (on the right). Granted that the scales are different, these show roughly that there is nothing unusual about German growth in that capital formation accompanied the growth of the economy. Perhaps this ought to be emphasized, however, since the literature tends to spend more time on what are largely peripheral issues about growth. Of course we are not necessarily talking about the causes of this growth, just noting an important characteristic.

The next topic concerns the broad relations among consumption, investment, government spending and national income. Figure 5.4 carries this information in ratio form. Very apparently, government spending is not a factor in the trends here, except at the very end of the period, being pretty much a constant at something usually less than 8 per cent of net national product, while the upward drift of the investment ratio is matched by the downward drift of the consumption ratio. This is not the pattern in the slower growing French economy, and it is also not the case, as we shall see in Chapter 6, of

National Product

Investment

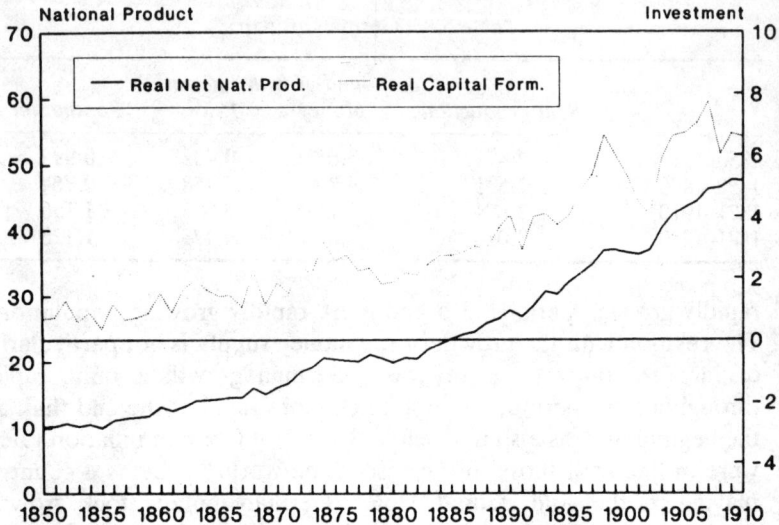

Figure 5.3 Growth and capital formation in Germany, 1850–1910

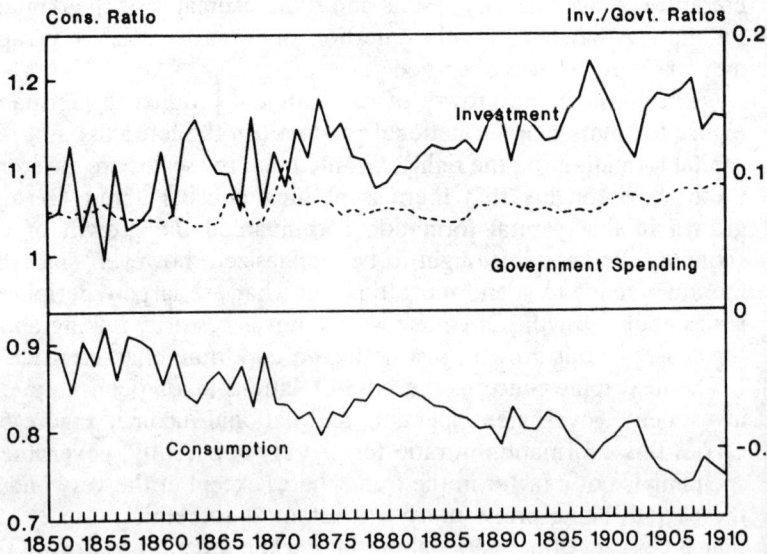

Figure 5.4 Spending ratios in real national product, 1850–1910

Table 5.9 C/Y, I/Y and G/Y averages by decade

	C/Y	I/Y	G/Y
1851–60	0.885	0.080	0.070
1861–70	0.856	0.106	0.071
1871–80	0.826	0.115	0.079
1881–90	0.819	0.119	0.071
1891–1900	0.797	0.142	0.074
1901–10	0.763	0.143	0.085

the rapidly growing Swedish economy. But the Germans saved to achieve their growth, and that is the bottom line.

We should look at the averages by decade given in Table 5.9, because there actually is something going on in the level figures just mentioned.[3] If these numbers should stand up over time, this is quite a remarkable upsurge of relative private investment, and is unlike anything we have to show for any of the other European economies. To dramatize this further, we note that the correlation coefficient between C/Y and I/Y for the entire period is −0.913 while that for the G/Y and I/Y is 0.151.[4] Clearly, whether interest rates were affected or not there is probably no crowding out by government spending here, and, if the usage makes sense, what really happened is that investment crowded out consumption.

Finally, we turn to the German business cycle. The raw figures for real NNP behind Figure 5.3 actually show a number of recessions in the 60-year period; the years of decline and the percentage decreases are as follows:

1853	4.41%	1875–7	2.86%	1891	3.36%
1855	5.88	1879–80	2.80	1894	1.34
1861	4.42	1882–80	0.83	1900–1	1.80
1869	5.78			1910	0.12

These events come in one of every four years (a very modern ratio, really), but only in one of every six years in the last 30 years of the period. They are also of decreasing severity as time goes on (and the weight of the more volatile agricultural sector diminishes). This oft-noted effect of industrialization has also been mentioned in the British and French data already discussed in this study.[5]

5.4   THE ROLE OF MONEY IN THE GERMAN EXPANSION

Now let us turn to the macro-financial questions that we have raised at earlier points in this study, on the 1850–1910 German data in this case. In the case of Germany, of course, there is considerable interest in exactly how the financial sector might have contributed to German growth. The story begins in Section 5.4.1 with the strongest statement for this effect, drawn from the historical literature essentially. This is a complicated issue, and so requires considerable space. Having established the hypothesis, then, the discussion turns in succeeding sub-sections to the macroempirical tests that we have been featuring. These begin with causality tests (that show no causality running from money to real income) and conclude with a discussion of financial sophistication and the demand for money. The results for the latter two topics do provide some possible support for the unique role of the German financial system, at the macroeconomic level of detail we have adopted.

5.4.1   The Development of the German Financial System

Modern-style banks of issue first appeared in Germany in the 1830s; the first was the Bavarian Mortgage and Discount Bank. The more important Prussian Bank of 1846 took over the assets and liabilities of the Royal Bank of Prussia; it was privately owned but regulated by the government in the central banking style of the times. Other states set up note issuing banks from 1847. Even so, private banks were the dominant form of banking enterprise, and they were ubiquitous throughout the period from 1815 to 1870. In Prussia alone there were 330 of these institutions in 1820/1 and their number grew to 642 by 1861 (Tilly, 1967).[6] But their direct contribution to industrial fixed capital was probably quite small. Banks that did lend to industry were the *Kreditbanken*, the first of which was the Schaaffhausen'schen Bankverein in Cologne, which was founded in 1848. Subsequently, attempts to emulate the apparent success of the French Crédit Mobilier motivated growth in this type of bank (after 1852).[7] Their growth in the 1860s was quite rapid.

The German currency has a mixed hard-and-paper standard up until the 1870s, but the Prussian Bank's note circulation dominated, reaching 40 per cent by 1865.[8] Tilly (1967) is, on the whole, very positive about the role of banking in this period, taking 'banking' in a very broad sense. Even as merely discounters of bills of exchange, he argues, banks became heavily involved in shaping the capital markets and (we should add) they surely played a major role in providing information on the credit worthiness of their customers to the general capital markets, whether they were directly involved in long-term capital projects or not. The notion that banks derive their rewards for providing information in an uncertain world is actually the theme of a second paper by Tilly (1986), that carries the story through to 1914. Tilly argues here that 'mixed banking' in Germany in the 1830–70 period was closely associated with the rapid development of the economy (especially that of the German railroads). Bankers guided (or even controlled) the finances of many major enterprises, and in some cases explicitly involved themselves in capital projects. Partly as a consequence, he argues, many banks born in the boom years up until 1870 were evidently based on shaky foundations (p. 124),

> In the wreckage of the financial crisis of 1873 and the long depression which followed it, large numbers of newly created corporate enterprises became insolvent. . . . Banks were especially hard hit. . . . According to one statistical count (for Prussia) more banks went down in the crash than had existed in early 1870.

The free incorporation law of 1870 is mentioned in this connection; this legislation was revised in 1884 in the direction of making incorporation more difficult. On net, then, Tilly believes that banks' portfolios became excessively specialized in certain risky ventures primarily as they served their main customers – the large industrial enterprises. As a postscript, the Reichsbank (the central bank) was established in the mid-1870s and Germany signed on to the gold standard in 1876. While their adherence to the gold standard may well have been half-hearted (see below), the ensuing period was certainly one of relative financial tranquillity.

Tilly's 1986 paper is mainly a contribution to a debate stirred up by Neuberger and Stokes (1974, 1975) over the role of the *Kreditbanken* in Germany's growth from 1883 to 1914. In contrast to, for example, J. Schumpeter (1939), Neuberger and Stokes argue (1974, p. 711),

> that the credit allocation policy of these banks was inhibiting rather than stimulating the Germany economy in the period for which data are available and that previous interpretations are in need of serious revision.

This view is based on a comparison of the benefits versus the costs that must have been incurred in allowing commercial banks so dominant a role in the control of the firm.[9] Neuberger and Stokes attempt to measure a *substitution effect* of higher cost accounts that leads to inefficiency, a *credit* (providing) *effect* that promotes growth, and an *institutional effect* of ambiguous sign.[10]

The way Neuberger and Stokes measure these effects – or rather, calculate the sign of the net effect – is to employ a growth model to calculate the 'credit-constant total effect' on the non-agricultural output of the German economy. A Cobb–Douglas production function is estimated with capital and labour as factors, and with their credit effect as a shift parameter. The estimated function shows increasing returns to scale and, more to the point, a negative effect of their credit proxy on growth – on, they argue, efficiency.[11] Indeed, subsequent calculations suggest to Neuberger and Stokes that the increasing returns to scale themselves (which they argue is evidence of an oligopolistic market structure) may have themselves been due to the operation of the selfsame *Kreditbanken*.

It is certainly possible to worry about the model – Are more factors relevant? Should the elasticity of substitution between capital and labour be assumed to be unitary (as the Cobb–Douglas does)? – or the data. Fremdling and Tilly (1976) question the latter, to some extent. Pointing out that the jury is not in on exactly how much the current account (a working capital account for large firms) drew from the fixed capital stock and how competitive the rates paid by banks were, they also question whether primarily serving large-scale industry necessarily leads to over-all inefficiency. More seriously, they believe that both the capital stock data and the current account credits data employed by Neuberger and Stokes do not correspond to the needs of their particular model. In the case of the former Fremdling and Tilly appear to be mistaken, but questions about data go with the territory in this sort of work and they should not be taken lightly, since what often appear to be small changes in the numbers all too frequently totally destroy an argument based on a certain significant coefficient.[12]

There is, of course, the possibility of employing other sorts of tests, and this Tilly does (1986), utilizing a model for measuring efficient portfolios. The approach requires identifying a set of portfolios for the German economy that (p. 131),

> are efficient in the sense of representing maximum yields for given variances and which, according to the underlying portfolio theory, contain no diversifiable risk.

This frontier is then compared with the portfolios of the credit banks (over the period 1880 to 1913). As it turns out, these banks appear concentrated in high-risk, high-yield sectors that are, in turn, major sectors in the rapidly growing German economy. Further, he argues, the portfolio appears to have been efficient, with the risky position stabilized by the low-yield corporate business that banks also engaged in (e.g., the current accounts discussed above). It (one observation, unfortunately) lies just within the efficient frontier. Thus it is possible that a different sort of efficiency was actually achieved by German banks,[13] although one must note that problems with the data (and with the working assumptions) are not absent from the Tilly study.[14]

Finally, let us return to a topic introduced a few pages back, and consider just how Germany participated in the international gold standard during this period. Germany joined the gold standard system in 1876; formally, they clearly did not play by the rules (Bloomfield, 1959) but, according to Sommariva and Tullio (1987, 1988), the evidence suggests that German central bank bahaviour can be explained with reference to the monetary approach to the balance of payments, a theory that provides an alternative channel of influence to the specie-flow mechanism usually advocated by the quantity theorists.[15] In particular, Sommariva and Tullio find that an increase in German output and prices induced a gold and silver inflow into Germany while an increase in Reichsbank domestic assets induced an outflow. The negative correlation between the domestic and foreign assets of the Reichsbank (the supposed violation of the rules of the game, as identified by Bloomfield) is attributed to bi-directional causation between the two accounts and not to a policy sterilization of gold flows. The Reichsbank did, however, play a role.

Looking further into the details, McGouldrick (1984) shows that gold inflows were actually cyclically neutral in Germany and that base money (p. 321) 'grew at a remarkably stable pace over German business cycles.' Indeed, base money actually had a slightly counter-cyclical tendency. He argues that the Reichsbank stabilized (not sterilized!) gold inflows in this period by means of bill discount rate policy. He concludes (p. 346),

> The contrasting relative stability of the monetary realm therefore stands as strong testimony to the advantages of the pre-1914 gold standard when properly ruled by a central bank.

But Germany grew very rapidly during this period, with substantial

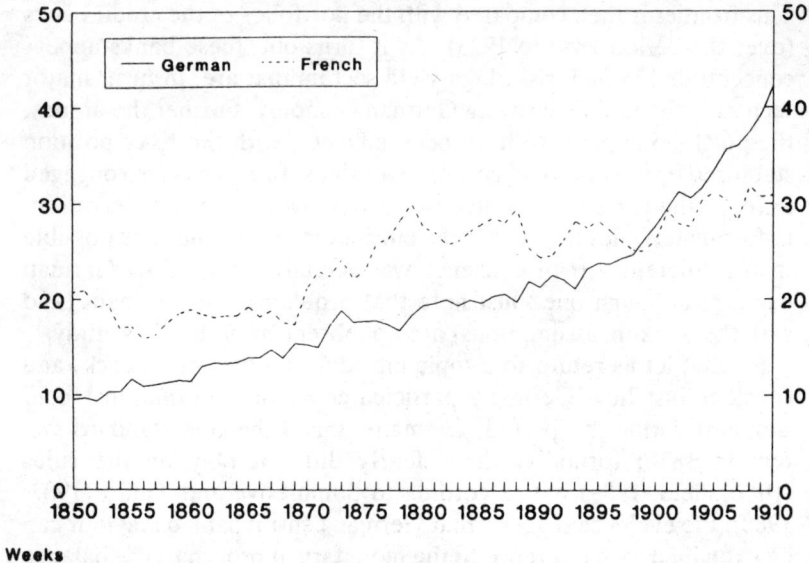

Weeks

Figure 5.5   Financial sophistication indices, 1850–1910

export earnings, and it is certainly hard to believe that the gold standard exerted any real pressure on the monetary authorities.

5.4.2   Germany's Financial Sophistication

We have raised the question of financial sophistication in the case of Germany. And, as elsewhere in this study, there is a direct, but of course very provisional way to deal with this. This is in the form of the financial sophistication index, expressed as the number of weeks of nominal net national product that the average German holds in the form of money. As we saw in Chapter 3, this velocity-based concept produced level figures for the British case, but a sharply-rising graph – interpreted as evidence of the increasing role of money ('sophistication'?) in the US case; the French result in Chapter 4 lay somewhere in between.[16] Here, partly for perspective and partly because it provides an interesting comparison in view of the debates in the literature, we present in Figure 5.5 results for Germany compared with France for the 1850 to 1910 period. Note that the measure of the money stock is M2 (broad money) on account of the notion that it is the broad activities of the banking system in which we are interested.

The German financial sophistication index, compared to the French, is quite low in 1850, at less than 10 in terms of the number of weeks of national product held in the form of bank money. Then, while the French index grows slowly and somewhat unevenly, the German holds to a fairly stable growth rate (not, though, in the early 1870s). From the late 1890s the index really spurts ahead, moving ahead of the French for the first time in 1899. 'Stability' might be a word that would leap to mind to describe the German experience before the late 1890s, but not 'leading sector', at least on this rather flimsy evidence.

5.4.3   Monetary Neutrality in Germany

Whether or not one is comfortable with the notion of 'financial sophistication' just described, it is apparent that growth of the money stock – and more particularly growth of the services provided by the commercial banking system (and any sector that benefited either publicly or privately) – was important to the German economy in this period. The next question, then, is whether (or, really, what) causal relationships stand out in this period, again as judged by the Granger-causality procedure.

The first set of tests involves the traditional test of neutrality between money and a measure of real output. If we believe in neutrality, then what we expect is that money will not Granger-cause real product; the converse test, though, of real product on money might easily show a Granger-causal relationship. Table 5.10 collects the results of tests of the standard Granger model, performing the test on log-level, log-detrended (by regression on trend), and differenced-logs of the per capita data on real output and money.

The results collected in Table 5.10 refer to three specifications simply because of the possibility that detrending in different ways could produce different (and therefore interesting) results. The results are a little mixed, on the whole, although by the most rigorous test (the differenced logs in the first five rows) there is no sign of causality in either direction. For the other methods of treating the data, monetary non-neutrality does appear; these results are suspect to some observers because the basic data themselves cannot be demonstrated to be stationary. On the whole, then, we would have to argue that monetary non-neutrality is not established on these numbers, although breaking the data into subperiods creates more than a suspicion that money helped boost the real economy along during the

Table 5.10 Neutrality tests for Germany. Money and real net national product (per capita form)

		1850–1910		1850–1880		1880–1910	
		$M \to Y$	$Y \to M$	$M \to Y$	$Y \to M$	$M \to Y$	$Y \to M$
Differenced-log	1	0.053	0.347	0.072	0.608	0.702	0.487
	2	0.123	0.256	0.079	0.466	0.122	0.593
	3	0.165	0.180	0.051	0.276	0.200	0.541
	4	0.298	0.334	0.124	0.429	0.404	0.131
	5	0.472	0.434	0.129	0.576	0.083	0.165
Log-DT	1	0.090	0.879	0.001*	0.910	0.086	0.846
	2	0.109	0.566	0.006*	0.656	0.066	0.726
	3	0.238	0.245	0.019*	0.381	0.154	0.726
	4	0.400	0.335	0.079	0.522	0.064	0.409
	5	0.618	0.496	0.104	0.551	0.074	0.288
Log-level	1	0.006*	0.860	0.000*	0.937	0.276	0.273
	2	0.017*	0.647	0.002*	0.834	0.460	0.323
	3	0.035*	0.366	0.003*	0.551	0.219	0.176
	4	0.119	0.306	0.021*	0.465	0.314	0.258
	5	0.190	0.453	0.008*	0.516	0.109	0.112

* Significant at 0.05 or less

period between 1850 and 1870. Our review of the historical literature suggests that this result would find a lot of support.

The argument in the literature that was presented earlier really focuses attention on the relationship between banks and the creation of fixed capital. Of course we would expect that the creation of fixed capital would, in turn, raise real output (at least if we were Keynesians, we would expect this), but we are already forewarned that by favouring large-scale firms, banks may have directed too much capital toward that sector, at the expense of faster growing and more useful smaller firms – or even firms in the non-industrial sector. The data exist on real capital formation, and so Table 5.11 undertakes a rerun of the test just described, this time probing for a Granger-causal relation between nominal per capita money balances and real per capita capital formation.

Actually, all three methods of treating the data show non-neutrality for the period as a whole as well as for both sub-periods (except for the differenced-log specification for the 1880 to 1910 period). Thus, one could argue that money helps drive investment in

Table 5.11   Neutrality tests for Germany. Money and real capital
formation (per capita form)

		1850–1910		1850–1880		1880–1910	
		$M \rightarrow I$	$I \rightarrow M$	$M \rightarrow I$	$I \rightarrow M$	$M \rightarrow I$	$I \rightarrow M$
Differenced-log	1	0.041*	0.749	0.131	0.878	0.396	0.529
	2	0.038*	0.613	0.081	0.707	0.075	0.809
	3	0.021*	0.488	0.049*	0.589	0.056	0.933
	4	0.053	0.694	0.158	0.683	0.104	0.312
	5	0.039*	0.757	0.105	0.812	0.204	0.126
Log-DT	1	0.010*	0.497	0.001*	0.868	0.262	0.276
	2	0.068	0.824	0.024*	0.880	0.134	0.649
	3	0.074	0.485	0.064	0.689	0.093	0.540
	4	0.058	0.603	0.109	0.764	0.017*	0.466
	5	0.154	0.780	0.321	0.839	0.021*	0.524
Log-level	1	0.000*	0.370	0.000*	0.641	0.047*	0.770
	2	0.001*	0.591	0.043*	0.909	0.079	0.977
	3	0.001*	0.286	0.019*	0.664	0.066	0.516
	4	0.003*	0.439	0.046*	0.745	0.019*	0.598
	5	0.004*	0.650	0.080	0.807	0.073	0.315

* Significant at 0.05 or less

Germany. More conservatively, in view of the doubts one might have
about the effect of using non-stationary data in the Granger-causality
test, the two detrended series show causality between money and real
investment only in the first 30 years of the 60 year period. This is not a
period for which the excess capital argument has been demonstrated
empirically, but we note that the real effect on investment was not
(with the two methods of detrending) accompanied by any real effect
of money on real product itself. But that is about as far as these tests
can take us.

There is one other thing that money is often alleged to do, and that
is to drive the price level. Actually, if it does not drive real income,
then, unless the price level is determined by some other factors,
money ought to drive that. A problem that is immediately apparent,
before looking at the results of a Granger test, was revealed in
Section 5.4; this is that the money stock grew at a compound rate of
3.85 per cent per year from 1850 to 1910, while the price level (the
NNP deflator) only grew by 0.40 of 1 per cent). Much of the difference was absorbed by the rapid growth of the economy, clearly, but

Table 5.12   Money and the price level in Germany. Broad money and the NNP deflator

		1850–1910		1850–1880		1880–1910	
		$M \to P$	$P \to M$	$M \to P$	$P \to M$	$M \to P$	$P \to M$
Differenced-log	1	0.565	0.330	0.745	0.318	0.593	0.928
	2	0.386	0.497	0.473	0.524	0.749	0.956
	3	0.742	0.067	0.755	0.170	0.205	0.438
	4	0.730	0.227	0.679	0.434	0.344	0.698
	5	0.480	0.111	0.839	0.136	0.033*	0.144
Log-DT	1	0.035*	0.819	0.726	0.469	0.074	0.432
	2	0.126	0.436	0.707	0.411	0.128	0.600
	3	0.111	0.421	0.848	0.601	0.103	0.818
	4	0.102	0.142	0.949	0.180	0.060	0.629
	5	0.248	0.265	0.669	0.231	0.136	0.809
Log-level	1	0.059	0.446	0.285	0.736	0.009*	0.091
	2	0.036*	0.199	0.088	0.652	0.033*	0.085
	3	0.036*	0.189	0.103	0.718	0.004*	0.118
	4	0.264	0.078	0.503	0.280	0.050*	0.156
	5	0.409	0.217	0.173	0.566	0.030*	0.047*

* Significant at 0.05 or less

as much as 2 per cent per year excess growth of the money stock cannot be directly attributed to that influence. As will be pointed out in the next section, it seems that this extra money was willingly absorbed into cash balances in that the demand may well have had an income elasticity well in excess of unity. The financial sophistication argument also leads one in this direction.

The results of the Granger-causality tests between money and the price level in Germany are set out in Table 5.12. This set of results does not show much influence of money on the price level, but what there is seems to be concentrated in the 1880 to 1910 period, when Germany was on the Gold Standard. That is not unreasonable, really, and suggests that to some extent, possibly at very long lags, the German central bank did permit the money supply (and hence prices) to conform to international norms (as adherence to the rules of the game in international payments would imply). But the evidence is not strong, being limited to a rather strong set of log-linear results (at all lags) and one lone result with differenced data (at a longish lag of five years).

Table 5.13   The German demand for money, 1850–1910 (logarithms of per capita real data)

	1850–1910		1850–1880		1880–1910	
Constant	−1.348	(0.15)	1.891	(0.12)	−10.080	(10.66)
Income	0.294	(1.88)	0.622	(2.16)	2.313	(21.23)
Interest rate	−0.060	(1.38)	−0.036	(0.46)	0.308	(3.08)
AR(1)	0.607	(4.32)	0.587	(2.69)	0.474	(2.45)
AR(2)	0.401	(2.81)	0.410	(1.78)	−0.218	(1.43)
DW	1.412		1.442		2.019	
R^2-bar	0.994		0.951		0.973	

The long-term interest rate variable is not in logarithmic form.

5.4.4 Money Demand

Obviously, the next job, and the last attempted in this chapter, aside from a badly needed summing up, is to see whether some of the suspicions just phrased, about the sub-periods being different with respect to the role of money *vis-à-vis* the real economy are upheld with respect to estimates of the demand for money. This turns out to be a very complex undertaking, as the following results will immediately suggest, because there is strong evidence that the demand for money is unstable (or at least different) across the sub-periods of the data. We will, accordingly, invest some space in investigating this issue, introducing some new tests as we proceed.

Let us, in order to try to get a fix on the situation, estimate several sets of completely conventional single-equation money-demand functions. These are in per capita real form and appear in Table 5.13. Putting aside the slightly better performance in terms of the coefficient of determination (at 0.996) in the overall tests, one must view with suspicion any statement that the demand for money might have been stable over the entire period, at least on this simple exercise. The income elasticity of demand is above 2 in the later period, which is what one might expect from an economy that is building its financial system from a relatively unsophisticated level, but, curiously, this is not shown for the earlier period. This, certainly, suggests where the money balances may have gone (idle, to some extent, as part of the cost of obtaining bank services in this period of rapid growth). It is possibly a little surprising that the value of the income

Table 5.14   The German demand for money. Two interest rate form
(logarithms of per capita real data)

	1850–1910		1850–1880		1880–1910	
Constant	1.581	(0.86)	4.724	(0.04)	–11.290	(11.62)
Income	0.643	(3.11)	0.293	(1.04)	2.446	(22.01)
Long rate	–0.039	(0.64)	–0.070	(0.86)	0.440	(4.29)
Short rate	0.000	(0.02)	0.008	(0.66)	–0.041	(2.53)
AR(1)	0.570	(3.48)	0.755	(3.03)	0.479	(2.45)
AR(2)	0.434	(2.59)	0.245	(0.94)	–0.232	(1.62)
DW	1.069		1.209		2.135	
R^2-bar	0.990		0.953		0.978	

The interest rate variables are not in logarithmic form.

elasticity is higher in the later period than in the earlier, when banks are given credit for helping to drive the system, but the results do fit in somewhat with some of the institutional material we have gone over.

The three tests are all run with AR(1) and AR(2) terms; this adjustment is significant (or close) in all three tests. Results were obtained for different AR structures, of course, and these are sometimes different across the three arrangements of the data, but the best specifications appeared to be those given; in any case, it is certainly convenient to have all specifications the same so that we can concentrate on the substantive hypotheses. What is peculiar, of course, is the sign of the long-term interest rate (positive) in the last period; this suggests quite strongly that there is some misspecification of the model, rather than non-stability, necessarily. That is, an increase in what is presumed to be the opportunity cost of holding money balances should not (normally) be expected to come in with a positive sign unless, of course, it is measuring something else (such as the direct productivity of money). If it is doing that, though, we would need to include an opportunity cost as well. A short-term rate is available (it did not work by itself in the above tests), and so Table 5.14 shows the results of including two rates in the same specification as given in Table 5.13. Only for the final period, as one might expect, does the short-term rate – a market discount rate – enter. Not only that, but it enters with a significant and negative sign, indicating that it could be representing the opportunity cost variable, with the long-term rate – with its significantly positive sign – representing the direct productivity of money, possibly. The fit of the model is slightly better, for the third period, in the case of the two-interest rate formulation, incidentally.

Results such as these are tantalizing, of course, and further work needs to be done. The most obvious problem here, which we now address, concerns the potential instability of the function across (at least) the two periods identified. In order to probe for structural instability (following Komlos's (1987) paper) we might attempt CUSUM and CUSUM-Squared tests. Unfortunately, these were not available for models with autoregressive error structures such as those just exhibited, so we have fallen back on a simpler structure, without those terms. This is not as bad as it seems, however, since the results for the two sub-periods are reasonably similar to those in Table 5.14 even without those terms.[17]

The CUSUM test plots the cumulative sum of recursive residuals against two lines that represent a confidence interval (at the 5 per cent level) around the residuals; should the plot lie outside these lines, then one can claim instability for those observations at (at least) the 5 per cent level. The formula for the CUSUM plot for the two interest rate model without AR terms is

$$W_p = \frac{1}{\sigma} \sum_{i=k+1}^{p} v_i \qquad p = k+1, k+2, \ldots, n \qquad (5.1)$$

Here σ is the standard error of the regression.[18] As Figure 5.6 shows, this test does not establish a case for instability except, of course, at the very end. A second test that is available, of the same sort, is the CUSUM-Square test, which works with the cumulative sum of squared residuals. The formula for this model is

$$WW_p = \frac{\sum_{i=k+1}^{p} v_i^2}{\sum_{i=k+1}^{p} v_i^2} \qquad p = k+1, k+2, \ldots, n \qquad (5.2)$$

Again, one plots two lines for an arbitrary confidence interval which is, in this case, 5 per cent.[19] In this case there does appear to be a period running from the mid-1890s into the 20th century, where the plot wanders outside the confidence intervals (indicating instability).

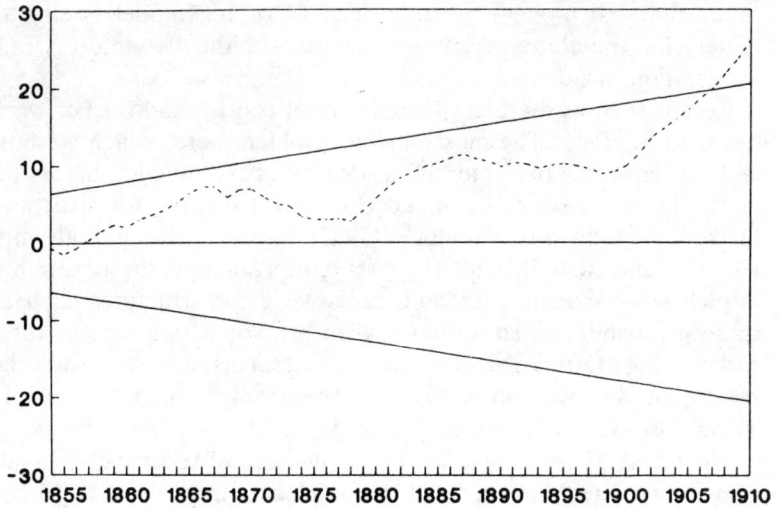

5 Percent Level

Figure 5.6   CUSUM test, German money demand, 1854–1910

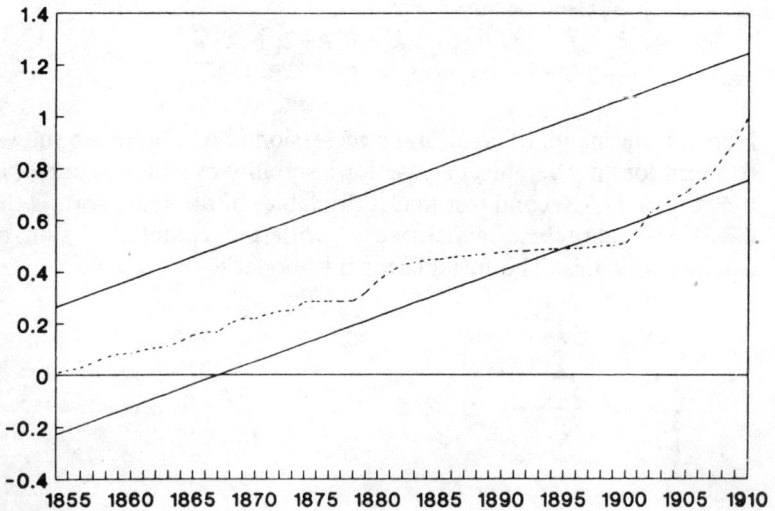

5 Percent Level

Figure 5.7   CUSUM square test, German money demand, 1854–1910

Table 5.15   The German demand for money. Chow-tested version

	1850–1878		1879–1910	
Constant	–4.772	(9.12)	–10.901	(13.59)
Income	1.587	(19.41)	2.418	(26.20)
Long rate	0.045	(0.50)	0.375	(4.67)
Short rate	0.002	(0.12)	–0.032	(2.06)
DW	1.638		1.196	
R^2-bar	0.937		0.973	

A more familiar test to some users is the Chow (1960) analysis of variance test for structural instability. This test also gives us a method for probing for the breaking point (if such is established) by searching over all possible splits for the highest F-value produced by the test. The test looks for equality of coefficients between two periods, conditional on having the two variances equal. For the two interest rate model this procedure produces a break in 1878, as shown in Table 5.15.

The value of the F-statistic here was 13.788, which is certainly significant at the 0.05 per cent level. This test, too, confirms that there is a dramatic change in the demand for money (if one can accept the simple model and the rather unsatisfactory Durbin–Watson statistic in the 1879 to 1910 result) during the period. It is worth remarking that the break occurs shortly after Germany went on to the Gold Standard (in 1876). Since the income elasticity of the demand for bank money did increase significantly during this period, it could be that the new system of regulation increased public confidence in the banking system; it produced, in effect, a superior financial product.

5.5 CONCLUSION

The story of Germany's successful rise to predominance among the European industrial powers has often been told. It is clear that what should be emphasized is the combination of human and natural resources along with a culture that responded to their new economic challenges in an appropriate way. What is not so clear, but an early theme in this chapter, is that what happened sometime in the 19th century is really a continuation of German development begun many centuries earlier. It is equally important to realize that while Germany benefited from its many advantages in the industrial race, she was matched step-by-step in many areas by at least some of her European counterparts during the period.

What leverage on these traditional topics does a macroeconomic perspective exert? For one thing, we have pointed out that two sectors given a lot of credit for playing a special role in the German case – the government and the commercial banking system – do not appear to have done so. For the government, this is possibly an overstatement, to be sure, but an inspection of the timing of the *Zollverein* (somewhat after the German expansion had begun), of the government involvement in railroads (quickly and effectively replaced by private enterprise) and of political unification (occurring after the industrial path was apparently joined) lend some credence to this view. For government expenditures, indeed, our conclusion is that they played no special role in the upsurge.

For the monetary sector, we found monetary neutrality, a typical result in this study, but neutrality of a rather special kind. In fact, there was a link between the money stock and real investment spending during the period studied, but either the model (and/or the data) was unable to identify the next link (to real GNP) or the literature is correct in suggesting that an inefficient allocation of investment resources was produced in this period by the specific strategies of the large commercial banks. Finally, one government policy that may have made a difference, possibly coincidentally, was the adoption of the Gold Standard (and the enfranchisement of the central bank) in the 1870s. The difference was possibly real, although there is no documentation to that effect in this chapter, but there certainly is clear evidence that a superior monetary product was created, evidence in the form of an apparent shift in the demand for money (in, that is to say, the demand for financial services). One manifestation of this was the sharply higher income elasticity of the demand for money later on.

Finally, we should note that while much of this chapter has been devoted to the German story, we have played our international theme from time to time. While the general interaction of the German economy was transparent, we went to special pains to document the similarity with France on an industry level. We also noted that German business cycles were similar to those in most of the other countries in this study in having decreasing amplitude as we approach

1910. Some of this is not fully documented in this chapter – nor is the Granger-causality evidence on German–European interaction in both real and nominal terms – in view of the extended discussion of these topics in Chapter 8.

6 Sweden during the Industrial Revolution

6.1 INTRODUCTION

Among the major European countries that are important in the industrial revolution, Sweden stands out as a particularly clear example of a country with a special role to play. Long before the industrial revolution, Sweden had a distinguished record as a European political power – even possessing a Baltic 'empire' in the 17th and early 18th centuries – and a solid economic base, based on the agricultural and extractive sectors of the economy, but it appears to have missed much of the first industrial revolution (to 1850), at least in the traditional product lines. Indeed, it has been claimed (Sandberg, 1979, p. 225) that Sweden was actually 'impoverished but sophisticated' in 1850, after as many as 150 years of a relative economic decline (meaning that it had a growth rate that was significantly lower than the European average). By 'sophisticated' Sandberg means that Sweden 'had a strikingly large stock of human and institutional capital' compared with the rest of Europe (p. 225).

> This conclusion is based on data on literacy levels, numbers of students attending schools and universities, the quality and quantity of scientific and technical research, infant mortality rates and life expectancy figures, and the remarkable size and efficiency of the modern financial system.

As a direct result, argues Sandberg, in the 60 years after 1850 'Sweden had the highest rate of growth of per capita GNP and the second highest rate of growth of total GNP' among the growing European countries. Since this comparison includes one with Germany, it is clearly a remarkable performance, to say the least.

Sweden differs from the British model of industrialization in several important respects. For one thing, Sweden had a relatively large agricultural sector with a population that derived a similarly large part of its income from farming and extraction; this contrasts with Britain or Belgium (but not France) among the early continental

190

developers. For another, like a modern developing country, Sweden's spurt in the 19th century, beginning as early as the 1830s, is related to very rapid growth in her export sector. The products involved, differing in relative importance from time to time, are mostly primary, with timber, oats and iron ore leading the way. At the same time, Sweden had a strong international position in specialty iron and steel products, although Swedish railroad development was not fully underway until the mid-to-late 1850s. The result of all this was a burst in the late 1800s that produced possibly the most rapid growth (per capita) in Europe. In any case, whatever the impetus, by 1910 Sweden was well on its way industrially, much like her closest competitors in the industrial race.

The puzzle in all of this concerns how a relatively impoverished economy that was as much as 90 per cent agricultural in 1850 could achieve such a record in only 60 years. It appears that no other European country moved so rapidly – that is, if we accept the description of Sweden in 1850 as at all accurate – and partly because it tends to damage the hypothesis of a long capitalistic preconditioning for successful industrialization, the Swedish case stands out as central to the debate over the *modus operandi* of the industrial revolution. It also stands as a potential success story for modern-day lesser developed economies. Sandberg, as already noted, has one possible answer – the Swedes had abundant human and financial capital – and needed only an opportunity to get going, which the industrial revolution in other countries provided. Another possible answer is, more prosaically, that the usual descriptions of Sweden's economic status from, say, 1700 to 1850 are simply in error. The kind of error one might expect is the failure to appreciate the extent of proto- or light industry or of the service sector, and of the development and deployment of movable human capital. In this chapter we will not address the question of Sweden's background directly, not having any solid macroeconomic data on which to base such a discussion, but we will certainly tackle questions of what happened during the rise after 1850 and offer points of comparison (and causal tests) involving the various hypotheses that have been lurking in the corners of this preliminary discussion.

The following sections stick to the arrangement of the other chapters in this study, but adapt it to the debates appearing in the Swedish literature. The discussion of population, agriculture, and industry appears in Section 6.2. This section features a discussion of the unusual population exodus that occurred; this was largely a flow from the farm directly to the United States although, of course, Swedish cities did expand with the industrial sector. Much of the explanation is tied up with conditions in the agricultural sector, but some place needs to be given to the unusual development of Sweden's human capital before the exodus.

For the macroeconomics, Sweden's growth is so rapid, and her cycles so infrequent, as to require us to use relatively little space to get this material across. This is done in Section 6.3. This particular section also considers the macroeconomic profile of Sweden at the time of her industrial spurt, in the sense of consumption, investment and government spending as proportions of national product. Section 6.4 undertakes a detailed discussion of the financial sophistication of Sweden during this period. This material is partly shaped by the literature – by Sandberg in particular – and partly by the opportunity, given the relatively good quality of the Swedish macro and financial data, to test models somewhat more detailed than one is usually able to do for a period prior to the mid-twentieth century. We discover, then, that financial sophistication in Sweden ran roughly parallel to that in the United States – across several sorts of tests – and considerably behind that in Britain. The chapter concludes with some simultaneous-equations work on the demand for money.

6.2 THE BACKGROUND TO MODERN GROWTH IN SWEDEN

For the period of Sweden's imperial activities, especially from the beginning of the Thirty Years War to 1718, historians are at pains to point out that Sweden became a major actor in the military drama without benefit either of significant population size or of unusual wealth. Sweden was, to be sure, a relatively well-off nation, with a strong agricultural sector and vigorous trade in furs, copper (to 1650) and iron (ore and finished products) as well as the possessor of a thriving timber trade in wood-starved Europe. Indeed (Roberts, 1979), largely because of these factors as well as a choke-hold on the Baltic trade that their earlier political successes brought them (they defeated the Danish on the seas, 1563–70), they even appear to have missed out on the 'secular stagnation' of the last half of the 17th century. We have no special call to assert numbers here, but on casual evidence, the per capita growth in Sweden during this period may well have exceeded the European average. Even so, the numerous and expensive wars of this time were only just bearable to the Swedes fiscally, and only, it seems, when their armies were successful. That is, the Swedish military success at this time generally is attributed to special administrative talents (of the aristocracy, primarily) and to a series of diplomatic manoeuvres and military triumphs which often laid the bulk of the expense on Sweden's enemies (and even on its allies, when this was possible). For our purposes, however, the important point is the strong suggestion that in this period Sweden was swept up in the accelerated economic growth of the 'preindustrial revolution', perhaps up to 1720 or so.

The conventional wisdom about the Swedes, from 1720 until the mid-19th century is that they had a thriving trade (in the products already mentioned), a high quality metallurgical industry dealing in specialized products, but, at the same time, no broad middle class. Foreigners, notably Dutch and German, provided both finance and ships. Instead, Sweden was characterized by its small farming units of free-holding peasantry who worked alongside an entrenched landed aristocracy. Indeed, goes the story, the way to get on in Sweden was to enter the military, work as a public servant, or act as a purveyor to the Crown. Sweden was apparently mercantilist in the 18th century, following the accession of Frederick of Hessen to the throne in 1720. This partly took the form of attempts at territorial expansion, mainly against Russia (and Prussia) with the last effort in 1788 against Russia perversely prolonging the Swedish monarchy in those revolutionary years. Along mercantilist lines, there were also numerous schemes at the time to promote 'royal manufactures' but Sweden's staple manufactured products were derived basically from iron, in which industry she had the world lead until Britain took over. Even so, it is at least arguable that the volume of Sweden's trade never declined for long in this period, particularly in real terms, even after the English large-scale exports arrived in the European metal markets toward the end of the 18th century. It is also probable (Heckscher, 1963) that Sweden grew in per capita terms from 1720 to 1815 and that growth was sufficient in the period from 1750 to 1850 to keep the standard of living of the labouring population relatively constant.[1]

During the early 19th century, a version of the open field system still dominated Swedish agriculture, but enclosure in the more prosperous farming areas apparently enabled the country to feed its growing population.[2] Following the Napoleonic Wars there was an economic slump that some argue lasted until 1830 with the ultimate turnaround only coming with a currency devaluation in 1834.[3] In any case significant social reforms began early in the century, perhaps as is sometimes alleged as a defence against the influence of the French Revolution, and culminated with compulsory school education in 1842, the abolishment of the guilds in 1846, the ending of town monopolies on trade and the lifting of export and import bans in 1847 and, in the 1864 statute, complete freedom of enterprise. Reform of the inheritance laws, improvement of the legal status of women, religious freedom, penal reform and local self-government also occurred in this period. At the same time, a growing commercial agriculture (and growing rural handicrafts), built a 'proto-industrial' population base in all but the poorest agricultural sections of Sweden. Social change and the spread of profit opportunities are factors in Sweden's sudden escalation, clearly. In any case, as we shall see, if one is looking for drama, it is not in agriculture or in social change, but in the effect of Europe's industrial revolution on a country that was actually resource rich, in primary materials (oats, timber, iron ore), in human resources, and, possibly, in the structure of its financial services industries.

6.2.1 Population and Human Capital, 1700–1910

Early population figures for Sweden suggest that Sweden was like much of the rest of Western Europe in having a significant population growth in this period. During the 19th century, Sweden had a growth rate of population that just reached double digits over a number of the decades around mid-century (Table 6.1).

We will point out below that Sweden's per capita national income slipped relatively in the period of its most rapid population growth (1820–60) and one can readily admit one possible explanation: this was a population growth that was quite rapid for an agriculturally-based economy. Even so, as Jorberg emphasizes, birth rates rose and death rates fell in this period and, by 1840, he also argues, Sweden's standard of living was clearly rising. So we are not, at the same time, suggesting that there was a Malthusian crisis underway in Sweden in this period.

Sandberg (1979) considers two of the major questions before us: why Sweden sat in such a relatively weak position in 1850 and, more importantly, what propelled it so rapidly shortly thereafter. Sandberg says that in 1850 (p. 227)

Table 6.1   Growth of population in Sweden

	Population (m)	Annual growth rate
1800	2.300	–
1810	2.348	0.21
1820	2.531	0.75
1830	2.827	1.11
1840	3.070	0.82
1850	3.405	1.04
1860	3.773	1.03
1870	4.075	0.77
1880	4.462	0.91
1890	4.676	0.47
1900	5.017	0.70
1910	5.393	0.72

Derived from Jorberg (1975).

> The great mass of the Swedish population was crowded into an agricultural sector based on poor land and a worse climate.

but that

> Starting around 1850, the Swedish situation changed rapidly: an economy with an effectively stagnant level of Y was propelled forward by a large exogenous increase in the international value and economic usefulness of its natural resources and in the availability of technological opportunities.

Further, says Sandberg, an important element in the rapid growth is the 'disproportionately large initial stock' of human capital in Sweden in 1850.[4] Other countries also made significant investments in education at this time, to be sure, but because human capital development is (assumed to be) a relatively slow process those countries would, in effect, be lagging *relatively*, as long as Sweden had a clear head start. Sandberg actually calls this large stock of human capital 'economically excessive' implying that in choosing education over, let us say, plant and equipment (well before 1850), the Swedes, as a matter of policy, put themselves into a state of 'sophisticated poverty'. Both of these ideas are hard to grasp formally – especially the 'economically excessive' comment. Perhaps, since none of the conclusions of Sandberg are affected thereby, it would be better phrased as a choice of

Table 6.2   Swedish emigration

	Within Europe	Emigration Outside Europe	Net[5]
1851–55	1 503	11 241	22 263
1856–60	424	3 732	8 312
1861–65	7 272	12 544	23 681
1866–70	22 056	80 575	122 646
1871–75	22 409	42 054	57 577
1876–80	22 359	60 447	81 177
1881–85	27 209	147 619	168 930
1886–90	21 687	179 886	178 355
1891–95	19 583	141 879	127 313
1896–1900	22 676	62 634	53 027
1901–05	17 932	129 746	123 133
1906–10	15 692	94 297	71 721
Totals	200 802	966 654	1 038 135

the Swedes, taken collectively, to put their investment kroner into schooling, a choice that turned out to be a type of consumption in the short run (perhaps, even, as intended *ex ante*) and possibly a profitable investment in the long run (judged *ex post*).

Another sign of Sweden's abundant human capital in 1850 is, of course, the oft-told story of the Swedish exodus to (mainly) the United States. The figures are given in Table 6.2 (Scott, 1965). Of these numbers, says Sandberg:

> The fact that Sweden in 1870 was very well endowed with human capital and very poorly endowed with natural resources meant that the population had to absorb a substantial 'negative rent' if it insisted on staying at home.

Negative rent or not, in mid-century, Sweden's rural population was growing relatively rapidly. Until the 1860s, what migration there was seems insufficient to narrow the gap between urban and rural real wages or to reduce the areas of extreme poverty in rural Sweden significantly.[6] From the 1860s, the pace of industrialization quickened, bringing with it higher real wages and a more stable source of income. From this point, both in-migration and large-scale emigration (largely to the United States) narrowed the gap between rural and urban real wages and reduced rural poverty (Söderberg, 1982). This is not to say that population was pushed from the Swedish farm by some sort of Malthusian crisis, for such did not exist in Sweden, probably from at least 1720 onward.[7] Rather, detailed analysis (of the 1871–81 period) shows that there was no effect, in Sweden, of poverty on migration; just the converse, as phrased above (Söderberg). It is, nevertheless, interesting that Sweden's emigration to the United States was largely to rural areas; it is also interesting that this population group brought with it a significant amount of additional human capital (in the form of education) in comparison with many other large national groups arriving in the United States at the same time.

6.2.2   The Transformation of Swedish Agriculture and Industry

As already pointed out, the immediate cause of Sweden's growth in this period was supplied by the demand for timber, iron and oats, from other countries that were already expanding rapidly. Indeed, Jorberg (1975) believes that an agricultural revolution preceded Sweden's industrial revolution and, because of its effect in terms of capital creation, population growth and the expansion of markets, provides the essential pre-history for Sweden's industrial revolution. He argues that what is different about the Swedish experience compared with Britain, France, etc. is that its *economic* take-off probably came before its industrial revolution. This view is certainly open to question, depending on what one means by 'industrial' for one thing. In particular, while we need not doubt Sweden's economic acceleration prior to industrialization, somewhat the same phenomenon seems to have occurred in the other countries we have considered in this survey. This pre-conditioning usually involves agriculture, commerce and pre-modern industry, as it did in Sweden.

Jorberg also puts some weight on structural changes that he believes occurred in the Swedish economy during this take-off period; he says that (pp. 101–2):

> During the introductory phase before 1870, Swedish society underwent a radical structural change. The relatively large increase in population may have resulted in overpopulation [in the sense that] . . . the rise in national income was slower than the increase in population.

although this last actually may not be true. Among the changes he emphasizes are enclosures and new agricultural techniques, and this is in keeping with his broadly agricultural thesis. In any case, the

Table 6.3   Swedish heavy industry, 1861–1910

Date	Coal output (000 t)	Coal imports (000 t)	Iron ore output (000 t)	Iron ore exports (000 t)	Pig iron output (000 t)	Railway line (miles)	RDP
1861	31	336	429	5.7	170	571	879
1870	37	465	616	13	300	1727	1128
1880	101	959	775	30	406	5876	1471
1890	188	1657	941	188	456	8018	1729
1900	252	3130	2610	1620	526	11303	2356
1910	303	4453	5549	4414	604	13829	3240
			Percent changes per year				
1861–1910	4.65	5.27	5.22	13.58	2.59	6.50	2.66
1861–1890	6.22	5.50	2.71	12.06	3.40	9.11	2.33
1890–1910	2.39	4.94	8.87	15.78	1.40	2.73	3.14

Source: Mitchell (1978).

agricultural sector needed capital for its expansion and thus it helped stimulate yet another structural change, in the form of a rapid growth of savings banks (2.3m Skr in 1834 to 29m Skr in 1860) and mortgage societies. But these numbers are really not adequate to the task, and small savings clearly did not play much of a role in specific investment projects, as we will argue further, below.

In the spirit of the topic of industrialization, let us look at a further disaggregation of the Swedish data, this time within the manufacturing sector. In particular, as Table 6.3 illustrates, Sweden's performance in this period is most impressive in its exports of a raw material – iron ore – to other, more industrialized countries. Of course, we do not want to exaggerate and so we see a coal-fed economic boom underway, with pig-iron output and (especially) the state-operated railroads being manifestations of this growth. Sweden's coal was largely imported, of course, and thus Sweden provides a good example of how the industrial revolution in Europe required and used 'role players' in various stages. Sweden's role was to provide high quality ore and timber, to absorb coal, and to provide high-quality manufacturing products – for both investment and consumption goods. However accidental all of this might have been, it turns out to have been very useful in the overall European scheme of things.

The broadest figures one might look at in this section actually have the most potential for disturbing the positions of the debaters. These refer, as illustrated in Figure 6.1, to the amount of real domestic product generated in the manufacturing and agricultural (and extrac-

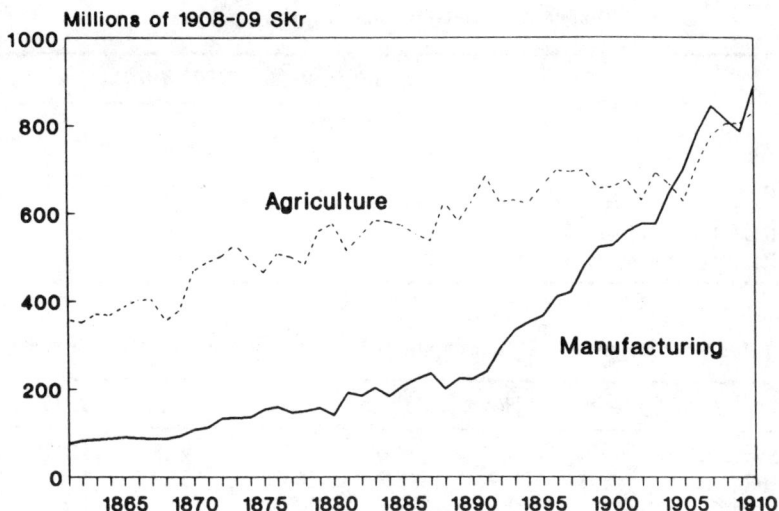

Figure 6.1   The composition of Swedish RDP, 1860–1910

tive) sectors, respectively. We know that the agricultural sectors of the heavily industrialized European countries are ultimately totally dominated by the manufacturing sector, and, while this process in Europe is relatively rapid in the long sweep of economic history, we usually imagine centuries going by as this process unfolds. Figure 6.1 indicates that from a position of being around one third of agriculture in 1890, the transition took only 14 to 20 years for manufacturing to pass agriculture in terms of generating a larger share of real domestic product. By 1910, indeed, manufacturing was ahead for good.[8]

To put Figure 6.1 into perspective, it is instructive to look at the compound growth rates of the two sectors, in this case compared to some more aggregate numbers. In Table 6.4 it is clear that agriculture is certainly growing – and growing considerably faster than population (food is imported into Sweden, too!) – while for fifty years manufacturing grew at the astonishing rate of 5.02 per cent. And it grew almost 7 per cent per year from 1890 to 1910. This speaks of general abundance, really, after 1890.

6.3   SWEDEN'S TAKE-OFF: MACROECONOMIC ASPECTS

Let us begin with some broad comparisons across countries that are so much of the traditional Swedish story. The figures in Table 6.5 are

200 *The Industrial Revolution*

Table 6.4   Growth in the Swedish economy

	1861–1910	*1890–1910*
Manufacturing	5.02	6.94
Agriculture	1.72	1.40
Real domestic product	2.66	3.14
RDP (per capita)	1.95	2.43
Population growth	0.71	0.71

Table 6.5   Relative GNP per capita in Europe (Europe = 100, each year)

	1830	*1850*	*1870*	*1890*	*1910*
Sweden	80.8	74.6	68.5	91.8	118.8
Belgium	122.9	145.2	164.1	162.4	171.1
France	110.0	117.7	121.7	132.7	136.3
Germany	102.1	108.8	118.7	138.4	141.3
Italy	110.4	97.9	86.9	80.2	73.3
Netherlands	144.6	150.9	140.9	151.0	146.1
UK	114.2	161.8	174.9	202.3	181.2

Source: Sandberg (1978).

taken from Sandberg (1978); they suggest that Sweden was losing ground to the rest of Europe until 1870. On the other hand, Sweden's relative position in Europe improved from 1830 to 1910, as did all but Italy in this table, and from 1870 to 1910, its relative position gained the most among these countries.

Turning away from international comparisons, the next topic, using the Krantz and Nilsson (1975) data, is represented in Figure 6.2; this shows the pattern of growth of the Swedish economy until 1910.[9] These figures show consistent growth with only a few contractions (especially after the 1870s); these are marked with asterisks in the figure. The picture also shows an apparent acceleration beginning either in the late 1880s or early 1890s. We can gain more leverage on these figures by looking at a set of estimated growth rates in Table 6.6. As is clear, the Swedish growth rate rose somewhat over the period, with the last period (1891–1910) being somewhat faster at 3.09 per cent per year and at 2.35 per cent per year, per capita. As we know, the latter is the highest in Europe at this time, but all of the figures in Table 6.3 are relatively high. The part of the Swedish

Millions of 1908-09 SKr

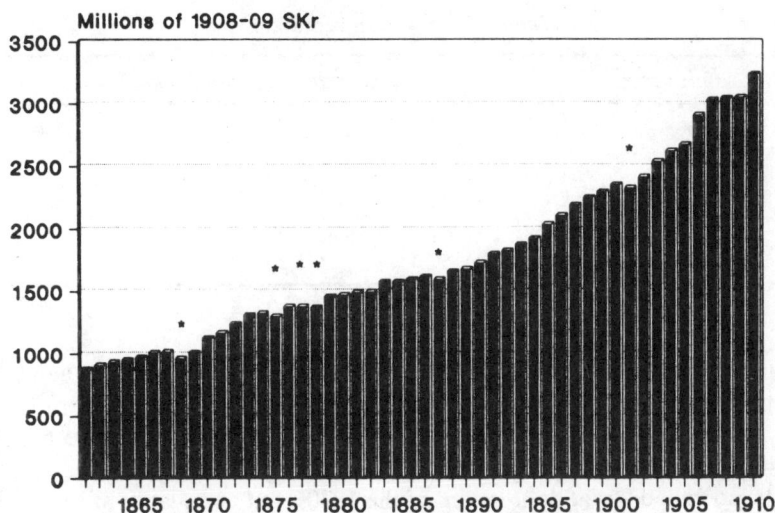

Figure 6.2   Swedish real domestic product, 1860–1910

Table 6.6   Swedish compound growth rates during the transition, 1861–1910 (standard errors in parentheses)

Period	Real Domestic. product	RDP per capita	RDP deflator	Real total consumption	Real investment
1861–1910	2.518 (0.042)	1.868 (0.041)	0.146 (0.075)	2.364 (0.040)	3.763 (0.211)
1871–1910	2.450 (0.060)	1.815 (0.057)	0.103 (0.115)	2.357 (0.055)	3.293 (0.272)
1881–1910	2.752 (0.071)	2.112 (0.065)	0.641 (0.122)	2.604 (0.066)	4.332 (0.321)
1891–1910	3.092 (0.084)	2.353 (0.086)	1.243 (0.132)	2.914 (0.086)	5.573 (0.539)

Source of data: Krantz and Nilsson (1975)

population that stayed behind actually enjoyed real consumption growing at 2.36 per cent in real terms (or 1.71 per cent per capita) over the entire period; this is an outstanding achievement.

Swedish growth during the period from 1861 to 1910 was not only rapid, it was remarkably stable. As the figures in Table 6.8 indicate, there were only six years in the fifty in which Swedish RDP declined

Table 6.7   Swedish recessions

Recession years	Per cent decline from peak
1868	5.40
1875	1.96
1877	0.07
1878	0.43
1887	1.42
1901	1.10

and in only one of these, in 1868, was this decline much more than a mild recession.

Note that a visualization of the cycles is available in Figure 6.2, above. To be sure, in Table 6.7, there is a bunching of bad years in the so-called 'great depression' of the 1870s, but as a glance at Figure 6.2 makes clear, the Swedish economy actually moved upward through this short period, having an RDP that *grew* from the peak in 1874 to the trough in 1878, by 3.62 per cent. (RDP grew 21.81 per cent from 1870 to 1878.) This is certainly slower growth than Sweden's usual rate but is still a very respectable performance.[10]

The downturn in 1868 is certainly due to agricultural failure; in this case, agricultural production fell 12.1 per cent, while manufacturing output did not change at all, over the year. The three recession years of the 1870s all showed agricultural declines, while industry did so only in 1877. It is worth underscoring that over the same years (1875–9), Italy, France, and Germany also had three or four years of recession (see Chapter 8). The international character of the events are probable. In the case of Sweden, Heckscher (1963), for one, feels that large grain flows from America to Europe, from the mid-1870s, were a major factor.[11] The year 1887 also brought a mild collapse of agriculture and a recession – not shared by Sweden's trading partners – as well as protective legislation for Swedish agriculture. In 1901, industry led the way and all three of the major European industrial powers were in recession. This was a mild decline, measured in per cent of real national product, but possibly among the first of a new breed of recession, being largely industrial and quite probably international in scope.

Another dimension to Sweden's economy is, of course, provided by a sectoral decomposition of the RDP figures. One way this has been done is to compare Sweden with other countries at comparable

Table 6.8 Comparative indicators

| | Per cent of gross expenditure in | | |
	Investment	Consumption	Government
Sweden (1900)	12.0	84.2	5.9
France (1870)	12.5	78.4	7.0
Germany (1870)	15.2	81.0	4.3
Great Britain (1840)	10.5	80.4	7.9

Source: Crafts (1984).

stages of development. What Crafts (1984) does is locate the dates at which various countries reached an arbitrary standard ($550 per capita, measured in 1970 US dollars) and then compare the broad sectors. The specific data vary from country to country, but even so, the differences are not remarkable, as Table 6.8 indicates. We see, then, that Sweden is around the average of the four countries in all but consumption. These numbers suggest broadly similar economies, at least judged by this simple macroeconomic decomposition.

Looking further into the details of the Swedish data, though, this simple tapestry unravels somewhat. While the numbers in Figure 6.3 are components of real domestic supply rather than gross expenditures, it is still apparent that the consumption ratio varies quite a bit over time, with what almost looks like a shift of consumption occurring between 1868 and 1874. More to the point, 1900, the year used by Crafts, does not look especially typical of the Swedish situation, if 'typical' is appropriate for any year in this series. With respect to the three ratios, then, Table 6.9 provides a decade-by-decade summary of their values. Actually, what emerges in this comparison – when the cyclical bumps are smoothed out of the data – is a remarkably steady performance from consumption after the 1860s, with government spending declining and investment rising over the period, in a kind of 'crowding-in' relationship similar to that in Germany.

Looking further into the possibility that the relative reduction of the role of the government might have been a key input into the growth of Sweden's physical capital stock in this period, we can consider the following simple correlations. The level figures are negatively correlated at −0.86; this shows a strong proximate crowding-in. On the other hand, both series are actually non-stationary (strongly-trend dominated in opposite directions) so that the data need to be transformed to render them stationary if such comparisons are to be

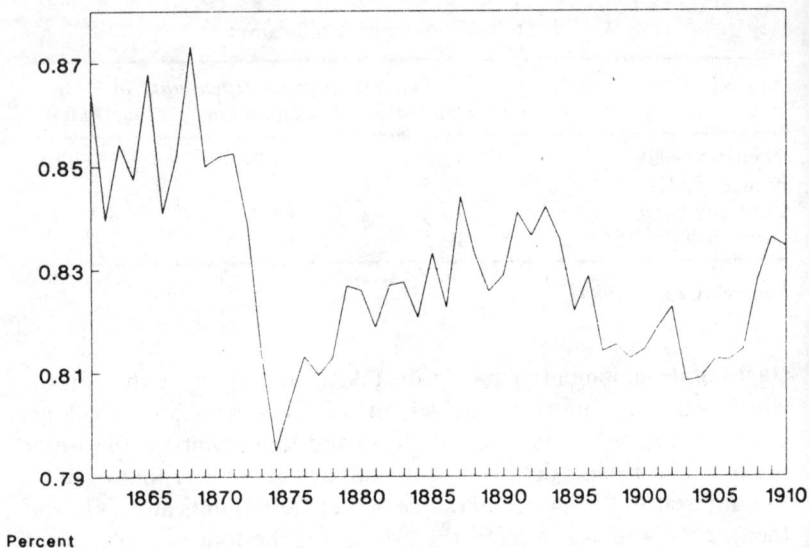

Percent

Figure 6.3   Swedish consumption ratio, 1861–1910

Table 6.9   Spending ratios in the components of real domestic product

	C/Y	G/Y	I/Y
1861–70	85.4	11.1	6.2
1871–80	81.9	9.6	9.1
1881–90	82.8	9.3	8.4
1890–1900	82.6	7.9	9.2
1901–10	82.0	6.4	11.5

made. Performing first a detrending (by log x on trend) and then a differencing, we produce Table 6.10. The last two calculations continue to exhibit the negative correlation that we have associated with possible crowding-in, although the correlation is certainly less decisive after the trend is removed.

One final look can be secured by plotting the two series produced by removing the trend from the raw series by regression (as in the second row of Table 6.10). These appear in Figure 6.4. Actually, this provides rather decisive pictorial evidence of a crowding-in phenomenon, although it must be admitted that the swings in the investment series are quite large compared with those in government spending. In any case, this is not a topic that has been investigated in

Table 6.10   Correlation coefficients (G/Y and I/Y)

Levels	−0.860
Detrended (regressive)	−0.569
Differenced	−0.489

Table 6.11   Money and real activity in Sweden, 1871–1910

	Levels of significance (p-values) for lags of			
	1	*2*	*3*	*4*
1. Bank assets causing RDP	0.74	0.92	0.48	0.15
RDP causing bank assets	0.0001*	0.01*	0.01*	0.05*
2. M1 causing RDP	0.83	0.85	0.95	0.86
RDP causing M1	0.07	0.003*	0.003*	0.002*
3. M2 causing RDP	0.50	0.68	0.40	0.13
RDP causing M2	0.00001*	0.002*	0.002*	0.01*
4. M1 causing prices	0.06	0.004*	0.06	0.02*
Prices causing M1	0.0003*	0.00001*	0.0002*	0.0001*
5. M2 causing prices	0.68	0.03*	0.19	0.20
Prices causing M2	0.52	0.09	0.48	0.56

* Significant results (at 0.05 level). The data are logarithms of per capita concepts.

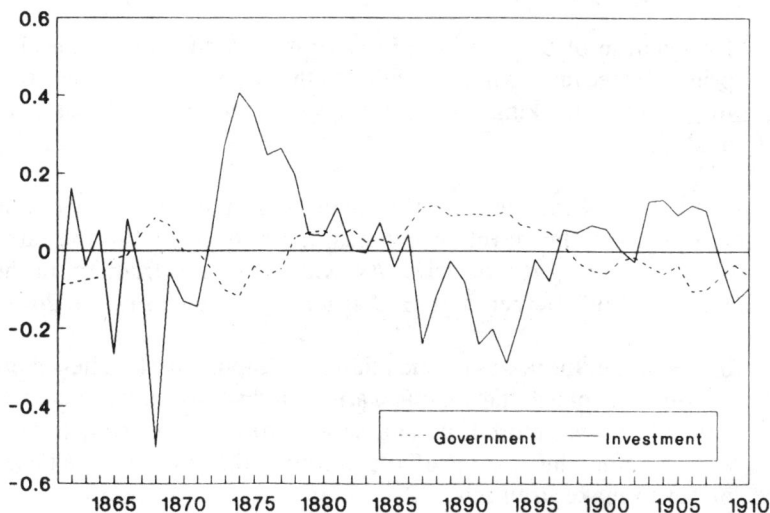

Residuals From Trend

Figure 6.4   Investment and government spending, 1861–1910

the Swedish literature, although on this evidence there might be some reason to do so, perhaps along the lines of the British data discussed in Chapter 2, or with co-integration tests.

6.4 SWEDEN'S FINANCIAL SOPHISTICATION IN THE 19TH CENTURY[12]

In this section we are interested in something we have already defined as 'financial sophistication', at several points in this study. Sandberg actually defines the concept in such a way that suggests the Swedish financial sector was well-developed around 1850 compared, let us say, with a European average. A version of Sandberg's (1978) argument could be phrased as the proposition that in 1850 something like 'relatively excess financial capacity' existed from which the Swedish economy was able to make withdrawals, as it were, over the next sixty-odd years. Such a concept can be labelled 'financial sophistication' certainly, but it would not be easy to grasp empirically. Furthermore, the notion that Sweden was in some sense well-developed at this time runs counter to the existing tradition in the literature. In particular, Kindleberger (1982) takes a sharply critical view of Sandberg's proposition, noting (p. 918)

> Designation of Sweden in 1850 as sophisticated raises a question primarily because so many writers on the subject take the view that the Swedish banking and credit system prior to 1850 was antiquated.

In *1870*, says Kindleberger, the financial system was indeed well developed, but this development was primarily related to the rapid growth of the export industries. As evidence of this tradition in the literature, Kindleberger cites Heckscher (1963), who says (p. 247),

> by and large, there was no such thing as a capital market; hence the distribution of capital among various industries as well as individual firms was more fitful and haphazard than was really necessary. Around the middle of the century, the influence of banks began to make itself felt, . . .

The sources of capital to industry, indeed, were the private savings of industrialists as well as foreign sources (pp. 247–8):

the influx of foreign capital was one of the main prerequisites for the expansion of the Swedish economy throughout practically the whole period ending with the outbreak of the First World War.

There are many other earlier writers, as Kindleberger notes, who could be taken to agree with this.[13]

In any case, in this section we will examine financial sophistication in a more precise way by studying financial variables in a series of time-series tests that are broadly consistent with the approach of Friedman and Schwartz in their recent *Monetary Trends* (1982). The concepts of financial development used here are based on (a) the behaviour of the velocity of money, (b) the magnitude of the income elasticity of the demand for money, and (c) the possible existence of economies of scale in commercial banking. Let us begin with a discussion of Sweden's financial setting.

6.4.1 Sweden's Financial Development: a Brief Review

By 1850, Sweden had in place a financial system that featured most of the technology of modern banking of the time, although it was geographically concentrated and possibly not very impressive when judged in per capita terms. As Nygren (1983, p. 45) puts it,

> the Swedish commercial banking system prior to the middle of the nineteenth century was notable for solidity and profitability, but it did lack liquidity. . . . Deposits were negligible. . . . the 1850s were the first decade to feature banking innovations and structural changes of significance for the future.

Indeed, the impression from Nygren's detailed and well-balanced discussion is that a significant contribution from bank development is more obvious from the 1870s onward than from the 1850s. There is little suggestion of significant financial development in 1850, but at the same time there is a distinct possibility that the financial industry actually provided a push after 1870, the period of most rapid growth.

In 1834, private banks (*enskilda* banks), aided by limited liability, began to issue currency and these issues grew to 43.2 per cent of the total note issue by 1859. The *enskilda* were inhibited by regulation of the interest rates they could charge; furthermore, their deposit business was small. In 1863 the Bank Reform Act established private banking on the joint-stock principle and permitted banks to lend at market interest rates. Banks, especially those outside Stockholm, quickly branched all over the country. From this point bank assets per capita rose from 47.9 Kr in 1860 to 523.1 Kr in 1910. Indeed, as a percentage of national income, they rose from 29.6 to 103.5 over the same period (a figure that was 13 per cent in 1830). During this period Sweden also had a central bank (the *Sveriges Riksbank* was chartered in 1656) that assumed 'lender of last resort' functions in the 1890s. So, indeed, there was considerable institutional development during this period.

A series of studies authored by Jonung contains much of what we know about the development of the Swedish monetary system between 1860 and 1910 (see 1976a, 1976b, 1978, 1983, 1984). An important consideration for our work is that from 1873 to 1910 Sweden was on the Gold Standard and maintained its position at an exchange rate that remained basically constant over the entire period (£ = Kr18.16, $ = Kr3.73).[14] Even so, as Jonung (1984) explains, the Swedish central bank and commercial banks were not rigorously tied to gold inflows and outflows by reserve requirements, so the money supply was at least partly able to react to internal pressures. From the point of view of this section, this finding suggests that the money stock should not necessarily be taken as exogenously determined, depending on what factors influence the note issue and bank deposit supply decisions, and, of course, depending on private decisions to use money in financial and commodity transactions.[15]

Another important question addressed in the Swedish literature concerns the steady decline of the income velocity of money during this period. As we shall argue below, this phenomenon is not unusual in less financially-developed countries, and the Swedish experience in this respect compares rather closely with that of the United States in the same period.[16] The general hypothesis is

> The downward trend in velocity is due to the process of monetization. This process is made up of . . . (1) the decline of barter and payments in kind . . . and (2) the rise of a commercial banking system supplying the public with notes and deposit facilities.[17]

These changes are institutional in nature say Bordo and Jonung, who study the velocity function in terms of a large number of potential determinants.[18] In any case, what we will do in the next two subsections of this chapter is undertake a formal causal analysis of the influence of such structural factors, and account for the direct

(Granger-causal) influence of money, bank assets, etc. on real income itself. We are also interested in the value of the income elasticity of the demand for money, since high values here might suggest a lack of financial sophistication in that it implies that money and bank services have not reached many potential users possibly because they are unaware of these services. The topic of the income elasticity of the demand for money will be considered at length in Section 6.4.4.

6.4.2 The Granger-causal Relation Between the Financial Sector and the Real Economy

To this point we have argued that financial development seems strongest just at (and not noticeably before) the period of most rapid growth in the real domestic product of Sweden. One can certainly argue that the economic climate was right for a broad and sustained upward surge in real output – and it clearly was, given the results – but a formal causal analysis, being sensitive to non-obvious leads and lags, seems better than leaving the financial hypothesis in such an imprecise position. The method used here is the Granger-causality test as applied in earlier chapters; we repeat the regression equation.

$$y_t = \alpha + \sum_{i=1}^{n} \beta_i \, y_{t-i} + \sum_{i=1}^{n} \delta_i \, x_{t-i} + e_t \qquad (6.1)$$

Again we note that in this setup, x will be said to cause y if the δ coefficients are statistically significant as a group. Significance here is judged by an F-test, carried out at a 5 per cent level of significance (and marked with an asterisk in the following tables).

The place to begin this discussion is with the traditional money-neutrality test, conditioned immediately by our interest in the development of the Swedish banking system. That is, the first empirical excursion here is related to the causation among financial assets, real income, and the price level but with the emphasis placed on the role of financial assets. These results are reported in Table 6.11 (p. 205). The variables here are bank assets and narrow and broad money (M1 and M2), and the potential objects of their influence are real domestic product (RDP) and its deflator.[19] Note that the tests in the table are expressed in pairs with direct causation appearing first and 're-verse' causation appearing immediately below; note, also, that all variables are in logarithms with the real and financial variables

Table 6.12   Money, investment and real income in Sweden, 1871–1910

	Levels of significance (p-values) for lags of			
	1	2	3	4
1. Bank assets causing RDI	0.08	0.0002*	0.01*	0.05*
M1 causing RDI	0.00001*	0.00001*	0.001*	0.0001*
M2 causing RDI	0.04*	0.002*	0.06	0.10
2. RDI causing bank assets	0.79	0.91	0.69	0.16
RDI causing M1	0.002*	0.08	0.55	0.80
RDI causing M2	0.77	0.84	0.70	0.17
3. RDI causing RDP	0.08	0.32	0.51	0.69
RDP causing RDI	0.02*	0.02*	0.04*	0.06

* Significant results (at 0.05 level).

sured in per capita terms. Finally, note that an asterisk indicates rejection at a 5 per cent or lower level of significance (i.e., it indicates that Granger-causality is established in this statistical sense).

The results in Table 6.11 strongly suggest that both bank assets and money, the latter defined as broad money (M2) or narrow money (M1), are Granger-caused by real income in this period and not the converse (a separate set of results, not shown, for 1861–1910 are very similar in this respect).[20] Similarly, both measures of money Granger-cause the price level. These are typical results in the causality literature, and they do not imply any special causal role for the financial sector as a leader in economic development. Note that the results in this table hold up, broadly, when the data are differenced in order to achieve stationarity.

There is an important exception in Table 6.11, though, and that is the strong suggestion in the second part of line (4) for M1 – but not for M2 – of what is often called 'reverse causation' between prices and money. This result, which shows that prices also drive money, is possibly related to Sweden's failure to play by the rules of the international gold standard. That is, it suggests that the Swedish money stock might be endogenous. Another sharp difference between the two measures of money (M1 and M2) will be seen in a moment, when we look at a financial sophistication index constructed partly from the money stock measures.

Table 6.11, then, does not suggest that the financial sector was unusual in this period, in that it was influenced by, but did not appear to influence, real output. According to the first test reported, that is to say, there is no direct link to per capita real domestic product.

Conversely, as suggested above, it appears to be rapid real growth that pulled along the banking system and the money supply. While this is certainly interesting, it is not remarkable. However, the possibility does exist that the links are less direct, as many writers have suggested, and that the influence of money is on capital formation (that is, on per capita real domestic investment) and then from investment to real income. To see if this is the case for Sweden, we can look at causal links (taken singly) between the financial assets and per capita real domestic investment (RDI) and then between investment and real income. Again, all variables are measured in the natural logarithms. The results are reported in Table 6.12.

In this case, in the first set of results, there appears to be a strong causal line running from financial entities to real per capita investment (the signs here are positive in the underlying regressions). Investment, in turn, in Set (3) appears to be Granger-caused by real income. It appears, then, that the Swedish financial system actually may well have played a role in stimulating Swedish investment during the industrial revolution. It also seems that Swedish investment spending was important to Swedish growth but that the Granger-causal link between bank assets and real income was dominated by the very strong demands of economic growth on the financial system. On net, these Granger-causality tests provide some but not a lot of support for the hypothesis that the financial sector had a special role to play, as judged by these time-series tests. Note, again, that the results in Table 6.12 hold up when the data are put into first-difference form.

6.4.3   Sweden's Financial Sophistication: Further Explorations

This section will consider how the behaviour of velocity – transformed into a 'financial sophistication index' – might both Granger-cause and be Granger-caused by the variables at hand. What Friedman and Schwartz (1982) do is take the velocity series of each country, invert it, and then multiply the result by 52. This index then gives the number of weeks of national income that the current money stock will finance. Of course, velocity itself has reasonable credentials as a measure of financial development, since high velocities might suggest inadequate stocks of money relative to spending. Indeed, in the early stages of development when financial markets present few liquid alternatives to money, it seems reasonable to employ velocity in this capacity, at least as a first approximation. In later stages of

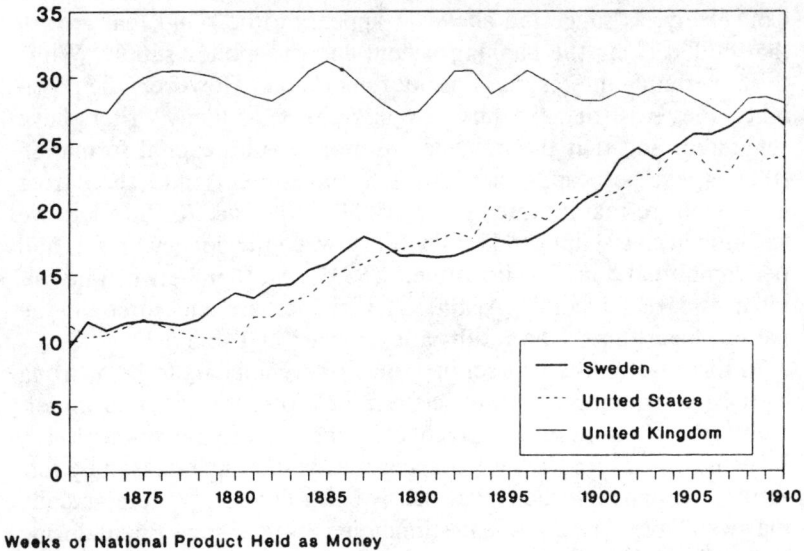

Weeks of National Product Held as Money

Figure 6.5   Financial sophistication indexes. Sweden, the UK and the US

development, however, when financial intermediaries come on stream (with money substitutes), this interpretation is not really credible. Indeed, in the later experiences of the developed countries, velocity often tends to rise as money substitutes are developed; it did so in Sweden.[21] But for the pre-1914 Swedish data for which velocity is declining steadily, we can possibly neglect the influence of intermediaries and if so, the decline of velocity/rise of the financial sophistication index can be interpreted as we do.[22]

In Figure 6.5 three countries (the United States, the United Kingdom, and Sweden) are compared in terms of the financial sophistication index just described. Here Sweden and the United States appear to have had common experiences over the period, while the UK index fluctuates around a constant level. For comparability, the money stock here is M2 in all cases. What Friedman and Schwartz say about the United States in the 1870s (compared with the United Kingdom) is (p. 146)

The United States, by contrast, though wealthier and more populous, was still financially backward, conducting its international trade largely in sterling. Nearly three-quarters of the population was classified as residing in rural areas, and half of the working force (male and female) was still in agriculture. . . . These differences meant a much higher demand for money relative to income by United Kingdom than by United States residents.

Indeed, say Friedman and Schwartz, much of the change to a sophisticated economy occurred between 1870 and 1906. In any case, as Figure 6.5 makes clear, Sweden's experience parallels that of the United States as judged by the financial sophistication index. And, as we saw in Figure 6.1, in 1875, indeed, the value of Swedish agricultural output in gross domestic product was four times that of its industrial output (the two were dead even in 1905). Needless to say, a significant majority of her workers also were in the agricultural sector.

The main issue in this section concerns the determinants of the Swedish financial sophistication index itself – of the inverse of velocity, that is to say – during the period of her industrialization. It is not hard to find suggestions for the determinants of velocity in the literature. The most obvious is bank assets per capita which could suggest, given the demand for bank services, a money supply influence on Sweden's financial sophistication. Interest rates are also often mentioned as determinants of velocity, since a fall in the nominal interest rate (as occurred in this period) would, other things being equal, increase money holding, decrease velocity, and, accordingly, increase the financial sophistication index. Then, too, there are non-financial influences. Bordo and Jonung (1981) and, separately, Jonung (1983, 1984), for example, mention the rise of industry and commerce and of urbanization and use the currency/money ratio, labour's share of GNP, the ratio of urban population to total population, the percentage of the labour force in non-agricultural activities, and the number of inhabitants per bank office among other institutional variables. These variables seem reasonable, certainly. Not all of these are available in time-series, of course, but many of these potential influences are considered in the following causal tests.

Table 6.13, then, groups the variables proposed into potential money-demand, financial structure, and industrial sector categories. The theme of the table is that of locating the factors that are the determinants of financial sophistication in Sweden and, in the last column, of identifying those financial or real entities that are themselves influenced by the financial sophistication index. The table contains the p-values obtained from the Granger-causality tests, and again we have marked with an asterisk those that imply significant

Table 6.13 Granger-causal influences on financial sophistication, 1871–1910

Causal agent	p-value for lags of 1	2	3	4	Sign	Reverse causation
Demand factors						
1. Interest rate – short	0.04*	0.06	0.06	0.12	+	No
2. Interest rate – long	0.33	0.36	0.49	0.61	:	No
3. Interest rate – Consol	0.41	0.03*	0.03*	0.05*	:	No
4. Real income per capita	0.002*	0.01*	0.01*	0.01*	:	No
5. Currency/M2 (C/M)	0.38	0.73	0.37	0.22	:	Yes
Financial structure						
6. Bank assets per capita	0.01*	0.06	0.14	0.14	+	No
7. Real money per capita	0.002*	0.01*	0.01*	0.01*	:	Yes
8. Reserves/deposits (R/D)	0.01*	0.19	0.29	0.20	–	No
9. Bank offices per capita	0.62	0.93	0.87	0.99	:	No
10. High-powered money (H)	0.22	0.85	0.97	0.99	:	Yes
Industrial structure						
11. Manufacturing/RDP	0.002*	0.07	0.19	0.32	+	No
12. Agriculture/manufacturing in RDP	0.01*	0.10	0.26	0.44	–	No
13. Non-agricultural employment per cent	0.01*	0.34	0.56	0.71	+	No

* Significant results (at 0.05 level).

causation. Note that the measure of financial sophistication uses M2, not M1, since the literature suggests that it is the banking sector as a whole that is involved and not just its demand deposit and note-creating dimension.[23] Note also that the rare instances of *reverse causation* – meaning that the index itself influences the variables listed on the left – are indicated in the last column of the table.

In these results there appears to be a mixture of structural, demand and financial supply influences on Sweden's financial sophistication index. Generally, financial sophistication does not affect any of the real variables in the system (see the last column in Table 6.13), so that seems to dispose of the possibility that the financial system was a (Granger-causally) leading sector. At the same time, variables from each of the arbitrary categories, demand, financial structure, and industrial structure factors, are shown to Granger-cause the financial sophistication index. Clearly, velocity in Sweden is driven by market and structural factors (and by real and financial factors). This is what the historical literature described above claims, although our tests provide an empirical corroboration of a different sort. Note that of the three 'proximate' determinants of money (C/M, H, and R/D), only R/D has an influence on financial sophistication, while causation runs the other way for H and C/M. This implies that the monetary determinants approach is invalid for Sweden; it may also imply that Sweden's money stock is endogenously determined as suggested above. In sum it appears that in a very broad sense the domestic economy drove Sweden's financial sector, with the banking sector showing an influence primarily on other financial variables rather than on real variables. The only exception we have found to this story resides in the investment/money figures discussed in Section 6.4.2.

6.4.4 Money Demand and Supply and Financial Sophistication[24]

In the quotation above from Friedman and Schwartz, reference was made to the demand for money. They point out that the income elasticity of money demand is higher in the United States than in the United Kingdom in this period and that, indeed, in the United States this income elasticity is significantly greater than unity (even when adjusted for the increase in financial sophistication in the United States). If so, then money (M2 in their case) is a luxury good in this period and this can be taken as further indirect evidence of a relative lack of financial sophistication in the United States. The same argument can be advanced for Sweden, of course, and so this section will look into questions concerning the income-elasticity of the demand for money. As we will see, though, the nature of the relationship forces us to estimate the demand for money in a simultaneous-equations framework. This is the result of the fact that the money stock is evidently at least partially endogenously determined in Sweden (as we have already argued). But, as we shall demonstrate, there is additional information on financial sophistication to be gleaned from the money supply function. This is sufficient reason to move in this direction.

For what it is worth, single-equation estimates of a standard log-linear demand for money function tend to support the idea of a lack of financial sophistication in this period, as revealed by the following results for the 1871–1910 period.[25]

$$M1_t = a + \underset{(5.12)}{0.535}\ M1_{t-1} + \underset{(4.71)}{0.742}\ y_t - \underset{(5.57)}{5.927}\ i_t \qquad \bar{R}^2 = 0.996$$
$$DW = 1.974$$

$$M2_t = a + \underset{(15.96)}{0.930}\ M2_{t-1} + \underset{(1.27)}{0.167}\ y_t + \underset{(0.97)}{0.898}\ i_t \qquad \bar{R}^2 = 0.990$$
$$DW = 1.772$$

The numbers in parentheses are t-values. Here the interest rate is the Bank of Sweden's discount rate (the only short-term rate available) and the long-run income elasticities for the two measures of money are 1.597 for M1 and 2.400 for M2. These numbers compare favourably with those produced by Friedman and Schwartz for the United States (for M2, the elasticity is not as high in the United States). These results just given are suggestive, of course, but have two major problems. Most obviously, perhaps, the result for M2 is poorly determined with only the lagged dependent variable being significant; this difficulty continues to trouble the experiments in the remainder of this section and so most of the reported results here refer to M1. The second problem is that the evidence of simultaneity that was discussed earlier is not dealt with by these ordinary-least-squares/single-equation models. Indeed, our discussion so far indicates that the money stock in Sweden was an outcome of an equilibrium determined *within* Sweden. That is, the Swedish money supply is partly endogenously determined although, of course, it is subject to exogenous factors from both national and international markets. In particular, we have shown – with Granger-causality tests – that the real sector of the economy equilibrates independently of the monetary sector while the money stock and interest rates are basically the outcome of the equilibration of the demand and supply of monetary services.[26] This, then, suggests the appropriateness of a model of money demand and supply in which the quantity of money and Swedish interest rates are determined endogenously.

Let us follow Klein (1974) in constructing such a model. Suppose, first, that the banking system is competitive. By this we mean that both the commercial banks and the *Riksbank* behave competitively (in their money supply behaviour). In practical terms this means that the depositors of these institutions are forced to bear the marginal costs of maintaining their deposits. This is clearly acceptable for the private banks, but whether Swedish currency was supplied on that principle, particularly after the *Riksbank* assumed total control of the note issue (after 1903), is certainly debatable. It is also certainly moot, since the data used here only run to 1910.

Let us assume that the demand for real money balances, is a function of the nominal interest rate and real income.[27] The supply of money, though, is not a function of the same variables (at least directly) because of the need to model technical factors in money supply. To do so, we need a model of the aggregate banking firm that reflects the fact that a higher real quantity of money will be supplied only in the expectation of a higher marginal profit in the banking industry. To make this notion operational then requires a specification of the price of money services that is relevant both to suppliers and demanders and is thereby capable of equilibrating the market for the services of banks.

Consider, first, the rental price of money faced by the representative consumer. Let us assume that the consumer can hold wealth in two forms: as (narrow) money or as an asset that generates no flow of monetary services; assume also that the non-money asset pays a nominal rate of interest of i. If currency pays no interest while at the same time interest is paid on deposits at the rate r_D, then the average return to holding money is $(D/M)r_D$, where D is deposits, C is currency (and $M = C + D$ is money). The opportunity cost of holding money, then, is $P_M \equiv iM - r_D D$ (i.e., $i - (D/M)r_D$). This is the price attached to the flow of monetary services and it is what we would want to put into the demand for money function, as follows.

$$M_D = f(y, P_M) \tag{6.2}$$

Above we said that because of our assumption of competition the holder of one krona in deposits must pay the actual marginal cost of producing that deposit. The marginal cost to the bank, we may suppose, is the opportunity cost of holding reserves against the deposit. Let us assume that the bank holds the quantity *MRD* (kronor) for each additional krona of deposits (*MRD* being the *marginal reserves to deposits ratio*) and that the bank's marginal investment opportunity cost is represented by the same nominal interest rate i. In this event, the marginal cost to the bank of providing a deposit is $[(MRD) \times i]$ per time period. Equating the deposit holder's cost per unit to the marginal cost of producing a deposit yields the equation $[i - r_D = (MRD) \times i]$ which is the same thing as

$$r_D = i(1 - MRD) \qquad (6.3)$$

This becomes the structural equation for *money supply* in a competitive financial system, because of the obvious dependence of MRD.

Increasing costs of providing banking services enter into this framework as increases in MRD, the marginal reserves-to-deposit ratio. In particular, it is possible that as banks expand into new locations, they make themselves less liquid and that this induces them to hold more reserves per deposited krona. MRD would then be increasing in M ($\equiv C + D$). Conversely, *economies of scale* in banking would be reflected in an *MRD* that declines with M. In either case – that is, whether one has increasing or decreasing costs – the actual quantity of money supplied is not predetermined and depends on where we land along the supply curve. That, of course, depends on money demand as well. In general that is to say both M and r_D are determined simultaneously by the supply function just given along with the demand for money.

To put the model into empirical terms, we can utilize the discount rate of the Bank of Sweden. This is the only short-term rate available and in terms of the discussion just undertaken, this rate is taken to be the endogenously-determined rate. Friedman and Schwartz (1982) have argued that there is a close integration of the American and British capital markets during this period. It seems likely that in the second half of the 19th century, the Swedish capital market might also have shared in the international capital pool and so it is at least conceivable that the opportunity cost of Swedish funds is the US corporate bond rate, as published by Friedman and Schwartz.[28] This will turn out to be a useful strategy in an empirical sense in what follows. Note again that the definition of money is an M1 measure and income is real domestic product.

Let us return to the demand function in Equation (6.2) and linearize it.

$$m_{Dt} = \beta_0 + \beta_1 P_{Mt} + \beta_2 y_t + e_t \tag{6.4}$$

Here m_{Dt} is per capita real money balances, P_{Mt} is the rental price of money defined above, y_t is per capita real domestic product, and e_t is a random error. Substituting in the definition of P_M yields the final estimating equation for money demand.

$$m_{Dt} = \beta_0 + \beta_1 \left[i_t - \left(\frac{D}{M} \right)_t r_{Dt} \right] + \beta_2 y_t + e_t \tag{6.5}$$

where $(D/M)_t$ is the deposit-to-money ratio and i_t is the US corporate bond rate. The real money and real income measures in Equation (6.5) are taken to be in per capita terms.

Table 6.14 reports a two-stage least-squares estimate of Equation (6.5). The two-stage least-squares approach is required because of the need to treat m_{Dt} and r_t and r_t as endogenous variables, as already discussed. In addition, the table lists two autoregressive (AR) coefficients; this proves to be necessary because of the pattern of serial correlation in the residuals (e_t) in Equation (6.5). Because of the AR terms, the method of estimation employed is nonlinear two-stage least-squares. The instruments used in the Table 6.14 estimates are i, y, the agricultural and manufacturing components of y, two lags of the preceding variables, and two lags of r_D and m. The fit of the model is quite good, with β_2 (on real income) and the AR coefficients particularly well determined.[29]

Table 6.14   Nonlinear two-stage least squares estimates of Swedish money demand

Parameter	Estimate	Asymptotic standard error
β_0	3.911	10.101
β_1	−3.270	1.630
β_2	0.110	0.019
AR1	1.161	0.150
AR2	−0.435	0.147

The Durbin–Watson statistic is 2.11.

The interest elasticity of money demand is that with respect to P_M, the rental rate of money. That elasticity, calculated at the sample means, is -0.169. The income elasticity of the demand for money from Table 6.15, evaluated at the sample means, is 1.055. It is significantly positive but is not significantly different from unity. M1, on this test, is not a luxury good in Sweden at this time and this aspect of a lack of financial sophistication thus is not supported in this test.

We also have an interest in the supply function that we derived above since it may have some bearing on the topic of financial sophistication. Indeed, a possible notion of financial sophistication has to do with how the marginal cost of banking services changes with changes in the quantity of money. Decreasing marginal costs would imply yet-to-be exploited economies of scale and financial unsophistication in this sense, while increasing costs would suggest a banking system without this potential.

The supply equation which we have postulated appears as Equation (6.3) above; it is a function of the marginal reserves-to-deposits ratio (MRD) and the opportunity cost (i_t) of funds to the banks. Let us assume that MRD is a linear function of real per capita money balances (m_t) as in

$$MRD_t = \delta_0 + \delta_1 m_t$$

If we substitute this into Equation (6.3), we then have our final estimating equation for money supply.

$$r_{Dt} = i_t (1 - \delta_0 - \delta_1 m_t) + u_t \tag{6.6}$$

Increasing costs in banking then would be represented by a positive parameter δ_1, while decreasing costs would appear as a negative value of δ_1. Using the same definitions of i, m, and r_D as in the money demand estimates, Table 6.15 presents the estimates of Equation (6.6). As in the case of the money demand function, there is an AR (2) structure to the residuals from Equation (6.7). The two AR parameters, along with the structural parameters in (6.7), are again estimated with nonlinear 2SLS. The instruments employed to deal with the endogeneity of m_t are the same as those used in the demand estimates: i, y, the agricultural and manufacturing components of y, two lags of the preceding variables, and two lags of r_D and m.

Table 6.15   Nonlinear 2SLS estimates of money supply

Parameter	Estimate	Asymptotic standard error
δ_0	0.3445	0.1382
δ_1	−0.0124	0.0033
AR1	1.0437	0.1391
AR2	−0.4607	0.1394

Durbin–Watson statistic = 2.234.

The most important result from Table 6.15 is the significantly negative estimate for δ_1, implying marginal costs of banking that *decline* with the quantity of money; that is, there appear to be *increasing* returns-to-scale in Swedish banking in the 19th century. The increase in returns to deposits is apparently due to the lower marginal cost of providing them at their new higher level. In addition, the mean-evaluated elasticity of r_D with respect to m is 0.459; that is, a 1 per cent increase in the real per-capita money supply will lead to a 0.459 per cent increase in the return to deposits.[30] The significance of this effect in the 1860 to 1910 period is that the total sample variation in the real per capita money supply over the sample period accounts for slightly more than half a percentage point in the variation in the return to deposits. More importantly, from the point of view of this study, it appears that the financial system of Sweden had unexploited economies of scale that were available as the demand for financial services expanded during Sweden's industrial revolution.

Finally, the two equations discussed in this section were estimated simultaneously with nonlinear three-stage least squares. As one would expect from a properly specified system, the coefficient estimates do not change much, but their standard errors are reduced. The system estimates and related statistics are shown in Table 6.16. The interpretations given after Table 6.14, of an income elasticity of the demand for money near unity and increasing returns to scale in money supply, are also maintained; in the 3SLS estimates, δ_1 is again significantly negative and the mean-evaluated income elasticity of money demand is 1.16 with a standard error of 0.17. Once again, the notion of an income elasticity of money demand in excess of unity is not supported for Sweden. Of course it is M2 which is the subject of such conjectures for the US and UK tests discussed in Friedman and

Table 6.16   Nonlinear 3SLS estimates of the money supply and demand system

Parameter	Estimate	Asymptotic std. error
Demand: (DW = 2.066)		
β_0	–3.301	9.467
β_1	–1.774	1.503
β_2	0.121	0.018
AR1	1.170	0.154
AR2	–0.427	0.151
Supply: (DW = 2.184)		
δ_0	0.263	0.147
δ_1	–0.101	0.003
AR1	1.037	0.141
AR2	–0.441	0.140

Correlation of supply and demand residuals = –0.523.

Schwartz, so this result for M1 is not necessarily damaging to that general idea of a lack of financial sophistication. The suggestion of economies of scale in banking is, however, a new result, leading in the same direction.

6.5   CONCLUSION

Sweden has an unusual position in our discussion of the industrial revolution, being later to arrive on the one hand, and, if any country has the right, a claim to have had an actual industrial *revolution* in the 19th and early 20th centuries. The foundation of this success was Sweden's trade in her natural resources – timber, oats and iron ore – but evidence also exists to suggest that Sweden had extra human and financial resources at this time that were unusually effective in shaping a quick transition to a modern industrial economy.

In this chapter, we have made a strong effort to pin down the financial resources part of the story, in terms of a study of Sweden's financial sophistication. It appears that by a crude measure of financial sophistication – based on the income velocity of money – Sweden is no different from the United States in her general usage of bank services. On the other hand, we found signs of a Granger-causal influence running from financial variables to real investment. Since investment grew significantly in this period, and undoubtedly made a special contribution to Sweden's successful transformation, the financial system must have been important in some sense. The problem we had is that the financial variables appear to be neutral with respect to having a Granger-causal effect on real output. This is a puzzle, really, although we also noticed it in the German case, where the claim was made that the lending policies of the commercial banks provided a lift to investment in fixed capital that went beyond that which was optimal. Perhaps the same is true of Sweden.

Our detailed study of the demand for money in this chapter reveals both the expected and the unexpected. The expected result is that the demand for money has an income elasticity greater than unity in the conventional money-demand tests; this result is expected if only because the relatively (financially) unsophisticated countries of the West tend to show this result during this period. What is unexpected is the successful testing of a simultaneous-equations model of the demand and supply of money. Normally the data are not good enough for such tests this far back in time – whether or not the model is appropriate. This test reveals an income elasticity smaller than that obtained in the single-equation tests, and, more provocatively, some evidence of what might be termed 'economies of scale' in the supply of bank services to the Swedish economy. These are provisional results, clearly, but interesting none the less.

7 Italy at the Time of the Industrial Revolution

7.1 INTRODUCTION

The fortunes of Italy without doubt are intermingled with those of Austria and Spain on account of the eight-century span of the Holy Roman Empire. The economic stories are very different, however, and, in view of the demise of the Empire in Napoleon's time – roughly at the time the present study begins – there is little need to treat the countries as a unit, except for an occasional aside.[1] What remains, then, is an example of how a country that was not especially rich in human or physical capital – but possessed enough to get the job done – eventually and somewhat unevenly joined the group of industrial nations.

For Italy the most general themes in the literature emphasize the unification of the country (from 1861), the arrival of politically liberal governments in the 1870s, and, most emphatically, the development of the railroad. While Italy clearly grew in real terms before 1870, it was with a performance that was substantially below the European average. Even after 1870, Italian economic growth was below average until its boom began, in the mid-1890s. Industrial growth after that, in the short stretch until 1910, was possibly over 6 per cent year and this definitely puts Italy among the European leaders in this category. But even at that time Italy was an economically divided country, with the strongest growth in industry occurring mostly in the North, while the South specialized in emigration it seems (600 000 people per year at its peak) as well as something as close to subsistence agriculture as we will see in our sample of countries. This chapter will, in any event, look at this record and makes the claim that northern Italian development is actually more impressive than economy-wide statistics suggest. Indeed, it might be better, in telling the general story, to emphasize the positive thrust generated by the manufacturers of the North, rather than to focus on the oft-mentioned political and social factors that held back growth.

The macroeconomic themes of the chapter begin with a discussion of Italy's relatively slow population growth and its broad causes.

Emigration is a major item in this discussion, and some parallels will be drawn with Swedish experience in this period. More formally macroeconomic is the discussion of the growth and cycles of the Italian economy from 1861 to 1910. We find that the real growth rate of GNP reached 2.5 per cent in the 1896–1910 period, with investment spending increasing over that same span at just under 9 per cent per year. Italian cycles, in contrast to those in the other countries we have discussed, do not get less frequent over time (GNP declines in one of every three years in the period), and they may even get more severe. This pattern needs to be explained, if possible.

Turning to monetary macroeconomics, we note, first of all, that Italian banking appears relatively stable during the period, although Italy has possibly the least financially 'sophisticated' economy in 1861 among the candidates discussed in this study. As times goes on, the role of the banks is increasingly evident in various ways, and there is an unusual finding for this study in the form of a (non-neutral) influence running from money to both real GNP and industrial production. The latter effect appears from 1881 to 1910 but not for longer time periods. Further, and equally unusually, for the same period there appears to be no Granger-causal effect from money to prices (measured either by the GNP deflator or by the cost of living index). Taken together, these are non-quantity theory of money results that are basically unique to the Italian case (as far as this study is concerned). Finally, the chapter pursues the strong suspicion that the 50-year period may not have financially similar experiences in its subperiods in terms of the behaviour of the demand for money. Here we utilize a model implanted in the recent literature by Spinelli (1980) that appears to confirm that the demand for money is not stable. The function does appear to be well-defined, though, at least for the period 1880 to 1910. We have had similar results for the other countries that have been considered.

7.1.1 Italian Population during the Transformation

In Chapter 1 we noted that Italian population grew moderately in the 18th and early 19th centuries. These figures, to repeat, are drawn from Maddison (1982), and are shown in Table 7.1. Here, the rates of growth are closer to the relatively slow pace of the Germans rather than to the heady pace of the British; it will be recalled that the UK rates were the fastest among the five countries, and were over 1 per cent per year in the second 60-year period.

Table 7.1   Population

	Population (m)	Annual growth rate
1700	13 300	. . .
1760	16 900	0.399
1820	19 000	0.195

Table 7.2   Population and migration (thousands)

	Population (m)	Annual growth rate	Emigration (decade to) (m)
1820	19 000	. . .	
1830	21 020	1.010	
1840	22 040	0.474	
1850	24 065	0.879	
1860	24 804	0.302	
1870	26 526	0.671	117
1880	28 211	0.616	317
1890	30 246	0.696	771
1900	32 416	0.693	1 471
1910	34 377	0.587	1 217

For the 19th century, at least for 1820 onward, Italian population growth continues at a relatively slow pace (compared with all but Sweden in this study). In Table 7.2, we see the decennial estimates from 1820 to 1910, still drawing on Maddison. Emigration is a major factor here, as the last column in the table indicates; furthermore, it is worth noting that the set of numbers in the first column is like both Sweden (where emigration was how the balance was achieved) and France (where it was not).[2] The French rate of economic growth was also much more steady during the entire period (from 1700, really) and did not feature the kind of spurt noticed in Italy late in the period.

In any event, not to gloss over a serious difference with developed Europe, in 1860 the Italian population of 26 million was 78 per cent illiterate and was 70 per cent in agriculture, and even by 1900 only 20 per cent of the gross national product was generated in the industrial sector.

Table 7.3   Agriculture/industry employment

| | 1870 | |
| | Percentage of employment in | |
	Agriculture	Industry
Italy	62.0	23.0
France	49.2	27.8
Germany	49.5	28.7
Sweden	53.9	NA
United Kingdom	23.0	42.3

Table 7.4   Percentage of labour in agriculture ($550 per capita standard)

	Per cent	Date
Italy	55.4	1910
France	49.3	1870
Germany	50.0	1870
Sweden	53.5	1900
Great Britain	25.0	1840

7.1.2   Agricultural Growth in Italy during the Transformation

Let us begin by documenting the employment situation in Italy in 1870 compared with the rest of the countries in this study. Maddison (1982) carries the summary given in Table 7.3 for these countries, in terms of the employment generated in the agricultural and industrial sectors. Clearly, at this date Italy is less developed in this sense than the other countries. A similar point, but with its focus on the stage of development, is provided by Crafts (1984) in Table 7.4. Here the method is to hold the stage of development constant (rather than the date); the arbitrary standard is $550 (US 1970) per capita. The notion is that this is a state at which countries might be referred to as developed in a comparative sense. By this comparison, Italy actually is close to the average of non-British Europe; this is, of course, even more obvious if we separate out the British numbers, as Crafts would have us do, on the grounds that their experience was simply different from that of the rest of Europe. In any case, Italy is still last in the calculation, although only marginally so.

The standard numbers on Italy's agricultural output during this

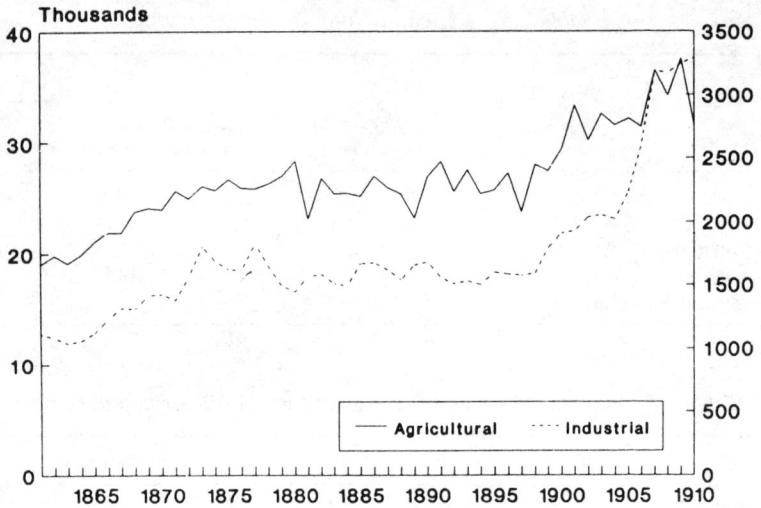

Figure 7.1   Industrial and agricultural production, 1861–1910

period are those of ISTAT (1957). As one might expect in this literature, the orthodox view paints a dismal picture of Italian agriculture, North and South, and much of the blame for the later industrialization of Italy is laid on an agricultural sector that appears to have the lowest productivity of any we have looked at in this study (Zangheri, 1969). In contrast, the aforementioned ISTAT numbers do not corroborate this story in significant ways, as we shall see. While we have no particular interest in the details of this controversy, the general numbers are relevant to this study (since agriculture is so important in GNP). We also note that in at least one important northern area – Lombardy – recent work by Barbiero (1988) confirms the more optimistic view of Italian agriculture and its assistance to industrialization in this period.

Figure 7.1 illustrates the relative growth of the industrial and agricultural sectors, as measured by ISTAT. Here the data are scaled differently, with the initial industrial number being 1119 million lire (measured against the right-hand scale) while the agricultural number at the beginning of the period is 19 019 million lire. Note that the agricultural figures, on the left axis, are thousand-millions. While the industrial figures move up faster than the agricultural over the entire period (with the gains mostly in the first decade of the 20th century), the agricultural figures are considerably above the industrial even by 1910 (the only country in that position in this study). Indeed, the industrial figures do not exceed the agricultural until World War II.

The point, then, is to note that Italian GNP throughout this period is bound to be dominated by the agricultural sector, both with regard to its trends and its cycles. We will see, below, that Italian cycles differ from those experienced by the other countries, in being roughly unchanged in volatility throughout the 1861 to 1910 period. The other countries we have looked at appear to have had their cycles damped by the strongly growing industrial sector, a benefit denied to the Italians. We note, finally, that the comparisons just made do not make use of the Fenoaltea data (to be discussed below) and thus show a somewhat more modest rate of industrialization than might actually be true. We are using the older numbers for purposes of comparability here.[3]

7.2 ITALIAN INDUSTRIALIZATION: BACKGROUND AND GROWTH

The background to Italian growth could easily reach to the days of the heady commercial successes of the Italian city-states in the Renaissance, but there is a danger in drawing so long a line since there could to be a strong tendency to downgrade Italian efforts in the First Industrial Revolution as if continuous economic supremacy over time were the standard to which the country should be held. From the beginning, but certainly from the time of the French occupation (1796–1814), Italy – especially Northern Italy – participated in European industrialization. The market was broad for European producers – and made broader still by the Continental System (1806). In this period textiles (cotton, wool and silk), metals and machinery producers were all active in Italy.

There is a traditional story about Italian development which tends to follow a mildly pessimistic line. It goes as follows. After Napoleon's downfall, from the agricultural collapse in 1816–17 when there certainly was famine in parts of Italy, it is said that there was prolonged depression until 1830 (Cafagna, 1976). Then, beginning in 1831 (stimulated by raw silk production and a stable (Austrian) government), there was relatively rapid economic development in the

North. The railroad had a lot to do with this, although the South remained stubbornly unaffected. In any case, it was the Piedmont and Lombardy that led the way, and Genoa and Milan became financial and industrial centres, although Naples was considerably more populous at the time. During the political turmoil in the period from 1848 to 1870, the North (especially the Piedmont under King Victor Emmanuel II and Count Cavour) developed a moderate and patronizing approach to development that seems to have maintained a positive pace for the industrial tradition in Italy. In any event, prosperity and skilful diplomatic manoeuvres put the Piedmont in the political and economic lead at the time of final unification in 1870.

From 1870 until the mid-1890s, overall Italian growth was not up to the European average in spite of its newfound status and stability. Partly, no doubt, this was due to the world-wide agricultural slack in this period which produced significant signs of depression in that sector. Then, too, periods of declining overall prices, such as this one, create an illusion of overall depression that not all observers appear to read correctly. Partly, further, it is the result of including the south of Italy – almost a different country economically – in the general statistical picture. But from 1896 until 1914, Italian growth was very rapid indeed. Much of Europe was moving ahead quickly at this time; interestingly, Italy came in with iron and steel as a major industry at this time.

Perhaps the best way to visualize Italy's growing industrial structure is to describe her production with both general and particular numbers. In Figure 7.2 two broad production indices are compared, one due to ISTAT (1957) and one more recent effort which is the work of Fenoaltea (1981). Real GNP is included for purposes of comparison (and for later reference). Here it is clear (from either set of industrial figures) that an industrial slowdown ran from the late 1880s until the mid-1890s. After that, industrial growth pulled the economy along, in the great industrial boom that was in full bloom by 1896. Notice that there are almost no 'industrial' recessions in Fenoaltea's data for the entire period. Indeed, in that series in only five years (1865 and 1889 to 1892) did Italian industrial production decline at all, and two of those declines (1865 and 1889) were essentially trivial. This suggests a much more robust picture of Italian industrial growth than the traditional view already outlined. The breakdown in Table 7.5 suggests how different the story is if one uses the ISTAT index (which follows the GNP figures quite closely) rather than the Fenoaltea revisions. These are compounded rates of growth

Index Numbers or billions of Lire

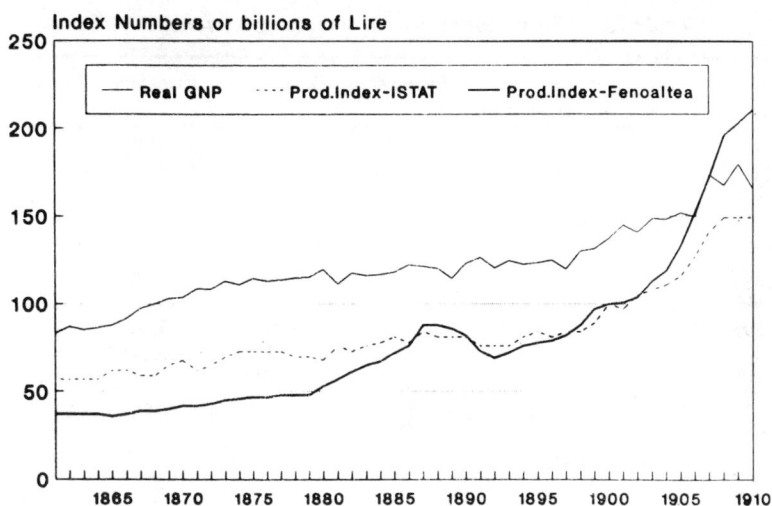

Figure 7.2   Italian industrial growth, 1861–1910

Table 7.5   ISTAT and Fenoaltea measures

	ISTAT	Fenoaltea
1861–1910	1.96%	3.55%
1861–1887	1.49	3.33
1892–1910	3.74	6.21

based on the end-points of the respective periods. The two views are dramatically different, of course, at least as a general picture of Italian industrialization, with the newer numbers showing rates of growth almost double the earlier estimates. More specifically, it is the 1879 to 1887 and 1902 to 1910 periods that produce the differences in these tabulations.

A breakdown of the major sectors responsible for the industrial spurt in Italy suggests just how broad-based the post-1892 boom actually was. These sectors include the traditional ones (cotton, iron and steel and mining) as well as the new ones of chemicals and utilities. Table 7.6, then, illustrates their performance at five-year intervals, with growth rates attached for the 1895 to 1910 period. What is really impressive in the table is the performance of the three

Table 7.6 The major industrial sectors in Italy, 1861–1910

	Cotton	Chemical	Iron and steel	Engineering	Construction	Extractive	Utilities
1861	·	·	61	102	396	35.4	8.3
1865	·	·	34	90	490	41.0	9.4
1870	10	·	43	117	341	48.5	11.7
1875	14	·	68	143	404	52.3	14.5
1880	25	·	101	173	440	69.3	17.6
1885	52	·	147	292	659	83.8	24.3
1890	73	·	284	311	586	84.5	34.4
1895	90	146	214	222	393	77.6	43.8
1900	102	369	307	312	391	98.4	61.2
1905	136	512	471	527	635	117.7	95.6
1910	152	1050	1013	1014	1135	136.0	163.6

Annual growth rate (1895–1910):

	Cotton	Chemical	Iron and steel	Engineering	Construction	Extractive	Utilities
	3.49	13.15	10.36	10.13	7.08	3.74	8.78

Note: Cotton, chemicals, iron and steel and engineering are in thousands of tons. Construction, extractive industries and utilities are in millions of 1911 lire).

Source: Fenoaltea, 1982a, 1982b, 1988a, 1988b.

manufacturing industries, whose compound annual growth rates were all over 10 per cent over the last fifteen years of the sample. Utilities (gas, elcctricity and water) also grew at a very rapid rate during the period, as did construction. Cotton and the extractive industries did not keep pace, but turned in respectable numbers, none the less.[4]

Italian development during its most rapid period seems to have depended on the growth of the railroad system, perhaps more than in the other countries considered in this study. In 1861 there were 2773 kilometres of track in operation (while in 1910 there were 18 090) and these were laid down steadily over the period with spurts in the early to mid 1860s and after 1872 (until around 1895). In 1861 the rail system was mainly in Northern Italy (70 per cent), linking Milan, Genoa, Venice, Bologna and Ancona, but by 1880 the national grid was filled in. The acceleration of northern industrial growth in the 1880s (at least by Fenoaltea's numbers) seems directly related to this pattern, but there was a lot of track laid in the 1880s and early 1890s as well, as noted in Table 7.7. The table, then, emphasizes the relatively rapid growth of industrial production, 1865 to 1890, accompanied by the railroad expansion from 1861 to 1895. By 1895 the railroad boom was over and the pieces were in place for the industrial

Table 7.7   Italian railroads and industrial growth, 1861–1910

Date	Track laid (km)	Average annual growth (%)	Industrial production index	Average annual growth (%)
1861	2 773	. . .	37	. . .
1865	4 591	16.39	36	–0.01
1870	6 429	8.01	42	3.33
1875	8 018	4.94	47	2.38
1880	9 290	3.17	53	2.55
1885	11 003	3.69	72	7.17
1890	13 629	4.77	82	2.78
1895	15 970	3.44	78	–0.01
1900	16 429	0.57	100	5.64
1905	17 078	0.79	133	6.60
1910	18 090	1.18	211	11.73

Source: Fenoaltea (1981).

acceleration that started in 1896. This picture is etched sharply in the figures of Table 7.7. We should note, though, that on a per capita or per-area basis, Italian railroads were possibly only half as dense as those in England and France in 1910. This, to be sure, is the statistical effect of including the relatively undeveloped south in the calculations.

An interesting hypothesis about the foregoing in the literature is that the Italian government, through the tax system, was able to appropriate the funds necessary to build the railroads – at the cost of starving industry of capital – at least until 1895.[5] Then, with the capital released and the transportation infrastructure in place, Italy was set for the industrial boom that followed. Clearly, this supposes a causal link between railroads and industrial growth that can be tested – perhaps by means of the Granger-causality test – but possibly with fairly long lags in view of the long gestation and building period for railroads. Bank assets may also be involved in the process in a somewhat different way than in other countries, in view of the arrival of the German-style industrial banks after 1894 (just at the time of the acceleration). Of course the alternative hypothesis is that there was no capital starvation, in view of Italy's participation in international capital markets.

A way to begin an evaluation of these questions is to look at some Granger-causal tests involving railroads. In the tests, shown in

Table 7.8   Railroads and Italian industrialization Granger-causal
investigations (log first differences of data)

| | \| p-Values for lags of | | | | | |
	1	2	3	4	5	Sign
1861–1910:						
RR causing industrial production	0.69	0.01*	0.02*	0.08	0.04*	ns
Industrial production causing RR	0.57	0.78	0.84	0.80	0.85	
1871–1910:						
RR causing industrial production	0.84	0.00*	0.00*	0.01*	0.02*	–
Industrial production causing RR	0.94	0.68	0.64	0.78	0.79	
1861–1890:						
RR causing industrial production	0.71	0.75	0.10	0.34	0.42	
Industrial production causing RR	0.94	0.86	0.66	0.75	0.55	

Note: ns indicates that the sum of the lag coefficients on the proposed causal
variable is not significantly different from zero.

Table 7.8, the Granger-causality model is employed on the log first
difference of the data, since the log-level figures proved to be non-
stationary.[6] These results indicate quite strongly that indeed there
was a Granger-causal link running from the railroad to industrial
production, and that it apparently occurred in the period from 1871
to 1910 (or possibly a little later). Interestingly, however, the influence in one case is not a positive one, as one might expect, but has a
negative sign, indicating that the influence of the railroad, while
possibly indiscernible in the early going, may actually have acted to
reduce economic growth during the period of Italy's most rapid
expansion.[7] This could imply overbuilding (or the capital market
effect discussed above), or it could reflect other problems in the data
employed or in the Granger test itself.[8] It is also interesting that for
the entire period, as indicated in the first lines of Table 7.8, there is
significant Granger-causation but the sign is ambiguous (indicated by
'ns'). Possibly, then, a positive early effect (not isolated in the table)
was mixed with a negative later effect. On the whole, this is what the
historical record would have predicted, as this is outlined above.

What we have seen, then, is that industrialization did arrive in Italy
at the same time as in the more developed countries of Western
Europe, but it was geographically concentrated and not on a very

large scale, relative to the major industrial powers. During the first 70 years of the 19th century, the foundations for an industrial spurt were laid, evidently. Political unity and market penetration seem in retrospect to have been important ingredients in this mix. In the 1870s and 1880s, the Italian economy certainly grew a little, but what is most impressive in the numbers is the sudden acceleration that followed the recession in the mid-1890s, carrying on into the 20th century. The railroad seems to have been important in laying the groundwork for this event, but, we conjecture, during the period of accelerating growth, new railroad construction may actually have provided a drag on growth although not enough, to be sure, to prevent the Italian economy from turning in some of the best growth figures in the world at that time.

7.3 THE ITALIAN MACROECONOMY IN THE LATE 19TH CENTURY

Figure 7.1 illustrates the growth of the Italian economy in various ways; included there is a plot of real GNP, which is actually quite flat over a substantial part of the period. To dramatize this important point further, and to attempt to pin down the exact time dimension of what appears to be a substantial period of relative stagnation, the breakdown given in Table 7.9 of real GNP (and other figures) is useful.[9] This table locates the period of relatively slow growth as ending in 1895 and from that point an investment-led industrial boom from 1896 to 1910. In this event real GNP grew at quite a rapid rate while investment grew at what is really an astonishing rate. It is also interesting that population growth apparently is not positively associated with this rapid growth then and, indeed, is at a lower rate during the period of most rapid growth. It will be recalled that emigration is a major part of this result. The per capita rate of growth, as a result,

Table 7.9   Estimated growth rates in the Italian economy, 1861–1910 (per cent per annum)

	Real GNP	Real investment	Population
1861–1910	1.177	2.274	0.651
1861–1895	1.078	1.484	0.657
1896–1910	2.574	8.783	0.580

is similar to, but at a faster rate than Germany during the same period, which puts it at the top of the European table for the time (for almost any time, for that matter). It is certainly clear that Italy did, indeed, have an important industrial boom underway by the end of the 19th century.

We need to note one other thing about the GNP figures that is possibly apparent in the graph but needs to be quantified more precisely. In 1875, real GNP stood at 114.403 in real (1913) lire. In 1889, after a period with numerous downturns, it stood at 114.571. Thus, for 14 years, the Italian economy produced essentially no growth (and declined in per capita terms). Furthermore, in 1897, eight years further along, the real GNP figure stood at 119.855. Now, while it is important to realize that this is a peak (1875) compared with a trough (1897), this still seems evidence of at least a tendency in the Italian economy of this era to dissipate the gains from expansion in rather deep (as we shall see) recessions. We note, also, that over the 1875 to 1889 period there was mild inflation (at 0.26 of 1 per cent per year) as well as relatively slowly growing investment spending.[10]

We have already noted that Italy appears to have had a classic investment boom during the period of her most rapid growth, and at this point some further quantification seems advisable. Drawing on the ISTAT (1957) data for comparability, and putting the data into ratio form, the correlations in Table 7.10 tell a remarkable story. Here we look at correlations of the C/Y and G/Y ratios with the investment ratio (I/Y). In both periods we see that consumption was negatively related to investment (in the first column) at about the same high level of correlation. That is, when C/Y was up, I/Y was down. In contrast, government spending (in ratio form) seems to have had little effect in the earlier period, but also contributed significantly to what we should call 'crowding in' in the later period. We have not seen both consumption and government contribute to investment in our earlier comparisons for other countries, done in a roughly comparable manner.[11]

Table 7.10   Correlations of *C/Y* and *G/Y* ratios

	C-ratio	G-ratio
Investment ratio		
1861–1890	–0.976	–0.140
1891–1910	–0.916	–0.849

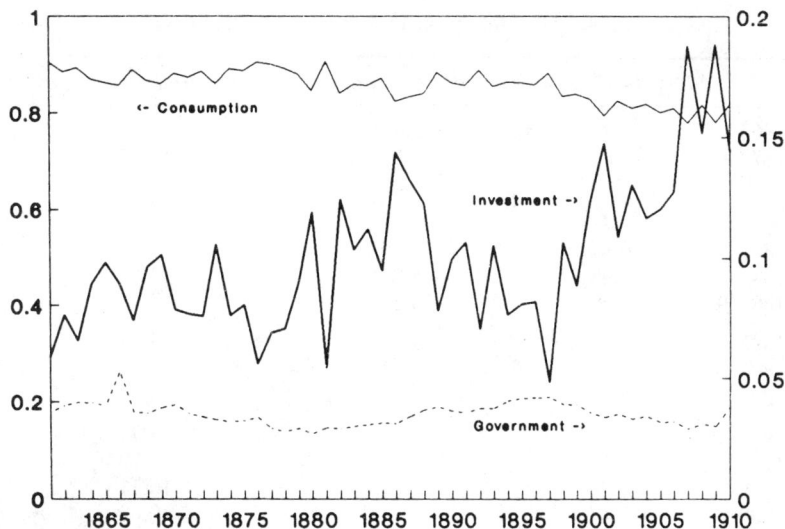

Figure 7.3   Spending ratios in the Italian economy, 1861–1910

As indicated, the story told here is not that of crowding out, but more of crowding in; a graph helps to make this clearer. In Figure 7.3 the three spending ratios are compared, with the consumption ratio on the left-hand axis and the investment and government spending ratios on the right-hand. Here we find the consumption ratio drifting steadily downward over the period, with a rather noticeable downward movement after 1895. Government spending, at less than 5 per cent of GNP was quite constant over the period, although it, too, drifted slightly downward after 1895. But most dramatic is the sharp upward movement in investment, again from the mid-1890s. The picture, thus, dramatizes what is clearly a good example of a boom that was partly shaped by significant new investment in plant and equipment.

The next topic concerns the cycles in the Italian data of this period. There are numerous downturns, measured by actual declines in the real GNP numbers (Table 7.11). In all, 17 of the 49 possible years showed downturns – meaning that the typical pattern was roughly for one lean year to be followed by two years of growth – with the more severe downturns scattered over the period (with the worst actually at the very end). This, too, is a pattern unlike that in the other European countries in our sample, where the cycles seem to become

Table 7.11   Italian business cycles (% changes)

	GNP	Agricultural production	Industrial production
1863	−2.16	− 3.48*	− 3.86*
1872	−0.15	− 2.80*	13.02
1874	−2.02	− 1.39	− 6.22*
1876	−1.16	− 2.89*	− 0.49
1881	−6.87	−18.50*	8.15
1883	−1.48	− 5.08*	− 4.68*
1887–9	−6.30	−10.55*	− 2.42
1892	−4.69	− 9.48*	5.71
1894	−1.57	− 7.71*	− 1.70*
1897	−4.07	−12.68*	− 0.44
1902	−2.84	− 9.48*	5.71
1904	−0.18	− 3.24*	− 1.70*
1906	−1.27	− 2.47*	16.11
1908	−3.44	− 6.31*	− 0.69
1910	−7.81	−15.90*	1.32

milder over the period and there are generally fewer years of recession compared with expansion.

Table 7.11 also provides a breakdown of the declines in the ISTAT
production figures for agriculture and industry. Here one finds agricultural production a prime suspect in 16 of the 17 declining years,
while industry figures in only five. This is indicated by an asterisk in
the cases when sectoral production declines more than real GNP. As
we noticed with the other countries in our sample, industrial output
tends to smooth the business cycle, although in the case of Italy, this
smoothing does not produce a very noticeable effect on GNP in view
of the relatively small share the industrial sector has in total GNP. In
a nutshell, Italy's cycles are clearly agricultural in origin, although the
industrial downturns of 1874, 1883, 1894 and 1908 have their counterparts in the (other) industrial countries of the world.

Another way to visualize the Italian cycles of this period is provided in Figure 7.4. The procedure used to generate this picture is to
plot the residuals of the regression that produces the first part of line
(1) in Table 7.9. As the residuals indicate, from the 1860s until the
1880s, Italy was doing very well, but it was not really until 1907 that
the Italian economy moved significantly above trend (at 1 per cent
growth in GNP). Indeed, the whole 'below trend' period covers 1881
to 1906, an incredible 25 years, although the turn-around begins

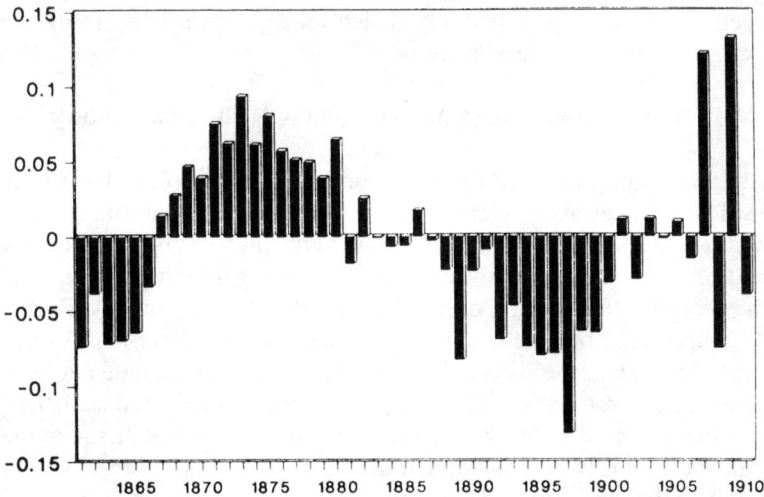

Figure 7.4   Italian business cycles, 1861–1910. Detrended logarithms of
real GNP

around 1896. It seems that in this respect, too, Italy's cycles are not
like those of the other countries we have looked at in this study.

7.4   MONEY AND THE ITALIAN ECONOMY

This section considers, in a fashion parallel to the treatment in earlier
chapters, the interconnection between Italian money and growth. As
with the other countries in our collection, the major empirical topics
covered are monetary neutrality and the behaviour of the demand for
money. In Italy, it seems, the former may not hold, while for the
latter we find a well-developed literature including some rare simultaneous-equations work that seems to lead in the direction of stability
of the demand for money over the period. We will not agree with the
literature on this point.

   We are also interested in the institutional development of the
Italian monetary system, and that work will actually precede the
empirical discussions. Indeed, before launching into the empirics this
chapter also takes a look at the financial sophistication index for the
Italian economy, in this case working on a comparison with France
and Germany. This background provides a structure that is helpful to

keep in mind in the essentially structureless empirical world of, for example, Granger-causality tests.

7.4.1   The Development of Italian Banking in the 19th Century

As mentioned above, Italy began operating as a political entity in 1861 – although its modern borders were not yet established – and had at that time an elected Parliament that oversaw monetary matters. In 1862, the lira was established as legal tender and in 1863 the official exchange rate of the lira with the British pound was set at 25.3 lira. This rate held during the intervals that Italy had a fixed exchange rate in the succeeding fifty years. There were nine banks of issue from 1861 until 1893 when failure and merger reduced their number to six; in 1894, then, a law concentrated the note issue in the Banca d'Italia, Banco di Napoli and Banco di Sicilia, a situation that survived beyond 1910. There was, though, no central bank, and (hence) no coordinated monetary policy, although as we shall discuss below the Italian government may well have attempted to adhere to the rules of the international gold standard through treasury operations (see below). But it is certainly true that Italy had a comparatively safe banking system in this period and, aside from the difficulties in 1892 to 1894, Italian banks may well have offered a superior product to their customers.

Above we mentioned that Italy was a gold-standard country for much of this period and it is now time to be more precise about that. What we should have said is that (Fratianni and Spinelli, 1984, p. 408),

> Despite the fact that Italy adopted the gold standard intermittently and for brief periods of time, her experience was not different from what it would have been had she adhered to the standard through-out, particularly from 1900 to 1913 . . . . Briefly put, Italy was guided by the norm of the gold standard.

By 'intermittent', then, is meant incovertibility from 1866 to 1884, a situation precipitated by the Austrian war effort (1966) and from 1894 to 1913, following a period of bank failure and the reorganization of the banking system. One way in which the Italian authorities 'adhered' to the gold standard was through attempts to control the size of the currency issue. At the same time, according to Fratianni and Spinelli, examination of the determinants of the monetary base, following a procedure employed by Cagan (1965), suggests that the commercial banks that carried out the policy were actually *sterilizing* foreign-exchange flows, a practice that is decidedly not in keeping with the gold standard rules. Their interpretation is that Italy's apparent adherence to the gold standard is explainable under the monetary approach to the balance of payments, by which means actual money altering gold flows are unnecessary, their place being taken by good flows and adjustments in the demand for money.

Before we begin our causal tests we should again note that Fratianni and Spinelli (1984) have done some formal work on the questions of international relations among nations at this time. What they find is foreign (British) prices Granger-cause the foreign components of the Italian monetary base – and Italian prices – while Italian prices themselves interact with British prices. Both of these results they regard as unsupportive of the monetary approach (the former is, at any rate) but this is not a comprehensive experiment, really, and so the question of exactly how Italy fits into the late 19th-century gold standard seems largely unanswered at this point. At a minimum, one needs to link monetary bases and price levels for all of the major players in the gold standard league.

7.4.2 Italy's Financial Sophistication

Among the countries of Western Europe, Italy is certainly one we would expect to exhibit financial sophistication, especially compared with the less developed European countries and possibly even to countries that possessed considerably larger per capita income and wealth. This is simply because Italian bankers had practically forever been in the vanguard of financial innovation in the world, especially, but not solely, in terms of international finance. Even so, part of financial sophistication is the extent of the domestic financial services system, and in Italy banking was not considerable outside the prosperous industrial and commercial centres. We would, then, expect the spread of the industrial revolution to coincide with an increase in the financial sophistication index in Italy, as it does with all but England during this period. The index, of course, provides a volume measure of financial services.

The two ways we are looking at financial sophistication in this study involve either the 'financial sophistication index' ($1/V$ times 52, measured in weeks) or the income elasticity of the demand for money. Considering what we have just said about Italian banking in this period, one might reasonably expect Italy to show a steadily increasing financial sophistication (however measured). This is what Figure 7.5 shows, where Italy is compared with France. Here we see a rise in Italy from just under 10 weeks to over 35 weeks (of GNP covered by money holdings), a rise that exceeds that in any other country we have looked at in this study, in percentage terms. It is interesting that the period from 1888 to 1903, a period in which the banking system was allegedly led to over-produce money, actually shows only a very small increase in the ratio of money to GNP (of 0.8 of a week, actually), but the depressed 1880s, in general, do show a strong rise. In comparison with France, still looking at the top half of the figure, we find that the Italians were apparently less well endowed with banking services in 1861, but by the late 1880s were on a par with the French.

Even so, one of the problems with such numbers is that the national income concepts (and banking statistics) vary across countries, so that absolute comparisons could easily be seriously misleading. To deal with that problem to some extent, and to provide an additional dimension to the discussion, the bottom panel of Figure 7.3 puts the two series just described, and the equivalent German numbers, on the same scale, with 1861 = 1. The resulting picture makes it clear that the relatively unsophisticated Italian financial system set the pace (of growth) in the period, although the Germans were rapidly closing at the end. France, on the other hand, seems to have developed relatively slowly in its financial sector in this period, providing a clear distinction across the three countries. Of course these comparisons reflect the relative sophistication already achieved by these countries at the point of the base year (1861). France was comparatively well developed, financially, at that time.

7.4.3 Monetary Neutrality

Considering the acceleration of the Italian money supply and the apparent increased use of, and growth of, the financial system even in the apparently dismal years of the Great Depression of the 1880s and early 1890s, it is interesting to examine the causal links between money and real income over the period. To begin, the growth of the money stock in this period breaks down as shown in Table 7.12 (using the end-points of the data). This shows very rapid monetary growth throughout, with very modest inflation, even during the boom period at the end.[12] This does leave a puzzle, since one would normally expect more spill-over from money onto prices, particularly when the economy is not growing very rapidly (as was the case from 1861 to

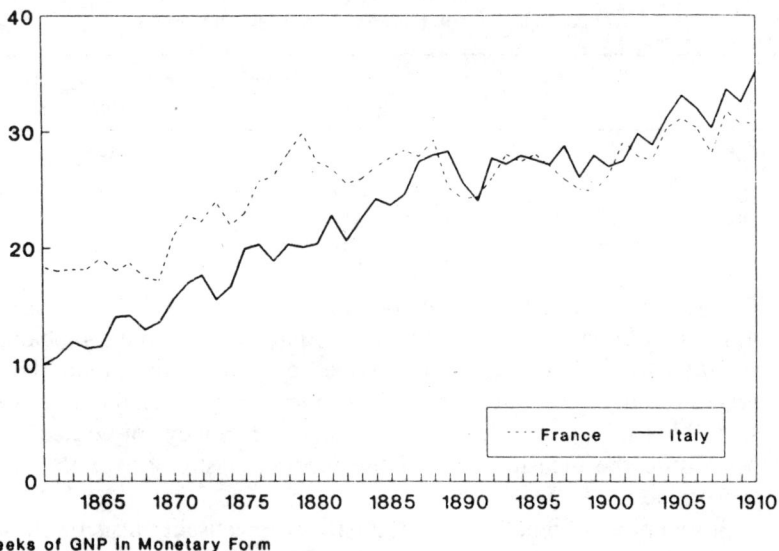

Weeks of GNP in Monetary Form

A. Financial Sophistication Indices
   Italy versus France

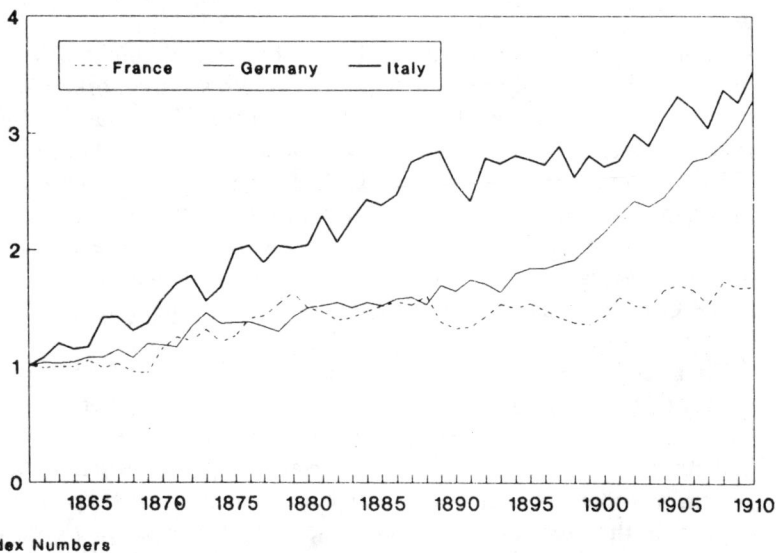

Index Numbers

B. Financial Sophistication Indices
   1865 = 1.00

Figure 7.5

Table 7.12　Growth rates of money and prices

| | Growth rates of | |
	Money	Prices
1861–1910	4.475	0.494
1861–1895	4.403	0.246
1895–1910	4.637	1.054

1895). It is possible that the demand for the services of banks might have something to do with this (i.e., that the customers of banks sought such balances for the services of banks other than those services provided in the form of the medium of exchange). If so, something might turn up in the demand for money, of course, especially in the measurement of the income elasticity over the two sub-periods.

Fratianni and Spinelli perform a battery of causality tests on these topics, using the monetary base rather than the money supply. They find that the monetary base had a causal influence on domestic prices *and real income* (so that money was presumably non-neutral), but not the converse. At the same time, prices caused real income; the period was 1867 to 1913.

Table 7.13 carries the basic results for the original empirical work on monetary neutrality in this section. These tests are worked with the money supply rather than the monetary base. Note that the data are (log) first differenced to achieve stationarity. There is, then, some sign of a monetary effect on real GNP (using the data provided in Fratianni and Spinelli), especially for the 1861 to 1890 period; there is also a touch of 'reverse causation' (of $Y -> M$) at five lags.[13] The most interesting effect, in some ways, in the table, however, turns up in the Granger-causal effect of money on real income in the 1881 to 1910 period.[14]

There do, then, appear to be two distinct periods here, in terms of money's effect on real variables, with banks having a general (real) effect on the financially unsophisticated economy in the early period and on the industrial sector itself during the period when Italian growth was more explosive. An explanation of this phenomenon that appears in the literature is due to Gerschenkron (1962) and detailed by Cohen (1967); these authors pin the result on the arrival of German-style industrial banks after 1894. These banks grew from nil to around 2 billion Lire in total assets by 1910. In Germany, as we

Table 7.13   Money and real activity in Italy Granger-causality tests
(per capita variables in log-first differences)

| | \multicolumn{5}{c}{p-Values for lags (in years) of} | |
	1	2	3	4	5	Sign
1861–1910						
M → Y	0.032*	0.095	0.153	0.226	0.368	+
Y → M	0.622	0.430	0.705	0.201	0.122	
M → I	0.684	0.457	0.762	0.375	0.235	
I → M	0.651	0.326	0.519	0.449	0.831	
M → IProd	0.245	0.204	0.319	0.533	0.133	
IProd → M	0.709	0.547	0.717	0.442	0.333	
1861–1890						
M → Y	0.007*	0.042*	0.087	0.165	0.324	+
Y → M	0.364	0.094	0.219	0.168	0.030*	+
M → I	0.430	0.447	0.919	0.334	0.355	
I → M	0.715	0.556	0.725	0.742	0.855	
M → IPROD	0.433	0.416	0.650	0.707	0.310	
IPROD → M	0.202	0.462	0.323	0.556	0.946	
1881–1910						
M → Y	0.346	0.313	0.266	0.302	0.494	
Y → M	0.953	0.613	0.899	0.588	0.590	
M → I	0.194	0.162	0.125	0.099	0.297	
I → M	0.680	0.609	0.984	0.879	0.973	
M → IPROD	0.021*	0.036*	0.027*	0.102	0.076	+
IPROD → M	0.233	0.422	0.520	0.661	0.327	

saw, there was a similar effect (on the investment spending of large industrial firms). But in any case, these matters are in dispute; one aspect of this involves the likelihood that the demand for money could possibly be described as stable even though it seems to be filling different needs at different times.

Another aspect of monetary neutrality, of course, lies in the effect of money on prices (there should be an effect). As noted above, Fratianni and Spinelli find that the monetary base affected the price level in this period, but, of course, that is not the same thing as testing for the money stock itself, although a monetarist, at least, would be surprised if the results differed. Table 7.14 reports the results of Granger-causal experiments for the same subperiods as Table 7.13, for the GNP deflator provided by Fratianni and Spinelli and for the consumer price index. These results show the expected effect very

The Industrial Revolution

Table 7.14 Money and prices in Italy Granger-causality tests (variables in log-first differences)

| | p-Values for lags (in years) of | | | | | |
	1	2	3	4	5	Sign
1861–1910						
M → DEF	0.059	0.001*	0.000*	0.000*	0.001*	+
DEF → M	0.951	0.974	0.882	0.442	0.283	
M → CPI	0.019*	0.001*	0.002*	0.005*	0.016*	+
CPI → M	0.755	0.883	0.926	0.261	0.407	
1861–1890						
M → DEF	0.156	0.005*	0.004*	0.000*	0.002*	+
DEF → M	0.716	0.988	0.937	0.838	0.576	
M → CPI	0.059	0.019*	0.040*	0.082	0.215	+
CPI → M	0.726	0.939	0.990	0.518	0.466	
1881–1910						
M → DEF	0.382	0.484	0.705	0.806	0.304	
DEF → M	0.164	0.480	0.405	0.215	0.275	
M → CPI	0.426	0.229	0.272	0.227	0.396	
CPI → M	0.810	0.556	0.697	0.801	0.955	

clearly over the 1861 to 1910 period, for both measures of the price level (of inflation really), without any suggestion of reverse causation from prices to money. On the other hand, the disparity of results over time that has been stalking us is even more apparent here than in Table 7.13, with a quantity-theory result apparent in the period when the economy was slowly growing, but not in the 1880 to 1910 period, when (after 1895) the economy accelerated. This latter period is, it will be recalled, a time when per capita money balances appear to have Granger-caused industrial production, so in that sense the two results are consistent, although money could easily have served both roles in the period. This is certainly not an anomaly, except, of course, to a monetarist, and it is broadly in line with the results of Fratianni and Spinelli.

7.4.4 The Demand for Money

The demand for money in Italy has received some attention in the literature, with the original and prevailing position being that of Spinelli (1980, p. 83).

The central result is that there exists a stable demand for money for Italy during this period. This function is homogeneous in prices and yields parameter estimates close to those found previously for other countries.

This covers the very long period of 1867 to 1965 on annual data. Since we have already found the possibility of disparate results across Europe – and over time within each country considered so far – it is interesting to see whether Italy is an exception for the period 1861 to 1910. It is also interesting that in a later paper (Calliari, Spinelli and Verga, 1984), it is acknowledged that there was an error in the money stock series and that the interest rate employed was an official discount rate and (thus) not a market rate. The later paper also deflates by the cost-of-living index rather than the GNP deflator. None of these adjustments need cause any problems; after all, the function could be homogeneous in either set of prices, and interest rates often do not seem to have much of an effect on money demand. Even so, one does wonder if the tests for stability were adequate to the task at hand. In addition, the later paper does not address the question of stability directly, although money demand is estimated over a comparable period to the one looked at here. So there is quite a bit to do, to try to advance the discussion beyond these preliminary results.

The model used in both papers features partial adjustment in money holding and smoothing in the computation of permanent income. Their models are equivalent to the following. Let the long-run demand for money be given by

$$m_t^d = \alpha_1 + \alpha_2 y_t^e + \alpha_3 i_t + u_{it} \tag{7.1}$$

where y_t^e is expected (permanent) income, and the adjustment in money demand is given by

$$m_t - m_{t-1} = \beta \, (m_t^d - m_{t-1}) + u_{2t} \tag{7.2}$$

Here β is presumably less than unity if adjustment is achieved in more than one year. Finally, let expected income be defined by the following conventional partial adjustment equation.

$$y_t^e = (1 - \gamma) \, (y_t + \gamma y_{t-1} + \gamma^2 y_{t-2} + \dots) \tag{7.3}$$

Here γ is less than unity. If $\gamma = 0$, then expected income would be equal to actual income in period t.

The solution to this model of money demand is given by substituting (7.1) and (7.3) into (7.2) and then performing the Koyck transformation (subtracting γm_{t-1} from each side of the resulting equation). The result is a 'reduced form' of

$$m_t = (1 - \gamma) \beta\alpha_1 + (1 - \beta + \gamma) m_{t-1} - \gamma (1 - \beta) m_{t-2}$$
$$+ \beta\alpha_2 (1 - \gamma) y_t + \beta\alpha_3 i_t - \gamma\beta\alpha_3 i_{t-1} + w_t - \gamma w_{t-1} \quad (7.4)$$

where w_t is a combination of the (presumed to be independent) errors of Equations (7.1) and (7.2). This equation has five parameters and five variables and is nonlinear in the parameters. It is reduced form – hence the inverted commas – only to the extent that y_t and i_t are exogenous to the money-holding decision. It is virtually the same function as that estimated in the Spinelli (*et al.*) papers.

Let us begin with some OLS estimates of the reduced form expression in Equation (7.4); we will consider nonlinear estimates in a moment. Table 7.15 fits the exact model with the moving average (MA) term estimated in rows (1), (4) and (7). Other specifications are attempted also, with rows (2), (5) and (7) dropping the second lags on money and interest rates (since they are not significant) and rows (3), (6), and (9) dropping the non-significant MA term. These adjustments do not change the story appreciably.

The main result here is that there appears to be a sharp contrast in the way the model fits over the two sub-periods, with a relatively well-defined function appearing in rows (7) to (9) for the period 1880 to 1910, while the same functions fitted over the earlier (overlapping) period are totally unsatisfactory. No claim for stability over time could be advanced on this (scant) evidence. There are two other things to notice about the result for 1880 to 1910. Firstly, the 'income' elasticities in lines (8) and (9) are 1.270 in both cases, recalling that income and money are measured in logarithms.[15] This is greater than unity, but not significantly so. Secondly, the second lags (on interest rates, money, and the error term) are all rejected, successively, as we move from row (7) to (9). These terms appeared when we used the smoothing equation for permanent income. The results, thus, reject the use of (this form for) permanent income in the model for money demand. Partial adjustment, as indicated by the initial lag on the money stock, is accepted. These results are not those of Spinelli

Table 7.15   The demand for money in Italy. OLS estimates

	Const.	m_{t-1}	m_{t-2}	y_t	i_t	i_{t-1}	MA(1)	$\bar{R}^2$	DW
1861–1910									
(1)	–0.125	0.898	0.007	0.364	0.003	–0.005	–0.061	0.986	2.000
	(0.55)	(1.64)	(0.01)	(1.70)	(0.14)	(0.24)	(0.11)		
(2)	–0.080	0.895		0.367	–0.004		–0.036	0.987	1.997
	(0.39)	(16.25)		(2.28)	(0.32)		(0.23)		
(3)	–0.080	0.895		0.367	–0.004			0.987	2.032
	(0.40)	(16.96)		(2.32)	(0.34)				
1861–1890									
(4)	–0.109	0.909	–0.032	0.424	0.004	–0.007	0.000	0.969	1.994
	(0.23)	(0.79)	(0.03)	(0.88)	(0.14)	(0.24)	(0.00)		
(5)	–0.034	0.873		0.378	–0.003		0.036	0.973	1.986
	(0.09)	(9.86)		(1.08)	(0.21)		(0.17)		
(6)	–0.034	0.874		0.378	–0.003			0.973	1.960
	(0.10)	(10.52)		(1.13)	(0.22)				
1880–1910									
(7)	0.838	0.736	0.057	0.271	–0.100	0.008	–0.226	0.985	1.988
	(1.40)	(1.83)	(0.18)	(2.08)	(2.15)	(0.12)	(0.50)		
(8)	0.878	0.785		0.273	–0.094		–0.276	0.985	1.990
	(2.36)	(11.81)		(2.38)	(2.89)		(1.26)		
(9)	0.880	0.784		0.274	–0.094			0.984	2.409
	(2.50)	(12.84)		(2.38)	(3.03)				

(1980) for a different time period that included this period as a sub-period (from 1867).

The next thing to do is to try to produce estimates of the structural coefficients in this model. The most direct way to do this is to use non-linear least squares; this employs an iterative technique to find the parameters. The reason this is done is that Equation (7.4) actually is over-identified since it has six variables (plus a second error term) but only four theoretical parameters. The results are shown in Table 7.16. The result in Row (3), then, provides a reasonable fit, in some ways, although the failure of the smoothing parameter on expected income to be significant and the slow adjustment inherent in the value of 0.205 for β may not please everyone. At least it is clear that this function, too, is not stable over the period 1861 to 1910 in the sense that convergence did not occur in the periods listed above row (3).

The existing papers in the Italian literature also consider whether the partial adjustment and smoothing hypotheses are valid. This is

Table 7.16   The demand for money in Italy. Nonlinear least squares estimates

	α_1	α_2	α_3	β	γ	$\bar{R}^2$	DW
Full model							
1861–1910			(Not converged)				
1861–1890			(Not converged)				
1880–1910	4.098	1.269	–0.443	0.205	–0.065	0.984	2.336
	(3.80)	(2.46)	(4.33)	(3.05)	(0.32)		
$\gamma = 0$ *(no smoothing)*							
1861–1910	–0.759	3.494	–0.036	0.105		0.987	2.032
	(0.36)	(2.75)	(0.39)	(1.99)			
1861–1890	–0.273	2.996	–0.026	0.126		0.987	2.032
	(0.10)	(1.63)	(0.25)	(1.52)			
1880–1910	4.066	1.267	–0.437	0.216		0.984	2.409
	(3.85)	(2.50)	(4.42)	(3.55)			
$\beta = 1$ *(instantaneous adjustment)*							
1861–1910	–0.070	0.334	–0.004		–0.106	0.987	2.031
	(0.38)	(2.52)	(0.36)		(2.00)		
1861–1890	–0.030	0.340	–0.003		–0.128	0.973	1.959
	(0.10)	(1.20)	(0.24)		(1.51)		
1880–1910	0.744	0.228	–0.079		–0.224	0.984	2.423
	(2.62)	(2.52)	(3.21)		(3.31)		

easily done in the model at hand. Firstly, in view of the failure of γ in the first set, we look at results of a test assuming that $\gamma = 1$ in Equation (7.4); this implies no smoothing. A set of three results appears in rows (4) to (6) of Table 7.16. In this case the model converges quickly in all cases. Again, there is a strong distinction between sub-periods, so that stability over the entire period is readily rejected for this formulation. The best fit, again, is for the 1880 to 1910 period, for which the income elasticity is 1.267 (as it was in Table 7.15); this value is clearly not significantly different from unity. This elasticity is 3.494 for the equation that describes the entire period, suggesting that it may have fallen over the period; if so, this would not be an unusual result for this period.

Finally, consider rows (7) through (9) in Table 7.16, where the smoothing hypothesis is retained and instantaneous (i.e., within one year) adjustment is assumed. Again the model converges readily for all periods and again the early period and the later period turn out differently, but this time not in the coefficients so much as in the overall fit. The values and the signs for the coefficients here are not especially attractive, however. That is, the income elasticity of money demand is implausibly low and the smoothing parameter (γ) is actually significantly negative. This seems like a mis-specification. One is left with a decided preference for the second set of results, with its result of slow adjustment of actual to desired money balances (which is not, a priori, unreasonable), and an income elasticity that may well have fallen over the period, finishing up near unity. In all cases, finally, the stability of money demand over this period does not appear to be a reasonable claim.

The role of money in the Italian economy has both similarities to, and contrasts with, that in the other countries we have looked at. Italy seems to have had a relatively turbulent financial history, at least in the sense of being able to maintain a position on the gold standard. She also started further back in terms of financial sophistication, and moved faster over the 50 years after 1861. Furthermore, there appears to be a non-neutral connection between the growth of money and Italian real growth that is not echoed in the other countries. This was not evident, though, in the gold standard period when, curiously, there also was no Granger-causal relation between money and prices. Echoing some of these problems, estimates of the demand for money in Italy suggest that this function might, indeed, be unstable, at least as formulated in this study.

7.5 CONCLUSION

In some ways, Italy is an outlier in this study. The main reason for this lies in the relative importance of the agricultural sector. Italy, in 1910, was involved in an industrial boom that most of the other countries were enjoying, but in this case the spurt was of a small sector – so small, indeed, that the relatively upward push in industrial activity was not sufficient to dampen the (mostly) agriculturally-based business cycles. The cycles were, in consequence, more violent in Italy than elsewhere (in this study).

At the same time, Italy does participate fully in the 19th-century industrial boom, and her financial sector appears to have developed at about the same time as Germany, Sweden and France. Curiously, though, monetary neutrality does not appear to have held for Italy at all times – but then neither did the gold standard for any length of time. Here, as elsewhere in Europe, the demand for money appears not to have been stable, although the model and, for that matter, the data, could readily be improved upon.

8 The European Macroeconomy

8.1 INTRODUCTION

This chapter looks at a series of tests of macroeconomic influences that run across national boundaries. Of course it is indisputable that the industrial revolution spilled across state lines, but whether the effects were broad enough to produce an interaction that can be discerned by means of macroeconomic time-series tests is certainly another matter. Indeed, because most of the formal tests proposed here require that the relationship hold up for a considerable time, the cards seem stacked against the general hypothesis. Even so, there are good reasons to believe that growth was an interactive process in Europe at this time, perhaps because of spillovers and perhaps because of the possibly increasingly pan-European nature of capital markets (and business cycles). Of course the adoption of the gold standard in this period by the countries covered in this study also increases the likelihood of there being discernible ties, particularly of financial variables.

What is proposed in Section 8.2 is to look at some broad numbers, first on population growth (in Section 8.2.1) and then on real growth (in Section 8.2.2). This discussion will draw together the material from earlier chapters in order to present a general picture. Population growth induces trend in level figures and trend generally produces non-stationarity in macroeconomic time-series variables. Section 8.2.3 considers the results of a series of Dickey–Fuller tests to measure this effect. The conclusion is that it would be best to difference the money and income data to avoid any questions (at least from this source) about the time-series material in this chapter.

Section 8.3, then, turns to financial integration. The discussion here is in terms of how financial sophistication fares across all six countries. Emerging in the discussion will be the proposition that the appearance of the gold standard had quite a lot to do with the apparent change in the demand for money over the second half of the period. Here, Granger-causality tests are conducted using the high-powered money stocks and price levels of the six countries (although

253

France is omitted from the first set of tests, on account of the state of the French data). We note that no summing-up is attempted for the demand for money in these economies in view of the generally poor results obtained with the functions attempted in the individual chapters.

Section 8.4 looks at standard tests (of Granger-causality) of the within-country monetary neutrality hypothesis. These results have appeared in other chapters, and so the effort here is to look for the general story – and to include the United States. The purpose of this exercise is to prepare the way for a discussion of the international business cycle in the period, with the results of an earlier study (Craig and Fisher, 1991) summarized in Section 8.5. Here both the monetary and real interaction hypotheses appear to draw some support in the context of late 19th-century business cycles.

8.2　A SUMMARY OF EUROPEAN GROWTH STATISTICS

The following material is designed to compare the level figures for the various European countries (and the United States) across data that we have used in earlier chapters. None of this will confirm the pan-European hypothesis, really, since each country has a unique historical record, but even at the level of comparison effected here, it is evident that strong industrial and financial growth and the transformation of the European economy into a predominantly industrial form generally moves quite rapidly in those countries that could still have this experience after 1871. That is, while the United Kingdom has already gone through the transformation revealed here, all of the other countries appear to be moving rapidly, with the details varying in interesting and somewhat characteristic ways.

8.2.1　Population Growth and the Macroeconomy

All of the economies of Western Europe grew in this period at rates rapid in comparison to most of their history, but the rates do differ a lot, both for population and for the growth of the economy. This chapter is striving for a general picture of the macroeconomic situation of Europe in the last half of the 19th century, and to that end Table 8.1 illustrates the growth rates of the three variables of concern to us throughout this discussion: population, real output, and the money stock. While the discussion of this section is mainly about

Table 8.1   Growth rates in Europe and the United States, 1871–1910

	Real output	*Population*	*Money stock*
France	1.42	0.21	1.71
Germany	2.67	1.16	4.92
Italy		0.65	2.68
Fratianni/Spinelli	1.05*		
Mitchell	1.24		
Sweden	2.45	0.63	5.16
United Kingdom		0.89	
Friedman/Schwartz	2.05*		1.76
Deane	1.89		
Capie/Webber			1.65*
United States		2.07	5.80
Friedman/Schwartz	3.69		
Romer	3.78*		
Balke/Gordon	3.82		

* These are the preferred measures. See below for a description of the data.

population, this is the context in which we will be operating; additionally, as already noted, population growth provides the main reason that (in Section 8.2.3) we feel the need to discuss the stationarity of the (real and monetary) data. Here we find the more rapid growth rates of money associated with the more rapidly growing economies, independently of population growth. This might suggest a causal relationship between money and output/income but, as we shall see below, Granger-causality tests generally do not locate such a relation for most of these countries. What we do find is that the role of money in growth is much more complex, involving the increased use of money by economic agents relative to the usual benchmark of income; there is also the suspicion that certain sectors of the economy benefited more than others from the services provided by the rapidly growing banking industry.

8.2.2   The Components of National Income Across Countries

The chapters that preceded this one have remarked on the changing structure of each economy in this period. What has been discovered is that the alteration of the structure was really quite rapid in most cases, undoing an economic milieu that had inched along for many centuries. While this study has located the primary impetus for this

Table 8.2   Ratio of agricultural to industrial production, 1871–1910

	France	Italy	Sweden
1871	1.58	18.56	4.32
1881	1.01	14.73	2.69
1891	0.90	18.21	2.87
1901	0.90	17.30	1.21
1910	0.71	9.60	0.93

development at an earlier time, it is still remarkable how dramatically the relative mix of agriculture and industry was altered in this period and, further, how complex the changing roles of the aggregate sectors themselves seem to have been. Here the reference is primarily to the behaviour of the investment ratio and to the changing influence of government expenditures on the ability of the economy to move resources into the rapidly growing sectors.

The first calculations are for the ratio of agricultural production to industrial production across the European economies; in Table 8.2 the state of the data limits the calculation to three countries. All ratios declined dramatically, although not always between 1881 and 1901, with Sweden's transformation the greatest in percentage terms. Since Germany and the United States also underwent such a transformation (the United Kingdom did not, although the ratio did decline), the generalization that in this short period the European economy underwent what is possibly its most dramatic transformation in this respect seems reasonable.

Moving on to more complete data for the five European countries, let us look at the behaviour of consumption, government spending, and investment – as ratios of national income – over the same period (Table 8.3). Generally what comes through the strongest here is the growth of the investment ratio in the case of the more rapidly developing economies. Most particularly, Italy, Sweden and Germany saw this. This was apparently paid for, possibly characteristically, out of consumption in the case of Germany and Italy and out of government in the case of Sweden. The government spending ratios did change a little over the period, with a decisive increase appearing in the United Kingdom and a decisive decrease in Sweden. By mid- to late 20th-century standards, of course, these are relatively low numbers. In any case, government related 'crowding in' may well have been a factor in this period, at least for France and Sweden.

Table 8.3   Spending ratios in the European economy, 1871–1910

	France	Germany	Italy	Sweden	UK
Consumption					
1871	0.79	0.83	0.87	0.85	0.83
1881	0.79	0.84	0.91	0.82	0.84
1891	0.81	0.82	0.86	0.84	0.86
1901	0.76	0.80	0.79	0.82	0.79
1910	0.78	0.74	0.82	0.83	0.77
Government					
1871	0.09	0.11	0.04	0.10	0.05
1881	0.05	0.07	0.03	0.10	0.05
1891	0.05	0.08	0.04	0.09	0.06
1901	0.05	0.08	0.04	0.07	0.10
1910	0.04	0.09	0.04	0.06	0.08
Investment					
1871	0.03	0.09	0.08	0.06	0.10
1881	0.09	0.10	0.05	0.09	0.08
1891	0.06	0.11	0.11	0.08	0.08
1901	0.07	0.12	0.15	0.10	0.11
1910	0.08	0.14	0.14	0.11	0.07

8.2.3   Dickey–Fuller Tests of Monetary and Real Quantities

This section briefly examines the basic data – on per capita gross domestic product and per capita nominal money stocks – to see if they are stationary. This is done because the tests that we carry out in Sections 8.2 and 8.3 are not as convincing in the presence of non-stationarity of the data. The stationarity check involves looking at Dickey–Fuller tests to see if trend dominates the data; it does, and so the data are converted to growth rates to render them stationary. This is the usual finding in the literature (Nelson and Plosser, 1982).

The usual tests for stationarity are the Dickey–Fuller (DF) and augmented Dickey–Fuller tests. The Dickey–Fuller test is performed on a particular series, x_t, by running the regression:

$$\Delta x_t = \alpha + \theta x_{t-1} + \mu_t \qquad (8.1)$$

If the data are non-stationary, that is, if there is a unit root in x_t, then one should not be able to reject the hypothesis that $\Theta = 0$. The results from Equation (8.1) for both money stocks and the real per

Table 8.4   Unit root Dickey–Fuller test results per capita real
domestic product and money

	Real product		Monetary quantities	
	Θ	t-statistic (Ho: $\Theta = 0$)	t-statistic (Ho: $\Theta = 0$)	
United Kingdom				
Log levels	−0.04	0.94	−0.01	0.18
Differences	−1.27	8.24*	−0.57	4.35*
Regression DT	−0.39	3.02	−0.08	1.30
France				
Log levels	−0.78	1.43	0.03	0.94
Differences	−1.24	7.95*	−1.08	6.52*
Regression DT	−0.40	3.21	−0.05	0.64
Germany				
Log levels	−0.00	0.16	0.01	0.46
Differences	−0.97	5.99*	−0.81	4.94*
Regression DT	−0.21	2.14	−0.10	1.22
Italy				
Log levels	−0.00	0.09	0.01	0.41
Differences	−1.31	7.94*	0.80	6.08*
Regression DT	−0.13	1.54	0.06	0.78
Sweden				
Log levels	−0.10	0.56	−0.02	0.79
Differences	−1.10	6.58*	−0.49	4.42*
Regression DT	−0.15	1.58	−0.14	1.79
United States				
Log levels	−0.03	1.36	−0.02	0.89
Differences	−1.04	6.46*	−0.55	3.69*
Regression DT	−0.27	2.66	−0.15	1.92

* The probability of obtaining a test-statistic smaller than this is less than
0.05. Critical values are from Fuller (1976, p. 373). Ho: $\Theta = 0$ identifies the
null hypothesis.

capita national products of the six nations are shown in Table 8.4.[1]
Our working hypothesis is that the basic series themselves will be
non-stationary, while their first differences will be stationary. This
result is in fact what we obtain. These results indicate that for both
monetary and real per capita data neither log-level nor regression
data are stationary, while the differenced data always are.[2] Note that
the regression detrending is done by regressing the log of the variable
on a constant and the trend term and then employing the residuals of

the regression as a (potentially) detrended series. In any case, the results certainly indicate that one should work with the differenced data in applications that are sensitive to non-stationarity.

8.3 MONETARY INTERACTION IN THE LATE 19TH CENTURY

The following subsections will undertake two major tasks. First, a cross-country comparison of the financial sophistication of the six countries will be considered. This will take the form of comparing the financial sophistication indices and parameters of the standard demand-for-money functions of these countries. The first task will be to look at the cross-country evidence on financial sophistication. This is only one aspect of interaction, of course, but there is already a literature on these topics (e.g., Friedman and Schwartz, 1982 and Craig and Fisher, 1991) that claims that financial integration blankets Europe and runs across the Atlantic, at least for the major European economies. We will look at the five European countries and the United States in these comparisons.

This section also considers a new hypothesis. During this period the international gold standard was broadly adopted, bringing the possibility of financial interaction insofar as all of the nations concerned actually played by the rules of the gold standard, as these rules are generally understood to apply. We will note, later in the chapter, that the money stocks of the European countries show considerable interconnection; this result was arrived at (in Craig and Fisher, 1991) using Granger-causality and cointegration tests for the same countries studied here. The current effort will be to establish whether Granger-causality can be established among the high-powered money stocks and among the price indices of the same countries. Here, though, we will lose France in the high-powered money calculations, since the data sources do not appear to contain a satisfactory approximation for that concept.

Even if high-powered money stocks are not tied together across nations – as they are – price levels may be, by the operation of the 'law' of one price. In this case, one might invoke the monetary approach to the balance of payments, a theory that works with goods flows and adjustments of money demand, rather than high-powered money movements (as in the classic specie-flow mechanism). Thus the evidence on the price levels completes the story, as far as these simple calculations can take us. They, too, are not Granger-causally linked in many cases.

8.3.1 Financial Sophistication Indices

In earlier chapters, we use an index based on the velocity of money, in order to measure financial sophistication. This index multiplies the inverse of velocity (i.e., M/Y) by 52, to measure the number of weeks of national product held in the form of money. The index itself also measures the influence of changing financial intermediation (among other things) and for much of the 20th century has declined, as money substitutes became more widely used. In this earlier period, however, it seems that both increasing availability and increasing quality have created the opposite trend, so that velocity has declined and the index of financial sophistication has risen. The term 'financial sophistication' would presumably not be evocative in the 20th century, and calculations such as this are generally not performed for periods later than the one studied here, at least for these particular countries.

Across nations, though, another complication arises, and that is simply that neither measures of money nor measures of national income are strictly comparable. The money stock used here is the broad money stock, partly because narrow measures (involving transactions balances only) are not generally available; but the details of the institutional structure are different across nations (as discussed in Chapters 3 to 7). The national income numbers differ significantly in concept, further, so that the safest comparisons are of percentage changes over time, rather than in the level figures. Even so, Table 8.5 presents the level figures, just to establish some visual contact with the subject, with the more useful percentage changes at the bottom of the table. Here we find four countries that more than doubled their financial sophistication (indices) with only the (clearly sophisticated) United Kingdom economy showing essentially no gain in this respect. The level was as low as 9.5 weeks of national product covered by money balances in Sweden in 1871 and as high as 42+ weeks for Germany during the period of her explosive growth. Using the United Kingdom as a norm, all but Sweden of the European economies exceeded the UK relative usage of monetary services by 1910, when none did in 1871.[3] Clearly, whatever else one can say about the industrial revolution in this period, there was a type of financial revolution going on. Even so, it needs to be noted that this is not a leading sector we are observing, at least in the sense of showing some

Table 8.5 Financial sophistication indices. Europe and the United States, 1871–1910

	France	Italy	Germany	Sweden	UK	US
1871	22.84	17.01	14.93	9.54	28.86	11.23
1881	26.89	22.85	19.55	13.20	28.56	11.79
1891	24.46	24.10	22.43	16.28	28.88	17.52
1901	29.24	27.56	29.53	23.68	28.90	21.31
1910	30.88	35.21	42.28	26.35	28.02	23.94
% Change	35.2	107.0	183.2	176.2	4.3	113.2

sort of clear causal link running from money to real activity (see below) except for a few subperiods of the data (for a few countries).

8.3.2 International Financial Integration

An important ingredient in the foregoing is the operation of the international gold standard. For much of the 1870 to 1910 period this was in operation in Europe, but two qualifications are certainly in order. First, not all countries in our sample were on the system at all times during the period, and second and more importantly, those that were may well not have played by the acknowledged rules of the system. Indeed, about the latter point, it seems logical that the rules would be suspended – unilaterally – at just the point at which an unexpected monetary shock from abroad might influence domestic real income.

The *United Kingdom* was on the standard throughout the period, but as the reserve-creating country in the system, generally did not have to play by the rules. The *United States*, with its rapid growth and substantial capital inflow, also may well have been exempted from the rules; they formally rejoined the system in 1878 (having suspended during the US Civil War). *Sweden*, who entered the system in 1873, may have played by the rules at least some of the time, but, again, rapid growth and substantial capital imports surely softened the effect. For Sweden, Jonung (1984, p. 392) argues,

> The long-run growth of the Swedish money stock during the pre-1914 gold standard era was . . . strongly related to the growth of the gold and foreign-asset holdings of the Riksbank . . . In the short run, there was no rigid link between gold flows and the money stock.

He also argues that domestic markets were well integrated with international and that the free flow of capital into Sweden from the financial centres of Western Europe (p. 393) 'was an engine for the transformation of the economy'. Lindert (1984), in contrast, argues that adherence to the gold standard exacted no penalties on Sweden in this period (p. 400),

> Sweden's participation in the international gold standard made no visible net contribution to the growth or stability of her national product, relative to a hypothetical world of flexible exchange rates for the krona.
> . . .
> Thus Sweden, like almost all other countries before and after 1914, observed the gold standard orthodoxy when it made no difference to the domestic economy, but abandoned it as soon as it began to bind.

He also doubts that 'adherence' to the gold standard played any major role in the accumulation of capital in Sweden's rapid take-off in this period.

In *Italy*, the gold standard was only in operation between 1884 and 1894. It is conceivable, of course, that the gold standard system was adhered to by the major Italian banks at other times, even though the government was not officially supporting it. Indeed, Fratianni and Spinelli (1984) claim that during this period Italy was guided by the norm of the gold standard, even though gold inflows were a relatively minor influence on the domestic money stock.

Germany joined the gold standard system in 1876; formally, they clearly did not play by the rules (Bloomfield, 1959) but, according to Sommariva and Tullio (1987, 1988), the evidence suggests that German central bank behaviour can be explained with reference to the monetary approach to the balance of payments, a theory that provides an alternative channel of influence to the specie-flow mechanism usually advocated by the quantity theorists.[4] In particular, Sommariva and Tullio find that an increase in German output and prices induced a gold and silver inflow into Germany while an increase in Reichsbank domestic assets induced an outflow. The negative correlation between the domestic and foreign assets of the Reichsbank (the supposed violation of the rules of the game, as identified by Bloomfield) is attributed to bi-directional causation between the two accounts and not to a policy sterilization of gold flows.

The Reichsbank did, however, play a role. Looking further into the details, McGouldrick (1984) shows that gold inflows were actually cyclically neutral in Germany and that base money (p. 321) 'grew at a remarkably stable pace over German business cycles'. Indeed, base money actually had a slightly countercyclical tendency. He argues that the Reichsbank stabilized (not sterilized!) gold inflows in this period by means of bill discount rate policy. He concludes (p. 346),

> The contrasting relative stability of the monetary realm therefore stands as strong testimony to the advantages of the pre-1914 gold standard when properly ruled by a central bank.

But Germany grew very rapidly during this period, with substantial export earnings, and it is certainly hard to believe that the gold standard exerted any real pressure on the monetary authorities.

The next task is to undertake some Granger-causality tests of the possible financial interactions among the European (and US) economies in the late 19th century. Existing studies of financial integration do not usually employ such methods, but the financial integration hypothesis is certainly a venerable one, and the recent study by Friedman and Schwartz (1982), which remarks on the close financial ties between the United Kingdom and the United States, is a case in point. In this section we are interested in the general topic of financial integration and, more particularly, in trying to pin down some of the influences of the international gold standard on the apparently rapidly increasing financial integration. Our hypothesis, again, is that it did not exert an influence, causally, and we will try to evaluate that by considering the obvious sub-periods of the data, as well.

In a recent study, Craig and Fisher (1991) found considerable financial interaction among the European economies, utilizing the money stock data of the same countries studied here, over the entire period 1871 to 1910. For Granger-causality tests, the statistically significant causal interactions were as follows:

UK	→	US
France	→	Germany
Germany	→	UK, France, Sweden
Italy	→	UK, France

Thus all countries were involved, with the rapidly growing German economy evidently at the centre of things. For cointegration tests over the same data space, less interaction was found, with all statistically significant effects involving the United States and none appearing among the major European economies. We will not undertake cointegration tests here, but will concentrate on the results of Granger-causality tests involving the high-powered money stocks and the price levels of these countries.

Examination of the relations among the high-powered money stocks of these countries is designed to reveal one end of the influence of international events, the pressure on monetary policy itself. Presumably capital and goods flows, however induced, are the (unidentified) agents of influence here. The Granger-causality test, to repeat, regresses a variable in which we are interested – let us say the British high-powered money supply – on its own lags and on the lags of another potential causal variable – say the German high-powered money supply. If the other variable adds significantly to the explanation of the dependent variable, then it is said to Granger-cause that variable; this is judged by an F-test.[5]

The overall results of the tests for the variables proposed here – the high-powered money stocks and the price levels – are a little surprising, really. Rather than produce tables of mostly non-significant numbers, we will simply concentrate on the overall relations that exist, such as they are.[6] First, for differences in the logs of high-powered money, it seems that the only relations that turn up for the period 1871 to 1910 are

Germany → Sweden
UK → Germany

For shorter periods (e.g., 1881–1910), the UK → Germany result holds up, but the other does not.[7] Even shorter periods were attempted, but there were really too few observations to give the hypothesis a fair chance in these cases. Thus there appears to be no *general* linkage of high-powered money stocks across the European economies, other than for the one case. This is considerably less interaction than for the money stock of these countries, as just discussed. This does not prove that these countries did not play by the rules of the gold standard system, but it is interesting, nevertheless, that high-powered money and money do not show the same pattern. We will attempt to reconcile this below, but there is one more piece to the puzzle.

The results just stated are not really surprising, in view of the suspicion in the literature that these countries did not abide by the rules of the game; what is surprising, though is that there is little price level interaction either, again as judged by the Granger-causality test. The data again had to be differenced (after taking the logarithms) although one price index (for Italy) was actually stationary in the level figures.[8] The results, for the entire period, do show a little more interaction, but still considerably less than for the money stocks.

Italy	→	US
France	→	Italy
Germany	→	Italy, Sweden

Shorter periods had less interaction. In this case Italy seems at the centre of things, but, more significantly, there are no interactions among the three major European economies at the time.

On net, then, while it is easy to understand the little interaction among high-powered money stocks and among price indices, the money stock results really do not seem to fit the pattern. It is possible, of course, that the data themselves are inadequate to the task, but taking the results seriously for the moment, one can contrive an explanation. First, the high-powered money result suggests that no general and repeated causes ran across borders; a policy of permitting the base to contract when gold flowed out, but preventing it from expanding when gold ran in, would tend to confound the Granger test attempted here. Second, close interaction among money stocks could reflect the operation of the 'monetary approach' to the balance of payments. In this theory, when the gold mechanism is shut off, the interaction is by goods flows; in this case domestic money stocks react to changes in the domestic demand for money. Thus if the underlying goods flows ran in one direction, even though the monetary authorities took themselves out of the game, the goods flows would induce money stock changes in one direction, *ex hypothesi*. Finally, and somewhat lamely, the relative lack of price level interaction could simply reflect the fact that other (domestic) factors (e.g., the weather) swamped the international influences on domestic prices. Certainly, as we noted in earlier chapters, it was only in the last ten years of the period that business cycles were coordinated clearly across these countries. There does appear to be a lot more work to do on these issues, however, even within the confines of the existing data.

This section has emphasized a rather dramatic fact: all of the European countries studied (except the United Kingdom) were relatively financially unsophisticated up to 1870 and thereafter quickly took on the character of the United Kingdom in terms of their relative usage of banking and monetary services. By 1910, the catching-up was complete. It is hard not to credit both the burgeoning international capital markets and the operation of the gold standard for much of this, but industrialization, rapid growth and real trade flows are also involved in the process. We should remind the reader, though, that there is good reason to suppose that these particular countries did not really play by the rules of the international gold standard. This would imply a somewhat greater role for capital and goods markets and a smaller role for central banks in the rapid transformation of the European economy at this time.

8.4 NEUTRALITY IN THE LATE 19TH CENTURY

We have employed the standard Granger-causality test at several points in this study, but now we wish to consider the results of a full battery of these tests across the data for the six countries in our sample. By 'full battery' we mean to include many of the important variations on the aggregate data, partly to see if the results are sensitive to the selection of a particular series and partly to try to establish a general result for Europe at this time.

The hypothesis, quite simply, is derived from the Quantity Theory of Money. Whatever version of that is espoused, the argument is that changes in the quantity of money do not induce changes in real variables *in the long run*. It is usual, in this theory, to think of money as exogenously determined (either by the central bank or the operation of the gold standard) and so the late 19th century, when the gold standard was employed by each of the countries included in this study, seems an appropriate time period to look at. We note, though, in view of the results of earlier chapters, that endogeneity of the money supply cannot be ruled out in this period. The reason given had to do with the possibility, as mentioned already, that central banks did not play by the rules of the international gold standard in this period, leaving the determination of the money stock to purely domestic considerations. The following tests do not really confirm this possibility in most cases, leaving the question unsettled, really.

The following results, again, are with the Granger-causality procedure, as repeatedly described above. The statistical test, an F-test, is used to see whether the exclusion of all of the exogenous terms in the basic regression would significantly reduce the explanatory power of the regression of the dependent variable on its lags. Conventionally,

Table 8.6   UK monetary neutrality tests, 1871–1910

		\multicolumn{5}{c}{p-values for lags of}				
		1	*2*	*3*	*4*	*5*
M2 – F & S						
	Y1	0.451	0.606	0.991	0.981	0.999
	Y2	0.977	0.245	0.126	0.277	0.372
	Y3	0.665	0.660	0.293	0.161	0.110
	Y4	0.588	0.639	0.319	0.120	0.080
	Y5	0.709	0.609	0.316	0.120	0.078
M2 – C & W						
	Y1	0.586	0.629	0.993	0.951	0.965
	Y2	0.822	0.985	0.830	0.996	0.738
	Y3	0.567	0.572	0.820	0.840	0.898
	Y4	0.460	0.591	0.749	0.802	0.886
	Y5	0.556	0.526	0.733	0.780	0.869

we will argue that Granger-causation is established if the probability that the proposed causal agent is not influential is 0.05 or less.

Table 8.6 presents the results of the test for the United Kingdom; what is shown there are the p-values for two measures of per capita money stocks and five measures of per capita national output. The money stock measures are those of

M2 – F&S = Friedman and Schwartz (1982)
M2 – C&W = Capie and Webber (1985)

While the real income measures are

Y1 = Real Net National Product, Friedman and Schwartz (1982)
Y2 = Real GNP at Factor Cost, Deane (1968)
Y3 = GDP in 1900 market prices, Feinstein, Table 5, Col. 8. This series is also used in Kormendi and Meguire (1990).
Y4 = GNP at Factor Cost, Feinstein, Table 5, Col. 13. This series is used by Capie and Webber to produce a GNP deflator.
Y5 = GNP at market prices, Feinstein, Table 5, Col. 10.

This collection largely covers the range for numbers employed in the literature in recent years. These results show no evidence of monetary non-neutrality.[9] Evidently, monetary neutrality is upheld for the United Kingdom.[10]

Table 8.7 Monetary neutrality in Europe and the US 1871–1910

| | \multicolumn{5}{c}{p-Values for lags of} | | | | |
	1	2	3	4	5
France	0.278	0.567	0.575	0.657	0.657
Sweden					
M1	0.652	0.838	0.761	0.324	0.565
M2	0.562	0.354	0.175	0.400	0.775
Germany					
M1	0.314	0.653	0.935	0.867	0.561
M2	0.144	0.330	0.779	0.850	0.568
Italy					
Y1	0.483	0.422	0.646	0.470	0.610
Y2	0.259	0.191	0.393	0.329	0.383
United States					
Y1	0.926	0.216	0.331	0.332	0.569
Y2	0.645	0.149	0.480	0.098	0.265
Y3	0.577	0.394	0.426	0.328	0.574

For the other countries in the study, there are several sets of income data, and little ambiguity about the results. Running out to five lags, Table 8.7 lists the results, again with some variations caused by the presence of alternative versions of some of the series. Here the different measures of money for Sweden and Germany represent narrow (M1) and broad (M2) money. The two measures of income for Italy are those of Fratianni and Spinelli (1984) and Mitchell (1978); for the United States, there are three different measures of real income, the old Friedman and Schwartz numbers (Y1), and the recent numbers of Romer (Y2) and Balke and Gordon (Y3). Whatever the measure, there is no evidence of monetary non-neutrality by means of these tests.[11] But the reader should be warned that other time periods do sometimes produce non-neutrality, as for Italy (1861–1910) and France (1830–70).

In the literature, there are causality-style tests of monetary neutrality for several of the countries in our sample, as well as other kinds of tests that bear on the same issues. Relying to some extent on the survey by Bordo (1986), we begin with the United Kingdom. For that country, Mills and Wood (1978), employing Sims's version of the Granger-causality test, find that output Granger-causes money in this period, but not the converse. Similarly, employing Granger-causality tests based on multivariate autoregressions, Dwyer (1983) finds that for the period 1870 to 1913 the money supply is demand-determined (as did Mills and Wood). In contrast, studying the UK cycle for 1833 to 1913 by methods similar to Dwyer's, Eichengreen (1983) finds real factors more important before 1880 and monetary factors thereafter. He employed high-powered money in these tests. These results suggest, on net, that monetary neutrality may hold in the United Kingdom, but that a closer examination of sub-periods is clearly warranted.

For the United States, Brillembourg and Khan (1979), using Sims's test procedure, find no Granger-causal relation between money and output (although they do establish a contemporaneous one). For Sweden, similarly, Fisher and Thurman (1989), for a variety of financial instruments, find no Granger-causality running from nominal instruments to real income (but do find the converse). For Italy, Fratianni and Spinelli (1984) argue that the monetary base Granger-causes real GNP, but not the converse, during a roughly comparable period.

The overall conclusion one might draw at this point has to be stated as conditional on the state of the data, on the arbitrary choice of time period and on the choice of the Granger-causality test for non-neutrality. Even so, it would seem that the general neutrality of money is pretty firmly established, particularly as the 19th century ends and Europe moves into a more closely integrated international economy. In this economy, business cycles are increasingly alike across nations, and real causes dominate financial in the determination of fluctuations in real output. The details of this are the subject of the next section.

8.5 THE PAN-EUROPEAN BUSINESS CYCLE

Most studies of the business cycle in late 19th-century Europe, while couched in local terms, appeal to some aspects of the international economy in explaining the causes of these events. Mention is made of fluctuations of exports (and, less frequently, imports), and there are frequent references to specific collapses of the European capital markets. There are also discussions of the international transmission mechanism – nominal and/or real – as it involves the gold-based, fixed-exchange rate system of the period. International real capital flows are also occasionally discussed in the cyclical context. The foregoing certainly is tangible, although often limited in scope. Even so, there appears to be a strong, but at the same time rather elusive, tradition that European business cycles actually are quite closely integrated in the late 19th century – or, in some versions, are integrated by the beginning of the 20th century. It is this general integration of business cycles that we intend to investigate in this section, following a line laid down by Friedman and Schwartz in *Monetary Trends* (1982). Indeed, we will argue that while there is strong general evidence of the financial interaction in the late 19th-century European economy, there are essentially no signs of real interaction, at least as judged by the macroeconomic procedures employed here.

As already discussed in Section 8.3.1, there is a strong tradition in the literature that financial crises in one economy spread to others, producing both financial and real contractions over a broad front. What is curious about this is the finding in the formal causality literature, as discussed in Section 8.4, that monetary influences on real events generally cannot be demonstrated. That is, for these cases at least, what is known in the modern macroeconomic literature as a 'real business cycle' explanation holds; this is that real cyclical events are produced by real (and not monetary) causes. We have already indicated the extent of this literature in this chapter, but we do want to emphasize that our results in this section are consistent with this real business cycle view – and hence with monetary neutrality – while at the same revealing a close financial integration of the European economy.

Section 8.5.1 contains some largely impressionistic illustrations of the cyclical interactions of these economies; these do not show particularly close integration. In Section 8.5.2, then, we discuss the results of earlier studies of the interaction hypothesis. The results discussed here suggest that monetary but not real interaction can be demonstrated.

8.5.1 Impressions of the Pan-European Cycle

The level and log-detrended data are not useless for all purposes, of course – and certainly not for some of the questions before us. In Table 8.8, for example, using the level figures we examine two sets of simple correlation coefficients across the six countries, one set for per capita nominal money balances (the top triangle) and one for real per capita gross domestic product. With the exception of the United Kingdom, the nominal correlations, as the literature implies, are

Table 8.8   Per capita monetary and real interactions, 1870–1910

		UK	France	Germany	Sweden	Italy	US	
Real	UK		0.767	0.875	0.853	0.754	0.839	Nominal
	France	0.902		0.969	0.976	0.976	0.960	
	Germany	0.962	0.933		0.991	0.968	0.987	
	Sweden	0.942	0.950	0.984		0.969	0.987	
	Italy	0.701	0.833	0.769	0.832		0.965	
	US	0.941	0.937	0.951	0.965	0.770		

higher in these comparisons, taking the period as a whole as the basis for the calculation.

A second way we might look at the level figures – on real domestic product this time – is to chart the recession years in the period for each of the countries, as in Table 8.9. Here a recession is defined as any year of declining real national product. Excluding the United States, the five European countries only had four years (1876, 1879, 1888, and 1892) when as many as three countries were simultaneously in recession. In no years were there four or five countries experiencing declining real product. This, too, does not show a particularly close integration of the real cycle in late 19th-century Europe.[12]

The log-detrended data also show cycles, although they have been justly criticized as showing somewhat too much cyclical activity (since every deviation from trend potentially generates a turning point). These data are, of course, non-stationary, as discussed above, but they are, in any case, an effective way to create a comparison of the common experiences in the real output of the European countries. The collection in Figure 8.1, then, is a representation of some of the more interesting cases, using the detrended data for comparisons. The figures are oriented around the German data, arbitrarily.

As already described in various ways, there seems to be considerable disparity when the real output numbers are compared in this fashion. There are some events in Figure 8.1A that Germany and the United Kingdom have in common, notably in the late 1880s, late 1890s, and 1907, but even in the 20th century, there are sharply opposing experiences. Germany and France (in Figure 8.1B) do seem more closely synchronized, but Germany and Italy (in Figure 8.1C) do not. The latter could easily be the result of the more agricultural nature of cycles in Italy than in Germany (than, indeed, in any of the other countries). Germany and Sweden (in Figure 8.1D) seem quite

Table 8.9   Years in which real product declined, 1870–1910

	UK	France	Germany	Italy	Sweden	US
1870						
1871			XXXX	XXXX		
1872						
1873	XXXX	XXXX				
1874						
1875					XXXX	
1876		XXXX	XXXX	XXXX		
1877			XXXX	XXXX		
1878		XXXX			XXXX	
1879	XXXX	XXXX	XXXX			
1880			XXXX			
1881	XXXX			XXXX		
1882						
1883		XXXX		XXXX		
1884	XXXX	XXXX				
1885	XXXX					
1886						
1887		XXXX			XXXX	
1888		XXXX		XXXX		XXXX
1889				XXXX		
1890						
1891			XXXX			
1892	XXXX	XXXX		XXXX		
1893	XXXX					XXXX
1894				XXXX		XXXX
1895						
1896						
1897		XXXX		XXXX		
1898						
1899		XXXX				
1900	XXXX					
1901		XXXX	XXXX		XXXX	
1902						
1903						
1904						
1905		XXXX				
1906						
1907						
1908	XXXX			XXXX		XXXX
1909		XXXX				
1910				XXXX		

closely integrated, particularly after the mid-1880s; they were both growing quite rapidly at that point and had few actual downturns in this period (as opposed to the deviations from trend that are shown in Figure 8.1). Finally, for the United States and Germany, their experiences seem very dissimilar until the mid-1890s; this echoes one of the results in Friedman and Schwartz (1982) that finds the real connection between the United States and the United Kingdom growing stronger at this time.

8.5.2 Previous Studies of the Pan-European Cycle

Our point of departure is the Friedman–Schwartz study (1982) of United States–United Kingdom interaction. What they find is that there is cyclical interaction between the United States and the United Kingdom, but that it is primarily monetary in nature. In particular (p. 6),

> Influences ran both ways across the Atlantic, though there is some evidence to suggest that real effects were stronger from the United States to the United Kingdom and price effects from the United Kingdom to the United States.[13]

These results were obtained from a variety of tests, the most effective being the 'phase of cycle' comparisons across economies. A test procedure that is similar to that used here – being of Granger-causality – is by Huffman and Lothian (1984) on US and UK cycles. The hypothesis of this study is that it is monetary shocks in one country that induce real reactions in the other – and that it is the operation of the specie-flow mechanism of the international gold standard that makes this possible. In their view, money is non-neutral in each country and money supplies are linked by the gold standard (p. 459),

> An unanticipated decrease in monetary growth in the United Kingdom . . . reduced output growth in the United Kingdom . . . [reduced the rate of growth of prices] . . . and induced a balance-of-payments surplus and hence inflows of specie and capital from the United States. Monetary growth in the United States decreased . . . and output growth . . . fell.

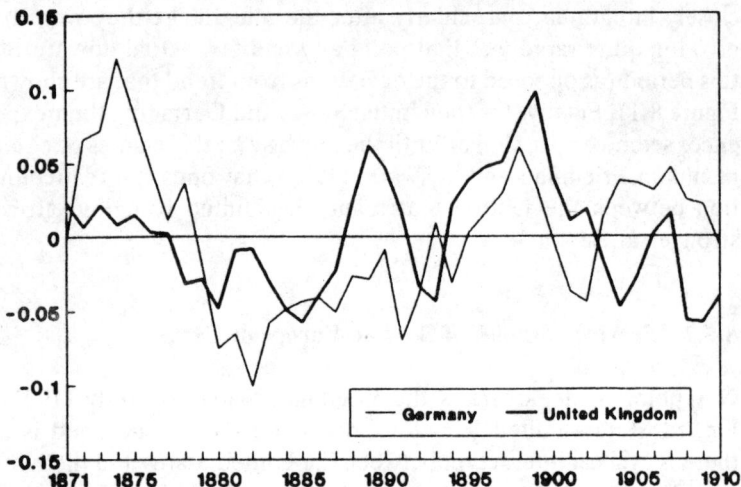

Detrended Logarithms of the Data

A. Germany and the United Kingdom
Cycles in Real Income, 1871–1910

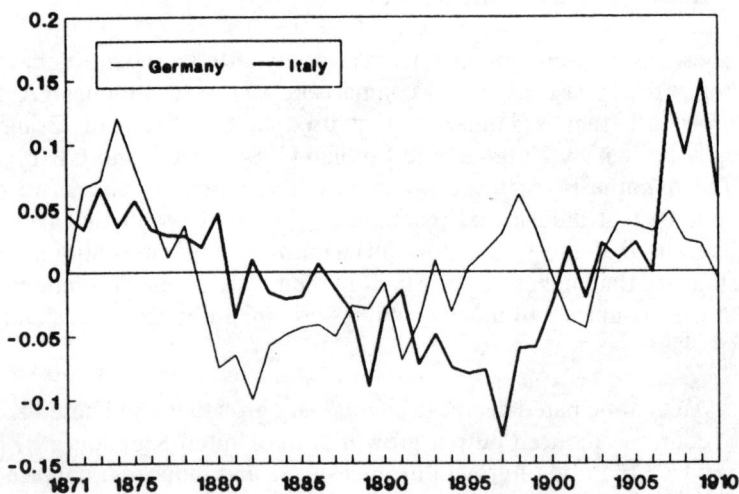

Detrended Logarithms of the Data

C. Germany and Italy
Cycles in Real Income, 1871–1910

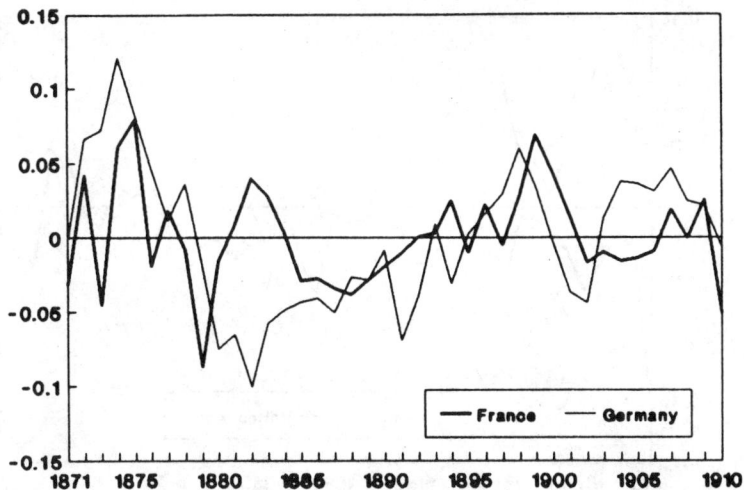

Detrended Logarithms of the Data

B. Germany and France
Cycles in Real Income, 1871–1910

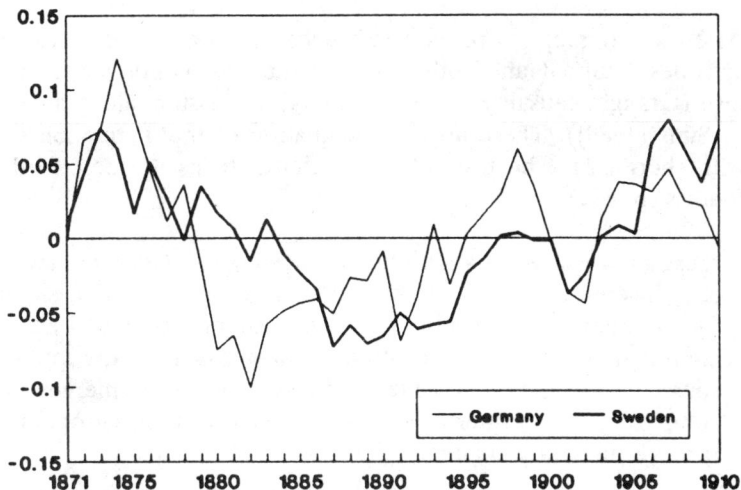

Detrended Logarithms of the Data

D. Germany and Sweden
Cycles in Real Income, 1871–1910

Figure 8.1   *continued on page 276*

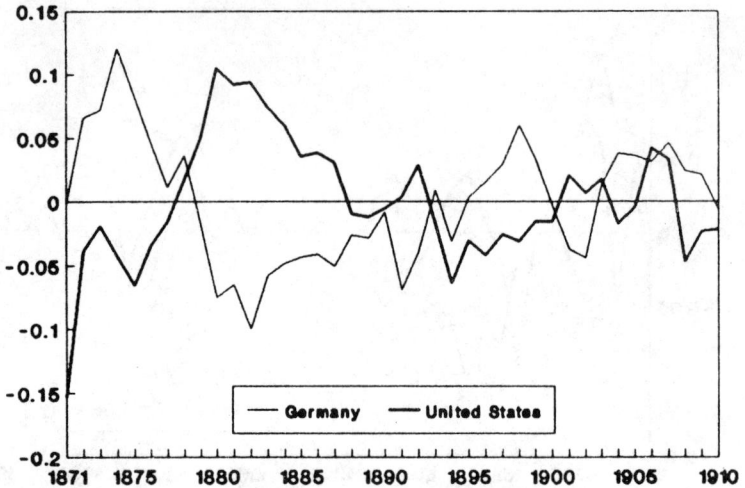

Detrended Logarithms of the Data

E. Germany and the United States
Cycles in Real Income, 1871–1910

Figure 8.1

After considerable work with reference cycles and with particular episodes, Huffman and Lothian turn to the aforementioned Granger tests (Granger-causality tests of vector autoregressions along the lines of Sims (1980)). These are single-equation or multi-equation tests with short lags. The tests of most interest to us are described as follows (p. 491),

> these show a clearcut association between own-country money and real income . . . The relationships, however, are not simple. Other-country money also has significant effects both on own-country money and on own-country real income in all the comparisons. . . . At the same time, additional evidence emerges of a complex system of interaction between the two countries operating through monetary channels.

They refer to the period 1834 to 1914. We must admit that our results – mostly for a different set of countries, for a different period, and, certainly, for a different test procedure – do not agree with theirs.

There is a Granger-causality study of real interactions among the

European countries in this period, by Easton (1984). The work here is on changes in real national income for somewhat different data than we employ below (and for the period 1881–1913). The results, for the countries that we are looking at, show Granger-causality (with a probability of 0.05 or better) only as follows,

Germany → United States
Sweden → Italy

In view of our broadly similar results below – on real interaction – it is worth underscoring Wood's (1984) concern that the Granger test, by mixing together positive and negative influences (e.g., demand or supply shocks) could, indeed, fail to record a cyclical interaction on net. Easton actually dealt with this problem by testing the absolute values of the changes in real national income, also to no avail. We do need to emphasize, in view of our results, that this approach searches for an overall direction of causation, by its very nature.

For the United Kingdom, a survey by Ford (1981) contains the international themes we are interested in. Ford discusses the causes of business cycles in this period – although his methods are not formally causal. He notes that Matthews (1959) and Coppock (1972) had previously argued for real interactions – overseas investment for Matthews and exports for Coppock – as well as for internal causes. In these very Keynesian-oriented studies, investment (usually domestic) or residential construction and exports dominate; both are usually taken as exogenous variables capable of unleashing multiplier effects. In fact, Ford also conducts empirical tests, using both regressions and cyclical phases across France, Germany, and Britain, and notes (p. 38)

> Particular international shocks could help to explain one major feature of the business cycle – the marked parallelism between Britain, France, and Germany, who were in the same phase of their reference cycles in 83 per cent of all months between 1879 and 1914.

Ford also runs separate regressions comparing the influence of money and exports on UK *nominal* national income; the value of exports wins hands down. This result, on the surface, is consistent with results by Craig and Fisher (1991), as discussed below, that reports nominal influences running from other European (France, Italy) countries to the United Kingdom. It says nothing directly about the business

cycle, though, since that topic normally refers to fluctuations in real
national product. This is especially the case if it is shown that nominal
factors do not themselves influence real.

In the Craig–Fisher study (1991), real interaction is shown (via
Granger-causality) in only three cases (at the 0.05 level of significance). These are

US	$\rightarrow$	France
UK	$\rightarrow$	Italy
Germany	$\rightarrow$	US

The only within-Europe case is the UK to Italy connection. There is,
in all this, a corroboration of the Friedman and Schwartz result that
there is no strong real interaction between the United States and the
United Kingdom. Even so, these tests reveal that there is, indeed,
real interaction across the Atlantic (the way Friedman and Schwartz
put it) involving a US influence on France and a German influence on
the United States. The latter, but not the former survives a recalculation with the actual data employed by Friedman and Schwartz (the
tests in the Craig/Fisher study employ the Romer calculations of US
GNP).

In summary, then, the results indicate that there is, indeed, some
merit to the general notion of the financial integration of Western
Europe during the last years of the 19th century; perhaps it was the
operation of the gold standard that brought this about. At the same
time, there is no firm evidence of real interaction, at least as judged
by the Granger-causality criterion. The most important thing we can
do at this point is to underscore the limitations of our results. Aside
from the usual caveats concerning the methods employed – and they
all are known to have low power statistically – we must especially call
attention to the nature of the data employed. In particular, annual
data such as these are not really the best vehicle for conveying
information about cyclical events that are certainly quite short and
sharp in the 20th century and probably more so in the 19th. That is, it
is probable that financial panics and their associated recessions were
quickly over in this period, leaving only occasional residues in the
annual data. Since some of the data will ultimately be available at a
higher frequency, the importance of this consideration will be assessed in due course.

A second problem, also alluded to in the above discussion, is the
problem that individual events could easily run one way and then
another – causally speaking – so that general tests such as these,

examining the hypothesis that causation ran one way over the entire period, could easily be confounded. Certainly the literature makes much of certain well-publicized events, such as the Crash of 1873 and the Baring Crisis of the early 1890s, which originated in different spots. But, at the same time, these are financial events and not real, and we have established some causation across financial regimes. Thus it is real events that should be covered by this qualification. Even so, the general impression is that the proponents of the shifting events hypothesis also seem to have put their faith in financial interconnections and have frequently inferred connections between the financial and the real. The strong evidence of financial integration muddies the waters here.

Finally, and by no means irrelevantly, we should note that the annual data themselves are subject to revision, and that different data sets can and do provide different results for these tests.

8.6 CONCLUSION

This chapter attempts to make a start on topics dealing with the macroeconomic issues in Europe's increasing economic integration in the late 19th and early 20th centuries. Generically, the topics are divided into real and nominal interactions, and there are both direct tests of the relationships and comparisons of standard numbers across the various countries.

Beginning with real factors, we noted that growth rates were dissimilar across countries, although an acceleration was generally apparent at the end of the period. In earlier chapters we noted that industrialization seems to be associated with a lessening of the severity of (mostly agriculturally induced) business cycles. Here we also notice that there is an increasing tendency for the business cycle to go international – for the same reason – and for countries to have broadly similar cyclical experiences as the First World War approaches. We also reported on Granger-causality and cointegration test results across these countries that show little real integration of business cycles for the period as a whole. It is true, however, that the test procedure does not permit examination of a period as short as 1895 to 1910 when, one suspects, real economic integration is probable.

For the case of nominal variables, there is evidence of general interaction by the same Granger-causality and cointegration tests;

these separately published results are described here. There are also two other areas of monetary interaction that are illustrated here. In one case it is suggested that for 1871 to 1910, taking the period as a whole, changes in the stock of money in each case did not affect real national product. This is not a surprising result, and it is also not a firm conclusion, since some of the earlier sub-periods of the data (in several cases) actually exhibited non-neutrality. With respect to the financial sophistication index, we discovered that these countries (except for the United Kingdom) showed rapidly increasing use of financial services – and, somewhat arbitrarily, every country was on a comparable level to the United Kingdom by 1910 (in this respect). We did not, finally, attempt a summary of results for the demand for money across these countries – even though there is a suspicion that income elasticities of that function were greater than unity for all but the United Kingdom. The reason for this omission was the deep suspicion that this function was either unstable or mis-specified in the individual country studies.

Endnotes

Chapter 1 The Background to the British Industrial Revolution

1. In fact, under neoclassical conditions there exists an optimal path known as the 'golden-age path'.

   A golden-age path is a growth path on which literally every variable changes over time (if at all) at a constant proportionate rate. (Phelps, 1966, p. 6)

2. We are here holding constant the effect of changes in technology and in labour force participation rates, for example.
3. The functional distribution of income is constant along the golden-age path of the neoclassical model.
4. Governments also can attempt to find ways to improve the lot of their people through territorial expansion.
5. E.g., by the extended family.
6. Adam Smith, David Ricardo and many others felt that the profit rate would fall with the increased growth of capital, but, as we have argued, this is not inevitable in a framework largely consistent with their views. Ricardo, among others, also thought that rents would swallow up GNP. Both arguments basically are drawn from the law of diminishing returns. This proposition is part of the neoclassical model (and provides one of its main properties as described above) but that model does not produce the result just stated, at least along the golden-age path of a growing (neoclassical) economy.
7. Crafts (1983) argues that the income elasticity of the demand for food is significantly below unity, in which case this measure understates the rise in the average standard of living.
8. Crafts (1983) argues that they are particularly suspect just at the point, 1770–1830, that is of most interest. Much of the problem is technical, although the use of a Laspeyres index (which is likely to overstate the growth rate) and the use of an excessively large weight for the cotton industry stand out. Crafts argues that a Divisia index should work better, but would require a homothetic utility function; he provides a useful discussion of the issues. Crafts calculates an approximation to the Divisia by cobbling together a Laspeyres and a Paasche index; this is how a Fisher Ideal index is produced, so the resulting construct is similar. The Divisia index, being an expression of the first-order conditions for the aggregate consumer's optimum, is an especially attractive construction (see Barnett, Fisher and Serletis, 1992). Note, however, that the full power of the Ideal index approach is not available unless the weights employed are recalculated each year in an annual index. The appropriate weights are budget shares for each of the categories in the index.
9. Of course, year-by-year numbers, which Minchinton lists, show a lot of

281

variation; we shall have more to say about cycles in this period later in this study. The decline in the 1740s is attributed to war (especially in 1744–8) by Minchinton. It should be pointed out that the figures in Table 1.9 are calculated using 1700 official (therefore 'constant') prices. Deane (1979, pp. 63–5) concludes that this procedure probably overstates the rate of growth of imports and that a better guess as to the growth rate would be to scale them back to a figure more comparable with the export growth figure. This, of course, suggests quite reasonably that England's markets may have been growing about as rapidly as England.

10. The detrending is by means of the regression of log Y on trend. The residuals are plotted in Figure 1.2. The data are drawn from Ashton (1959, p. 189). Two missing observations are interpolated.

11. The values given are the ratio of military spending to trend national income.

12. And up to 1910, for that matter.

13. Money creation is a factor in the Napoleonic wars, when (from 1797 to 1821) Britain was off the gold standard and could pursue such an independent monetary policy. This will be discussed in Chapter 2.

14. Thus, says Williamson (1984), a country that fights a lot of wars, as England did between 1700 and 1815, would be expected to grow significantly slower than it otherwise would have. This is a contribution to the 'why did England grow so slowly during the industrial revolution' debate that we will consider in more detail in Chapter 2.

15. The data actually run from 1665 to 1815.

16. We note, however, that the 1800 figure is 12.9 per cent and the 1810 figure 18.2 per cent, indicating somewhat of a change in the government's techniques. O'Brien notes that for the wars referred to above, taxes paid about 20 per cent of the total bill; in the 1793–1815 wars, however, the amount financed by taxation rose to 58 per cent of the total.

17. The timing one might expect here depends, of course, on what has happened to the age distribution of the population. For example, if the population growth in this period is primarily the result of the falling death rate of infants, one would not expect a falling real wage in the same decade, necessarily.

18. The purpose of this calculation was to present a detrended result.

19. The annual prices, as before, are from Phelps Brown and Hopkins (1956), while the annual English population is taken from Wrigley and Schofield (1981).

20. These rates were obtained by the regression of log X on the trend variable.

21. Another issue that arises concerns the possibility that firm size varies over the period, growing larger toward the end. This could produce a trend (or conceal a trend) in the data depending on the direction of scale economies or diseconomies. Weighting the profit rates by firm size would be one way to deal with this possibility.

22. Mirowski has also published a paper on Adam Smith and profit rates (1982). In the *Wealth of Nations*, Smith claims that the profit rate fell over much of the 18th century. Using the (biased) mean profit series

contradicts this (over Smith's life); even with the adjusted series, there is no downward drift.

23. Recall that the profit index, when adjusted, also has no clear trend.
24. A considerable number of ARMA models were attempted here, but the choppiness of the series inhibited this work. The winner is

$$\pi_e = \underset{(0.85)}{0.95} - \underset{(2.95)}{0.75}\,MA(2) - \underset{(1.63)}{0.22}\,MA(3) + \underset{(1.01)}{0.21}\,AR\,(1)$$

These were judged by the adjusted R^2, which in this case was 0.296 and by the residuals, which showed no trend. When the nominal rate was adjusted by the predictions of this equation, the resulting real rate also proved to be trendless.
25. In Hoppit, the bankruptcies are those reported in the *London Gazette* (and other official sources). Mirowski notes that bankruptcies have a procyclical pattern typically (so that a rise is not necessarily a crisis). He also rightly complains about the usefulness of Hoppit's long moving average (61 quarters) because the technique tends to alter frequencies and shift peaks and troughs. Nobody has the perfect index, it seems.
26. We should note some problems with the Mirowski profit index. The Mirowski index and the Hoffmann index are not particularly well correlated, at 0.343. In turn, Mirowski's adjusted profits index, which he claims is a useful method of identifying cyclical factors, has fifteen distinct peaks (which is the most of any series at 3.53 years per cycle) as well as a curious tendency to fall relatively slowly and steadily after each sudden upward surge. It also appears to be random in that its ARMA representation over a reasonably large grid of possibilities is ARMA (0, 0); this was a statistical determination over a very volatile series.
27. Ashton (1959) thinks the depression was short; he mentions exports and (especially) the building trades in this connection.
28. In Mirowski's (1985) quarterly index, East India Company stock in the first quarter of 1774 stood 38 per cent below its peak in the second quarter of 1771.

Chapter 2 The First Industrial Revolution in Britain, 1780–1860: National Income and its Distribution

1. According to Feinstein's (1981) calculations, agricultural investment was £2.5m per annum in 1761–90 (31 per cent of the total), £4.0m in 1791–1810, £4.5m in 1821–40 and £6.5m in 1841–60 (12 per cent of the total). While its relative position clearly was undermined, at the same time the agricultural capital stock more than doubled. Indeed, Feinstein refers to the period after 1840 as the 'golden age' of British farming.
2. Following Dahlman (1980), the open field system can be characterized by five stylized facts that set up a representative description of what it might have been during its heyday.

(1) The farming community divided its lands into arable and non-arable land and part of the arable lay fallow.

(2) The fields were large and were subdivided into long and thin strips.
(3) The strips each had separate owners (not necessarily being those who worked the land) and an individual's holdings were typically scattered around the community.
(4) There were large areas – the commons – that were owned by the community as a whole; these were generally for grazing.
(5) This pattern changed from year to year, so that land would be common one year and arable the next, without altering Points (1) to (4) just stated.

3. It is important to recognize that all of Europe saw enclosures, especially in the parts that had the potential to enter the growing world-wide agricultural markets.
4. The spinning jenny (Hargreaves patented this in 1770) went from 8 spindles to over 100 between 1764 and 1800 and initially produced a cheap yarn in bulk. The water frame (Arkwright's patent was 1769) was a factory machine powered by water and then steam that produced a strong yarn. A smoother, finer, yarn was produced by the combination of the two in the form of the mule (Crompton's patent was 1779). Collectively, these developments led to a dramatic decline of costs, a shift of production from the home to the factory and a significant reorientation of the work force. They also produced profits.
5. It actually did not matter all that much which of the Laspeyres, Paasche, Fisher's Ideal, or Divisia index was used and for the first two, it did not matter much what base was used. This is, though, a calculation carried out only at a few points rather than for an annual data series, so the full power of the 'ideal' index number approach is not utilized.
6. Note that the linked index numbers just referred to are for England and Wales in the one case and Great Britain in the other. The reader is free to perform other calculations if this seems unacceptable.
7. In the IS–LM framework, of course, income is endogenous.
8. For population growth economic growth will directly inspire population growth (as it raises incomes) as long as children are not inferior goods or medical care – broadly interpreted – is itself a superior good (as it seems to be in more recent times). For foreign demand we can argue that expansion in England, for example, raises incomes in France and, thereby, inspires a greater French demand for products from England.
9. See Lucas (1973) and Lucas and Rapping (1969).
10. Investment was £17.5 in the decades of 1791–1800 and 1801–10 and £22.5 in 1811–21 (Feinstein, 1981).
11. The reference cycle, following procedures established by the National Bureau of Economic Research, provides a set of turning points identified judgmentally by examining (in this case) over 200 time series of economic variates.
12. This index grows from 54.6 in 1790 to 159.9 in 1850, at a compound growth rate of 1.79 per cent per year.
13. Normally one would want to difference the logs of such a series to obtain a stationary series. As it turns out, however, while the GRS index may possess a unit root (at the 1 per cent but not 5 per cent level), the series

produced by Equation (2.1) does not. The test employed is the Augmented Dickey–Fuller test as described in Chapter 3. Non-stationarity, thus, is not a problem for the residual version of the GRS index.

14. U_{EMS} comes from Phillips (1958), I/GNP from Deane (1968) and W from Bowley and Wood.

15. The time series in the Gayer index are

	Weight
Hoffmann's index of industrial production	1
Kondratieff's index of textile production	2
Number of bankruptcies	2
Total value of inland bills of exchange created	2
Brick production (excise)	2
Index of share prices	2
Volume of domestic good exports	3

16. Note that in the neoclassical growth model, along the golden path, both shares (all shares) would be constant. If the relative price term does not change, then a rise in labour productivity (a fall in L/y) would be expected to be associated with a rise in real wages along the path.

17. This does not necessarily mean workers' incomes were worse since L/y may well have risen during this period (although in Table 2.7 we showed a fall in L/y from 1760 to 1800).

18. Ashton had dared to suggest there was an improvement in workers' standard of living from the 1820s.

19. The literature on the standard of living covers many topics that are not directly relevant to a macroeconomic study. This list is long and includes detailed studies of particular areas or sets of workers, the expectation of one's length of life at birth, attempts to measure caloric intake and even *ex-post* measurement of the height of individuals. None of these are unreasonable and, in time, one might expect to have a general (and hence macroeconomic) picture built up in this way for this period.

20. There is clearly unfinished business here. A second study of this sort is by Mokyr and Savin (1978), again referring to the Flinn paper. The traditional statistical problems concern aggregation and in particular both temporal and spatial aggregation (see Gourvish, 1972) in this period. There are also 'time series' problems peculiar to this period of which end points to pick, of the high variances, especially around turning points and of autocorrelation in the basic numbers. Their work basically concludes that there is too much noise in the data to make a strong statement one way or the other.

Chapter 3   The United Kingdom in the Second Half of the 19th Century: Maturity and Relative Decline

1. For a start, look at McCloskey (1971) and Floud and McCloskey (1981). Some industries – for example, chemicals – are probably exceptions to the generalizations suggested by Table 3.1.

2. The original compromise in Feinstein's series is produced by averaging two other series. The compromise suggested by Solomou and Weale

takes account of the different reliability of the numbers; they feel the estimates are 'maximum likelihood' under certain conditions. They refer to them as 'balanced estimates'.

3. Since the Deane figures are at factor cost, the estimates in Feinstein are taken from Table 1, Column 11. These are nominal and are converted to real using Deane's implicit GNP deflator. Rather than abandon the GNP comparisons in favour of GDP to accommodate the recent Solomou/ Weale data, we have simply incorporated the new GDP figures in the table. The slower growth rate shown there also appears in a comparison with Feinstein's GDP compromise estimates.

4. The GNP figures are the same as those used for Figure 3.1.

5. Note that Feinstein does not provide a GNP deflator for this series; consequently, Deane's implicit deflator was employed on both series.

6. These are drawn from her Table B, where Y is here defined as the sum of the first columns $(C+I+G+(EX-IM))$.

7. Across the two sets of data, the correlations are 0.99 for consumption and government spending and 0.96 for investment. The difference is probably due to the handling of inventory investment in Feinstein's calculations (the variance of investment is much higher in Feinstein's figures).

8. The income and consumption figures are from Deane (the longest series available) and are in real terms. The population figures are from Feinstein (1972).

9. These are the data employed in Friedman and Schwartz (1982) and in many of the latter tests in this chapter and in Chapter 8.

10. δY_{t-1} is referred to as an autoregressive (AR) term. If μ and α were equal to zero and $\delta=1$ (indicating a unit root), then Equation (3.5) would be that of a random walk. See below for a discussion of AR and moving average (MA) models.

11. The Deane GNP deflator is used here to convert these nominal figures to real.

12. This is a recession if GNP figures are used. This was quite possibly the worst (or second worst) such event in the period, but is roughly comparable with some of the more severe post-World War II downturns in the West.

13. We will discuss the annual numbers on liabilities below. They exhibit considerable cyclical variation in this sector in the period, which is not surprising.

14. This paragraph leans heavily on a recent survey by Dowd (1989).

15. One of the problems was the tendency to lend at Bank Rate, whatever the market rate. This practice was changed in 1878 to a policy of lending to its regular customers at market rate and to others at a penal rate (Bank Rate).

16. Goodhart (1984) suggests that this simple dichotomy does not reflect the fact that the Bank had multiple instruments and multiple objectives and at times could be interpreted as mixing this brew differently.

17. Results for the United States produced AR terms that were very close to unity and were often unstable. UK interest rates did not seem to work

well in the United States, but this is not a firm result since the model was evidently rejected.

18. We should note, though, that Friedman and Schwartz actually fit a somewhat different model to the data, with two interest rate terms – the 'differential yield on money' and a 'proxy yield on physical assets'.
19. In contrast to the MA process, the AR has a direct connection with potential non-stationarity. This is implied by the fact that Equation (3.5) is a difference equation of order 1 whose single root might be explosive.
20. Most generally, it is possible to have an ARIMA process driving the data, where the differences of the data (of order n) are taken. This would be denoted as ARIMA (p, n, q) where n is the number of times the data are differenced (one time in the data, below). In the literature, n is also referred to as the 'degree of integration'.
21. A second way in which one might examine these data – and a slight variation on the foregoing – is by means of the Wold Decomposition described above. This proposition is that an economic time series can be completely described by a moving average process consisting of a deterministic part and a series of moving average terms of possibly infinite order. The hope in practical cases is that a relatively small number of moving average terms will do the job in the sense of producing a good fit, statistically. For the two velocity series, the table below represents the best fits for a moving average model; these were, indeed, decisively better than shorter or longer configurations in each case. Here it is clear that only a few terms work (longer series added only statistically insignificant terms). Note that the terms across the table are the individual moving average terms. For both series a relatively low order fit was achieved, but the optimal length and the fit differ between the two velocity series. It is simply untenable to assert – based on the identification process undertaken here – that the two series are drawn from a common pool. They are clearly driven by different processes.

Velocity models

	Constant	MA1	MA2	MA3	MA4	$\bar{R}^2$
UK	1.824	1.028	0.354			0.523
	(233.24)	(6.29)	(2.18)			
US	3.276	1.159	0.794	0.269	0.316	0.835
	(46.51)	(5.51)	(4.91)	(1.66)	(2.75)	

t-values in parentheses.

22. The argument here is that by including AR(1) terms or by looking only at the longer lags of Granger-causality tests, one essentially removes the effects of non-stationarity. Chapter 8 recalculates some of these tests in first difference form, however, as a check on some of these results.

Chapter 4   Industrialization without Revolution: the French Case

1. Roehl (1976) has a considerably more detailed bibliography and discussion. One point that he makes seems especially worth repeating and that concerns a tendency in the literature not to be clear whether it is absolute or relative (to England) retardation that is being attributed to the French economy. We have already had this discussion in Chapter 3 with respect to the British, where the boot was on the other foot, relatively.
2. Let us cut one level down to the next stratum of detail (see Caron, 1979). For the entire period, this result was produced mostly by a rapid drop in the birth rate (accompanied by a very slow decline in the death rate). Evidently, the culprit is birth control, largely in the form of later marriages. Immigration actually held the numbers up, from 1866 to 1886, but this source was snuffed out by the Naturalization Act of 1889.
3. The original numbers appear in Mitchell (1978).
4. See the survey of this literature in Goldsmith (1984).
5. Kindleberger (1964), calling on a variety of French sources, notes that the potato was introduced from 1740 to 1770, clover and other forage crops from 1770 to 1790, corn (in the south) and sugar beets (in the north), all by the end of the century. This, he alleges, put the squeeze on the fallow-field system and produces the judgment (p. 211),

   > the greater part of France participated to some degree in the agricultural revolution of the eighteenth century.

6. Morineau (1970) reports figures of Toutain (from 1963) that suggest that output increased

   | 1700–1750 | 0.3% per annum |
   | 1750–1780 | 1.4% per annum |

   which would have placed the former around or a little below population growth and the latter considerably above.
7. Speaking for the critics of the established view, Goldsmith (1984, p. 177) feels that what has gone wrong in this debate is

   > In accepting uncritically the popular notions of static agrarian systems and the eternal order of the field, early modernists misconstrued the findings of the geographers and confused historically distinct aspects of farming. The morphology of agrarian systems was not the same as the economic use of land. There was always a broad range of intensification and factor mixes possible without any change in morphology.

   This, too, is approximately the view taken in Slicher van Bath's essay for the *Cambridge Economic History of Europe* (1977). See Weber (1976) and, especially, Braudel (1967) for contrasting views.
8. In this connection official studies indicate that, in 1840, grain yields were relatively low in a broad area that covered the south and reached almost to Paris. For example, in this region, 27 per cent of the arable land was in fallow (in 1847) of which 20 per cent was essentially useless.

9. O'Brien and Keyder claim that quality of land, meteorological temperament, choice of crops (which is also influenced by demand) and availability of capital all influence measured productivity to some extent. The question, in a nutshell, is whether there is a measurable difference for a comparable piece of land, standardized for the above factors. Their answer is (p. 137)

> Only to a small extent should the backwardness of agriculture in France be conceived as a problem of small peasants slow to innovate or to copy the superior techniques deployed by farmers in Britain.

The problem is high labour densities in the context of a system of property rights that held labour in the countryside and depressed the rate of capital accumulation in agriculture. Even so (p. 137),

> In the livestock sector or the cultivation of industrial crops there is no evidence of French backwardness.

10. Or from 54 per cent of its 1909 level, since 1910 was a very bad year for the agricultural sector.
11. Incidentally, the comparable growth figure for industrial production from 1815 to 1840 is 2.73 per cent.
12. The figures for industrial output are (in index numbers):

	1700	*1780*
France	100	454
England	100	197

13. Fohlen argues (1970, p. 203),

> The industrial revolution in France thus covers a period of approximately a century, from 1750 or 1770 to 1870 . . . . The long duration of this transformation is sufficient to indicate the slowness of industrial progress.

In fact, he feels, the term 'industrial revolution' does not fit the French, who, he argues, seemed 'reluctant' to turn aside from their well established major industries of coal, iron and silk, if such comments make economic sense.
14. Actually, in the literature on French development, one encounters frequent references to a coal problem (as in Kindleberger, 1964). This was a French perception from the 1820s, apparently, as is often mentioned in explanations of why they lagged behind the British. The table below provides the basic numbers. It is abundantly clear from these figures that the French typically imported coal as needed, and, when coal demands

Coal production and consumption in France (000 tons)

Date	Production (000 tons)	% Change (p. a.)	Consumption (000 tons)	% Change (p. a.)
1815	882			
1820	1 094			
1825	1 491	6.90		
1830	1 863	7.01	2 492	
1835	2 000	3.41	3 256	
1840	3 000	6.10	4 184	6.79
1845	4 207	11.04	6 220	9.10
1850	4 434	4.78	6 985	6.69
1855	7 400	7.59	12 000	9.29
1860	8 300	8.72	14 200	10.33
1865	11 000	4.87	18 500	5.42
1869	13 400	6.14	21 300	5.00

n. b. The % change is decadel.

Source: Fohlen (1970), p. 208.

really escalated, they met the increased pressure by importation. This is, indeed, an obvious example of an international market in coal at work and is not necessarily an indication of retardation (if such there was).

15. Looking at another set of statistics provided by Crouzert (1970), we see that it was both primary metals and metal fabricating that were involved in this lead, and that the French rates of growth for a century were really quite rapid for the basic industrial sectors. These are (for 1815 to 1914), mining 4.2 per cent, primary metal 3.5 per cent, chemicals 4.2 per cent, metal fabricating 3.4 per cent, food 2.3 per cent, miscellaneous new industries 4.0 per cent and textiles 1.5 per cent.
16. The French edition of their book was published in 1985.
17. They were English-style in that they used coke and considerably more capital-hungry types of equipment. Firms employing charcoal-based smelting technologies fared much better. It is, of course, possible that these firms succumbed because they did not have sufficient time to get established.
18. In 1839, in particular, the railroad companies were liquidated.
19. This is phrased in this way in view of the opinion in the literature (e.g., LLB) that the disastrous harvests in 1847–8, in which grain prices doubled, were followed by overabundance to the point of 'toppling the market'. This is referred to as the 'scissors' in the literature. The same is alleged by the same authors to be true of the harvests in 1854–6 and the grain market after 1856. Looking at Toutain's figures for the agricultural component of nominal GDP we see (in m francs):

	GDP (AG)	AG production index
1845	5007.1	71.6
1846	5319.5	69.4
1847	7341.0	87.9
1848	5451.4	85.5
1849	4917.7	82.2
1853	5643.6	69.3
1854	6938.1	78.1
1855	6899.9	72.1
1856	7520.1	76.5
1857	8411.8	89.2
1858	7931.2	96.5

The scissors effect certainly does seem to have occurred in 1847–9, but the agricultural production index in 1854–6, while down from the abundance of the late 1840s, is not that low historically, and 1857 and 1858 are both better years (in contribution to nominal GDP) than any of the previous years. On this level of generality, the second coming of the 'scissors' is not obvious.

20. The particular domestic event here is the effect of the Freycinet construction plan (of 1878) for railroads that might have set off an echoing boom in other kinds of construction and in municipal schemes. Cancelled projects and vacancies appeared in the wake of the 1882 financial collapse. This, by itself is not proof, since modern cycles typically exhibit such behaviour, but is suggestive, none the less, of how complicated the situation becomes, once an economy modernizes.
21. The Bank of France replaced an earlier bank, the Caisse de Comptes Courants, which had been founded in 1796. Note that much of the following discussion is drawn from Cameron (1967), but amended as noted.
22. Below, we will suggest that the money stock figures are not very useful prior to 1860 or so. One reason, quite possibly, is that other securities provided many of the services of money, albeit very imperfectly and inconsistently (and, worse, immeasurably).
23. The first of the savings banks dates to 1818; by 1845, there were more than 350 of them not, apparently, serving the working classes.
24. The first of these was Jacques Laffitte's Caisse Général du Commerce.
25. Lucas used a procedure that permitted infinite lags, but tests out to 100 lags on these data produced no meaningful differences in the results, so no attempt was made here to stretch the data any further. The length of the lag is j, in Equation (4.1).
26. A bond is a contract to deliver a nominal sum of money at some future date and so would be the generic item here.
27. In addition, the econometrics that support its estimation are suspect, it forecasts badly and the monetary data on which it rests are suspected to

be inconsistent with those required by economic theory (see Fisher, 1989 and Barnett, Fisher and Serletis, 1992). All of these things (unfortunately) hold for the work in this section, but the state of the data leave us with little choice of approach.

28. There is further work with structural variables in Chapter 6 – for Sweden. See the extended discussion of such variables in the Bordo–Jonung (1987) study of velocity. France is not one of the countries those authors studied.

29. Even so, in view of the close relation between the government and the banking system, and in view of the fiscal difficulties of the government surrounding the 1870 war, it is not hard to conjure up explanations of why the demand for money might be hard to locate.

Chapter 5 The Development of the German Macroeconomy

1. A counterbalance, of sorts, resides in the control of 39 states by Prussia after the Napoleonic wars; this territory included the industrially important Westphalia and the Rhine, and is certainly the heart of the industrial area.

2. Germany's first steam engine, *Der Adler*, was built by George Stephenson.

3. Note that there is a large and variable balancing item in these accounts so that the ratios can and do add up to a number greater than unity at times.

4. For the last twenty years, the correlation between C/Y and I/Y is -0.714 while that between I/Y and G/Y is an insignificant -0.038.

5. Perhaps we should also point out that the 'great depression' of 1875 to 1882 is more accurately a 'great stagnation' since the bottom figure of 1882 is only 0.70 of 1 per cent below the peak of 1874.

6. These banks did not issue notes but they did considerable business in banker's acceptances and discounts. They also dealt with the government, sometimes on a very large scale (e.g., the Rothschilds of Frankfurt).

7. Tilly (1967) uses the felicitous phrase 'joint-stock promotional banks' to describe these institutions.

8. It is sometimes alleged that the Prussian Bank's activities are (positively) causally linked to the growth of the financial sector, but this is hard to establish in view of the data and, indeed, quite possibly not correct, at least up until 1870. See Tilly (1967) for a discussion.

9. Banks, to the extent they could, would direct business to their own (not necessarily low cost) firm and would guide risky choices according to the risk-return preferences of their own (conservative?) shareholders.

10. The last named is positive when the new institutions aid firms in reaching new capital sources and negative when bankers' positions on the board lead to capital decisions that are less than optimal for the firm.

11. The actual variable used is current-account credit divided by total credit. The 'current account' is a special and widespread account much favoured by German banks in their dealings with their corporate customers. The adverse effect comes about via the direction of too much capital to heavy industry and too little to light.

12. Komlos (1978) raises the question of whether multicollinearity in the independent variables renders the results sensitive to small changes in the data. The ensuing debate partly concerns whether this is a problem (it certainly could be). Komlos also questions the assumption of Neuberger and Stokes that labour and capital were unemployed at the same rate; since they appear not to have had any real choice in this matter, this (and most of the debate) must await new data.
13. We note, as Tilly does, that a comparable British test shows considerably less efficiency in the British banking sector than in the German.
14. Aggregation problems among the diverse German banks and their customers leap to mind.
15. As discussed, for example, in Friedman and Schwartz (1982).
16. Chapter 8 carries a summary of this index for all six countries discussed in this study, for the 1871 to 1910 period.
17. The results for the simpler model are as follows:

	1850–1910		1850–1880		1880–1910	
Constant	–6.289	(11.09)	–4.930	(8.78)	–11.273	(14.43)
Income	1.944	(31.34)	1.657	(19.78)	2.438	(27.71)
Long rate	–0.090	(1.50)	–0.008	(0.09)	0.449	(5.33)
Short rate	0.003	(0.24)	–0.002	(0.14)	– 0.039	(2.56)
DW	0.850		1.474		1.227	
R^2-bar	0.977		0.931		0.974	

18. The formula for the straight lines establishing the 5 per cent confidence interval is:

$$W = \pm \left[0.948\sqrt{n-k} + 1.896 \frac{(p-k)}{\sqrt{n-k}} \right]$$

19. The line in this case is

$$WW = (\pm)a_0 + \frac{p-k}{n-k} \qquad p = k+1, k+2, \ldots, n$$

See Harvey (1981) for further explanation.

Chapter 6   Sweden during the Industrial Revolution

1. See the discussion in Söderberg (1982).
2. We note that in outlying rural areas, until 1860, population growth (and extreme poverty) apparently forced the subdivision of agricultural plots.
3. These are well-worn but doubtful assertions that survive in the literature partly because of the absence of good data.
4. Sweden, in 1850, had 90 per cent literacy. In 1859, only 1.4 per cent of its children received no formal education. Universal education, though, dates to the Act of 1842, as mentioned above.

5. The last column is the net of emigration and immigration, with some attempt made to count unregistered migrations.

6. In this connection, Sandberg looks at wages in the United States among different populations of European origin – in order to try to measure the human capital element – and finds, usually, the Swedes at or near the top of the wage distribution. This also seems suggestive.

7. See the discussion in Söderberg (1982) and Heckscher (1963).

8. The data are from Krantz and Nilsson (1975).

9. Before we go on, we should describe the data that are available to us. The Swedish aggregate data for the last half of the 19th century are possibly the best available for any country in that period. The national income accounts are complete on an annual basis and have been carefully built up from raw materials that are both very reliable and very detailed; the source used here is the work of Krantz and Nilsson (1975). The monetary data are equally precise and are largely the work of Jonung (1975). The latter, too, are built up from individual records for each year, but they also enable a separation of the money stock into an M1 and an M2 series, although the latter is the most useful for comparisons across countries. The growth rates are estimated by regressing the logarithm of real GDP on the trend variable.

10. Note that there was a decline in prices in that same period (the RDP deflator was 1.023 in 1974 and fell to 0.796 in 1894). This may have confused some observers.

11. Note (Craig and Fisher, 1991), that Sweden's real sector is cointegrated with those of these same three countries over the entire 1871 to 1910 period. It is hard to believe that the agricultural sector is not an important part of this interaction. Note that large supplies of grain came from the Ukraine into European markets, as well.

12. Many of the results of this section, down to subsection 6.4.4, appear in Fisher and Thurman (1989).

13. In defence of Sandberg we should point out that his notion requires a comparison with other countries *at similar stages of development*. Thus the appropriate comparison, for example, would be with an English financial system of approximately a century earlier, in which case Sweden's system would certainly look a lot better, *relatively*.

14. Actually, Sweden, with Norway and Denmark, formed the Scandinavian Monetary Union over this period.

15. In the standard setup of Cagan (1965), the contributions to the money stock of the currency–money ratio (C/M), the reserves–deposit ratio (R/D) and the monetary base (generally defined to be bank reserves plus currency in the hands of the public) can be calculated under the assumption that these 'proximate determinants' are uncorrelated with each other. Over the 1871 to 1896 period, Jonung (1976b) finds that the monetary base contributes slightly less than 50 per cent to the growth of the money stock while from 1897 to 1913 it has a much closer relation to money growth. The two (presumably endogenously-determined) ratios provide the remainder of the effect.

16. The United Kingdom in this period is clearly relatively financially soph-

isticated. In the United Kingdom the velocity of money rose very slightly over the same period.

17. Bordo and Jonung (1981, p. 98). In an earlier work, Jonung (1976b) puts forward roughly the same view.
18. Proxies suggested and used by Bordo and Jonung are the percentage of the labour force in non-agricultural activities, the currency–money (C/M) ratio and the ratio of non-bank financial assets to total financial assets. These also appear in Friedman and Schwartz (1982). A broader set of financial variables is tested separately by Jonung (1983) over the 1875–1913 period. Here C/M, the ratio of cash payments to the total wages of farmhands, labour's share in national income and the ratio of urban population to the total population produce significant coefficients in a log-linear test of the velocity equation.
19. The national income and price data come from Krantz and Nilsson (1975), while the financial and monetary data are from Sandberg (1978) and Jonung, (1975). Michael Bordo kindly supplied corroborating data and a long-term interest rate used in a study with Jonung (1987).
20. In the tables that follow, generally only results for 1871 to 1910 are presented. In every case where it was possible, the tests were extended back to 1861. There were only rare cases where this made any difference and those cases are reported either in the tables or in the footnotes. The 1871 results are presented solely for consistency of display, since some numbers are not available for the entire period.
21. In their recent study of the behaviour of velocity, Bordo and Jonung (1987) argue that the period of declining velocity is the result of the monetization process, whereas the period of rising velocity is the result of increasing financial sophistication. 'Financial sophistication' in this case is defined as *both* the emergence of a large number of substitutes for money and the development of various methods of economizing on money balances. We are, of course, suggesting that monetization itself is a form of financial sophistication and, in any case, are studying only the period of declining velocity.
22. Of course, there are other forms of money. For example, commercial bills are certainly in increasing use in this period, although in the absence of really good figures on their volume, it is not possible to offer more than the conjecture that they did not influence the situation sufficiently to disrupt our proposition.
23. In any event, the same tests were run using M1. There are some differences, with interest rates affecting the M1 version of the financial sophistication index, and with the industrial structure variables *not* providing any effect on the M1 measure of money.
24. This section is the result of joint, unpublished work with Walter N. Thurman.
25. The variables are narrow (M1) and broad (M2) money and are measured in log real per capita form. The Cochrane–Orcutt adjustment was employed to deal with serial correlation in the residuals.
26. Recall that Swedish GDP Granger-causes money but not the converse.
27. We will further assume that both the demand and supply functions used

here are stable over the 1871–1910 period.

28. Bordo and Jonung (1987) and Jonung (1984) suggest using the British bond rate to measure the opportunity cost for holding money. This was attempted in what follows, but the results were not as well determined as with the US corporate bond rate.

29. The estimates of Table 6.14 are consistent under the maintained hypothesis of simultaneously determined r_D and m. Is there other evidence that r_D is endogenous in the demand for money? The evidence comes from a Wu–Hausman test of the predeterminateness of r_D in (6.5). See Wu (1973) and Hausman (1978). The Wu–Hausman test compares (nonlinear) OLS estimates of (6.5) with the (nonlinear) 2SLS estimates. Under the null hypothesis of a predetermined interest rate, both OLS and 2SLS are consistent and their difference should be small. If their difference is significantly different from zero, then the Wu–Hausman test rejects the null hypothesis. The Wu–Hausman statistic, which is asymptotically standard normal under the null hypothesis, takes the value 6.082 for the specification reported in Table 6.14, thus rejecting the exogeneity of r_D.

30. Put differently, the sample mean of r_D of 4.722 per cent implies that a 1 per cent increase in the real quantity of money will increase the return to deposits by approximately two basis points.

Chapter 7   Italy at the Time of the Industrial Revolution

1. We are not saying that political and religious styles are not involved in the economic stories that will unfold here, nor are we saying that the countries are not interrelated. Instead, the claim is that in the 19th century these three countries are probably not sufficiently economically interrelated to require imposing a group view.

2. The emigration figures are from Fenoaltea (1988a).

3. The ISTAT publication offers two sets of numbers, one based on actual borders and one based on modern borders. We have employed the latter set of numbers here, arbitrarily. See the critique of these data in Toniolo (1990).

4. Fenoaltea (1988a) provides evidence that construction spending was sensitive to financial conditions in general and the international supply of capital in particular.

5. See Fenoaltea (1981) for an explanation and critique.

6. In fact, though, the conclusions from the log-level figures are roughly the same as those for first differences.

7. The sign was calculated from the sum of the coefficients of the lagged causal agent.

8. The results here differed only marginally with the ISTAT index (Table 7.8 uses the Fenoaltea index). Nothing turned up for the real GNP numbers, however, again indicating how important it is to resolve the difficulties with the Italian data.

9. This table uses estimated rates mainly because 1910 is a dramatically bad year for the real variables. The estimation is by regression of log x on the trend (and a constant).

10. The inflation calculation is by means of the GNP deflator. By the cost-of-living index there was mild deflation during this period. These numbers were calculated just using the endpoints in the data and so are not strictly comparable with the numbers in Table 7.9.
11. Note that government here is represented by the item called 'public consumption' in the ISTAT calculations.
12. The price index used is the GNP deflator in Fratianni and Spinelli (1984). The consumer price index gives even lower estimates of inflation (0.332 over the entire period, for example).
13. The Mitchell data do not show these effects. Note that the investment data, the second set for each grouping, are taken from Mitchell.
14. These periods are overlapping in order to provide a comparable and adequate number of observations for each set. This was arbitrary, and no attempt was made to find the dating that would produce a specific result, although this could be done, of course.
15. If we are using the model described above to interpret this result, then this reduced form coefficient is not an income elasticity, but a composite of the several coefficients modifying the income term in Equation (7.4). Of course if $\gamma=0$ and $\beta=1$, then it could be so interpreted. Below, we report the same value for the elasticity, approximately, as that given here, under the first of these conditions.

Chapter 8 The European Macroeconomy

1. The real product numbers used in this table and in much of the remainder of this chapter come from the following sources: France, real gross domestic product (Toutain, 1987); Germany, real net national product (Mitchell, 1978); Italy, real gross national product (Fratianni and Spinelli, 1984); Sweden, real domestic product (Krantz and Nilsson, 1975); United Kingdom, real net national product (Feinstein, 1972 as employed in Friedman and Schwartz, 1982); and United States, real gross domestic product (Romer, 1989).

   The monetary quantities used are generally for a broad measure of money, at an annual frequency. The US data are taken from Friedman and Schwartz (1982), while those for the United Kingdom are drawn from Capie and Webber (1985). For Sweden, we used the stock of M2 as published in Jonung (1975), while for Italy, the data employed are published in Fratianni and Spinelli (1984). The German data appear in Tilly (1973), while the French data appear in Saint Marc (1983).
2. Results from an augmented Dickey–Fuller test are provided in Craig and Fisher (1991) for approximately the same set of data. The model is

$$\Delta X_t = \alpha + \theta X_{t-1} + \sum_{i=1}^{p} \beta_i \Delta X_{t-i} + \delta T + U_t$$

   where p is the number of lagged dependent variables and T is a trend. The results given there are virtually identical to those reported here for the Dickey–Fuller test.
3. A word of caution is required here, since these calculations do not

account for the possibly greater introduction of money substitutes in the United Kingdom.

4. As, for example, Friedman and Schwartz (1982) do in their discussion of US and UK interactions in this period.

5. See Chapter 1 and the attendant discussion for more of the theory and some cautions about the procedure.

6. The results for the entire period 1871 to 1910 are available from the author.

7. In some of the shorter periods attempted, there was some interaction between Sweden and the United States.

8. The national product deflators were used in these tests in all cases.

9. Tests show 'reverse causation' – real per capita income Granger-causing per capita nominal money balances – did occur in five cases in the table. These were for the Friedman and Schwartz data in the first row, and for four of the five tests in the second set (only the Deane measure of real income did not Granger-cause the Capie–Webber measure of money).

10. Recall that in Chapter 3 we noted some non-neutral results for several of these measures at very long lags.

11. There is one instance of 'reverse causation' between real income and money. That is for the Swedish test for M2.

12. Note that the figures for the United Kingdom used here reflect the Friedman and Schwartz measure of national product. In the paper by Craig and Fisher (1991) a different measure was used, based on a recent revision of some of the data by Feinstein (1988). This shows a larger number of downturns for the UK case, but does not alter the broad conclusions drawn from this table.

13. Note that this summary judgment refers to the period 1867 to 1975.

Bibliography

Ashton, T.S. (1949) 'The Standard of Life of the Workers in England, 1790–1930', *Journal of Economic History* (Supplement).

Ashton, T.S. (1955) *An Economic History of England: The 18th Century* (London: Methuen).

Ashton, T.S. (1959) *Economic Fluctuations in England, 1700–1800* (Oxford: Clarendon Press).

Balke, N.S. and R.J. Gordon (1989) 'The Estimation of Prewar Gross National Product: Methodology and New Evidence', *Journal of Political Economy* (Feb.).

Barbiero, T. (1988) 'A Reassessment of Agricultural Production in Italy, 1861–1914: The Case of Lombardy', *Journal of European Economic History* (Spring).

Barnett, W.A., D. Fisher and A. Serletis (1992) 'Consumer Theory and the Demand for Money', *Journal of Economic Literature*, forthcoming.

Barro, R.J. (1987) 'Government Spending, Interest Rates, Prices and Budget Deficits in the United Kingdom', *Journal of Monetary Economics*, (Sept.).

Black, R.A. and C.G. Gilmore (1990) 'Crowding Out During Britain's Industrial Revolution', *Journal of Economic History* (Mar.).

Bloomfield, A.I. (1959) *Monetary Policy under the International Gold Standard, 1880–1914* (New York: Federal Reserve Bank of New York).

Borchardt, K. (1976) 'The Industrial Revolution in Germany, 1700–1914', in C.M. Cipolla (ed.), *The Emergence of Industrial Societies* (New York: Barnes and Noble).

Bordo, M.D. (1986) 'Explorations in Monetary History: A Survey', *Explorations in Economic History* (Oct.).

Bordo, M.D. and L. Jonung (1981) 'The Long Run Behaviour of the Income Velocity of Money in Five Advanced Countries; An Institutional Approach', *Economic Inquiry* (Jan.).

Bordo, M.D. and L. Jonung (1987) *The Long-run Behavior of the Velocity of Circulation: The International Evidence* (Cambridge MA: Harvard University Press).

Bordo, M.D. and E.N. White (1990) 'British and French Finance During the Napoleonic Wars', Working Paper No. 3517, National Bureau of Economic Research (Nov.).

Braudel, F. (1967) *Capitalism and Material Life* (London: Weidenfeld and Nicolson).

Brillembourg, A. and M. Khan (1979) 'The Relationship Between Money, Income, and Prices: Has Money Mattered Historically?' *Journal of Money, Credit and Banking* (Aug.).

Cafagna, L. (1976) 'The Industrial Revolution in Italy, 1830–1914', in C.M. Cipolla (ed.), *The Emergence of Industrial Societies* (New York: Barnes and Noble).

Cagan, P. (1965) in *The Determinants and Effects of Changes in the Stock of Money, 1875–1960* (New York: Columbia University Press).

Calliari, S., F. Spinelli and G. Verga (1984) 'Money Demand in Italy: A Few More Results', *Manchester School* (June).

Cameron, R.E. (1958) 'Economic Growth and Stagnation in France, 1815–1914', *Journal of Modern History* (Mar.).

Cameron, R.E. (1967) 'France', in R. Cameron (ed.), *Banking in the Early Stages of Industrialization* (Oxford: Oxford University Press).

Capie, F. and A. Webber (1985) *A Monetary History of the United Kingdom*, Vol. I (London: Allen and Unwin).

Caron, F. (1979) *An Economic History of Modern France* (New York: Columbia University Press).

Chow, G.C. (1960) 'Tests of Equality Between Sets of Coefficients in Two Linear Regressions', *Econometrica* (July).

Cipolla, C.M. (1980) *Before the Industrial Revolution* (2nd edn) (New York: Norton).

Clapham, J.H. (1921) *Economic Development of France and Germany, 1815–1914* (Cambridge: Cambridge University Press).

Clapham, J.H. (1926–38) *An Economic History of Modern Britain* (Cambridge: Cambridge University Press).

Clough, S.B. (1972) 'Retardative Factors in French Economic Growth at the End of the Ancien Régime and during the French Revolution and Napoleonic Periods', in M. Kooy (ed.) *Studies in Economics and Economic History* (Durham NC: Duke University Press).

Cohen, J.S. (1967) 'Financing the Industrialization in Italy, 1894–1914: The Partial Transformation of a Late-Comer', *Journal of Economic History* (Sept.).

Cole, W.A. (1973) 'Eighteenth-Century Economic Growth Revisited', *Explorations in Economic History* (Sum.).

Cole, W.A. (1981) 'Factors in Demand, 1700–80', in R. Floud and D.N. McCloskey (eds), *The Economic History of England Since 1700* (Vol. 1) (Cambridge: University Press).

Collins, M. (1983) 'Long-Term Growth of the English Banking Sector and Money Stock, 1844–80', *Economic History Review* (Aug.).

Coppock, D.J. (1972) 'The Causes of Business Fluctuations', in D.H. Aldcroft and P. Fearon (eds), *British Economic Fluctuations, 1790–1939* (London: Macmillan).

Crafts, N.F.R. (1976) 'English Economic Growth in the Eighteenth Century: A Reexamination of Deane and Cole's Estimates', *Economic History Review* (May).

Crafts, N.F.R. (1977) 'Industrial Revolution in England and France: Some Thoughts on the Question, Why was England First?', *Economic History Review* (Aug.).

Crafts, N.F.R. (1980) 'National Income Estimates and the British Standard of Living Debate: A Reappraisal of 1801–1831', *Explorations in Economic History* (Apr.).

Crafts, N.F.R. (1983) 'British Economic Growth, 1700–1831: A Review of the Evidence', *Economic History Review* (May).

Crafts, N.F.R. (1984) 'Economic Growth in France and Britain, 1830–1910:

A Review of the Evidence', *Journal of Economic History* (Mar.).

Crafts, N.F.R. (1985) *British Economic Growth During the Industrial Revolution* (Oxford: University Press).

Craig, L.A. and D. Fisher (1991) 'Integration of the European Business Cycle, 1871–1910', *Explorations in Economic History*, forthcoming.

Crouzert, F. (1970) 'An Annual Index of French Industrial Production in the 19th Century', in R. Cameron (ed.), *Essays in French Economic History* (Homewood, IL: Irwin)

Dahlman, C. (1980) *The Open Field System and Beyond* (Cambridge: University Press).

Davis, R. (1962) 'English Foreign Trade, 1660–1700', in W.E. Minchinton (ed.), *The Growth of English Overseas Trade* (London: Methuen, 1969).

Deane, P. (1968) 'New Estimates of Gross National Product for the United Kingdom, 1830–1914', *Review of Income and Wealth* (Mar.).

Deane, P. (1979) *The First Industrial Revolution* (2nd edn) (Cambridge: University Press).

Deane, P. and W.A. Cole (1962, 1967) *British Economic Growth, 1668–1959* (Cambridge: University Press).

Domar, E.D. (1946) 'Capital Expansion, Rate of Growth and Employment', *Econometrica* (Apr.).

Dowd, K. (1989) 'The Evolution of Central Banking in England, 1821–1890', mimeo, University of Nottingham (Apr.).

Dutton, J. (1984) 'The Bank of England and the Rules of the Game under the International Gold Standard: New Evidence', in M.D. Bordo and A.J. Schwartz (eds.) *Retrospective on the Classical Gold Standard, 1821–1931* (Chicago: University of Chicago Press).

Dwyer, G. (1983) 'Money, Income, and Prices in the United Kingdom, 1870–1913', mimeo (Emory University).

Easton, S.T. (1984) 'Real Output and the Gold Standard Years, 1830–1913', in M.D. Bordo and A.J. Schwartz (eds), *A Retrospective on the Classical Gold Standard, 1821–1931* (Chicago: University of Chicago Press).

Eichengreen, B. (1983) 'The Causes of British Business Cycles, 1833–1913', *Journal of European Economic History* (Spring).

Eversley, D.E.C. (1967) 'The Home Market and Economic Growth in England, 1750–1780', in E.L. Jones and G.E. Mingay (eds), *Land, Labour, and Population Growth in the Industrial Revolution* (London: Arnold).

Feinstein, C.H. (1972) *Statistical Tables of National Income, Expenditure and Output of the U.K., 1855–1965* (Cambridge: University Press).

Feinstein, C.H. (1978) 'Capital Formation in Great Britain', in P. Mathias and M.M. Postan (eds), *The Cambridge Economic History of Europe* (Vol. III) (Cambridge: University Press).

Feinstein, C.H. (1981) 'Capital Accumulation and the Industrial Revolution', in R. Floud and D.N. McCloskey (eds), *The Economic History of England Since 1700* (Vol. 1) (Cambridge: University Press).

Feinstein, C.H. (1988) 'National Statistics, 1760–1920', in C.H. Feinstein and S. Pollard (eds), *Studies in Capital Formation in the United Kingdom, 1750–1920* (Oxford: Clarendon Press).

Fenoaltea, S. (1981) 'Railways and the Development of the Italian Economy to 1981', mimeo (Jan.).

Fenoaltea, S. (1982a) 'The Industrialization of Italy, 1861–1913: A Progress Report', mimeo, Cliometrics conference

Fenoaltea, S. (1982b) 'The Growth of the Utilities Industries in Italy, 1861–1913', *Journal of Economic History* (Sept.).

Fenoaltea, S. (1988a) 'International Resource Flows and Construction Movements in the Atlantic Economy: The Kuznets Cycle in Italy, 1861–1913', *Journal of Economic History* (Sept.).

Fenoaltea, S. (1988b) 'The Extractive Industries in Italy, 1861–1913: General Methods and Specific Estimates', *Journal of European Economic History* (Spring).

Fisher, D. (1989) *Money Demand and Monetary Policy* (London: Wheatsheaf-Harvester).

Fisher, D. and W.N. Thurman (1989) 'Sweden's Financial Sophistication in the Nineteenth Century: An Appraisal', *Journal of Economic History* (Sept.).

Flinn, M.W. (1974) 'Trends in Real Wages, 1750–1850', *Economic History Review* (Aug.).

Floud, R.C. and D.N. McCloskey (eds), (1981) *The Economic History of Britain Since 1700* (Cambridge: University Press).

Fohlen, C.B. (1970) 'The Industrial Revolution in France', in R. Cameron (ed.), *Essays in French Economic History* (Homewood, IL: Irwin).

Fohlen, C.B. (1976) 'France, 1700–1914', in C. Cipolla (ed.), *The Emergence of Industrial Societies* (New York: Barnes and Noble).

Ford, A.G. (1981) 'The Trade Cycle in Britain, 1860–1914', in R.C. Floud and D.N. McCloskey (eds), *The Economic History of Britain Since 1700*, Vol. 2 (Cambridge: University Press).

Fratianni, M. and F. Spinelli (1984) 'Italy in the Gold Standard Period, 1861–1914', in Michael D. Bordo and Anna J. Schwartz, *A Retrospective on the Classical Gold Standard* (Chicago: University of Chicago Press).

Fremdling, R. and R. Tilly (1976) 'German Banks, German Growth, and Econometric History', *Journal of Economic History* (June).

Friedman, M. and A.J. Schwartz (1982) *Monetary Trends in the United States and the United Kingdom, 1867–1975* (Chicago: University of Chicago Press).

Fuller, W.A. (1976) *Introduction to Statistical Time Series* (New York: Wiley).

Gayer, A.D., W.W. Rostow and A.J. Schwartz (1953) *The Growth and Fluctuation of the British Economy, 1790–1850* (Oxford: Clarendon Press).

Gerschenkron, A. (1962) *Economic Backwardness in Historical Perspective: A Book of Essays* (Cambridge: Harvard University Press).

Gilboy, E.W. (1932) 'Demand as a Factor in the Industrial Revolution', in A.H. Cole (ed.), *Facts and Factors in Economic History* (New York: Kelley (1967)).

Goldsmith, J.L. (1984) 'The Agrarian History of Preindustrial France. Where Do We Go from Here?', *Journal of European Economic History* (Spring).

Goodhart, C.A.E. (1972) *The Business of Banking* (London: Weidenfeld & Nicolson).

Goodhart, C.A.E. (1984) 'Comment', in M.D. Bordo and A.J. Schwartz (eds), *A Retrospective on the Classical Gold Standard, 1821–1931* (Chicago: University of Chicago Press).

Gourvish, T.P. (1972) 'The Cost of Living in Glasgow in the Early Nineteenth Century', *Economic History Review* (Feb.).

Granger, C.W.J. (1969) 'Investigating Causal Relations by Econometric Models and Cross-Spectral Methods', *Econometrica* (July).

Harley, C.K. (1982) 'British Industrialization Before 1841: Evidence of Slower Growth During the Industrial Revolution', *Journal of Economic History* (June).

Harrod, R. (1939) 'An Essay in Dynamic Theory', *Economic Journal* (Mar.).

Harvey, A.C. (1981) *The Econometric Analysis of Time Series* (London: Phillip Allen).

Hatton, R., J. Lyons and S. Satchell (1983) 'Eighteenth Century British Trade: Homespun or Empire Made', *Explorations in Economic History* (Apr.).

Hausman, J.A. (1978) 'Specification Tests in Econometrics', *Econometrica*, (Nov.).

Heckscher, E.F. (1963) *An Economic History of Sweden* (Cambridge: Harvard University Press).

Heim, C.E. and P. Mirowski (1987) 'Interest Rates and Crowding-Out During Britain's Industrialization', *Journal of Economic History* (Mar.).

Hicks, J.R. (1946) *Value and Capital* (2nd. edn) (Oxford: Clarendon Press).

Hicks, J.R. (1969) *A Theory of Economic History* (Oxford: University Press).

Hobsbawm, E.J. (1957) 'The British Standard of Living, 1790–1850', *Economic History Review* (No. 1).

Hoffmann, W.G. (1955) *British Industry, 1770–1959* (trans. by W.O. Henderson and W.H. Chalconer) (Oxford: Oxford University Press).

Homer, S. (1977) *The History of Interest Rates* (New Brunswick, NJ: Rutgers University Press).

Hoppit, J. (1986) 'Financial Crises in Eighteenth-Century England', *Economic History Review* (Feb.).

Hueckel, G. (1973) 'War and the British Economy, 1793–1815: A General Equilibrium Analysis', *Explorations in Economic History* (Summer).

Huffman, W.E. and J.R. Lothian (1984) 'The Gold Standard and the Transmission of Business Cycles, 1833–1932', in M.D. Bordo and A.J. Schwartz, *A Retrospective on the Classical Gold Standard, 1821–1931* (Chicago: University of Chicago Press).

ISTAT (1957) *Indagine Statistica Sullo Sviluppo del Reddito Nazionale dell'Italia del 1861 al 1956* Annali de Statisica Serie 8, Vol. 9 (Rome: Instituto Poligrafica di Stato

Jones, E.L. (1981) 'Agriculture, 1700–1800', in R. Floud and D.H. McCloskey (eds), *The Economic History of Britain Since 1700*, Vol. I (Cambridge: University Press).

Jonung, L. (1975) *Studies in the Monetary History of Sweden*, Ph.D. Dissertation, University of California (Los Angeles).

Jonung, L. (1976a) 'Money and Prices in Sweden, 1732–1972', *Scandinavian Journal of Economics* (No. 1).

Jonung, L. (1976b) 'Sources of Growth in the Swedish Money Stock, 1871–1971', *Scandinavian Journal of Economics* (No. 4).

304   *Bibliography*

Jonung, L. (1978) 'The Long-Run Demand for Money – A Wicksellian Approach', *Scandinavian Journal of Economics* (No. 2).

Jonung, L. (1983) 'Monetization and the Behavior of Velocity in Sweden, 1871–1913', *Explorations in Economic History* (Oct.).

Jonung, L. (1984) 'Swedish Experience under the Classical Gold Standard, 1873–1914', in M.D. Bordo and A.J. Schwartz (eds), *A Retrospective on the Classical Gold Standard, 1821–1931* (Chicago: University of Chicago Press).

Jorberg, L. (1975) 'Structural Change and Economic Growth in Nineteenth Century Sweden', in S. Kolbik (ed.), *Sweden's Development from Poverty to Affluence, 1750–1970* (Bloomington, Minn: University of Minnesota Press).

Kemp, T. (1962) 'Structural Factors in the Retardation of French Economic Growth', *Kyklos* (No. 2).

Keynes, J.M. (1936) *The General Theory of Employment, Interest, and Money* (New York: Harcourt, Brace).

Kindleberger, C.P. (1962) *Foreign Trade and the National Economy* (New Haven: Yale University Press).

Kindleberger, C.P. (1964) *The Economic Growth of France and Britain, 1851–1950* (New York: Simon & Schuster).

Kindleberger, C.P. (1982) 'Sweden in 1850 as an "Impoverished Sophisticate": A Comment', *Journal of Economic History* (Dec.).

Klein, B. (1974) 'Competitive Interest Payments on Bank Deposits and the Long-Run Demand for Money', *American Economic Review* (Dec.).

Komlos, J. (1978) 'The Kreditbanken and German Growth: A Post script', *Journal of Economic History* (June).

Komlos, J. (1987) 'Financial Innovation and the Demand for Money in Austria-Hungary, 1867–1913', *Journal of European Economic History* (Winter).

Kormendi, R.C. and P. Meguire (1990) 'A Multicountry Characterization of the Nonstationarity of Aggregate Output', *Journal of Money, Credit, and Banking* (Feb.).

Krantz, O. and C. Nilsson (1975) *Swedish National Product, 1861–1970* (Lund: CWK Gleerup).

Lee, R.D. (1973) 'Population in Preindustrial England: An Econometric Analysis', *Quarterly Journal of Economics* (Nov.).

Lee, R.D. and R.S. Schofield (1981) 'British Population in the Eighteenth Century', in R. Floud and D.N. McCloskey, *The Economic History of England Since 1700* (Vol. 1) (Cambridge: University Press).

Lévy-Leboyer, M. and F. Bourguignon (1990) *The French Economy in the Nineteenth Century* (Cambridge: University Press).

Lindert, P.H. (1984) 'Comment', in Michael D. Bordo and Anna J. Schwartz (eds), *A Retrospective on the Classical Gold Standard, 1821–1931* (Chicago: University of Chicago Press).

Lindert, P.H. and J.G. Williamson (1983) 'English Workers' Living Standards During the Industrial Revolution: A New Look', *Economic History Review* (Feb.).

Lucas, R.E. (1973) 'Some International Evidence on Output-Inflation Tradeoffs', *American Economic Review* (June).

Lucas, R.E. (1980) 'Two Illustrations of the Quantity Theory of Money', *American Economic Review* (Dec.).

Lucas, R.E. and L.A. Rapping (1969) 'Price Expectations and the Phillips Curve', *American Economic Review* (June).

Maddison, A. (1982) *Phases of Capitalist Development* (Oxford: University Press).

Malthus, T.R. (1798) *Essay on the Principle of Population* (Ann Arbor: University of Michigan Press).

Marczewski, J. (1988) 'Economic Fluctuations in France, 1815–1938', *Journal of European Economic History* (Fall).

Mathias, P. (1983) *The First Industrial Nation* (2nd edn) (London: Methuen).

Matthews, R.C.O. (1959) *The Trade Cycle* (Cambridge: University Press).

McCloskey, D.N. (ed.), (1971) *Essays on a Mature Economy* (Princeton: University Press).

McCloskey, D.N. (1976) 'English Open Fields as Behavior Towards Risk', *Research in Economic History* (Vol. 1)

McGouldrick, P. (1984) 'Operations of the German Central Bank and the Rules of the Game, 1879–1913', in M.D. Bordo and A.J. Schwartz (eds), *A Retrospective on the Classical Gold Standard, 1821–1931* (Chicago: University of Chicago Press).

Mills, T.C. and G.E. Wood (1978) 'Money-Income Relationships and the Exchange Rate Regime', *Review*, Federal Reserve Bank of St. Louis (Aug.).

Milward, A.S. and S.B. Saul (1973) *The Economic Development of Continental Europe, 1780–1870* (London: Rowman and Littlefield).

Minchinton, W.E. (1969) 'Introduction', in W.E. Minchinton (ed.), *The Growth of English Overseas Trade* (London: Methuen).

Mirowski, P. (1982) 'Adam Smith, Empiricism and the Rate of Profit in Eighteenth-Century England', *History of Political Economy* (Summer).

Mirowski, P. (1981) 'The Rise (and Retreat) of a Market: English Joint Stock Shares in the Eighteenth Century', *Journal of Economic History* (Sept.).

Mirowski, P. (1985) *The Birth of the Business Cycle* (New York: Garland).

Mitchell, B.R. (1978) *European Historical Statistics, 1750–1970* (New York: Columbia University Press).

Mokyr, J.B. (1977) 'Demand vs. Supply in the Industrial Revolution', *Journal of Economic History* (Dec.).

Mokyr, J.B. and N.E. Savin (1978) 'Some Econometric Problems in the Standard of Living Controversy', *Journal of European Economic History* (Fall/Winter).

Morineau, M. (1970) 'Was There an Agricultural Revolution in 18th Century France?' in R. Cameron (ed.), *Essays in French Economic History* (Homewood. IL: Irwin).

Nelson, C.R. and C.I. Plosser (1982) 'Trends and Random Walks in Macroeconomic Time Series: Some Evidence and Implications', *Journal of Monetary Economics* (Sept.).

Neuberger, H. and H.H. Stokes (1974) 'German Banks and German Growth, 1883–1913: An Empirical View', *Journal of Economic History* (Sept.).

Neuberger, H. and H.H. Stokes (1975) 'German Banking and Japanese

Banking: A Comparative Analysis', *Journal of Economic History* (Mar.).

Newell, W.H. (1973), 'The Agricultural Revolution in Nineteenth Century France', *Journal of Economic History* (Dec.).

Nygren, I. (1983) 'Transformation of Bank Structures in the Industrial Period, The Case of Sweden 1820–1913', *Journal of European Economic History* (Spring).

O'Brien, P.K. (1988) 'The Political Economy of British Taxation, 1660–1815', *Economic History Review* (Feb.).

O'Brien, P.K. and C. Keyder (1978) *Economic Growth in Britain and France, 1780–1914* (London: Allen & Unwin).

Phelps, E.S. (1966) *Golden Rules of Economic Growth* (New York: Norton).

Phelps Brown, E.H. and S.V. Hopkins (1956) 'Seven Centuries of the Prices of Consumables, Compared with Builders' Wage-rates', *Economica* (Nov.).

Phelps Brown, E.H. and S.V. Hopkins (1957) 'Wage Rates and Prices: Evidence for Population Pressure in the Sixteenth Century', *Economica* (Nov.).

Phelps Brown, E.H. and S.V. Hopkins (1959) 'Builders' Wage-rates, Prices and Population: Some Further Evidence', *Economica* (Feb.).

Phillips, A.W. (1958) 'The Relationship Between Unemployment and the Rate of Change of Money Wage Rates in the United Kingdom, 1861–1957', *Economica* (Nov.).

Pippinger, J. (1984) 'Bank of England Operations, 1893–1913', in M.D. Bordo and A.J. Schwartz (eds), *A Retrospective on the Classical Gold Standard, 1821–1931* (Chicago: University of Chicago Press).

Price, R. (1981) *An Economic History of Modern France, 1730–1914* (London: Macmillan).

Riden, P. (1977) 'The Output of the British Iron Industry before 1870', *Economic History Review* (Aug.).

Roberts, M. (1979) *The Swedish Imperial Experience, 1560–1718* (Cambridge: University Press).

Roehl, R. (1976) 'French Industrialization: A Reconsideration', *Explorations in Economic History* (July).

Romer, C.D. (1989) 'The Prewar Business Cycle Reconsidered: New Estimates of Gross National Product, 1869–1908', *Journal of Political Economy* (Feb.).

Rostow, W.W. (1962) *The Stages of Economic Growth* (Cambridge: University Press).

Saint Marc, M. (1983) *Histoire Monétaire de la France, 1800–1908* (Paris: Presses Universitaires de France).

Sandberg, L.G. (1978) 'Banking and Economic Growth in Sweden before World War I', *Journal of Economic History* (Sept.).

Sandberg, L.G. (1979) 'The Case of the Impoverished Sophisticate: Human Capital and Swedish Economic Growth before World War I', *Journal of Economic History* (March).

Schumpeter, E.B. (1960) *English Overseas Trade Statistics, 1697–1808* (Oxford: University Press).

Schumpeter, J. (1939) *Business Cycles* (New York: McGraw-Hill).

Scott, F.D. (1965) 'Sweden's Constructive Opposition to Emigration', *Journal of Modern History* (Sept.).

Shapiro, S. (1967) *Capital and the Cotton Industry in the Industrial Revolution* (Ithaca, NY: Cornell University Press).

Sims, C.A. (1972) 'Money, Income, and Causality', *American Economic Review* (Sept.).

Sims, C.A. (1980) 'Macroeconomics and Reality', *Econometrica* (Jan.).

Slicher van Bath, B.H. (1977) 'Agriculture and the Vital Revolution', *Cambridge Economic History of Europe* (Vol. v) (Cambridge: University Press).

Söderberg, J. (1982) 'Causes of Poverty in Sweden in the Nineteenth Century', *Journal of European Economic History* (Spring).

Solomou, S. and M. Weale (1991) 'Balanced Estimates of UK GDP, 1870–1913', *Explorations in Economic History* (Jan.).

Sommariva, A. and G. Tullio (1987) *German Macroeconomic History, 1880–1979* (London: Macmillan).

Sommariva, A. and G. Tullio (1988) 'International Gold Flows in Gold Standard Germany: A Test of the Monetary Approach to the Balance of Payments, 1880–1911', *Journal of Money, Credit, and Banking* (February) pp. 132–40.

Spinelli, F. (1980) 'The Demand for Money in the Italian Economy: 1867–1965', *Journal of Monetary Economics* (Jan.).

Tilly, R.H. (1967) 'Germany, 1815–1870', in R. Cameron (ed.), *Banking in the Early Stages of Industrialization* (Oxford: University Press).

Tilly, R.H. (1973) 'Zeitreihen zum Geldenlauf in Deutschland, 1870–1913', *Jahrbuchen für Nationalokonomie und Statistik* (Band 187, Heft 4).

Tilly, R.H. (1986) 'German Banking, 1850–1914: Development Assistance for the Strong', *Journal of European Economic History* (Spring).

Toniolo, G. (1990) *An Economic History of Liberal Italy, 1850–1918* (London: Routledge).

Toutain, J.-C. (1987) 'Le Produit Intérieur Brut de la France de 1789 à 1982', *Économies et Sociétés* (No. 15).

Tucker, R.S. (1936), 'Real Wages of Artisans in London, 1729–1935', *Journal of the American Statistical Association* (Mar.).

Von Tunzelmann, G.N. (1979) 'Trends in Real Wages, 1750–1850, Revisited', *Economic History Review* (Feb.).

Weber, E. (1976) *Peasants Into Frenchmen* (Stanford: Stanford University Press).

Weiller, K.J. and P. Mirowski (1990) 'Rates of Interest in 18th Century England', *Explorations in Economic History* (Jan.).

Williamson, J.G. (1984) 'Why Was British Grown So Slow During the Industrial Revolution?', *Journal of Economic History* (Sept.).

Williamson, J.G. (1987a) 'Has Crowding Out Really Been Given a Fair Test? A Comment', *Journal of Economic History* (Mar.).

Williamson, J.G. (1987b) 'Debating the Industrial Revolution', *Explorations in Economic History* (July).

Wood, G.E. (1984) 'Comment', in M.D. Bordo and A.J. Schwartz (eds), *A Retrospective on the Classical Gold Standard, 1821–1931* (Chicago: University of Chicago).

Wrigley, E.A. (1969) *Population and History* (New York: McGraw-Hill).

Wrigley, E.A. and R.S. Schofield (1981) *The Population History of England, 1541–1871: A Reconstruction* (Cambridge, Mass: Harvard University Press).

Wu, D.-M. (1973) 'Alternative Tests of Independence between Stochastic Regressors and Disturbances', *Econometrica* (July).

Zhangeri, R. (1969) 'The Historical Relationship Between Agriculture and Economic Development in Italy', in E. Jones and S. Woolf (eds), *Agrarian Change and Economic Development* (London: Methuen).

Index